Ernest Gellner and Contem

Ernest Gellner was a unique scholar whose work covered areas as diverse as social anthropology, analytical philosophy, the sociology of the Islamic world, nationalism, psychoanalysis, postmodernism, East European transformations and kinship structures. Despite this diversity, there is an exceptional degree of unity and coherence in Gellner's work with his distinctly modernist, rationalist and liberal world-view evident in everything he wrote. His central problematic remains constant: understanding how the modern world came into being and to what extent it is unique relative to all other social forms. Ten years after his death, this book brings together leading social theorists to evaluate the significance of Gellner's legacy and to re-examine his central concerns. It corrects many misunderstandings and critically engages with Gellner's legacy to provide a cutting-edge contribution to understanding our contemporary post-9/11, global, late modern, social condition.

SINIŠA MALEŠEVIĆ is a Lecturer in the Department of Political Science and Sociology at the National University of Ireland, Galway. His recent publications include *Identity as Ideology: Understanding Ethnicity and Nationalism* (2006), *The Sociology of Ethnicity* (2004), *Ideology, Legitimacy and the New State* (2002) and *Making Sense of Collectivity* (co-edited with Mark Haugaard, 2002).

MARK HAUGAARD is a Senior Lecturer in the Department of Political Science and Sociology at the National University of Ireland, Galway and was Jean Monnet Fellow at the European University Institute, Florence. His recent publications include *Hegemony and Power* (2006), *Power: A Reader* (2002) and *Making Sense of Collectivity* (co-edited with Siniša Malešević, 2002).

Ernest Gellner and
Contemporary Social Thought

Edited by

Siniša Malešević and Mark Haugaard

CAMBRIDGE
UNIVERSITY PRESS

CAMBRIDGE UNIVERSITY PRESS
Cambridge, New York, Melbourne, Madrid, Cape Town, Singapore, São Paulo

Cambridge University Press
The Edinburgh Building, Cambridge CB2 8RU, UK

Published in the United States of America by Cambridge University Press,
New York

www.cambridge.org
Information on this title: www.cambridge.org/9780521882910

First published 2007

Printed in the United Kingdom at the University Press, Cambridge

A catalogue record for this publication is available from the British Library

ISBN 978-0-521-88291-0 hardback
ISBN 978-0-521-70941-5 paperback

For our children Alex, Luka and Vanessa

Contents

Notes on contributors

THOMAS HYLLAND ERIKSEN is Professor of Social Anthropology at the University of Oslo and holds a Special Chair in Anthropology at the Free University of Amsterdam. He has published numerous books in Norwegian and English, including *Ethnicity and Nationalism* (1993/2002), *Small Places – Large Issues* (1995/2001), *A History of Anthropology* (2001, with F. S. Nielsen) and *Engaging Anthropology* (2006).

JOHN A. HALL is the James McGill Professor at the Department of Sociology, McGill University, Montreal. He is the author, co-author or editor of twenty-two books, including *Powers and Liberties* (1985), *Liberalism* (1989), *Coercion and Consent* (1994), *International Orders* (1996), *Is America Breaking Apart?* (2001), *The State of the Nation* (Cambridge, 1998) and *The Anatomy of Power* (Cambridge, 2006). He is currently completing an intellectual biography of Ernest Gellner.

MARK HAUGAARD lectures in the Department of Political Science and Sociology at the National University of Ireland, Galway, and was Jean Monnet Fellow at the European University Institute. His publications include *The Constitution of Power* (1997), *Power in Contemporary Politics* (2000), (co-ed.) *Making Sense of Collectivity* (2002), (ed.) *Power: A Reader* (2002) and (co-ed.) *Hegemony and Power* (2006).

MICHAEL LESSNOFF recently retired as Reader in Politics and is currently Honorary Research Fellow at the Department of Politics, University of Glasgow, Scotland. He studied at the University of Glasgow and Balliol College, Oxford. Among his publications are *The Structure of Social Science* (1974), *Social Contract* (1986), *The Spirit of Capitalism and the Protestant Ethic: An Enquiry into the Weber Thesis* (1994), *Political Philosophers of the Twentieth Century* (1999) and *Ernest Gellner and Modernity* (2002).

ALAN MACFARLANE is Professor of Anthropological Science at the
University of Cambridge and a Fellow of King's College. He is the
author of over a dozen books, including *The Origins of English
Individualism* (1978), *The Riddle of the Modern World* (2000) and *Letters
to Lily: On How the World Works* (2004). His next book, *Japan through
the Looking Glass*, will be published in 2007.

SINIŠA MALEŠEVIĆ lectures at the Department of Political Science and
Sociology, National University of Ireland, Galway. Previously he was
a research fellow in the Institute for International Relations (Zagreb)
and the Centre for the Study of Nationalism (Prague). He has also
held visiting research fellowships in the Institute for Human Sciences
(Vienna) and the London School of Economics. His books include
Identity as Ideology: Understanding Ethnicity and Nationalism (2006),
The Sociology of Ethnicity (2004) and *Ideology, Legitimacy and the New
State* (2002).

MICHAEL MANN is a Professor at the Department of Sociology,
University of California, Los Angeles. He is the author of many
prominent publications including a prize-winning series *The Sources of
Social Power*, vol. I: *A History of Power from the Beginning to 1760 AD*,
and vol. II: *The Rise of Classes and Nation-States, 1760–1914*
(Cambridge, 1986, 1993). Recent highly successful books include
Incoherent Empire (2003), *Fascists* (Cambridge, 2004) and *The Dark
Side of Democracy* (Cambridge, 2005), winner of the 2006 Barrington
Moore award of the American Sociological Association. He is
currently working on the third volume of *The Sources of Social Power:
The Globalization of Capitalism, Empires and the Nation-State*.

NICOS MOUZELIS is Emeritus Professor of Sociology at the London
School of Economics. He is author of many influential books
including *Modern Greece: Facets of Underdevelopment* (1979), *Politics
in the Semi-Periphery* (1986), *Back to Sociological Theory* (1992),
Sociological Theory: What Went Wrong? (1995) and *Bridges: Between
Modern and Late Modern/Postmodern Theorising* (forthcoming).

KEVIN RYAN lectures at the Department of Political Science and
Sociology, National University of Ireland, Galway, and is the author
of *Social Exclusion and the Politics of Order* (2007). He is interested in
social exclusion and marginality, and is currently researching
contemporary innovations in the governance of social difference.

PETER (PETR) SKALNÍK is a social anthropologist specialising in politics
and Africa. He taught at Charles University, Comenius University of

Bratislava, University of Leiden and University of Cape Town, and at present teaches social anthropology at universities in Pardubice, Czech Republic and Wroclaw, Poland. He first met Ernest Gellner in 1976 in the wake of his escape to the West following his steady opposition to communist dictatorship. Since 1997, together with Jiři Musil, he has convened in Prague a monthly Gellner Seminar, a respected platform for discussion among Czech and foreign social scientists. Skalník's publications include *Outwitting the State* (1989), *Political Culture* (2004) and *The Early Writings of Bronislaw Malinowski* (Cambridge, 2nd edn, 2005).

Acknowledgements

This work emerged out of a conference held at the National University of Ireland, Galway in May 2005, to commemorate eighty years since the birth of Gellner, in 1925, and ten years since his death, in 1995. In order to bring this conference together we received support from many quarters. In particular we would like to thank the following for their help and support: the Social Science Research Centre (NUI, Galway); the Department of Political Science and Sociology (NUI, Galway); the Arts Faculty (NUI, Galway); the Sociological Association of Ireland; and the Czech Embassy in Dublin. Without the assistance of these bodies, this conference, and consequent book, would not have been possible. Many individuals also gave us their assistance, especially Josef Havlas, the Czech Ambassador, for opening the conference, Fiona Bateman with organisation, Maria-Alexandra Gonzalez, who committed the proceedings to digital video, Gerard Delanty for reading and commenting upon the manuscript, and Kevin and Patricia for proofreading.

Introduction: an intellectual rebel with a cause

Mark Haugaard and Siniša Malešević

With his exceptionally independent and uncompromising mind, Ernest Gellner was a rare breed of intellectual. Unshakable in his defence of Enlightenment, and a self-proclaimed 'rationalist fundamentalist' (Gellner 1992: 80), Gellner had his fair share of followers and sympathisers. Yet he never really belonged to an identifiable collectivity, whether a religion, nation, state, class or status community, or indeed an academic school of thought, paradigm or intellectual circle. Even though, on a personal level, he missed the warmth of communal bonds as they extend beyond the immediate family circle,[1] he remained an adamant ontological individualist in his academic, political and, to a certain extent, personal life. An intellectual maverick who openly expressed disdain for fashionable philosophies and hegemonic systems of thought, it is perhaps no surprise that he found himself on the fringes of the academic mainstream. In this sense he was a true intellectual rebel: a stubborn rationalist and materialist when the Wittgenstein-inspired idealism of linguistic philosophy was in its heyday; a liberal anti-Marxist and fierce anti-communist when Marxism and socialist ideals dominated British sociology; and an unyielding positivist and anti-relativist as postmodernist and poststructuralist thought rose to prominence in the fields of anthropology and cultural studies.

Yet despite, or perhaps because of, his lifelong defence of rationalism and individualism, Gellner's intellectual passion drove him to understand, to explain and to empathise with shared values, forms of life and ideological systems of belief that were otherwise alien to his own. He had a genuine and sincere appreciation – both sociological and personal – of life under state socialism, Sharia law or postcolonial autocracies, perhaps more so than many Western-based intellectuals who built successful careers through the criticisms of orientalist, imperialist or ethnocentric thought. Gellner's individualism was a spur rather than a hindrance in comprehending the collective nature of human sociability, and he was

---

[1] This is most clearly expressed in Gellner's interview with John Davis. See Davis (1991).

1

one of the few twentieth-century thinkers who managed to combine successfully the study of sociology, philosophy, anthropology and history in developing creative, original and persuasive explanations of the macro-structural changes that have shaped our world. His uniqueness lay in his gift as a polymath, and Gellner left his mark in areas as diverse as social anthropology, analytical philosophy, the sociology of the Islamic world, nationalism, psychoanalysis, postmodernism, East European transformations and kinship structures.

As John Hall points out in chapter 10 (and more extensively in Hall 1998), Gellner's intellectual outlook is deeply ingrained in his biography, which in many respects parallels the history of Central Europe from the late nineteenth century, with the break up of empires, world wars, genocides, a proliferation of radical political ideologies and rise of dictatorships, but also the unprecedented economic growth, intensive industrialisation, the expansion of city life, secularism, development of the welfare state and the birth of mass educational systems. Gellner witnessed most of these tectonic shifts, which undoubtedly influenced his thought at an experiential level. Born in 1925 in Paris and raised in the multiethnic city of Prague, in the heart of Europe shaken by the Great War, the young Gellner lived amid the remnants of the post-Habsburg world. The bilingual son of German-speaking Jewish parents, he would become trilingual after attending the Prague English Grammar school. Despite a strong anti-semitic environment, Gellner seems to have enjoyed the vibrancy and cultural diversity of a typical *Mitteleuropa* city. The advent of the Second World War exposed Gellner to change of seismic proportions as the world he knew was literally blown apart by political forces and ideological currents that sought either to obliterate difference or to mould it into some form of uniformity. The rise of Nazism and the collapse of Masaryk's Czechoslovakia forced Gellner's family to move and settle in England in 1939, where Gellner continued his education at St Albans County Grammar School. He was an excellent student and as a result won a scholarship to Oxford's Balliol College.

At Balliol he studied philosophy, economics and politics. Although he was fond of all three subjects, the dominance of Wittgensteinian ideas in Oxford at that time contributed to Gellner's preference for the social sciences over philosophy. He briefly interrupted his studies to fight in the war as a soldier with the Czech Armoured Brigade (and was involved in the siege of Dunkirk). As the war was ending he was longing to return to Prague, where in 1945 he attended Charles University for one semester before witnessing the new Czechoslovakia becoming a Soviet satellite state and the intolerance of the radical right giving way to that of the political left. From Gellner's perspective one rigid collectivism had simply replaced another. All of this compelled him to settle in England for good. He graduated from Oxford with first class honours in 1947 and was appointed lecturer in philosophy in the same year at the University of Edinburgh.

After only two years Gellner moved to the London School of Economics where he joined the department of sociology. Upon the completion of his fieldwork in Morocco he successfully defended his PhD thesis 'Organisation and the Role of a Berber Zawiya' in 1961. Just a year later he was appointed Professor of Philosophy with a Special Reference to Sociology. In 1974 he was elected to the British Academy. After nearly thirty-five years spent productively at the LSE Gellner moved to Cambridge in 1984 where he was William Wyse Professor of Social Anthropology and a fellow of King's College. Following his retirement in 1993 and the collapse of communism, he returned to Prague to head the Centre for the Study of Nationalism at the newly established Central European University. It was here in the apartment block in Prokopova Street – which he shared with his first cohort of the Centre's PhD students – that Gellner died on 5 November 1995, just one month short of his seventieth birthday.

Although his education at Oxford equipped Gellner with the intellectual tools that would eventually help him to articulate his most influential theories, he could never reconcile the dominant ideas of 1940s and 50s Oxford with the realities he had experienced in Central Europe. In Wittgenstein's philosophy of language – espousing the view that there is no such thing as a private (individual) language, so that humans are chained in autarkic and self-validating cultural worlds – Gellner saw echoes of the rigid collectivisms that had nearly destroyed Europe. Rejecting the political paralysis that such relativist views seem to invite, Gellner began his inquiry into their origins and development, subjecting the Wittgensteinian turn to rigorous sociological and historical analysis.

His first book *Words and Things* (1959) was simultaneously a rebuke of linguistic philosophy and a sociological analysis of its influence and function. Gellner argued that the esoteric character of this philosophy requires no argumentation or justification as it ideologically reaffirms the common sense of 'the Narodniks of North Oxford'. He described it as a populist, philistine mysticism and parodied it as 'philosophical form eminently suitable for gentlemen' (Gellner 1959: 264–5). He also found many parallels between the *Weltanschauungen* of Oxford dons and Berber tribesmen as he wrote *Saints of the Atlas* (1969), his only empirical book. However, his most important early work is, without any doubt, *Thought and Change* (1964), where he lays the contours of his theories of modernity, social change, nationalism and historical transformation. It is here that one can really chart the worth of his socio-historical method as he sets out a powerful sociology of specific philosophical doctrines and ideologies, from utilitarianism and Kantianism to nationalism. Instead of analysing philosophies in terms of their internal coherence, Gellner attempts historically to contextualise and explain the reasons behind their origins and influence. It is here that he also charts the unique, unprecedented and exceptional character of modernity which is sustained by continual economic growth and a degree of cultural uniformity.

His Moroccan field study generated another long term interest – Islam. In many of his publications, but most of all in *Muslim Society* (1981), he was preoccupied with the question of why the Islamic world, like no other, has proven to be so resistant to secularisation. Combining Ibn Khaldun's and David Hume's ideas, he offered an original interpretation by pointing out the peculiar cyclical nature of social change which characterises the urban/rural relationship in traditional North Africa. By differentiating between popular folk orgiastic Islam and high ascetic Islam of the Book, he argued that Islamic modernisers are in a better position then many other late developers as they are able to draw on, and invoke, rich traditions of the existing high culture in order to modernise without a need to sacrifice cultural authenticity. In this context Gellner saw in the high culture of Islam an equivalent to Weber's Calvinist ethic, a potential generator of intensive economic development.

However the book which has without doubt received the most attention from Gellner's opus is *Nations and Nationalism* (1983). This book expanded on the chapter from *Thought and Change*, providing a highly original, sophisticated and in many respects still unsurpassed theory of nationalism. On the one hand Gellner demonstrates the intrinsic modernity of the desire for supposedly primeval national attachments, and on the other hand he underlines the necessity of cultural homogeneity for the smooth functioning of post-traditional societies, which links into questions of ideology and practice. In this book (together with *Culture, Identity and Politics*, 1987; *Encounters with Nationalism*, 1994 and *Nationalism*, 1997) Gellner made a major breakthrough by capturing the intrinsic paradox at the heart of nationalist doctrine, explaining that 'nationalism is a phenomenon of *Gesellschaft* using the idiom of *Gemeinschaft*: a mobile anonymous society simulating a closed cosy community' (Gellner 1997: 74).

His interest in nationalism, Islam and industrialisation was never distinct from his philosophical interests and he often switched from one to another in the same essay – part of an intellectual style which connected issues as diverse as tribal kinship structures and linguistic philosophy in a masterly and imaginative style; Platonic ideals and agricultural production; Freudian unconscious and original sin; Adam Ferguson and Imam Khomeini; Emile Durkheim and Lenin – whom Gellner nicely described as the 'Ignatius Loyola of Marxism'.

Much of his philosophical work, for example *The Devil in Modern Philosophy* (1974), *Legitimation of Belief* (1975), *Spectacles and Predicaments* (1980), *Relativism and the Social Sciences* (1985a) and *Reason and Culture* (1992) were written in defence of rationalism and empiricism. Gellner launched an unyielding attack on a variety of relativist and idealist styles of thought, from hermeneutics and phenomenology to existentialism and postmodernism. Although clearly influenced by Popper, Gellner claimed a greater commitment to realism in the historical sense of the word, and he successfully sociologised Popper's epistemology by arguing that 'the positivists are right for Hegelian reasons' (Gellner 1985a: 216).

In *The Psychoanalytical Movement* (1985b) Gellner provided a socio-historical explanation of this argument, honing his analytical strategy to perfection as he carefully and argumentatively untangled one of the most interesting puzzles of recent times: why did psychoanalysis achieve such an astonishing degree of popularity in the second half of the twentieth century? The answer was to be found as much in its falsification-resistant doctrine and its closed systems of initiation as it was in its ability to provide a sense of personal salvation, intellectually stamped comfort and therapeutic relief in a highly secular age. While psychoanalysis may be illuminating at the diagnostic level, in the concept of Unconscious Gellner discovered 'a curious offspring of Descartes' Daemon, Kant's Thing-in-itself, and Schopenhauer's Will', declaring its promise of cure utterly unfounded (Gellner 1985b: 216)

If Freudianism was a potent individualist and secular doctrine of salvation, Marxism was for Gellner its collectivist counterpart. In numerous articles and book chapters and in two separate books, *State and Society in Soviet Thought* (1988) and *Conditions of Liberty* (1994), Gellner subtly dissected the origins and structure of state socialist movements and Marxist-Leninist ideology. Marxism, unlike other faiths, had experienced almost irrecoverable collapse which, according to Gellner, had less to do with its 'formal elimination of the *transcendent* from religion' and more to do with its 'over-sacralisation of the *immanent*' (Gellner 1994: 40). In other words, echoing Durkheim in reverse, Gellner argues that fully functioning societies require the profane as much as the sacred – the routine, ordinary, banal – and the Soviet world obliterated the profane. Stalin's terror could not destroy the mass belief but the muck of Brezhnev's era did the job:

When *nomenklatura* killed each other and accompanied the murderous rampage with blatantly mendacious political theatre, belief survived: but when the *nomenklatura* switched from shooting each other to bribing each other, faith evaporated. (Gellner 1994: 41)

With the publication of *Plough, Sword and Book* (1988) Gellner offered a systematic historical sociology of human development. Although he identified the three principal stages of human history as the hunter/ gatherer, agrarian and industrial worlds, the focus was firmly on the contrasting images of economically stagnant, culturally polarised and coercive *agraria* versus vibrant, culturally homogenous, literate, growth- and cognition-oriented *industria*. The main idea behind this work was to reaffirm the Weberian tripartite vision of social development as against a singularist Marxist view; that is, to see history as the interplay of politics, economics and culture rather than solely through the prism of economic modes of production.

Gellner's last book, *Language and Solitude* (1998), is a condensed, almost autobiographical reflection on the many themes he struggled with throughout his career. While it is the ideas of Wittgenstein and Malinowski that come under the spotlight, Gellner's real target is the sociological underpinnings of post-Enlightenment and post-Romanticist thought, where Wittgenstein and Malinowski stand for two different articulations of human experience. For Gellner this is the world split between the individualist Robinson Crusoe tradition (stretching from Descartes, Hume and Kant to neo-positivism and neo-liberalism) and the collectivist, organicist 'village green' tradition (extending from Herder and de Maistre to nationalists, populists and eventually social Darwinism 'mediated by Nietzsche'). Whereas Gellner places himself firmly on the side of individual autonomy, which for him is the pre-condition for cognitive and economic growth, as a sociologist he follows Weber in acknowledging that 'shared culture alone can endow life with order and meaning' (Gellner 1998: 186). However, this is less a nor-mative problem of personal preferences and more an open-ended his-torical process of change: the gradual and in some way inevitable move from the intrinsic warmth of a cosy but inefficient and oppressive *Gemeinschaft* to contractual, rational and efficient yet solitary and cold *Gesellschaft*.

Despite the variety of topics that appear in Gellner's books there is an exceptional degree of unity and coherence in his life's work. His intel-lectual world-view is evident in everything he wrote, from his early studies on language and kinship, to his mature analyses of nationalism, Islam and modernity, to his philosophical critiques. Unfortunately the reception of his work has tended to be partial and incomplete, creating a lot of misunderstanding with respect to his key concepts and theories. Today he is generally represented either as a theorist of nationalism – one of the 'founding fathers' of nationalism studies – or as Bauman calls him, 'the master of metaphor', a reference to his witty style of writing.

As a result, much of his philosophical, anthropological and historico-sociological work has been neglected.

The aim of this book is to rectify this foreshortened reception of Gellner's contribution, calling attention to the many and varied contributions he has made to social and political analysis. We aspire to shed light on the broader scope of Gellner's work by showing how the questions he raised and the ideas and analyses which are his legacy to us are as relevant today as they were at the time of their inception. In other words, our aim is to go beyond the image of Gellner as a theorist of nationalism or a witty essayist so as to emphasise the contribution he has made in other areas of research. For example his queries on Islam and modernity may have much to offer in understanding the social dynamics of our post-9/11 world; his philosophical doubts on relativism and the nature of cognition could provide invaluable insights on the nature of modern thinking; and his macro-historical analyses of social transformation from the agricultural polyglot empires to the industrial monoglot nation-states and beyond provide fruitful insights regarding the form, content and structure of global change today. However, none of this is to say that Gellner had the last word on such burning questions. The tone of this introduction – deliberately acquiescent and uncritical as it is – might indicate that we will be paying homage to Gellner's thoughts on sociology, anthropology and philosophy. Nothing of the sort. Following this brief review of Gellner's life-work, the studies in this book chart a sociological, philosophical and anthropological critique of Gellner's position. Although the majority of contributions build on Gellner's legacy or work within a broadly Gellnerian perspective, none is oblivious to the ontological, epistemological or socio-historical imperfections of Gellner's arguments. As George Lichtheim (1965) pointed out so long ago in his review of *Thought and Change*, even when you remain unconvinced by Gellner's solutions you are always struck by the degree of originality and the relevance of the questions he asks.

The structure of the book

This book has been divided into three parts. In the first part, entitled 'Civil society, coercion and liberty', we analyse the circumstances of emergence of modern industrial society and the way in which they provided the unique conditions necessary for freedom of thought through the institutions of civil society. Relative to these debates there is a Gellner who, like the great classical sociologists (Durkheim, Simmel and Weber), is fascinated by the transition to modernity. However, there is also a less sanguine Gellner who is driven with a burning intensity by a quest born out of the Holocaust. Like Bauman, he wishes to understand the specific aspects of modernity which allow for freedom of thought, because he is acutely aware that modernity not only has a liberating potential but, equally, can destroy freedom with a thoroughness which traditional societies could never have dreamt of, even in their most totalitarian moments. In the second section, entitled 'Ideology, nationalism and modernity', we pass under the cloud of these totalising tendencies. Nationalism represents a system of thought, an ideology that is unique to modernity, which creates the conditions necessary for mass extermination of peoples within the state and mass mobilisation against the enemy externally. However, this is not a simple story of good and evil. Modernity is like a Janus head with faces that are both opposing yet inseparable. According to Gellner, nationalism was necessary for industrialisation and, more ominously, from some of the chapters in this work it emerges that it was also a precondition for democracy. In the last section, 'Islam, postmodernism and Gellner's metaphysic', we juxtapose three systems of thought. According to Gellner, the genesis of modernity is derived from a specific form of openness that is historically unique. Like nationalism, Islam is functionally commensurable with modernity but unfortunately both ideologies have a predisposition to closure. Their functionality entails that once modernity has come about, or has passed its stage of genesis, there is no sociological reason why these closed forms of thought might not be more successful than the open spirit of Enlightenment reason. This concern is compounded by the fact that, in the historic heartland where Enlightenment reason developed, the spirit of openness has become radicalised into a form of relativistic nihilism. Postmodernism is the outgrowth of the same kind of modern communitarian thinking that resulted in nationalism in early modernity but which, in advanced modernity, has combined with a misguided radicalisation of Enlightenment openness. Islam presupposes a fusion of fact and value that leads to dogmatism, while postmodernism entails a relativism which renders falsification impossible. Islam is sociologically compatible with modernity, as a kind of functional equivalent of Protestantism. In contrast, while most forms of contemporary liberalism are normatively robust defences of openness, they are sociologically weak because they suggest a disenchanted world devoid of belonging. While postmodernism recognises the significance of community, it is philosophically incapable of defending modernity because of its implicit relativism. In contrast to these ideologies, Gellner's intellectual quest is driven by a desire to develop a metaphysic which has the capacity to constitute a philosophically robust defence of liberal openness while, simultaneously, being sociologically defensible.

In historical sociology there are two dominant schools of thought: those who see history in terms of historical continuity and those who view it as characterised by discontinuity. The former view history as an incremental evolution towards the present, while the latter think of history as constituted of layers of social life which are qualitatively different. To borrow an image from Foucault, the discontinuists view history in the manner of an archaeological site in which there is a stone age, a bronze age and an iron age layer each of which is clearly distinct from the others. Most conventional historians belong to the former school while historical sociologists tend towards the latter. There is a theoretical reason for this. Most sociology (with the notable exception of methodologically individualist stances, such as rational choice theory) presumes that social life is systemic or relationally constituted. This assumption need not be as strong as in structural functionalism, but the sociological imagination is premised upon the idea that social order is reproduced through unintentional effects, which feed back to create the contextuality of social action. When a social actor reproduces structures, that act of structuration entails drawing upon a contextuality of action which, while the unintended effect of intentional action, shapes the conditions of possibility for felicitous structuration practices. Of course, one does not have to be determinist in this. It may be the case that a specific actor within a traditional society may shape his or her actions premised upon an individualist orientation, but what is determined is that other actors within the system will lack the background interpretative horizon to react appropriately, and so the exceptional individualist remains an anomalous or deviant actor. Consequently, certain characteristics cannot develop on their own. Freedom of thought presupposes individualism, which is premised upon weak social ties, which presupposes that social order is no longer sacred and so on. In the continuist vision of history, freedom of thought might be viewed as a long process of conflict between free thinkers and those of a closed mind-set. According to this view Socrates, Galileo, J. S. Mill and Solzhenitsyn would be part of a continuous movement. To the discontinuists, on the other hand, freedom of thought became possible only because of fundamental changes in social order as a whole. Even if it is acknowledged that such individuals are necessary for freedom of thought, they are not considered a sufficient condition.

In the first chapter, Alan Macfarlane begins by outlining Gellner's perception of the unique conditions particular to modernity which made liberty possible. Central to this was the separation of spheres of social life. The pursuit of power became confined to the political sphere, wealth to the economy, social warmth to kinship, and the sacred became confined to the realm of religion. Out of this division arose 'civil society', which is a realm within which freedom can flourish free from domination by the specialists in coercion, religious dogma or tradition. This separation of spheres was a unique phenomenon which is not the normal condition of humankind. In Gellner's interpretative horizon this separation constitutes a fundamental discontinuity both with the past and also, in the present, with communist and Islamic societies where this separation has not taken place.

The discontinuist view of history tends to be holist, in the sense that social configurations are relationally self-constituting. The separation of spheres presupposes the individualised self of Protestantism and the division of labour of capitalism, where the economic activity becomes separated from private affective life. It also presupposes an economy which is sufficiently productive so that the specialists in coercion can be 'bought off'. This productivity is premised upon innovation, which is conceptually impossible if the individualised self is not free from custom and superstition. So the circle from separation of spheres to civil society, to liberty, to Protestantism, to individualism, to innovation, to productivity, to dominance of the economy over the polity and clergy, to freedom and so on, is complete.

Characteristically such a view of history has difficulty providing conceptual space for half-way stages. However, in this chapter Macfarlane shows that the advent of civil society partly owes its emergence to a half-way historical phenomenon, which is between traditional society and modernity. On the basis of the research of F. W. Maitland, Macfarlane shows that the English phenomenon of the 'Trust' is such an intermediary institution which is neither, yet both, *Gemeinschaft* and *Gesellschaft*. The Trust creates a unique set of rights around the institutionalisation of what is essentially a fictitious person. As such, it straddles the divide between community and association, status and contract, and mechanical and organic solidarity – the oppositions that divide traditional from modern society. Because it is an intermediary stage it could survive in the feudal world while, at the same time, creating the contractual preconditions for civil society. The Trust allowed the personal rights of feudalism to become transposed into the property rights of industrial society and it allowed religious institutions, clubs, trade unions and insurance companies to gain a legal standing as separate entities which had rights, as freestanding entities, which were separable from the particular rights of the individuals who were their members. This created the preconditions for the separation of spheres essential to modern liberty.

Having established the significance of intermediary institutions to modern liberty, Macfarlane looks at their future. Gellner argued that the conditions of modernity which allow for freedom are unique, so it is reasonable to suppose that they can easily be undermined. Macfarlane analyses the current 'war on terror', which Gellner died too soon to witness, and argues that the condition of perpetual war against an invisible enemy creates circumstances which are antithetical to modern freedom. Returning to his idea of intermediary social forms, Macfarlane argues that freedom may be better protected in a social order which constitutes such an intermediary form.

Macfarlane argues that Japanese society is a contemporary inter-mediary form, in the sense that it is both an advanced industrialised society, yet traditional in so many ways. Japan is like a giant industrial-ised 'tribe', which is democratic. Because it still retains sufficient elements of *Gemeinschaft* it can deal with external threat as a holistic entity and, as such, does not have to curb freedom to provide unity. In a manner which is reminiscent of Aristotle's desire for balance, moder-ation and mixed forms, Macfarlane invites his readers to contemplate Japan as a utopian model which will allow stabilisation of the freedoms of *industria* through *agraria* – a vision for which Gellner's discontinuist social theory did not provide conceptual space.

In the second chapter, Michael Mann takes up Gellner's theme con-cerning the uniqueness of Western, liberal, industrial societies. Certain critics of this thesis have argued that Western Europe's industrial surge forward was based not upon a unique social formation, rather upon two accidents of history: the supply of coal in Britain and raw material from the colonies. Siding with Gellner, Mann argues that this is not the case. However, this does not imply total agreement.

Part of Gellner's hypothesis is that Western uniqueness was based upon the fact that, for the first, and only, time in history, those who acquired wealth through power and coercion became subservient to those who created wealth through production. Central to this inversion of power was the change in interpretative horizon associated with liberty. Within the Gellnerian framework, the demise of the dominance of pre-dation over production created the possibilities for the liberties of modern democracy – freedom of speech and expression, and the absence of barbarous forms of domination, such as slavery. This is coupled with a general removal of coercion from everyday life, except in instances of punishment for wrongdoing, in which circumstances coercion is strictly moderated in accordance with the rule of law and the democratic will of the people.

While Mann accepts that there was a fundamental shift in modernity, the implicitly normatively affirmative view, of increasing liberty and minimisation of coercion, is put under radical scrutiny. Mann argues that Gellner underestimates the role of coercion and overstates the centrality of liberty.

At the core of Mann's reinterpretation of the Gellnerian picture is the concept of empire. The non-coercive, liberty-enjoying, view of social order in advanced Western societies is only correct when viewing states internally. In the nineteenth century and the first half of the twentieth while British society enjoyed liberty at home, its foreign policy was directed at building an empire which entailed continual war and domination. It was only at home that the producers were dominant, while throughout the empire the reverse was the case, and it was only at home that liberty was the order of the day while in the empire it was sadly neglected.

Gellner recognises that the period of European state formation was indeed bloody and he attributes this to the normal state of agrarian societies in which those who wield the sword dominate those who use the plough. However, Mann argues that in fact, even by the worldwide standards of traditional societies, Europe of the late middle ages and early modernity was actually exceptionally warlike. Mann argues that European state formation was in fact a process of empire building within Europe. We tend to think of the Habsburg lands as empire but not of Britain, France, Spain and Italy as such. In reality, they are also the outcome of empire building within Europe. Once the European empires reached a kind of *modus vivendi* (essentially because there were no more small militarily weak states that could be invaded) European states turned their empire building intentions outward and made war over the rest of the globe. Arguably, the current administration in the USA is continuing that tradition. What is clear in this picture is that, where empire is being carved out, coercion dominates production. Consequently, when the empires were being carved out in Europe there is no question of production dominating coercion, and liberty played second fiddle to domination. When production dominated coercion within Europe it was only because empire building had shifted outside. This leaves the paradox that liberal democratic states practise freedom at home but make war and govern through coercion abroad.

This does not constitute a falsification of the Gellnerian hypothesis that freedom presupposes a domination of the specialists in coercion by the producers. However, it does imply that such a relationship between coercion and production has not been reached in the unambiguous way in which Gellner argued that it had.

While Mann convincingly argues that Gellner underestimated the role of coercion in modernity, Mark Haugaard subjects Gellner's account of power, as synonymous with coercion, to radical critique. Haugaard argues that coercive power, which is based upon violence, is only one kind of power (coercive power) but that stable social order actually presupposes what he calls 'social power', which is premised upon a strong internalisation of certain structuration practices.

In the power literature, there are essentially two scalar views of power. On the one end of the scale there are theorists who view power entirely conflictually: power is exercised 'over' others, against their interests, and is by and large the outcome of coercive threats based upon violence or severe deprivation of some kind. At the other end of the scale, thinkers like Hannah Arendt (1970) and Barry Barnes (1988) argue that power is capacity for action which actors derive from their membership of a social or political system. In this chapter Haugaard steers a middle course between these two positions, emphasising that power is both 'power to' and 'power over', and that both manifestations of power are based upon resources other than purely coercive ones. This applies not only to modern systems of domination but equally to traditional ones.

The implication of this for Gellner's theory is that the transition from traditional *agraria* to modern *industria* is not simply a question of a move from the dominance of coercive power to economic power. Rather, the transition entails this plus the replacement of one kind of social power by another. According to Haugaard's analysis of power, traditional societies cannot simply be characterised as dominated through coercive power but they also maintain social order through forms of social power which have a consensual base in the internalised socialisation of the traditional actors involved. Of course, as these traditional systems were going into decline this social power became weaker, with the consequent tendency to replace social power with coercive power – hence the rise of revolutionary and counter-revolutionary violence in the late feudal age.

While the advent of modernity did entail a decline in violence inside the system, this was not simply an overcoming of coercive power. Rather it represents the emergence of new kinds of social power. While Haugaard argues that social power is ultimately consensually based this should not be taken to imply, as it does in Arendt, that this power is necessarily benign. Consent has to be *created* and this always entails false essentialism and the manipulation of social consciousness. This allows Haugaard to link the decline of coercive violence inside modern states with the rise of the discourses of modernity, including nationalism. This gives us the implicit paradox that it is not the Enlightenment but also its converse, the manipulation of knowledge, which allows for the lowering of coercion, and consequent rise of freedom, within modern states. Because the social power of modernity arises inside systems, Mann's observations that these systems are violent externally does not constitute a falsification of

Haugaard's hypothesis, because outside these systems the basis of social power is absent owing to the fact that these Western systems were confronting social actors who did not have the 'appropriate' mode of socialisation.

For Gellner the liberties of industrial society are premised upon civil society which, as we have argued, presupposes the dominance of coercive power by economic power and the separation of religious belief from both polity and economy. In contradistinction from this perspective, Marxist theory is based upon the hypothesis that economy always dominates the polity (that civil society is a mask for bourgeois freedom as opposed to freedom in general), and, in practice, Marxism entails the fusion of economy polity and religious belief into one. As a consequence, it can be argued that both the theory and the practice of Marxism are in fundamental opposition to Gellner's perspective. However, as is argued by Peter Skalník in chapter 4, Gellner's interest in Marxist perspectives, in particular Marxist anthropology, suggests a more complex and nuanced relationship to Marxism than such an opposition would imply.

According to Gellner, Marx devalues the political in favour of the forces of production. Contrary to Marx's self-perception, this makes him an essentially bourgeois social theorist. The bourgeoisie owed their domination to the fact that they subdued the specialists in coercion. In the bourgeois social order, labour dominates coercion, and owing to the Protestant work ethic, labour is the measure of all things. Marxist utopia is a state of affairs where the state has withered away and those who labour become kings – hence, a quintessentially bourgeois utopia. The reason that any attempt at communism did not actually result in such a utopia is, of course, because this bourgeois interpretative horizon downplays the role of coercion. Communism was in fact yet another society in which coercion dominates production.

While communism does not allow for the freedoms of Western industrial society, from a sociological perspective it is a logical development beyond feudalism. As argued by Skalník, both communism and Islam are the functional equivalents of Protestantism, in the sense that both belief systems contribute to a gradual disenchantment of the world and an orientation towards rule-following which are both necessary for the creation of a society based upon industrial production. Where they differ from Protestantism is in the fact that they do not entail the kind of individualism and separation of interpretative spheres necessary for an open liberal society. Hence, they are modernising, leading to *industria*, but not liberalising.

For Gellner, the normative worth of Western liberal-democratic societies did not lie in their capacity to industrialise or, possibly more surprisingly, in their practice of democracy. The latter is largely an illusion as most of social life and social change is not touched by democratic institutions, nor can the election of elites every five or so years really be construed as government by the people. Following Popper, what makes these societies worthwhile is that they are fundamentally open societies, in which freedom of thought flourishes and the contestation of ideas is part of everyday life. Gellner's emphasis upon openness made him fascinated by alternative systems of thought, including Islam and communism as alternatives to Western modernity. As a true Popperian, Gellner views the existence of an alternative normative order as a prerequisite for contestation; consequently both these, admittedly closed, systems provided food for the kind of dialogic practice which is integral to openness. Thus, Gellner's attitude to the collapse of the Soviet experiment was mixed.

For Gellner, Marxism made itself immune to falsification. In this respect it is akin to religious belief. Lack of openness made it conceptually difficult for Marxism to deal with social orders and phenomena which had the potential to falsify Marxism. One such social order was the so-called Asiatic mode of production and one such phenomenon was ethnicity and nationalism. As argued by Skalník, studying how Soviet social theorists and anthropologists dealt with these phenomena fascinated Gellner as they showed the workings of a closed system under stress from possible falsifiers. In this regard, Gellner analysed how Soviet anthropologists dealt with the power of ethnic phenomena. On the one hand, Marxist orthodoxy has no conceptual space for it, yet, on the other, anthropology is based upon the study of ethnos and, furthermore, these studies were taking place within an empire which was constantly creaking under the stress of ethnic tension. According to Skalník, Gellner was particularly fascinated by Bromley's account of *etnos*, which he interpreted as implicitly coming close to a non-economic freestanding account of ethnicity but which, because of the epistemic closure, could not quite make that final move. However, the theory did point to some cracks in the Marxist monolith and, as such, a possibility, not fully grasped, yet there, for Popperian openness.

Skalník argues that Gellner actually exaggerates the extent of Bromley's departure from orthodoxy, but Gellner's interest tells a lot about his desire for an understanding of the conditions of possibility for an open society and how he believed that the study of closed systems of thought could further this project.

While Islam and Marxism provide ideological alternatives to the open society, nationalism is an ideology which is found within liberal democratic societies that is essential to industrialisation (thus the emergence of liberty) and yet constitutes a constant fundamental threat to the openness of these societies. In part II nationalism becomes the central focus of analysis.

Gellner argued that nationalism is associated with industrialisation but, as has been frequently observed by many commentators, the actual emergence of nationalism in many parts of the world, for instance in the Balkans, is not associated with industrialisation. According to Popperian criteria, this fact has the potential to falsify Gellner's theory. However, as is argued by Nicos Mouzelis, the essence of the theory can be saved by modification. In particular, Mouzelis argues that the concept of *industria* should be replaced by that of modernity. Such a move would deal with this potential for falsification and make better sense of the elective affinity between nationalism and the kind of society that has emerged since the eighteenth century. As will be explained, this substitution also has the consequence of rescuing Gellner's account from possible tele-ology, thus making it a genuinely legitimate functionalist account.

Mouzelis starts from the premise that Western modernity entails an irreversible decline in traditional non-differentiated community coupled with an unprecedented mobilisation and inclusion of the population in the centre. In this regard the rise of the modern state is paradigmatic as it entails the massive transfer of infrastructural power from the peripheries to the centre. However, there is a prima facie tension between the desire to transfer everything to the centre and the simultaneous decline of non-differentiated community. As has been argued by Parsons, the dif-ferentiation of institutional roles generates a problem of social integration. After all, the more situationally specific logic of differentiated roles, the separation of economy, polity and religion, coupled with the rise of individualism, has the potential to lead to system disintegration. According to Mouzelis, nationalism performs this integrative function while at the same time accelerating the process of modernity through homogenisation.

This theory entails an adjustment of Gellner's perspective. While it may be the case that in advanced modernity the economy dominates the polity, what made the great shift from traditional society to modernity possible was the dominance of the polity over the economy. It was state expansion that was the motor of modernisation, which ultimately undermined localised feudal practices. The modern state could not tol-erate the mediated power (feudal hierarchy) of traditional society, thus destroying the segmental world of traditional society. Part of the ideology that made this possible was nationalism, which served as a legitimation for the desires of centralising elites. The centring of infrastructural power coupled with the rise of nationalism created the conditions of homogenisation whereby the peoples (plural) of the feudal world could be transformed into a people (singular). The hypothesis that modernity presupposes a period of dominance by the polity would be consistent with Mann's account whereby the formation of modern European states was actually highly coercive, and only became less so within Europe when these states were stabilised and infrastructural power could be brought to the centre. It was only in those circumstances that the economy had the possibility of becoming dominant and industrialisation followed. In Haugaard's language, coercive power creates the social order, while social power is responsible for its routine reproduction.

The theory that polity had a periodic dominance in early modernity, which was also associated with nationalism, removes a possible teleology implicit in Gellner's position. In Gellner the economy *needs* a homogenised population and nationalism performs that function. However, the genesis of nationalism remains obscure. If it arose from these economic needs, we have a teleological theory whereby needs result in outcomes. However, in Mouzelis' adjustment, nationalism arose from the actions of state-building elites who were consciously looking for an integrative ideology. Using the empirical case of Greece, Mouzelis demonstrates how such elites went about using the past to create the imagined community of the Greek nation. Once the Greek nation-state was formed, of course, it began to industrialise, and was facilitated in so doing by the existence of the Greek imagined community. However, that community was not created to serve the needs of industrialisation but there was an elective affinity between the two since industrialisation could not have taken place if it had not been for the creation of a homogeneous Greek society.

In chapter 6, Siniša Malešević begins from the same irrefutable fact as Mann: while modernity preaches peace, the modern world is characterised by greater violence than any other social order. In the twentieth century up to 120 million people were massacred through ethnic cleansing and over 200 million in war. While moderns show revulsion at the ritualised violence of the past – public hangings and so on – they have developed the capacity for mass killing, along lines of industrial efficiency, to an extent which the cruellest tyrants of the past would have marvelled at. Against this fact stands Gellner's optimistic view of modernity in which the producers dominate the coercers. Furthermore, Gellner argued that the cognitive framework of modern man has shifted from a condition of traditional thought in which myths that are functional to social integration are prioritised over empirical facts. For modern social agents, with their orientation to innovation, the empirical world is separated from normative judgement and social integration, which allows for the unhindered pursuit of empirical truth.

Malešević challenges Gellner's account on both these fronts. Not only is modernity characterised by violence, but it is also driven ideologically by a belief system in which social integration clearly dominates truth. That ideology is, of course, nationalism. Not that Gellner did not take account of nationalism, of course; that is what he is best known for. But Gellner always took an optimistic Enlightenment view whereby nationalism is a phenomenon of early modernity which the Enlightenment logic of late modernity would overcome. Consequently he predicted the long-term demise of nationalism. In contrast, Malešević argues that modernity does not imply a transition to a society in which socially integrative falsehoods are given second place to truth, consequently the advance of modernity does not, and will not in the future, entail a decline of nationalism. Rather, we witness its dominance over other ideologies, or its integration into them through banal nationalism.

Gellner's optimistic reading of modernity is based upon the idea of a disjuncture whereby social order shifted from being coercively based, in traditional society, to being largely normatively based in modernity. As we saw, Macfarlane argued that in fact this normative base first developed in traditional society around the idea of Trusts. Haugaard similarly argued that traditional society was based upon consent but the nature of this consent was different. What is implicit in all of this is unease at the idea of a shift in the conceptualisation of the basis of social agency.

Malešević also feels this dissatisfaction but he turns the argument the other way around: in traditional societies social order was maintained by coercion and that continues to be the case; similarly, in traditional societies knowledge was subservient to the myths of social integration and that is also the case in modernity. In fact, just as in traditional society, violence and ideology are fused. Internally, modern states may appear at peace but the truth of the matter is that tranquillity is maintained by a constant vigilance at our borders where coercion keeps out those who are likely to contaminate the nation – the thousands of potential 'illegal aliens'. The whole war-making capacity of modern states is based around the internalisation and routinisation of 'banal' nationalism. As argued by Billig, 'banal' does not mean benign. The internalisation of the myths of the nation is absolutely central to the mobilisation of the mass machinery of war, which the modern state has developed to an unprecedented scale. The events of 9/11 were a trigger which allowed the banal nationalism of the everyday life of Americans to be mobilised into a war in which thousands are being killed. In the crucial early stages, when the trajectory to war was being laid, those who opposed war were excluded from the discourse of the true, not by falsification of their ideas (as in a Popperian open society) but by the labelling of their position as 'unpatriotic'. In other words, their position was 'wrong' because it was contrary to the myths of social integration – banal nationalism.

In the last chapter of part II, Thomas Hylland Eriksen reflects upon the pertinence of Gellner's model of nationalism for the contemporary world. In particular Eriksen wishes to know if Gellner's paradigm can provide conceptual space for contemporary reactions to immigration of minorities and the increasing rise of multiculturalism in what were previously more homogeneous nation-states.

As we have argued, the central element of Gellner's theory is the correlation between nationalism and homogenisation. This raises the obvious question: what happens to those who resist the forces of homogenisation? These are what Gellner terms entropy-resistant groups. He has two answers: if they share territory they secede and form their own nation-state or, if that option is closed to them, they form a diaspora group who have, or aspire to having, a nation-state elsewhere. In other words, they reproduce the discourse of nationalism whereby nation and state are one or should be one, situated somewhere in geographical space. However, neither of these descriptions corresponds to the current reality of complex identity formation. Pakistanis living in Oslo are neither Ruritanians wishing to secede from Megalomania nor the equivalent of the Jewish diaspora of old.

According to Eriksen, this insufficiency in the Gellnerian model is symptomatic of two conceptual premises in Gellner's theory. First, Gellner does not distinguish between culture and identity. He assumes that a person's identity is defined by culture, which frequently is not the case. In Trinidad people of Indian ethnic origin are culturally integrated, yet they preserve their ethnic identity. However, the ethnic identities of Caribbean peoples of African origin may be weak yet they may maintain strong cultural similarities and continuities. So, you can have cultural variation without ethnic variation and vice versa, which is not to deny that there can be a correlation between both.

When Gellner theorised entropy-resistance he took for granted that the basis of this resistance was cultural, but if culture and identity are no longer congruent this assumption is not justified. A group may be culturally the same as the majority of society but may have an identity which makes them entropy-resistant. This disjuncture may be a matter of choice but, all too frequently, it is forced upon the group in question. With regard to the latter, Eriksen relates the anecdote of a Norwegian of Pakistani ethnic origin who owned a flashy BMW. Within a short period after purchase, he was asked for his credentials by the traffic police ten times. In contrast, seven ethnic Norwegians who owned the same type of car were only stopped once between them. The former had an entropy-resistant ethnic identity irrespective of the extent to which he was culturally Norwegian or not. Reversing the theoretical logic, it also happens that identity can be created out of nothing and cultural characteristics can be acquired or invented to suit that identity. Of course, Gellner was aware of this phenomenon in the creation of nation-states, but failed to appreciate that the same thing can take place at a sub-national level. In our increasingly global world, where communication is easy, ethnic minorities are frequently strengthening ties with other members of the same ethnic group, thus reinforcing their sense of identity. In the past, a move from Pakistan to Oslo was for life; now there is the possibility of return during the holidays and continual email and text contact. In fact, Pakistanis who were born in Oslo, and whose parents also were, can set up contact with their 'home' village in the Punjab.

The second premise of Gellner's theory, which made it unable to provide conceptual space for contemporary multiculturalism, is Gellner's taken-for-granted view that identity is linked to geographical space. You are a diaspora nationalist because you are living in a geographical space which is 'wrong' for you. There is a sense of incompletion in this. The diaspora Jew living in pre-1949 Europe was yearning for completion with the state of Israel. However, the minorities of the contemporary world are not situated in space in this way. We are living in a transnational world in which there is no longer the expectation that social actors change identity based upon situatedness in geographical space. New immigrants maintain their language, not necessarily because they live in ghettoes but because they choose to maintain links with others of the same identity half-way around the world. Recently an anthropologist researching the Dominican Republic found that he could not complete his endeavours without fieldwork in New York.

Aside from the pace of globalisation, whereby transnationalism was not as obvious in the 1980s and early 1990s, there is another reason why Gellner might have been blind to this phenomenon. As we have repeatedly emphasised, Gellner argued that national identification was functional to the economy. However, transnational minority identification does not follow this functional logic.

While Eriksen makes a strong case for globalisation entailing a form of transnationalism which transcends Gellner's model, he also recognises that there is a curious and significant way in which Gellner is still correct. While the social agents involved do not view themselves as diasporas in need of integration, state policy reflects a Gellnerian world-view. While there is official lip-service to cultural difference, this is only acceptable in some instances. In Britain, while curry may be a 'British dish', in the eyes of the state Islamic social practice is an unacceptable form of entropy-resistance, which is in need of integration and homogenisation.

In part III we analyse Gellner's account of Islam and the relationship between his defence of Enlightenment reason and postmodern epistemology. The first chapter of this section, by Michael Lessnoff, is a positive critique of Gellner's account of the relationship between Islam and modernity.

Gellner's account of modernity stresses two elements: it is a mode of cognition (openness to falsification) and a mode of production (*industria*), and both are interrelated. The spirit of cognitive openness makes invention possible, which advances industrial production, and that, in turn, gives the productive classes the resources to dominate the specialists in coercion. Following Weber, the initial trigger for this was Protestantism because, on the cognitive side, it removes magic from the world and teaches rule-following, and, on the economic side, it instils a work ethic in which sensuous excess is avoided.

Gellner argues that traditional societies are divided between literate 'high' culture and 'folk' culture. As modernity is a mass literate society, there is a tendency for 'high' culture effectively to colonise 'folk' culture. In Western Europe, Protestantism, with its emphasis upon the text of the Bible, was partly responsible for this colonisation of folk culture. Because of the Protestant emphasis upon rule-following and the absence of magic, it also contributed to the creation of a critical mass of people within society who had the appropriate cognitive framework for *industria*.

This ideal-type characterisation of the relationship between *industria* and a specific cognitive framework leaves the success of Islam a mystery. Unlike Christianity, which is either in decline or being confined to the 'private realm', Islam does not seem to be in any way weakened or confined by industrialisation. It seems that Islamic societies can industrialise without Westernising. The solution to this apparent contradiction between Gellner's modernising hypothesis and the success of Islam is that there are two forms of Islam, magical Islam which is in decline, and a more puritanical Islam of the Book which is the functional equivalent of Protestantism. The latter form of Islam is similar to Protestantism in the sense that it represents a return to the text, and in its emphasis upon rule-following and rejection of local miracles. Gellner argued that from a class point of view it was largely urban middle class and thus can be characterised as 'high' culture.

While Lessnoff argues that Gellner is correct to argue that magical Islam, Sufi Islam, is in decline, the analogy between 'high' Islam and Protestantism is fundamentally flawed with regard to the parallels in cognitive framework. Yes, it is true that there is a high Islam, with an emphasis upon the Book, and a low Islam which includes local saints and other kinds of magic. The essence of Gellner's thesis concerning Protestantism is that it was more commensurable with Popperian openness, thus more functional to innovation, than Catholicism. However, the parallel does not hold for Islam.

While modernising Western society is scientific, in the early middle ages it was the Islamic world that was at the cutting edge of astronomy. According to Lessnoff's research, they effectively challenged some of the fundamental premises of Ptolemy's astronomy and, in so doing, laid the groundwork for modern astronomy. However, the ultimate breakthrough came in the West with Copernicus, Galileo and Newton. If Gellner's theory that high Islam was a kind of Protestantism were correct, then one would expect that the initial advances were made by these 'protestant' Islamic movements and that, for whatever reason, the decline of Islamic science in the late middle ages would be in some way attributable to a temporary advance by folk Islam. However, Gellner is correct that folk Islam was displaced by high Islam as modernity advanced, but, contrary to the hypothesis of an elective affinity between Protestantism and science, this was the reason for decline of Islamic astronomy. It was mystical Islam which nurtured the scientific spirit and it was Islam of the Book that killed it. To simplify, Sufism was a kind of theological monism in which God was cotermininous with the natural world. This had the implication that the world was a sacred space, which is a form of mysticism but, simultaneously, also has the implication that studying the natural world constitutes a theological exercise. If the work of God and God himself were inseparable, studying nature and astronomy is a sacred mission. Furthermore, Sufis tended to interpret the Quran symbolically rather than literally, which also contributed to a certain openness. In contrast, Islam of the Book devalued the significance of the natural world relative to that of the sacred text, and the latter was interpreted literally and dogmatically.

If we look at the work of Newton we find a profoundly religious man who believed that in studying the laws of physics he was uncovering the laws of God. As argued by Lessnoff, this belief derives from the Western tradition of natural law. According to this tradition, the law of nature was created by God and is discoverable by humans aided by the faculty of reason, which God has implanted in us for this purpose. Of course, there is also revelation, which gives us divine law, but the latter does not invalidate the former. Consequently, as in Sufism, the astronomer is discovering God in uncovering the laws of nature. In reading the Book of Nature, Newton was looking for a natural law, which was sacred. In contrast, in high Islam, Islam of the Book, nature did not have the capacity to reveal God's law, which was entirely confined to revealed law of the Quran. Furthermore, the interpretation of the Quran which became dominant within Sunni Islam is a literal one, in which underlying principles are discarded in favour of the literal word. Hence, looking for coherence and regularity became played down in favour of memorising.

In conclusion, contrary to expectations from Gellner's 'high' culture versus 'low' culture, Protestant versus magical enchantment, hypothesis, Islam of the Book is not the functional equivalent of Protestantism, in that it closed the mind to innovation and falsification. In fact, there was a greater elective affinity between Sufism, which is magical, and the scientific spirit.

In chapter 9, Kevin Ryan engages Gellner in a debate with postmodernism. Gellner, of course, wrote specifically about postmodern thought in *Postmodernism, Reason and Religion* (1992) and discusses it in several of his later works. Gellner views postmodernism as one of the latest manifestations of modern relativist irrationalism, which has it roots in communitarian thought. For Gellner the intellectual roots come from Wittgensteinian and hermeneutic traditions. Postmodernism is part of a tradition of communitarian thought whereby actors are locked into systems of self-referential signifiers from which there is no escape. This retreat into language directly parallels the Wittgenstein-inspired retreat into ordinary language. Sociologically speaking, both derive from the same yearning as the nationalist dream of a retreat into the 'village green', which was a self-referential world of cosy 'localness' that was a pure extension of a particularised self – the self of the nation.

A premise of Ryan's critique of Gellner is that, despite his writing about postmodern theory, Gellner did not actually engage with it in a serious manner. Effectively he slots it into the intellectual universe of the open society and its enemies, placing it in the enemy camp without serious consideration of the nuances of postmodern theory. As presented by Ryan, the objective of postmodern theory is not to revel in the parochialism of local language games; rather it is to be open to the contingency of meaning. Both the followers of Popper and those of Foucault are, in fact, driven by the same Kantian problematic: the desire to engage in a permanent critique. Where the difference lies is in terms of emphasis.

Postmoderns are more conscious of this critique as self-directed. It is an ontological self-examination, in which the systems of thought that constitute our being-in-the-world are critiqued. In contrast, moderns direct their critique at the specific problems which they confront at a given moment and which they consider external to them. This constitutes postmodern theory as *problem-driven* research which conceptualises the conditions of possibility of specific problems in our ontology. Modern *problem-solving* has a greater tendency to take problems as given, thus solely confining its critique to the answers to the problems: can specific answers be falsified or not?

Following Ryan's logic, in a curious reversal of the Gellnerian world-view, it is actually the problem-solving Popperians who are local. It is they who take their community of scientists as 'the world' and do not concern themselves with the bigger question of where that world came from. In essence, the problem-solvers are the ones on the village green. In contrast the postmodern Foucauldian approach seeks constantly to probe the boundaries of the village green: to know how 'we' internalise a particular system of thought that delivers these specific local problems for resolution.

There is a clear parallel here with the Kuhn/Popper debate. The postmodern problem-driven researcher asks why and how they came to internalise a particular local paradigm, while the problem-solvers are the 'ordinary scientists' who solve problems within a paradigm without being aware of the possibility that their paradigm is just a village green. The difference between Kuhn and postmodern theory is, first, in their definition of localness – research paradigms versus systems of thought. The second and more significant difference is that postmodern theorists are conscious of how the village green is kept 'clean'. To extend the analogy with nationalism, as has been forcefully argued by Mann and Malešević, nations are created through ethnic cleansing, whereby those who do not belong are excluded. This creates the conditions for 'democratic' dialogue among those who belong to the nation. Similarly, a problem-solving scientific community polices its borders, excluding doubtful and deviant forms which have the potential to introduce 'irrelevant' problems into their shared local community. By a curious twist, when Gellner engaged with postmodern theory there was a constant tendency to lump these theories with irrational forms (with religion and nationalism), and in so doing, by an ironic twist of fate, it could be argued that Gellner joined the locals on the village green building boundaries between 'them' and 'us', thus keeping the village green tidy by sweeping 'doubtful forms' off the neatly clipped grass.

Such an observation may seem a harsh judgement of a thinker who otherwise devoted his life to open dialogue. As a qualification, it is important to remember that Gellner's treatment of postmodernism was motivated not by the desire to keep the village green tidy (even if that was the unintended result) but by the belief, which may be correct, that postmodern social theory is not open to falsification. Habermas is arguably the chief exponent of open society today and he holds a similar view of postmodernism.

In the last chapter of the book, Hall attempts to distil the Gellnerian metaphysic of openness which is implicit in so much of his work. Given Gellner's consciousness of philosophy and sociology, it is a metaphysic which should be both philosophically sound and capable of self-defence (like liberalism but unlike postmodernism), while simultaneously being functional (as Islam and nationalism are, but which some forms of contemporary liberal thought are not) and sociologically plausible in terms of its portrayal of human agency (as contractarian liberalism is not).

Hall begins by observing that Gellner's metaphysic has a strong grounding in his personal history. Gellner began life in a cosmopolitan world which crumbled in the face of nationalism. After fleeing Central Europe, he found himself in Britain, the intellectual centre of liberal openness but where at that time intellectuals were being seduced by relativism derived from Wittgenstein. While an outgrowth of the Enlightenment, this metaphysics was incapable of defending the open society against its rivals.

While Gellner fully appreciated the appeal of relativism, he insisted on the need for universal standards. In his search for foundations, Gellner debates the conceptual opposition between Hume and Kant. Empiricism is criticised as a metaphysical system because it presupposes an implausible solipsistic disencumbered reasoning agent. Hume's empiricism and Skinner's behaviourism (the latter is the logical outcome of the former) both suggest an implausible concept of the self as repetitive automaton. In this regard, Chomskian Kantianism is suggestive of a more plausible description of human agency. Here the social agent is not a being who simply repeats social practices but one who creates social life out of his or her cognitive capacities. However, there is a tendency for these capacities to lie behind the social agent in a manner that renders agency meaningless because 'cognitive structures' displace the 'I' as a source of causation. Thus the 'I' is replaced by an 'it'.

In the end, Gellner seeks his foundations in a kind of ontological sceptical empiricism, which is justified through pragmatism. It is an empirical fact that scientific knowledge is powerful and has the capacity to deliver the resources necessary to render human suffering through deprivation unnecessary and thus obscene. Hence, with the move from scarcity to affluence comes an ontological transformation which renders the social agent normatively resistant to the kind of radically stratified inequality and suffering that characterised premodern social orders. Once this transformation takes place a number of arguments for liberty become persuasive which, while neither mutually consistent nor persuasive singly, collectively amount to a qualified endorsement of the moral principles underpinning liberty.

While Hall is clearly not entirely satisfied with Gellner's metaphysic as a normative defence of liberty, he argues that the premises of Gellner's account are stronger than any current rivals. The broad tendency in modern social theory is to suggest that out of a current plurality of world-views there can be convergence through open discussion because, after all, humans share so much in common. In contrast the strength of Gellner's position, which was tempered in the crucible of his experiences of Nazism, Stalinism and understanding of Islam, lies in his profound understanding of the Weberian point that different systems of thought are constituted through incommensurable metaphysics. In this sense the contemporary fashion for multicultural dialogue is premised upon dis-respect for real difference, while Gellner's metaphysic arose out of a profound understanding of the radical implications of divergence of world-views. However, while his premises may be superior, his solution itself is not entirely satisfactory because it has to be acknowledged that Gellner's metaphysic presupposes a questionable feedback loop from the technical to the moral sphere.

In conclusion, what remains of Gellner's thought after these various critiques? Arguably what is most impressive is that, ten years after his death, his research problematic – the questions he raised and the way he answered them – is still at the cutting edge of social theory. While several of the chapters in this book are critical of Gellner's solutions, none of them argues that his concerns are no longer relevant. When theories no longer speak to our concerns there is no longer a need to falsify or modify them as the chapters in this book have done. As we stated at the beginning of the introduction and have continually re-emphasised, Gellner was a thinker who devoted his life to openness and in this spirit we hope that these critically engaged essays are a fitting tribute to him.

References

Arendt, H. 1970. *On Violence*. London: Penguin.
Barnes, B. 1988. *The Nature of Power*. Cambridge: Polity.
Davis, J. 1991. An Interview with Ernest Gellner. *Current Anthropology* 32 (1): 63–71.
Gellner, E. 1959. *Words and Things*. London: Victor Gollancz.
    1985a. *Relativism and the Social Sciences*. Cambridge: Cambridge University Press.
    1985b. *The Psychoanalytic Movement*. Evanston, IL: Northwestern University Press.
    1992. *Postmodernism, Reason and Religion*. London: Routledge.
    1994. *Conditions of Liberty: Civil Society and Its Rivals*. London: Hamish Hamilton.

1997. *Nationalism*. London: Weidenfeld and Nicolson.

1998. *Language and Solitude*. Cambridge: Cambridge University Press.

Hall, J. A. 1998. Introduction. In J. A. Hall (ed.), *The State of the Nation: Ernest Gellner and the Theory of Nationalism*. Cambridge: Cambridge University Press.

Lichtheim, G. 1965. Review of *Thought and Change*. *The New Statesman* 69: 6.

Part I

Civil society, coercion and liberty

1   Ernest Gellner on liberty and modernity

Alan Macfarlane

Ernest Gellner was in many respects a late Enlightenment thinker. His central theme, like Montesquieu, Hume and de Tocqueville, was summarised in the title of one of his last books, *The Conditions of Liberty.* In this chapter I will summarise what he thought those conditions were. I will then look at three areas where his interpretation can be expanded or challenged. The origins of civil society are somewhat neglected in Gellner's scheme and I shall examine one theory to explain how, against the odds, a new kind of civilisation emerged. The fragility of the Open Society in the aftermath of 9/11 and the 'war on terror' was not something he could address, and I shall do so briefly here. Finally, I shall consider whether there is an alternative to the type of divided modernity which Gellner both defended and mourned.

Gellner believed that liberty arose out of the central characteristic of modernity, namely the separation of spheres or institutions. The pursuit of power (politics), wealth (economics), social warmth (kinship) and meaning (religion) had become separated and balanced each other. 'The really fundamental trait of classical capitalism is that it is a very special kind or order in that the economic and the political seem to be separated to a greater degree than in any other historically known social form' (Gellner 1980: 285). None of the institutions is dominant, there is no determining infrastructure, but a precarious and never stable balance of power.

In the majority of agrarian societies, and in communist and some Islamic societies, nothing is separated, so 'political, economic, ritual and any other kinds of obligations are superimposed on each other in a single idiom' (Gellner 1994: 7). Yet 'Civil Society is based on the separation of the polity from economic and social life'. This 'separation is an inherent feature of Civil Society, and indeed one of its major glories' (1994: 80). Indeed, this is a defining characteristic of civil society, which 'refers to a total society within which the non-political institutions are not dominated by the political ones, and do not stifle individuals either' (1994: 193). So that the 'emergence of Civil Society has in effect meant the breaking of the circle between faith, power and society' (1994: 141).

Gellner's experience of 'closed', integrated worlds, in communism, Islam and Morocco and in his readings on classical societies, led him to realise intensely what many had forgotten, but the Enlightenment knew only too well, that this was one exception to the normal tendency for power to accumulate at the centre, for inequality to grow, and for thought to become imprisoned. There is almost always a negative feedback as wealth grows, and predations dominate over production.

What particularly interested him were the inhibitions on thought, the antithesis to Popper's 'open society'. 'The dependence of the individual on the social consensus which surrounds him, the ambiguity of facts and the circularity of interpretation are all enlisted in support of the fusion of faith and social order. This is the normal social condition of mankind: it is a viable liberal Civil Society, with its separation of fact and value, and its coldly instrumental un-sacramental vision of authority, which is exceptional and whose possibility calls for special explanation' (1994: 140).

Gellner realised the contingent, accidental and unlikely nature of this balanced, open and free world and puzzled about its origins. He adduced various theses. He followed Weber in seeing the role of religion as central. The ascetic, anti-magical tendency in part of Christianity, flourishing with Protestantism, was essential. The fact that the clerics and the rulers fell out with each other and broke the Caesaro-Papist compact, allowing religion and politics to be separated, was another peculiarity.

Secondly he explains the balancing of economy and politics, the emergence of production as a force as powerful as predation, largely by invoking the development of technology and science. The process whereby 'commerce and production … take over from predation and domination' for the first time in history perpetuated itself because it was 'accompanied by two other processes – the incipient Industrial Revolution, leading to an entirely new method of production, and the Scientific Revolution, due to ensure an unending supply of innovation and an apparently unending exponential increase in productive powers' (1994: 73).

Why did this first happen in Europe? Here Gellner uses the widespread insight of the Enlightenment that it was because the geography and history had created a number of medium-sized states, no single one able to dominate for long. The multistate system protected liberty.

Gellner's attempt to specify the question, which is the question of why, against all the odds, in that place and that time, a new form of liberty emerged, is excellent. His answer picks up parts of the Enlightenment answer. But as I have written elsewhere, when comparing him to his predecessors, he misses a great deal that is worthwhile in their answers. All the 'middle part of the Enlightenment solution, the contrast between China and Europe, the analysis of the Roman failure, the nature of the feudal contract and the feudal gate, the loss of the balance in much of continental Europe, the peculiar case of England and why it developed differently, and the consequences in America, all this is missing' (Macfarlane 2000: 262).

I suggest that Gellner's omission of this was due to several reasons. He had not grasped the main point made by Maine and Maitland, which is that the movement from status to contract had already been made within feudalism. As de Tocqueville points out, it was then reversed in much of continental Europe, which relapsed into status again, which is probably what misled Gellner.

He also simplified and distorted history by believing too strongly in tripartite, evolutionary stage models – a point which is encapsulated by the title of his book *Plough, Sword and Book*. In fact, here are many paths, and no uniform stages. There are reversions, deviations, different and mixed forms. There are only tendencies and patterns, no laws. Here I would like to add to my suggestion of ways in which his work could be elaborated and modified by briefly exploring three further themes.

The nature and origins of civil society in Europe

The first is the nature and origins of civil society. Gellner seems to assume that civil society, that is the plethora of institutions which lie above the individual and family, but are not part of the state, emerges naturally if the separation of spheres occurs. It might be more profitable to think of a more active process. In other words, if there are institutional forces to protect and expand these intermediary institutions, they will grow within the social system and push apart the spheres. This creates the conditions for liberty and the separation of spheres.

It is a curious fact that one of the great revivers of the interest in and analysis of civil society should have been so uninterested in its roots. Perhaps it was basing himself on Adam Ferguson rather than Montesquieu, Adam Smith and de Tocqueville that did it. For whatever reasons, we do not get a moving picture of what the roots and nature of civil society and hence the cornerstones of liberty were.

Where we do get it is in the camouflaged political philosophy of F. W. Maitland whose early Trinity dissertation on 'Liberty from Hobbes to Coleridge ...' bore fruit in his last, sick, years in a wonderful explanation of how civil society emerged accidentally in England in the technical device of the 'Trust'.

What Maitland showed was that, through a technical and accidental set of events in the fourteenth century, there developed a device for avoiding properties reverting to the crown at death. In essence, medieval lawyers had originally set out to get round the payment of taxes at death to the king. So they had set up a device whereby groups of friends were entrusted with the property of a major landholder for their lives. When the landowner died, the king could not take the property for it was not owned by the recently deceased person. The entrusted individuals then passed it on to the heir.

This was the 'trust', a curious mixture of status and contract which Roman lawyers and scholars found impossible to understand, but which was protected by the Lord Chancellor and grew rapidly through the centuries. It provided the 'tough shell', as Maitland described it, which allowed civil society to flourish. Corporations were set up by the state and could be wound up. Trusts were independent and their expansion, as Hobbes feared, hemmed in the economic, political and religious powers.

It is a hugely important device, overcoming the central tension in modern civilisations between status and contract and becoming the basis of that civil society which Gellner recognised as the quintessential nature of liberty. Maitland gave a detailed account of how trusts combined the two parts of our lives in an illogical, impossible, yet working hybrid. It could not occur, according to many continental lawyers of Maitland's time, and people are still disbelieving that such a thing can exist. Here I will omit the technical details which I have elaborated elsewhere and move on to sketch out a few of the ways in which the device of the trust spread out from its original narrow legal origin to create the conditions for liberty.

The effects of the introduction of this apparently restricted device, as it spread out throughout the whole of English civilisation, and then into the largest empire on earth, were enormous. Trusts were decisive in tipping the balance against the king in the mid-seventeenth century, for the Inns of Court were trusts. They were behind many political associations, from the political clubs to the trades union, which made democracy possible. They were the basis for local and regional self-government. They instilled the idea that power was held in trust for others, and was not a possession of the rulers. Even the British Empire was held 'in trust' for those who were in it.

Trusts allowed sectarianism and religious liberty. The Methodists, Baptists, Quakers and others were set up and made possible by trusts. Currently, the Roman Catholic Church in England is a registered trust. They allowed the expansion of the economy as a separate and counterveiling force to the polity. The joint-stock companies, Lloyds Bank and Insurance, Sun Alliance, the London Stock Exchange and myriad other organisations were set up as trusts.

Trusts encouraged social groupings of numerous kinds. The sporting clubs (Jockey Club, MCC and a host of others) formed quasi-political pressure groups as well as being centres for sport. They were the foundation for high-class clubs (the Garrick, Carlton, etc.), as well as working men's clubs. They were the basis of science and arts (the Royal Society, British Academy, Lunar Society and others). Many voluntary associations – Oxfam, Royal Societies to protect birds, animals, children, Boy Scouts – all sorts of manifestations of people coming together to do things were encouraged.

More difficult to measure, but equally important, trusts encouraged that openness and self-confidence in the population without which democracy cannot work. It led to the ethic of trust and disinterested public service (as with magistrates and many others) which underpin an open society.

And, very importantly, all this was taken to and flourished in America. So that when de Tocqueville reported on what made America a great and liberal society, he laid a suitably heavy stress on its associational, trust-based nature. But he was not able to find its roots, for it needed a historian cum political philosopher of Maitland's stature to do this.

I only stumbled on Maitland's idea of the trust by accident and never had a chance to discuss it with Ernest, for he was dead. But he would have seen that Maitland has provided an account of the main key which, over the centuries, allowed civil society and hence liberty to flourish. We now have a description of what happened, and how, through a set of chances and unlikely balances, liberty was maintained and flourished against the normal tendencies.[1]

The threat to liberty posed by war and terrorism

A second theme, which Gellner's death did not allow him to consider, was the threat to liberty posed by war and particularly the so-called 'war on terrorism'. Gellner's picture of modern liberty has a deep ambivalence on the question of how secure liberty is. On the one hand the 'escape' into modernity is permanent. Once out of the 'enclosure', once through the 'gate', there is no going back. On the other hand he is well aware that the tendencies to predation, the normal tendencies furthered by the enemies of the Open Society, are very strong. There is no permanence. History has not ended. We are likely to go back into that dark night which Weber predicted, though it is a somewhat different night.

[1] For a fuller account of Maitland's vision, see Macfarlane (2002: chapter 7), or the website www.alanmacfarlane.com (under Maitland).

I think if he had seen what has happened since 1995, and particularly since 9/11, he would have stressed the dangers more. In order to remind us of these dangers, which require far greater treatment than I can give here, let me allude to just one thinker whom I find most insightful on this, Alexis de Tocqueville. What he showed was that liberty and the open society almost always collapse in the face of war, fear and terror.

In the earlier nineteenth century de Tocqueville pointed out that 'all nations that have had to engage in great wars have been led, almost in spite of themselves, to increase the powers of the government. Those which have not succeeded in this have been conquered. A long war almost always faces nations with this sad choice: either defeat will lead them to destruction or victory will bring them to despotism' (de Tocqueville 1835: 207). So he noted that 'All those who seek to destroy the freedom of the democratic nations must know that war is the surest and shortest means to accomplish this' (de Tocqueville 1840: 842). The process, he believed, could be sudden or gradual, but either way a prolonged war will destroy democracy. 'War does not always give democratic societies over to military government, but it must invariably and immeasurably increase the powers of civil government ... If that does not lead to despotism by sudden violence, it leads men gently in that direction by their habits' (de Tocqueville 1840: 842).

The obvious point is that liberty and truth are the first casualties of war. As soon as a war is declared, even if there is no fighting, a government feels itself justified in taking 'any necessary action' to protect its citizens. There is little tolerance of criticism. Suspected opponents are to be locked up; the media are to be censored; due process of law with open trials and juries is to be suspended; the Official Secrets Act is strengthened; all questioning of the government is treason. Even free and open parliamentary elections may have to be postponed until the 'emergency' is over.

People will obey these commands, on the whole, because they have to, either from fear or from the threat of force. All open dissent is treason. In a few seconds several centuries of careful opening up of the political and mental world can be reversed. The lights go out, not one by one, but turned off by one master switch.

This rapid collapse of almost all civil liberties and formal democracy has happened many times in the past, from republican Rome through to the Second World War. Sometimes it can be reversed if the war is of limited duration and the democracy is very strong and emerges triumphant, as happened in 1945. Yet in a vague 'war' against a perpetual foe, as with the 'crusades' against infidels, Jews, witches and other 'terrorists', the war is unending. So democracy and the rule of law, the freedoms of civil society and the balance of power, can never safely be restored.

As the shoots of freedom begin to creep out of the ground, the sharp frost of another panic or perceived terrorist 'threat' will wither them. The tree of the state will be bare, just power and order, a machine for fighting an endless war.

This suppression of democracy through fear of war is the normal human condition and has occurred in almost all great civilisations from China to Spain. There were small-scale exceptions – Athens, early Rome, the early Italian city-states, the Dutch – but there have only been three larger exceptions. These were cases where, by an accident of history, a water boundary protected a growing nation from the threat of landed attack. These were Japan, Britain (particularly after the unification with Scotland) and North America.

For a few hundred years from the seventeenth to the twentieth century these three 'islands' guarded themselves at sea, with naval forces or coastal fortifications. They did not need and had no standing armies, armies which almost always tend to lead to military-based despotisms. So they built up and enjoyed the precarious delights of a balance of powers and a certain openness and popular representation which made them into democracies of a sort.

'Of a sort' is important to stress, for in Japan it was not a democracy, but it was for a very long period a peaceful and balanced political system. This lasted until it became threatened by European powers and America from the middle of the nineteenth century. Out of this there developed the militarism which quickly switched the nation into an imperial aggressor in the middle of the twentieth century.

Britain had the most powerful technology on earth when it became the first industrial nation. Combined with its fleets and great empire, it could feel relatively unthreatened. This enriched its balanced democracy, which just survived the turmoil of the twentieth century.

In the case of North America, it feared no landed neighbour for over two centuries and could pursue the path of quiet democratic growth. Its enemies, particularly the Soviet Union, were far away and its troops were stationed abroad. There was no temptation to military dictatorship and no threat that could be plausible enough to persuade its populace, even in the height of the Cold War, to abandon its open political and social system.

All this began to change towards the close of the twentieth century, but we did not notice it at first. The fear and panic was being sown within the powerful Western nations by prophets who foresaw a 'clash of civilisations'. They called for moral and military rearmament and the strengthening of the state. For a while the confidence and separateness of North America prevented most people from hearing their calls and they were brushed aside. They appeared as a lunatic fringe of deeply conservative extremists whom no one could really take seriously with their talk of a 'conspiracy of evil' which had taken over from communism.

All this was symbolically and actually changed by September 11th, 2001 and the two planes that crashed into the twin towers in New York. In a few seconds America joined the land-masses of Eurasia. It became, in effect, a continental power with vulnerable borders, rather than being a safe island. It joined the powerful tendency towards fear and the desire to use pre-emptive force from which it had been shielded for those two and a half centuries of its growth.

War, with its associated fear and tendency to increase political centralisation, will almost always destroy liberty. The views of the great political scientists were clear. A republic (including democracies) is particularly vulnerable to these pressures and will turn into a dictatorship very fast. So only a short and finite war, lasting four or five years, can be endured before freedom and the separation of spheres is permanently lost.

What has happened since 9/11 is that both of these conditions for liberty have been lost. Nowhere is an island now. America has, in a split second, been joined to mainland Eurasia, even more so than by Pearl Harbour. The seas have melted away, as they did for Britain in 1914 and 1939 with the air-raids. Yet in 1918 and 1945 the wars ended, with the possibility of freeing the illegally interned Japanese and others. Now that we are in a perpetual war, and a war where the enemy are within as well as without, there is no chance for liberty to return.

We are in danger of entering a one-way process. The constant diminution of civil society and liberty as a means towards an end has become instituted. It is 1984, as predicted, with Big Brother at last ensconced with the smiling face of certain right-wing politicians whose names change, but whose messages become ever more menacing. These are things which would have deeply troubled Gellner and we miss his penetrating analysis of the traps we are entering.

The costs and necessity of modernity: the exceptional case of Japan

Gellner was well aware of the consequences of the Enlightenment transformation. He believed that Western industrial-capitalist society is 'without any shadow of doubt, conquering, absorbing all the other cultures of this Earth' (Gellner 1988: 200). The single occasion when men escaped from the embedded pre-industrial world has 'transformed the entire world' (1988: 277), for the 'modern industrial machine is like an elephant in a very small boat ... [it] presupposes an enormous infrastructure, not merely of political order, but educationally, culturally, in terms of communication and so forth' (1980: 288).

One central theme in Gellner's work is the growth of rationality or the disenchantment of the world. There is a 'radical discontinuity' which exists 'between primitive and modern mentality' (1988: 42). This is the 'transition to effective knowledge', which Gellner describes many times.[2] This is, of course, not unlike the work of Karl Popper, whom Gellner admired. But Gellner's stress is on the fact that 'the attainment of a rational, non-magical, non-enchanted world is a much more fundamental achievement than the jump from one scientific vision to another'. Popper 'underestimates the difficulty' of establishing an open society (Gellner 1979: 182).

Yet this 'freedom of thought' is bought at a price. Gellner takes from Kant and Weber, among others, his analysis of the consequences of this disenchantment. The modern world 'provides no warm cosy habitat for man ... the impersonality and regularity ... which make it knowable are also, at the same time, the very features which makes it almost ... unadaptable' (Gellner 1979: 184). Our world is 'notoriously a cold, morally indifferent world'. It is notable for its 'icy indifference to values, its failure to console and reassure, its total inability to validate norms and values or to offer any guarantee of their eventual success' (Gellner 1988: 64–5). The open predicament is one where logical consistency and openness is bought at the price of social and moral inconsistency. We are simultaneously strictly rational and open-minded, and totally lost and confused. Within the new world 'there also is and can be no room either for magic or for the sacred' (Gellner 1988: 66). 'Revelation offers one vision and science offers, not another, but none' (Gellner 1995: 239).

Yet we cannot go back to innocence. '*The* central fact about our world is that, for better or worse, a superior, more effective form of cognition does exist.' Thus the 'world we live in is defined, above all, by existence of a unique, unstable and powerful system of knowledge of nature, and its corrosive, unharmonious relationship to the other clusters of ideas ("cultures") in terms of which men live. *This* is our problem' (Gellner 1992: 60). This 'atomized, cognitively unstable world, which does not underwrite the identities and values of those who dwell in it [,] is neither

---

[2] For example, see Gellner (1979: 169, 173).

comfortable nor romantic'. All we can do is realise that it is mistaken to believe that 'the price need not be paid at all, that one can both have one's romantic cake and scientifically eat it' (Gellner 1987: 181–2).

A living experience of different worlds also made Gellner more aware than many of the 'cost' of disenchantment. The 'insulation' of various spheres of life has its own costs. Although it allows people to think 'freely' and to act 'rationally', it is, of course, caught in the deeper contradiction that the real world is *not* separated into watertight compartments. We have to *believe* that religion and politics, morality and economics, kinship and politics are separable and can live amicably alongside each other. But the garment is thereby torn apart arbitrarily; reality is a seamless web, as people living in the majority of human societies have realised. Marx recognised this in his concept of 'alienation', Durkheim in 'anomie', Weber in 'disenchantment'. Gellner adds his own voice to elaborating these contradictions.

Like his famous predecessors, Ernest Gellner believed that there is no alternative. Either we have meaning, warmth, community, or we have rationality, efficiency, liberty but coldness and loss of meaning. Yet Gellner may have missed the one real alternative system which provided a bridging of this antithesis in a way which is more acceptable than the two which he spent his life considering – communism and Islam.

Gellner never explored Japanese civilisation. An encounter with Japan on a visit to Osaka in his later years which I discussed with him left him bemused and irritated. He could not see how the Japanese could behave so deferentially, apparently find it so hard to communicate with outsiders and generally inhabit an obviously embedded world full of 'sticky' social relations, yet simultaneously run the most efficient economy on earth. He playfully suggested to me that all the behaviour he observed was an act, put on for outsiders. When top Japanese managers went into their boardrooms they dropped all this type of behaviour and became the plain-speaking rationalists who lay behind the mask. He never pursued this odd contradiction and entered the mysterious looking-glass world which is Japan. If he had done so, he might have seen the one possible exception to all the grand sociological generalisations which he took for granted.

The essence of the difference between the three great forms of human civilisations, tribesmen, peasants, industrial-capitalist, is as follows. In tribal societies nothing is separated off. Beliefs about the world (religion), relations with people (society), ways of keeping order (politics) and the methods of producing and consuming wealth (economy) are all mixed together. There are no distinct institutions. It is not possible to isolate 'the economy', 'the religion', 'the society', 'the polity'. This is a joined or holistic world.

Until I had studied Japan, I thought that such unified holism was only to be found in very small, barely surviving, oral cultures such as those studied by anthropologists in remote places. It had become obvious to me that almost all such societies had been destroyed when the next great stage of human history occurred, that is the settled peasant civilisations which came to dominate the world from about five thousand years ago.

A characteristic of 'civilisation', as opposed to tribalism, was the beginning of institutional divisions. Usually they were represented by the three great orders. The military and rulers became specialists in power and politics, the state was born. The priests and writers became specialists in belief, a religion was born. The peasants, merchants and craftsmen became specialists in production, an economy was born, though it was still undivided to a certain extent from society since the main unit of production and consumption was through the family.

This happened in the long period between about 5000 BC and about 1500 AD. Then, in the capitalist, scientific, industrial revolutions, the Enlightenment and the French and American revolutions, the already partial separations become firmer and more universal. First in north-west Europe with Protestantism, and then in America, and then over much of the world, the world of full separations (in theory at least) emerges.

The final separation, often equated with capitalism and the end of feudalism in the later middle ages, heralded our world. Now the market emerged as a separate and discrete entity. The peasant mode of production was shattered and the 'economy as an instituted process' was inaugurated with private property, the universal acceptance of monetary values, production exclusively for exchange. Furthermore, the pact of church and state which had often been instituted in peasant civilisations was broken apart, as with Protestantism, and our modern world of full institutional separation (in theory at least), where only the individual is part of all four worlds, had emerged. Like Ernest Gellner and his predecessors, in particular Weber, this is what I took 'modernity' to mean.

The extraordinary discovery I have only recently made about Japan is that, by filtering and modifying the pressures from outside, it has managed to avoid these separations. Starting off as holistic and integrated, it has remained so. While appearing to be very modern, and perhaps indeed postmodern (in its fusion between spheres of life), it has reached this stage without going through the stage of modernity. Emiko Ohnuki-Tierney offers us a choice. The Japanese case 'challenges the assumption that modernization undermines the symbolic realm of the people; either the anthropological distinction between primitive and modern cultures is incorrect, or Japanese culture is "primitive"' (Ohnuki-Tierney 1984: 50). I would argue that the distinction, as I had understood it when Ernest Gellner was alive, is indeed incorrect. If we do retain the opposition, then Japan is certainly 'primitive' or tribal.

The jibe that America is the only country that went from barbarism to decadence without the intervening phase of civilisation, could be adapted for Japan to state that it was the only nation that went from tribal to something outside modernity, without the intervening stage of modernity. It has always been an embedded, holistic, tribal society. Edwin Reischauer is roughly right when he says that 'the Japanese formed a sort of gigantic modern tribe' (Reischauer 1988: 396).

This explains many odd things I have encountered in my study of Japan. Schoolchildren I met could not answer the question of what religion they believed in because there was no such thing as 'a religion'. Likewise it explains why much of economic activity is embedded in social relations, and vice versa, so that it exhibits a form of 'capitalist communism'. It explains the odd feeling of a porous kinship, both spreading out its emotional impact onto relations of power and production and belief, yet in itself weak and fragmented at the institutional level. It explains why all parts of life are fused together through aesthetics and style, which, by emphasising process and form, can unite people when there is nothing else to do so. It explains why all of ethics is multistranded, contextual and ad hoc.

The feeling I have, after living in a tribal society (the Gurungs of Nepal) and after reading and teaching about many of the classic tribal societies in Africa, India, South America and the Pacific, is that Japan is in some ways like a gigantic tribal society. It comprises not just a few thousands or tens of thousands of persons, but over 120 million. The surface of Japan, particularly the technology and material world, at first look familiar enough. Yet below that is a set of relations between parts of what makes a society work which is totally different from what I have experienced elsewhere.

Japan is, as the famous image states, a *natto* society. The intertwined roots of the fermenting soya beans move together as we stir one part of the mixture. Hardly any action or relationship is single-dimensional or stranded. Almost everything involves simultaneously what we would divide off as a separate political, economic, social and religious dimension. This is a huge burden for the Japanese since it means that each interpersonal relationship tends to be multilevel. It explains why many Japanese find it such a relief to live in the fragmented West.

Yet the multilevel and intertwined nature of the society is also a great source of strength since the famous anomie (rootlessness) and point-lessness, the draining of meaning when we separate out our institutions and which Gellner lamented, is mitigated in Japan. Every gesture or action, for example working or painting or drinking tea, has a wealth of meanings beyond the thing itself.

The fusing of fields or institutions, which makes living in Japan in many ways like living in the enchanted and largely undivided world of a Himalayan village, but with 120 million rather than two thousand people to interact with, can be seen in the field which we label religion or belief.

In Japan, nothing is split apart. Mind and body are on one continuum, part of the same entity, not separate as in the modern West. The material world of the senses and the supernatural world of spirit are not opposed and different; they are interfused in the way that the poet Wordsworth tried to describe. Everything is simultaneously material, and infused with spirit. The sacred and the profane, the individual and the group, the natural and the supernatural, the mind and the body, all the recent Western oppositions are negated.

In my visits and reading I sense a vast integrated world which has somehow survived on the edge of Eurasia. It has not gone through the dissociations of modernity which Gellner, along with all the great classical sociologists, assumed to be the only path to a relatively open industrial-scientific world. It has managed to achieve an orderly, efficient, sophis-ticated and aesthetically beautiful civilisation while maintaining this holistic cohesion.

Evidence for this interpretation comes if we ask the question, what is the determining institution in Japan? In tribal societies there is nothing that dominates, although kinship, which includes what we term religion, politics and economics, often draws everything together. In many peasant civilisations, it is the combination of religion and politics. In modern capitalist societies, it is the economy which is the infrastructure or determinant. But with Japan?

Kinship is not a candidate, for it is both very weak, constructed and fragmentary, though, as a sentiment and metaphor, it stretches out into all spheres. Religion it is not. Japan is not another India, where religion has been so important. Religion in Japan does not exist as an infra-structure; it is fragmented; it is simultaneously, like kinship, everywhere and nowhere at the same time. Political power is important traditionally and the strong feudal traditions make it come closer to a determining fact, but again it seems to mingle into the family and economy and not to be the generator of all worlds. And economic activities, as we have seen, while very important, do not prescribe, but reflect other pressures.

This explains why it is unsatisfactory, when asked to say what permeates or holds Japan together, to suggest that it is the normal institutions we are familiar with – law, politics, economy, religion, kinship or class. Instead, we begin to talk of aesthetics, etiquette, feelings, shared experience, history.

It feels in Japan as if there is no infrastructure in the Marxist sense, no base or foundations on which Japan is built. Rather it is, like the traditional houses, held together not by the strong foundations but by the horizontal ties between different parts. It is glued by manners, purity, aesthetics, good behaviour, respect. It is the only large civilisation I know of where 'custom' (or *habitus*, as it is now known to anthropologists) really *is* king. That is to say the unexamined, invisible rules of behaviour are all that hold people together. You *are* Japanese, and you behave accordingly. Nothing can be or needs to be written down. There is no shell or outer carapace – except the physically bounded country which provides a tough casing for what, inside, is flexible, soft and constantly in movement.

Other contemporary industrial societies are structured by the institutional areas, so that individuals behave within each of them, performing institutional roles as workers, family members, voters, worshippers. In the absence of institutional spheres, everything is connected to everything else in Japan. Everyone and everything is a relation, not a thing in itself. In Japan we have *Homo holisticus*, holistic or undivided humanity.

In Japan, everything is enchanted, and yet nothing is. There are no separations of mind and body, spirit and matter, natural and supernatural. This is the Wordsworthian solution. Likewise the normal opposition of art and life is negated. Life is art, art is life. Likewise with class – there are no intrinsic (caste) or manufactured (class) divisions between people, all of whom are held in a hierarchical yet equal web, moving out from the centre (the Emperor) to the outside, like a spider's web, rather than like a chest of drawers. Likewise the division of labour and leisure is absent. We work to live, and live to work.

What is extraordinary is that all this 'enchantment' and fusion of head and heart, of pre-Cartesian associations, can subsist alongside an extremely successful, urban, industrial, market economy. That is the mystery and something which Gellner, with his somewhat binary thought system, found it very difficult to approach. It is amazing that writing, money, markets, cities, all those things which are supposed to bifurcate and drain our world fail to do so and the total, holistic, structural, relational and pre-dissociated world can continue serenely on its way.

This throws light on the Gellnerian problems of how we can overcome the bifurcation of modernity, but from a different tack from that in Maitland. It addresses a problem which, like Ernest Gellner, I have faced throughout my adult life. How can we preserve the totality and integration we find in childhood or in tribal societies, yet alongside this include the benefits of industrialism, freedom of thought and high technology?

Previously it looked as if, as Ernest argued, one could only have one or the other – cosiness and poverty, or coldness and wealth. The Japanese show that, to a considerable extent, we can have our cake and eat it. Japan has adopted the opposite solution to America and Europe, who have gone for separating off the worlds.

All this is important to say at a time when the Western models are being questioned and simultaneously China and India are looking for a philosophy which will give them both wealth and meaning. The Japanese case may not be possible to emulate. Yet it does show that there is an alternative, that history has not ended.

This is not the 'Confucian' way; it is anti-Confucian. Yet it is an alternative way, reintegrating a shattered experience. Our interest in it comes not only because of our growing awareness of global inter-dependence, but also because we feel increasingly dissatisfied with the artificial separations of modernity. Gellner was likewise always dissatis-fied, but never saw a solution to the apparently inevitable contradiction. In the West we are moving to something else, often loosely called postmodernity. Yet the shape of this move in the West, from modernity to something else, is very different from the shape in Japan from pre to post. So Japan is a fascinating thought experiment for us.

The fact that Japan has managed to be a hugely successful 'modern' technological and economic power, while remaining in essence 'non-Axial', 'non-Cartesian' and non-capitalist, is amazing. It subverts the 'laws' of sociology, including the formulations of Marx, Weber and Durkheim. It undermines all standard stories of the developmental sequence of civilisations. It suggests that there are different paths to the present, and hence to the future. It is thus an important example for many non-Western societies, including China and India. Now that commun-ism has collapsed, Japan is the only viable and successful alternative to Western individualistic capitalism.

Of course, other societies do not need to take as radically different a path as Japan. Nor do they have to be as periodically savage or contorted in their relations to others. Yet the assumption that it is only by splitting off the parts of our life, as Gellner and I assumed, that is, the natural and the supernatural, the heart and the mind, the body and the soul, the material and the spiritual, that we can we be prosperous and competitive is shown to be questionable. We find a place where the economic, pol-itical, ideological and social are united, yet efficiency is possible. Japan is the large exception to all the normal tendencies of human history and the 'stages' through which we were supposed to arrive at our predestined end result.

Japan leapt from tribal to postmodern without the intervening 'stages' of semi (peasant) and full (industrial/capitalist) modernity, just as its technology in the nineteenth century leapt from a pre-wheel, largely feudal level, to a post-wheel, post-industrial level, without the intervening stages.

In the book I am currently writing on this subject, I have tried to explain how the Japanese have managed to retain an essentially integrated, holistic, 'non-modern', civilisation alongside behaving very effectively as a modern industrial power.[3] It is the way in which they have solved this problem, coming up with a unique solution as to how to be both 'modern' and 'ancient', that might teach us something useful.

Japan is relatively egalitarian, with little disorder, high artistic standards, satisfaction in a life full of meaning. All this has been described for certain early tribal societies. Yet in Japan it happens alongside a hyper-efficient modern industrial production system and urban way of life. In some ways, the Japanese have achieved Marx's dream of a non-alienated wealthy society, they have solved Durkheim's problem of overcoming anomie, they have escaped from Weber's iron cage.

The Japanese seem to have largely overcome one of the great dichotomies, forcefully restated by Ernest Gellner when he argued that we can have either efficiency or warmth, but not both. The Japanese, despite many difficulties, have evolved a package which ensures a great deal of order, stability, safety, meaning, beauty and comfort, combined with a superbly efficient and successful economy.

If we compare those other alternatives to Western capitalism to which Gellner devoted considerable attention, the Japanese solution seems rather attractive. Islam often shares many of the features of intolerance of other religions of the Book, as Gellner pointed out. Although there are many variants, there is a tendency toward anti-intellectualism, to bureaucratic corruption and economic inefficiency which has at times sent Islamic societies towards the same dire situation as their Christian alternatives. It has its attractions, but it is not intrinsically better as a total package than Western capitalism. It is morally more co-ordinated, but intellectually (and for many women) not very satisfactory.

Likewise the communism derived from the teachings of Marx and Lenin, despite its high ideals, has shown a great set of weaknesses. It does not work effectively as a way of organising the economy. It often leads to

---

[3] This section on Japan was written in August 2005 at an early stage of writing my book *Japan through the Looking Glass* (Profile Books, 2007).

another form of absolutism and savage brutality towards its minorities and dissidents. It does not even banish inequality. It has lost its allure, and certainly did not hold Gellner in its spell.

So, without the case of Japan there is no large-scale alternative left in the world. We can either turn away from the Japanese experiment, or we can learn something from this. Many have done the former. As Robert Smith writes, 'we seek to reassure ourselves by denying the implications of what we see, for otherwise we should be forced to concede that a system different from our own, without becoming like us, has achieved goals we have long taken to be uniquely ours' (Smith 1983: 139).

We may not wish to be Japanese, yet we cannot but be intrigued by the Japanese struggle to create a decent, beautiful and meaningful society along lines totally different from those of Western, individualistic capitalism. It suggests alternatives to the modern Western way in its attitudes to ecology, polity, society and religion. We learn that we do not have to consume so much, to empty our life of meaning, to become ever more unequal, to believe in a single God, to have high crime rates and a lawyer-dominated society. The Japanese example provides us with choices. There is a working alternative in the twenty-first century. It is alive and flourishing and we can step through the magical glass for the price of an air ticket or a few hours in a good art gallery or museum. Yet Japan remains invisible unless we un-think a great deal of what Ernest Gellner believed to be the necessary nature of modernity. The Enlightenment partially blinded him, as it did so many other great thinkers.

Gellner might suggest that liberty is constrained in the Japanese solution, and in many ways it is. Maruyama Masao, in particular, saw that the absence of the isolated subjective individual was a problem in Japan.[4] Yet it is hard to argue that Japan is either totalitarian or anti-individualistic. It holds up another solution to the question of how to organise our world which I believe Gellner would have been delighted to explore if he had been around with us today.

I have argued that basically Gellner specified the problems very well in terms of accident and uniqueness and the tension between open and closed. He addressed the deepest questions he had posed in a brilliant way. What I have tried to do here is to add three qualifications or modifications.

Gellner never explained satisfactorily how the open society, resting on civil society, could emerge against the predatory tendencies which he so graphically outlined. F.W. Maitland's solution, a combination of

---

[4] See Macfarlane (2005) for my interpretation of Maruyama.

accident, islandhood and a number of chance yet powerful events, partially helps to complete Gellner's story in this most important element of his general account.

Gellner was well aware of the fragility of the world of liberty and was apprehensive about its continuation. He would have been even more so if he had lived for another ten years and witnessed the exact consequences of what de Tocqueville had predicted, and George Orwell was later to elaborate in *1984*, namely that a perpetual war will destroy liberty step by step. The most important condition for liberty is a freedom from fear, and the unholy collusion of some Western governments with their mirror foes, I suspect, would have distressed him.

Finally he might well have found an intriguing solution to his antitheses between meaning and efficiency, warmth and openness, community and association, if he had thought more about Japan. He was well aware of the importance of Karl Jaspers' work on the axial transformation. He might therefore have grasped the implications of the recent work of S.N. Eisenstadt (1996) and Robert Bellah (2003), who have shown how Japan failed to go through the axial transformation and hence took a different path. Whether he would have been able to revise his whole orientation to take account of a civilisation which lies outside the sociological categories which have become established in the West since the Enlightenment it is difficult to say.

What is clear is that we confront a great mind circling over the patterns of human history. It is a mind which we miss greatly. So it is a particular pleasure to have been able very recently to rescue the film of an eight-hour seminar on models of social change held in Cambridge in 1977. Gellner was at the height of his power and was surrounded by some of the intellectual heavyweights of the time: Edward Thompson, Raphael Samuel, Keith Hopkins, Jack Goody, Edmund Leach, Maurice Godelier and others debated the virtues of various interpretations of history, in particular Marxism. We see many of the assumptions and interpretations which I have alluded to here expressed in Gellner's inimitable style and for a moment time is suspended and he is still with us.[5]

References

Bellah, R. 2003. *Imagining Japan*. Berkeley: University of California Press.
Eisenstadt, S.N. 1996. *Japanese Civilization*. Chicago: University of Chicago Press.
Gellner, E. 1979. *Legitimation of Belief*. Cambridge: Cambridge University Press.

[5] The seminars can be seen at www.alanmacfarlane.com/ssrc/ssrc1977.html

1980. *Spectacles and Predicaments: Essays in Social Theory.* Cambridge: Cambridge University Press.

1987. *Culture, Identity and Politics.* Cambridge: Cambridge University Press.

1988. *Plough, Sword and Book: The Structure of Human History.* London: Collins Harvill.

1992. *Postmodernism, Reason and Religion.* London: Routledge.

1994. *Conditions of Liberty: Civil Society and Its Rivals.* London: Hamish Hamilton.

1995. *Anthropology and Politics: Revolutions in the Sacred Grove.* Oxford: Blackwell.

Macfarlane, A. 2000. *The Riddle of the Modern World: Of Liberty, Wealth and Equality.* Basingstoke: Palgrave.

2002. *The Making of the Modern World: Visions from the West and the East.* Basingstoke: Palgrave.

2005. *Fukuzawa Yukichi and Maruyama Masao: Two Visions of Japan.* Berkeley University Maruyama Lecture.

Ohnuki-Tierney, E. 1984. *Illness and Culture in Contemporary Japan.* Cambridge: Cambridge University Press.

Reischauer, E.O. 1988. *The Japanese Today.* Tokyo: Tuttle Publishing.

Smith, R. 1983. *Japanese Society.* Cambridge: Cambridge University Press.

Tocqueville, A. de 1968. [1835, 1840]. *Democracy in America*, 2 vols., trans. George Lawrence. London: Fontana.

2 Predation and production in European imperialism

Michael Mann

Introduction: a defence of the European Miracle (and of Ernest Gellner) – in Europe

In the first and second volumes of *The Sources of Social Power* I gave an account of 'the European Miracle' which owed a considerable personal debt to Ernest Gellner – and also to John Hall, through our LSE Seminar Series 'Patterns of History'. There we invited eminent scholars, experts on a great range of societies in time and place, to speak on the major issues of their field. We did this in order to pillage knowledge from them which would be useful in our own budding theories of social development. I greatly admired my two colleagues' abilities to cut to the chase of major issues, especially John through his incisive questioning and Ernest through his theory-rich one-liners. Over the 1980s Ernest, John and I then gave overlapping accounts of the 'European Miracle' in which we argued that the essential breakthrough to modernity came in Western Europe, and that its origins and dynamic lay deep-rooted in the continent (Gellner 1988; Hall 1986; Mann 1986). So also did Jean Baechler, with whom we collaborated in a book (Hall et al. 1988), and so have economic historians like Ernest Jones (1987) and David Landes (1998).

Since the 1990s this viewpoint has been attacked by economic historians styling themselves as 'anti-Orientalists', especially Kenneth Pomerantz (2000), Bin Wong (1997) and André Gunder Frank (1998), buttressed by demographers (Lee and Cameron 1997; Lee and Feng, 1999) and sociologists (Goldstone 2002; Hobson 2004). They contend that only in the nineteenth century did the European economy – more specifically, the British economy – overtake the Asian economy, specifically the economy of the lower Yangtze, Asia's most advanced region. Before the eighteenth century they see Asia as having been ahead, while in the eighteenth century the two continents and regions were broadly level, both caught in the Smithian 'high equilibrium' trap of agrarian economies, followed up by the Malthusian population trap. 'Smithian development' could extend the division of labour and markets, but without major technological or institutional breakthroughs no further surge of development was possible, and then population growth would wipe out most of the gains. They say that only the industrial revolution, essentially occurring after 1800, enabled first Britain and then Western Europe to surge forward into global dominance. They add that this surge was not deep-rooted, but due to two 'accidents'. First, Europe/Britain (unlike China) happened to have coal near its industry, reducing costs and enabling technological virtuous cycles to develop between its industries. Second, Europe/Britain acquired New World colonies which happened to provide sugar, timber, cotton and especially silver, which boosted its domestic economy and living standards and enabled it to trade substantially for the first time with Asia.

If these arguments are true, then a large part of Gellner's account of modern development, given specially in his *Conditions of Liberty* (1994) – and my own in *The Sources of Social Power* – falls to the ground. I have discussed the issues more fully elsewhere (Mann 2005). Here I repeat only my conclusions in order initially to flourish my membership card of the Gellner fan club, before turning to a more critical vein.

Though the anti-Orientalists make many good points, they fail to undermine the twin notions that the European breakthrough came earlier and that its dynamics were deep-rooted. The demographic data on England (Wrigley and Schofield 1989; supplemented by Hart 1998, and Wrigley 1998) reveal that living standards were already higher than in China by the early eighteenth century. Soon after 1700 the relationship between food prices and mortality rates, already weak, had disappeared completely, and there were no more famines. Both problems remained in China, as Lee and Feng have conceded (1999: 45, 110–13). Malthusian crises had already been banished from England and not from China, concludes Deng (2003). The crucial economic data concern labour productivity. Brenner and Isett (2002) show it increased by a massive 60 per cent in England from just before 1700 to just before 1800, at a time when Chinese labour productivity was declining. Thus Britain could expand agriculture yet also at the same time (uniquely) release labour into the towns and into industry. Agricultural imports were unnecessary until after 1820 or 1830. Smithian limits were being breached from the early eighteenth century, before the industrial revolution. As for coal, British luck had also come early. Even by 1700 England produced five times as much coal as the rest of the world put together, and fifty times as much as China. After 1700 Chinese coal output declined while British output grew steadily. Economic growth also diffused fairly evenly across the whole English economy (Crafts 2004). Temin (1997) measured the efficiency of early nineteenth-century English industry in terms of its ability to lower prices of its exports in relation to imports. Substantial lowering occurred across most industries, revealing (he says) that a general entrepreneurial, innovative economic culture was already in place by 1800. Capitalist economic institutions did also exist in China, but they now dominated England.

It is true that trade remained more developed in Asia. At the beginning of the nineteenth century Europe contributed a much smaller proportion of world trade than Asia did. Frank observes that Europe had essentially nothing China wanted, except silver, whose export from the Americas to Asia was the only product enabling the Europeans to receive the many Chinese goods they desired. But in finance Europe led decisively. Asian dependence on silver, itself a commodity, as a generalised means of exchange, indicates a primitive banking and credit system. In Western Europe capitalist credit-money developed, from the fifteenth century in Italy to the late seventeenth century in England. This allowed debts to be transferred to third parties, to circulate as private money, and to be issued as bank money. Three-way relations between the state, rentiers and taxpayers appeared, mediated and reproduced by a public central bank, backed by an infrastructurally powerful state and a sovereign parliament which represented both creditors and debtors. An elastic supply of credit-money issued by banks and the state enabled England to defeat France, and was a precondition for the diffuse entrepreneurial spirit mentioned above. I am delighted to report that Ingham concludes his masterful account of these developments by saying that the evolution of capitalist credit-money may be traced to the 'multiple, insecure, acephalous political jurisdictions' of Europe which I had identified in the first volume of *Sources* (Ingham 2004: chapter 6; quote from p. 109). As Ingham observes, there was nothing remotely comparable in China – not even a single currency, let alone generalised forms of credit.

There were no longer Malthusian or Smithian cycles in Britain soon after 1700, while a modern financial system was also in place. Uniquely, the limits of agrarian societies had been breached. The European economic miracle was underway a century earlier than the anti-Orientalists say. It had emerged over a long period of time and contained dynamics of varying temporalities, some of them quite old. Of course, it did not yet dominate the world – this only happened after 1850, and then it was only to last for a century or so.

But an *economic* miracle was never Gellner's primary concern. He believed that industrialism had important consequences in homogenising societies and creating nations, but in itself it was little more than a 'universal bribery fund', its growth keeping everybody more or less content while more valuable progress was made elsewhere. Far more important for him were the political and ideological liberties causing and reinforcing the miracle: political freedoms, and freedom of thought and expression from all authority – secular, spiritual and magical. The result was a genuinely creative force allowing human society to escape from 'predation' into 'production', into a society where for the first time increasing wealth would not be seized by 'kings, cousins and thugs', but distributed more fairly through the population as a whole. And indeed this key transition from predation to production did transpire in Western Europe. In explaining the miracle, Gellner also consistently stressed causal factors connected to individual freedom and reason – especially forms of Protestantism which were (through design or circumstance) relatively rational, tolerant and independent of the state; a competitive multi-state system; and a scientific revolution which proved techno-logically productive (Gellner 1988, 1994, 1995). For Gellner the core of the miracle lay in a broader liberalism growing in European and espe-cially British society.

Recent historical research has given Gellner much support. The technologies of the industrial revolution have been traced back to the English 'scientific revolution' of the seventeenth century (e.g. Goldstone 2002). Though most inventions came through the 'micro-technologies' of engineers and artisans, they had imbibed the scientific ideology that natural phenomena were orderly and predictable, mastered by exact measurement and reproducible experiment. Not absolute truth, but instrumental, incremental knowledge was their goal (Mokyr 1992, 2000). Even the anti-Orientalists concede that after about 1650 the Europeans, not the Chinese, were making the important scientific and technological breakthroughs – however much the Europeans had earlier borrowed from Chinese science and technology (Hobson 2004). There is also agreement that the scientific revolution owed much to Protestant rationalism. Scientists believed that the laws they discovered were God's laws. Leibnitz, Boyle and Newton embedded their theories amid Protestant theology. Margaret Jacobs (1997, 2000) notes that many of the scientists, entrepreneurs and engineers of the industrial revolution were Protestant Dissenters, committed to values of probity, order and faith. In Catholic Europe science blossomed later, embedded in the anti-religious ration-alism of the Enlightenment. But even in Charles Darwin's time in the mid-nineteenth century, most researchers defined their work not as 'science' but as 'natural theology'. All this sounds very Gellnerian.

Yet Gellner's liberal model seems much less suited to the taking of the miracle overseas. Europeans did not simply out-compete the rest of the world; they conquered it and then imposed empire upon it. So far as I know, Gellner did not write about these empires. In his essay 'War and Violence' (in Gellner 1995), he passes from agrarian to industrial societies without a word about empires, except for the Soviet type. This is odd, since the leading edge of overseas imperialism, as well as of capitalism, passed from Catholic authoritarian to Protestant constitutional countries, and most especially to Britain. British imperialism also involved the same kinds of actors and institutions as those responsible for the economic miracle at home. Merchant trading companies almost invariably preceded formal colonial rule. African expansion was spearheaded by 'freelance promoters', adventurers, missionaries, entrepreneurs and soldiers-for-hire, men like Stanley, Rhodes, Goldie and Lugard, hired mostly by trading companies, with blank treaty forms in their pockets, and a desire to expand the three Cs – Commerce, Christianity and Civilisation – in their hearts. Even the king of the Belgians formed his own private company (Pakenham 1991: xxiv). The science useful for empire and boosted by it also usually came from individual 'adventurers' like Joseph Banks, while the maritime explorers mixed science and enterprise, as their ships' names reveal – *Discovery*, *Resolution*, *Adventure*, *Endeavour*; *Géographie*, *Naturaliste*; *L'Astrolabe* and *La Boussole* (Drayton 2001: 245). Empire, like the miracle at home, embodied intense, rational, scientific competition, between individuals, enterprises and states. The culminating British Empire, ruler of a quarter of the earth's land surface in 1920 – as well as its nearest equal, the French Republican Empire – was considered a 'liberal' empire. Empire was obviously part of the same miracle.

And yet the imperial part of the miracle looks very different from the domestic one, especially if one stresses – as Gellner does – liberalism. For all their liberal virtues at home, the Europeans – and especially the British – initially took overseas not political and ideological liberties but mass killing, slavery, racism and authoritarian government. The word 'liberal' for any of this seems very problematic. It also seems to require a more nuanced view of the relations between production and predation than that given by Gellner. In the empire, one did not simply replace the other; they were engaged in close, sometimes symbiotic, sometimes contradictory relationships well into the twentieth century. In the rest of this chapter I will trace these relations in the British Empire, structuring my argument in terms of my four sources of social power.

Militarism and empire

The Europeans were highly militaristic, as the anti-Orientalists Pomerantz and Hobson emphasise. In Europe intensive inter-state warfare had been common for many centuries. Keen (2001: 5) says a 'martial secular culture' was, along with Christianity, 'one of the two chief defining features of … medieval European civilisation'. War also dominated the rise of the European state, as Charles Tilly (1990) and I (Mann 1986, 1993) have demonstrated. Europe may even have been uniquely warlike. Though Latin America became a multistate system in the early nineteenth century, inter-state wars were much less frequent and severe than in Europe, as Miguel Centeno (2002) has shown. Postcolonial Africa has also contained a multistate system, but has also seen very few inter-state wars, as Jeffrey Herbst (2000) has noted. Both authors regard their continents as exceptions to the Tilly/Mann path of modernisation, but maybe it was Europe that was the exception. I have not seen comparable comparative studies of Asia, but it seems there were also relatively few inter-state wars in the late precolonial period, and certainly few in postcolonial Asia. For a very long time East Asia was dominated not by warring states but by a single 'stand-alone empire', whose tributary system was largely symbolic and peaceful.

Why were Europeans so warlike? European wars are generally said to have been between kingdoms, then national states and then nation-states. But try instead 'empires'. A standard definition of empires sees them as centralised political systems acquired by violence and maintained by routinised coercion through which a core dominates peripheral societies, serves as intermediary for their main interactions, and channels resources from and between the peripheries (see Motyl 2001: 21). In fact, Europe was long composed of such rivalrous empires, but they were initially located within Europe itself. The continent comprised a series of core 'mini-empires' gobbling up numerous peripheral 'minnow states'.

The process derived from a combination of feudal social relations and the geopolitical opportunities presented within Europe by the combination of the collapse of the Roman Empire, the barbarian invasions, and an era of local defensive warfare by lords who had castles and a few armed and horsed knights and retainers. Europe in the early medieval period included areas which were rather depopulated, areas of near-virgin land, many small states, and some areas which were cultivated but stateless. As Bartlett (1994) pointed out, the better-organised lords and kings of the core European lands expanded by conquering and colonising the underpopulated or stateless or weak-state lands of the periphery in a process lasting from the tenth to the fourteenth century. Latin Christendom expanded from its base in France, west Germany and north and central Italy, the English colonised the Celts, Germans emigrated to eastern Europe, Spain and Sicily were reconquered, and Christianity was imposed upon Bohemia, Hungary, Poland and Scandinavia. Together this comprised what Bartlett calls 'the Europeanisation of Europe', imposing fairly uniform social relations over the continent. If its spiritual core was Latin

Christianity, its material core was the coupling of lord–vassal relations with tying peasants forcibly to the land. Expansion was also encouraged by the dominant single-son inheritance system, which gave incentives for acquisition of land and its peasants by the militarily trained younger sons of lords and knights. So while big states expanded, so also did the number of feudal mini-states run by counts, free knights, merchant oligarchs and prince-bishops.

The combination produced many states varying greatly in size. Even in the sixteenth century, Europe contained over two hundred political units, mostly tiny. Inter-imperial wars then involved the swallowing-up of these minnows. The Ottoman, Romanov and Habsburg states in the eastern part of the continent are conventionally called 'empires'. But we do not today use the term for those further west: Britain, France, Spain, Prussia/Germany and Italy. Yet they all began in exactly the same way, swallowing up the minnows, sometimes by dynastic marriages, but more often through war and conquest. The western winners, who were the ones who went on to found empires in other continents, were already 'mini-empires' in Europe, ruling at first indirectly, then directly, over territories acquired mostly by military conquest and intimidation. When the mini-empires expanded into the world – and briefly dominated it – there was a global Age of Empires, one that was extremely warlike.

In Western Europe we occasionally use the terms 'empire' and 'colony' teleologically, to describe states which spread over the boundaries of today's states – as in the Norman Empire or the English colonisation of Ireland. We do not refer to the Empire of France or the colonisation of Wales, though they involved almost identical processes. This is because the latter empires were so successful that they became invisible. All the most successful empires do this disappearing act. What we call 'nations' in Western Europe, as opposed to the 'multinational' eastern empires, included the subjects of many of the initially small and peripheral polities, usually conquered by force or intimidated by force into submission, who were then assimilated into the core imperial cultural identity. The French and (to a lesser extent) the English and the Castilian Spanish were European equivalents of the Romans or the Han of earlier times. They 'civilised' and culturally assimilated conquered peoples in a process lasting centuries.

Nations and homogeneous modes of rule, as opposed to imperial centre–periphery rule, emerged quite late. The Act of Union giving all of Great Britain one form of rule came in 1701, and even then Ireland remained precariously integrated. Only the Revolution brought unitary rule to France, abolishing the seventeen regional parliaments and the 366 legal codes the country still contained in 1789. Eugen Weber (1976) famously put the conversion of peasants (with multiple local and regional identities) into Frenchmen in the nineteenth century. The British and French were already embarked on imperial projects outside of Europe by the time of their consolidation. The British had already practised their colonial policies in Scotland and Ireland (see various essays in Canny 2001). Germany and Italy were not unified until the 1860s and 1870s and promptly embarked on their empires as soon as they had consolidated. The bigger European states were more imperial than national *throughout* their history, first in Europe and then in the world. The Russian Empire also expanded fairly continuously across both Eastern Europe and North Asia.

So there were powerful rational inducements towards war in Europe because bigger states could swallow up smaller states without incurring too much suffering. In wars between the major states, the winners generally took territory not from their main rivals, but from the smaller states. For the bigger states, this was often a game where you could greatly win, but not greatly lose. War was worth it. This fills in a hole in the original Tilly/Mann argument. We could explain why wars generated modern constitutional and absolutist states, but we could not explain why Europeans were so enthusiastic about war in the first place – especially given its cost and the resistance it provoked among their subjects. We tended to assume the normalcy of war, but war was unusually desirable for the bigger and better-organised states, and not going to war might involve eventual losses if one's rivals increased their power while one did not. Pre-emptive strikes to avoid being threatened or encircled are typical of inter-imperial wars – for example, the Scramble for Africa, at the end of the nineteenth century. But it came at the end of a very long Scramble for Europe. So I make two amendments to Gellner. First, predation was not merely the normal feature of pre-industrial societies – it had been unusually prominent in pre-industrial Europe. Second, contrary to Gellner, predation continued right through into industrial modernity in the twentieth century in the form of European empires which systematically and unequally extracted the raw materials of the colonies for the manufactured products of the imperial core.

Through repeated wars inside the continent, Europeans had been able to refine weapons and military organisation by which quite small forces on land and sea could pour intensive fire-power onto the enemy and defeat them. Since the mini-empires were quite small, they could only afford small forces. The compact power of the charging knights and then pikemen formations first gave victory in Europe. Then, from the Spanish *tercio* of the 1530s, combining harquebuses with pikemen in defence of Spanish possessions in Italy, Europe specialised not in large armies but in concentrated fire-power. A similar process occurred in naval warfare. In their wars with each other, Europeans invented batteries of cannons mounted on 'ships of the line', and then organised 'line ahead' formation, increasing fire-power further. Eventually, this meant that no state elsewhere in the world, however large, could withstand Europeans in fixed battle, first at sea, then on land. But this only happened gradually. Three centuries of European expansion into the world predated the industrial revolution – from cannon on Portuguese ships, supplemented by the heavily armoured, horsed and musketed Spanish infantry, to the fast and quick-firing Dutch, French and British naval squadrons of the mid-seventeenth century onward.

Imperial expansion began with military techniques and organisations refined in intra-European wars well before the capitalist and industrial revolutions. This military miracle – just like the economic miracle – had a deep-rooted dynamic, centred on focused fire-power. These small European forces could early conquer America and use their shipboard fire-power to intimidate along coastlines elsewhere. Asia and even Africa initially had more formidable states and larger land armies. But in India what was decisive from the mid-eighteenth century was the co-ordinated fire-power of well-drilled European infantry and artillery, given effective logistical support (Fissell and Trim 2005; Lenman 2001: 159; Marshall 2001: 499).

Multistate competition was as crucial for the imperial as for the domestic economic miracle. Yet the European states, being small, with few personnel to spare, could not pacify or rule unless aided by many settlers or powerful native elites. In India after the battle of Plassey, the East India Company assumed the government of Bengal in 1765. Yet it was still careful to act formally as the Mughal emperor's agent. Even after the British government acquired formal sovereignty over India in 1858, it was forced to rely on the local authority of Indian elites, in effect ruling indirectly. Empire was wrested by the gun, but consolidated by political negotiation (Bayly 1998; Marshall 2001). This was due less to liberalism than to logistical necessity, dictated by paucity of numbers. Even though the industrial revolution later generated steam-ships, magazine rifles and Maxim guns, giving Europeans extraordinary fire-power superiority, they still needed either settlers or native allies.

Imperial economics: production through predation

Since the Europeans could increase production through predation, they did so. They seized the land and its agricultural and mineral resources by force. They killed or drove off or enslaved the natives. They used military power, especially navies plus marines, to enforce unequal terms of trade, and they also forced them to use British ships to carry their goods. Trade centred until the early nineteenth century on the triangular exchange of manufactured goods from England, slaves from Africa and slave plantation produce from the Americas. Silver from the Americas also permitted trade with Asia, as the anti-Orientalists say. Then there was an 'eastward turn', as Indian wealth financed the Empire as a whole and allowed Britain to run a balance of trade deficit and the world's reserve currency. With India as a partial exception, the mature British imperial economy, like most other imperial economies, centred on raw materials from the colonies in exchange for manufactured goods from the imperial core.

The most lethal predation occurred where there were many settlers, in the temperate zones. There they wanted the land, but not native labour. So they used their fire-power to drive them off. They were most ruthless where they were Protestant and effectively self-governing, and most of these colonies were British. In the territories now forming the continental states of the United States, there had been anywhere between four and nine million native Americans at the initial point of contact. By the 1900 census there were 237,000, a loss-rate of at least 95 per cent. In Australia there were probably more than 300,000 aborigines at the time of the First Fleet. In the census of 1921 there were 72,000, a loss-rate of 75 per cent. Though disease was the biggest killer in both continents, deliberate mass killings, rolling waves of genocide, also figured large. The more representative and 'liberal' the political practices among Europeans, the higher the rate of killing of natives (all details from Mann 2005: chapter 4). The more the political liberalism, the greater the slaughter.

In comparison, slavery seems rather mild. In Europe in the sixteenth century it was dying out, but it was revived for overseas use and expanded through the seventeenth and eighteenth centuries. In all, about 13 million slaves were taken from African coasts and transported to the New World. About 2 million died en route as a result of overcrowding, poor nutrition and cruel policing. Though slavery had been first revived by the Portuguese in Brazil, by 1650 the British were carrying more slaves than anyone else, and by the 1770s they were carrying the majority. British colonies used most of the slaves, and British slave plantations developed the most efficient regime of mass production, geared to the first mass consumer markets. It was 'the first least-camouflaged expression of ... capitalist logic' (says Blackburn 1997: 554; cf. Eltis 2000: 37; Richardson 2001). Though coercion at the point of capture was wielded by African chiefs and Arab traders, once on board ship mostly British merchants, planters and colonial authorities enforced slavery. Coercion also shaded off into other forms of bonded, corvée and other semi-free labour statuses, especially where resources were abundant but labour scarce, as in Africa. Wallerstein rightly stressed that this conjunction of free labour in the core and coerced labour in the periphery was a structural property of modern imperial capitalism.

But even without genocide or slavery or bonded labour, the entire imperial enterprise was one of seizing territory and resources. Francis Xavier, the Jesuit proselytiser of the East Indies, said that empire was 'to conjugate the verb to rob, in all its moods and tenses' and no one conjugated it better than the British (Marty and Appleby 2001: 97–8). India was initially simply plundered (Ray 2001: 514–16), and this initial stage continued on the frontiers of the expanding empire well into the twentieth century. The return of plunder to England was enthusiastically greeted there, and wars were generally presumed to pay for themselves (Marshall 2001: 5). Even 'informal empire' (where the peripheral state remained sovereign, but with its autonomy constrained by the imperial power) involved gunboats, especially in its early years, as in the 'unequal treaties' imposed on the Ottoman Empire, Persia, China, Japan, and Latin American and Caribbean states. Between 1899 and 1929 the 'liberal' United States invaded Latin American and Caribbean states on thirty-two occasions to reinforce its supposedly 'informal' control of their economies. Militarism was not incidental to imperialism, but its heart. This was an Age of Empires, and empire meant predation, well into the twentieth century.

It is true that British liberals felt uncomfortable with this. Like Americans today, in the mid-nineteenth century many were in denial about empire. They criticised imperialism, identified it with conservatism, and talked of Britain only as the leader of 'free trade' across the world (Porter 2005: chapter 5). The power of the Royal Navy was to be used only to open up the world to the virtues of free competition. When endorsing 'empire', they meant what is now called informal empire, especially its milder institutionalised forms, relatively free of punitive interventions, as was the case for Britain in Latin America after mid-century. Yet the empire kept on expanding by force and liberals were willy-nilly engaged in the process. Gladstone said he did not like empire, yet he sent in the gunboats and the soldiers as much as any prime minister except Salisbury. In the USA the liberal Woodrow Wilson was later to be caught in a similar contradiction during his presidency.

How central predation was to the European/British economic miracle remains controversial. The anti-Orientalists stress it. I downplayed it in *Sources* (1993) because most economic historians then estimated that colonial trade was fairly small, providing less than 1 per cent of British annual GDP. O'Brien (2001: 76; forthcoming) has recently argued that while the data are too poor to allow definite conclusions, we should take seriously the belief shared by most contemporaries that empire brought economic progress, national security and the integration of the kingdom – all useful for economic growth. Debate about whether empires paid their way continues, though the British Empire, the king of the Belgians and the Japanese Empire probably did make a profit, while most others did not. At one particular point, in the 1770s during the industrial revolution, the profits of slavery provided between 21 and 55 per cent of total British investment capital, while its sugar mills and plantation labour control methods also influenced the organisation of British factories (Blackburn 1997; Morgan 2000). Overall, the benefits of British imperial predation seem more like a useful boost to an economy already booming than a major cause of the economic miracle itself.

The biggest economic impact came from the worst predators, the white settlers. Niall Ferguson (2003, 2004) has recently extolled the economic beneficence of the British Empire. He displays tables showing consider-able growth in some parts of the Empire in the late nineteenth and early twentieth centuries. Yet bizarrely his figures are for Australia, New Zealand and Canada – the White Dominions. They had the highest growth rates in the world – above even the USA, which Ferguson should really have included as well, since it contained the same kind of white settlers. Some Latin American countries also had rather lower but nonetheless quite impressive growth. Deepak Lal (2004) produces almost identical arguments and data. At the time the statistics were produced, these were largely free and independent states, under mild informal empire at the most. But to get to this level of achievement, the settlers had displaced and often exterminated the native populations, seized their lands, and then put their capitalist skills to work on a presumed *terra nullius*, an 'empty land' filled with abundant natural resources. This had hardly been a triumph of *liberal* empire.

Yet as empires – especially the British Empire – proceeded, they did tend to become milder. Slavery was abolished. Unfree labour forms lessened in established colonies, and when their cruelty in newer colonies was exposed in the British media, scandals ensued which sometimes produced reform. The British authorities also tended to favour milder methods than did the settlers. This remained evident in southern Africa and Kenya even into the second half of the twentieth century. Conquest, once stabilised, brought a lessening of militarism, though later intermit-tent rebellions brought savage repression, with mass killing of males and sometimes of women and children too. The last bad case was the putting down of the Mau Mau rebellion in the 1950s. Again, repression might cause an outcry in Britain if exposed. In the end there was even a little economic development in many British colonies.[1] Perhaps production was finally supplanting predation. But to understand these contrary and seemingly liberal dynamics, we must turn to the other sources of social power.

Imperial politics: representative government, eventually

In imperial politics logistical necessity far outweighed any liberal constitutional principles. Outside of settler colonies, there were so few British people in the colonies that political alliances with native elites were absolutely essential for stable rule. This move towards some form of what is called 'indirect rule' (rule through native elites) happened in all colonies regardless of the constitution of the mother country – and so involved the exclusion of the native masses from political power. Indeed, there was an ever-widening contradiction between representative government in Britain itself and authoritarian government over non-white natives abroad. In the late nineteenth century – and not before – the British began to claim that they were bringing freedoms, including eventual self-government to the natives, but they envisaged this as being a long way off. The white settler colonies soon enjoyed suffrages wider than in Britain itself. But no natives enjoyed representation at even the local government level until after World War I, though in Asia there were a few appointed native members of governors' councils. Most African countries did not get even this until after World War II. Some restricted-franchise local governments were won between the wars. After World War II, full self-government was achieved. Perhaps a liberal story might be told here too, and Ferguson (2003, 2004) and others have tried to tell it.

But every improvement was achieved by struggle, after demonstrations, strikes and riots by native movements (Louis 1999). Without this, the authoritarian empire would have lasted much longer, since the

---

[1] There was much less than Ferguson or Lal suggest. Ferguson (2003) presents fuller data, especially on India. There he relies on Tirthankar Roy who has produced the most favourable recent survey of the economy of the Raj. But his data show that Indian GDP grew between about 1880 and 1920 by less than 1 per cent per annum; then it levelled off and in the 1930s it declined (Roy 2000: 218–23). Between 1858 and 1947 there was an overall rate of development of about 0.2 per cent per year – at a time when Britain itself experienced massive development. Life expectancy seems to have also remained fairly static (ILO 1938). In other colonies economic growth was rarely visible until the late 1940s. Though colonial administrators had kept calling for development funds, the home government said it had not the cash to spare. The French Empire experienced the same problem.

British saw self-government as being in the distant future. The Viceroy of India, Lord Curzon, told the Bengal Chamber of Commerce in 1905:

> if I felt that we were not working here for the good of India in obedience to a higher law and a nobler aim, then I would see the link that holds England and India together severed without a sigh. But it is because I believe in the future of this country, and in the capacity of our race to guide it to goals that it has never hitherto attained, that I keep courage and press forward ... We have to answer our helm, and it is an imperial helm, down all the tides of Time ... wherever ignorance or superstition is rampant, wherever enlightenment or progress [is] possible, wherever duty and self-sacrifice call – there is, as there has been for hundreds of years, the true summons of the Anglo-Saxon race. (Gilmour 2003)

In 1923 Governor Clifford told the Nigerian Legislative Council: 'In a country such as Nigeria, which in too many areas has not yet emerged from barbarism, a strong, and within limits, an autocratic government is essential' (Wheare 1950: 42). In 1922 Frederick Lugard, then the doyen of colonial policy, declared: 'The verdict of students of history and sociology of different nationalities ... is ... unanimous – that the era of complete independence is not as yet visible on the horizon of time' (1922: 197). As late as 1938 the Colonial Secretary, Malcolm Macdonald, said: 'It may take generations, or even centuries for the people in some parts of the Colonial Empire to achieve self-government. But it is a major part of our policy, even among the most backward peoples of Africa, to teach them and to encourage them always to be able to stand a little more on their own feet' (quoted by Marx 2002: 151).

Lugard and MacDonald were thought of as fairly liberal administrators, but they had a very different time-frame from the 'backward peoples' themselves, who soon did achieve self-government – by leaving the empire. This was due partly to their own efforts, partly to the unintended consequences of two World Wars, especially the second one. This forced the British to recruit almost 3 million colonial natives into their armed forces, while military logistics also forced them to develop colonies' infrastructures (military pressures had also caused the development of Indian infrastructures earlier). Promises of self-government after the war had been largely betrayed after World War I. So the British had to be more specific in World War II. In 1942 India was promised full self-government after the war, and when the war did end the British government knew it lacked the power to hang on. Africa's reward was not self-government but the continuation of wartime development programmes. This was intended to prolong the life of empire, and, initially, to solve Britain's chronic sterling crisis by providing raw materials that could be sold for dollars or be substituted for imports paid for in dollars.

The post-World War II programmes amounted to what historians have called 'a second colonial occupation'. Economic development was expected to increase 'non-European stakeholders in the imperial enterprise' and 'enhance the empire's efficiency and its propensity for effective exploitation for metropolitan benefit' (White 1999: 9–10, 35, 49). But the effect of economic development, just as in India earlier, was the opposite. It increased the power of urban workers, teachers, lawyers and civil servants. Unfortunately for the British, from their ranks came nationalist malcontents. Through the twentieth century the British tried to counter these middle-class nationalists by building up the powers of traditional upper classes – in Africa chiefs, in India princes and Brahmins. They had also sought to divide and rule between ethnic and religious groups. Such tactics only further alienated the middle class. It had benefited from imperial rule through education, it lived quite well, and it implemented imperial rule at an everyday level. Yet it was not loyal. Sharkey puts it well for the Sudan: from its ranks came 'colonialism's intimate enemies, making colonial rule a reality while hoping to see it undone' (2003: 119).

If Britain had helped the natives towards self-government, this had been mostly unintentionally. Yet, when faced with determined nationalists (in India in the 1940s, later in Africa), the British did at least depart more gracefully than others. The Spanish, German and Japanese empires were forcefully ended by other empires. The French, Dutch and Portuguese tried to resist longer before being forced out. British grace seemed to derive from an ability to avoid defining departure as defeat. The Foreign, Colonial and Sudan Offices had models to hand from the gradual grant of self-government to the white Dominions, and they believed exit would actually mean 'the preservation of post-colonial "influence", as opposed to the complete negation of empire' (White 1999: 35, 98–100). During the nineteenth century the British informal empire had become larger than its direct colonial rule. Now the whole empire would supposedly become informal, renamed as the 'Commonwealth'. Faith in informal empire was indeed distinctively liberal. This trajectory also characterised the larger progress of the American empire, from direct colonies in the Philippines and Puerto Rico, plus regular military interventions in the early twentieth century, to the informal empire punctuated by only occasional interventions practised from the 1930s to the 1980s. In the long-run empires (and up to Bush the Younger) the Anglo-Saxon empires did become milder. So there was eventually something in the notion of a liberal empire, though the liberal content was arrived at slowly and through a circuitous and largely unintended route.

Imperial ideologies: freedom, racism, nationalism

From the mid to late nineteenth century, the central ideological thrust of both British and American imperialism was the paradoxical claim to be entitled to dominate less fortunate peoples by virtue of being the freest peoples on earth. The core of 'Orientalism' was the belief that Middle Easterners and Asians were habituated to despotism, and this led to static, if not degenerate, societies (Said 1979). Africans were believed to be at much more primitive levels of rule. The British responsibility was to enlighten them all, apply our modern dynamism to them, and lead them very gradually towards freedom. Lugard declared that 'the ideal of government can only be realised by the methods of evolution which have produced the democracy of Europe and America, – viz., by representative institutions in which the comparatively small educated class shall be recognised as the natural spokesmen for the many'. Even in the case of the more civilised races who he perceived were 'more capable of rule', like the Fulani of northern Nigeria, he warned British colonial officers to exercise 'ceaseless vigilance' over them to prevent 'misrule and tyranny' by them over others (1922: 193–7). The argument is similar to Kant's in *What Is Enlightenment?*: educated elites must gradually spread enlightenment among the ignorant and benighted masses. This was the rather restricted liberalism of Empire.

Obviously, genocide and slavery contradicted liberalism. But slavery bore a more complex relationship to freedom. Precisely because Europeans as a whole constituted a free moral community, they could not be enslaved to work on New World plantations. This was ideologically taboo, yet the economics of new world sugar, tobacco and coffee required such labour. Since labour was scarce there and it is always difficult to enslave anyone in their own country (they can escape), slaves had to be brought from elsewhere. Luckily, Africans had no such taboo against enslaving those outside their own kin networks. Nor did Africans have any taboos concerning women working, as Europeans did. So Africans could be used to help enslave other Africans, women as well as men. 'The rise of slavery in the Americas', says Eltis (2000: 279), 'was dependent on the nature of freedom in western Europe'. That is one reason why it was led by the freest people of all, the British.

Yet this changed when the evangelical revival gave a more religious slant to British conceptions of freedom. Since all people had souls, no one should be enslaved. By 1800, though slavery remained profitable, it was being seen as contradicting religious norms. Slaves were also beginning to mount more resistance, and they had become somewhat more economically independent in the Caribbean heartland of British slavery. Slavery was finally abolished throughout the British Empire in 1833, and British armed forces then spent much effort trying to repress slavers instead of slaves. As I found in my study of colonial ethnic cleansings, churches and missionaries, Catholics as well as Protestants, were normally a restraining influence on settler maltreatment of natives.

But at the same time as the British were abolishing slavery, they were intensifying racism. The Spanish had not been racist. They had not doubted that Aztec, Inca and other elites in America were highly civilised. They converted and married them, as is visible today in the vast numbers of mestizos in the American continent. At first, cohabitation and inter-marriage were also fairly common where British settler populations contained a surplus of males. In the Americas slavery was encouraging racial conceptions of superiority, but this was not then apparent in Asia, where the British expressed admiration for the civilisations con-fronting them. Inter-marriage, cohabitation and concubinage were all common in India. One third of British men in India in 1780 who left wills left everything to Indian women (Dalrymple 2002). Yet between 1786 and 1795 the East India Company shifted policy to discourage mixed marriages, which it had earlier encouraged. It also removed sons of 'mixed blood' marriages from its employ, having previously given them preferential treatment. Lesser occupational niches were found for 'half-castes'. Bayly (1999: 219) locates a jump in racialist stereotypes in the 1830s; while Sen (2002: 143; cf. Collingham 2001) says that blood and civilisation were now thought of as 'much the same thing': 'the calibration of blood became of vital significance for the colonial order'.

There were several reasons for this shift. The arrival of larger numbers of European women tended to damp down racial inter-marriage, and the women also had an interest in reducing the supply of native brides. The British were also attempting to define their own imperial identity as against the more multiracial practices of the Portuguese and French. From the late eighteenth and early nineteenth centuries, again under the influence of evangelicalism, British sexual mores were tightening, and women were the main carriers of these influences into the colonies. Cohabitation and concubinage were now considered immoral, and even marriage outside of the community of the faithful was frowned on. More generally, the British were increasingly bringing to their colonies notions of 'improvement', both material and moral. But while Britain itself was improving, Asian and Indian societies were believed to be declining. Hindu society was 'decadent', 'spineless' and 'corrupt', Muslim 'cor-rupt' and 'despotic'. Indeed, European entry into Asia did coincide with a period of imperial decline there (as the anti-Orientalists admit).

There was a growing gulf between European conceptions of moral improvement in their own society and the seemingly degenerate quality of other societies. British administrators expressed increasing frustration at their inability to get Indians to modernise. They denounced them as *incorrigibly* idle and corrupt – a stereotype with racial flavouring.

Despite growing racism, the British had to rule through natives in Asia and Africa. Macauley explained the ideological task: 'We must do our best to form a class who may be interpreters between us and the millions whom we govern, a class of persons Indian in blood and colour, but English in taste, in opinions, words and intellect.' Indian and even African elites were culturally assimilated. The British class system and Indian caste merged, as princes, Brahmins and Muslim notables became the 'gentry leaders of a caste-based society' (Cannadine 2001).

But not even elites could assimilate in the private sphere. The intimate lives of the British and the natives were kept apart and Indian caste and religious barriers increasingly reinforced this. Hindu notions of purity centred on the intimate issues of who could marry and who could dine with whom. Contact cannot be made with the unclean. Nor did higher-rank Hindu or Muslim women mix much outside of their religious community. In a sense, the British adapted such caste and religious prohibitions into their own racism to texture their private lives. They changed their style of dress and comportment to one of 'bodily closure', abandoning loose Indian garments in favour of the uniformed, buttoned-up, top-hatted or topeed sahib and his crinolined, corseted memsahib. Comfort was sacrificed for the sake of a stiff bureaucratic dominance. An 'affective wall' was built between the body and the environment and peoples of the tropics (Collingham 2001). Natives were kept out of the social clubs and the sporting associations. Though Indians watched and soon took to cricket, there were no integrated cricket clubs. Above all, inter-marriage remained rare. By the end of the nineteenth century it was taboo for all except very low-status British men to marry or even associate much with Anglo-Indians or Indians. The British interacted intimately only with native servants. In Africa the British (and French) passed laws against inter-marriage, in contrast to the many mixed marriages found in the Portuguese colonies.

Under the late nineteenth-century impact of biological racialism linked to Social Darwinism, the emphasis on racial purity intensified. Racial 'degeneration' was now seen as explaining stagnant and backward societies, so careless sexuality and inter-breeding must be avoided. Yet patriarchal, not Darwinian, models dominated. More civilised races who were militarily inferior to the Europeans were termed 'effeminate'. The more backward were 'child-like' – though there was a special place of masculine respect given to disciplined, loyal warrior groups. Sir Lepel Griffin, a senior official in India explained:

the characteristics of women which disqualify them for public life and its responsibilities are inherent in their sex and are worthy of honour, for to be womanly is the highest praise for a woman, as to be masculine is her worst reproach, but when men, as the Bengalis are disqualified for political enfranchisement by the possession of essentially feminine characteristics, they must expect to be held in such contempt by stronger and braver races, who have fought for such liberties as they have won or retained. (Sinha 1995; cf. Sen 2002)

As Stoler (2002: 78) says: 'sexual control was both an instrumental image for the body politic ... and itself fundamental to how racial policies were secured and how colonial policies were carried out'.

These intimate notions prevented all but a few natives from assimilating into a British identity. They might be attracted by the higher level of civilisation, the order and the law they saw the British as (imperfectly) embodying, but the British repelled them, bodily and socially. Indians who finished their education amid upper-class institutions in Britain would later complain that it was only the British in the colonies who treated them so badly. Intimate racism prevented the British, the French and the Dutch empires (though not the Portuguese) from taking the Roman or Han Chinese route to cultural assimilation. Thus it doomed their imperial project.

It is often said that native nationalists were influenced by British (and other Western) notions of liberties, often learned in imperial schools. 'Indians as well as French Canadians and Afrikaners quoted John Locke, Lord Durham and John Stuart Mill' (Louis 1999). Liberalism was indeed adapted for local rebellious use (as later were socialism and fascism). Yet the natives could see clearly the contradiction between Mill's liberalism when applied to the British and his view that Indians, Chinese and Africans were incapable of self-rule because of their long-standing oriental despotism and defective domestic life. They were unlikely to buy his form of liberalism. But maybe such glaring hypocrisy fired them up to achieve genuine liberties more quickly.

But were these great British theorists really necessary? The combination of racist exclusion plus authoritarian rule would have appalled any colonised people in any period of history. Self-rule is a universal aspiration, and it was expressed by countless Indians and Africans. In this period, native traditions, especially Hinduism and Islam, also gave rich sources of support for collective identity and claims to self-rule. In the early period, resistance to the British by the declining Mughal gentry and merchants had involved some sense that they were defending an 'India' which was essentially under alien occupation. Bayly calls this 'patriotism', the loyalty then being more to a state than to a nation. He suggests that European conceptions of nationalism, based on resistance to empire, made considerable sense to occupied peoples across the rest of the world. Then British development of communications infrastructures in the late nineteenth century (designed to move troops around India and money back to Britain) tended to integrate the Indian elite and generated more of a common sense of identity and resistance. There was an emerging sense of a single 'Hindu religion' or 'culture' out of what had been a plethora of cults and sects (Bayly 1998, 2004: chapter 6; Ray 2003). The British did also produce orderly and efficient government and this came wrapped up in a secular ideology of modernisation and reform. This often initially stirred up a conservative cultural proto-nationalist reaction, later itself becoming more secular, and claiming to be more genuinely modern than the British themselves, who were still backing 'traditional' chiefs and princes (Gelber 2001: 152–61).

In India by the inter-war period Gandhi, Congress and the Muslim League were between them mobilising mass movements. Their unity depended less on the existence of an actual Indian nation (they were deeply divided along religious, caste, ethnic and left/right lines), than on a common hostility to the racist British and the blindingly obvious validity of the demand for self-rule. This was even truer in Africa, where there was little sense of being a 'nation' in the conventional sense of attachment to a country, territory or colony. In the couplet 'African nationalism', 'African' denoted not a national identity but an essentially racial one. This was a union of blacks against whites (Muslims against Christian whites in the far north), diffusing rapidly from the more advanced African nationalist movements to the others. Such 'nationalism' was generated by a racist and so a self-destructive Empire. It was more anti-imperialism than nationalism, at least as conventionally understood.

Conclusion

I have shown that Europe had long entwined production and predation and that the British Empire continued doing so as it expanded, until well into the twentieth century. In its first two or so centuries predation dominated over production. Those who profited were British merchants, investors, plantation owners and settlers – plus some native clients. Even the British as a whole may have benefited a little. But most natives initially suffered, and very large numbers died. The Empire was then rendered a little milder by Protestant-flavoured liberalism – but it was rendered milder still by the constraining logistics of rule by the few over the many. As indirect rule became stabilised, it tended neither greatly to harm nor much to benefit the natives. After 1870 in India, and in the 1940s in Africa, some limited investment for production for the benefit of natives began finally to accompany predation, spurred on by the need for defence against rival empires. There were also a few genuine success stories, generally resulting from imperial-assisted transplanting of crops to other continents (as in Malayan rubber). But all these developments were also accompanied by racism and divide-and-rule tactics exposing the hypocrisy of liberal imperialism and fuelling nationalist movements of resistance. These ironically became unstoppable when production actually did overtake predation, and when liberal empire became reality. Thus this finally liberal empire rapidly fell – to be replaced by a combination of production and predation from within, by native governments themselves (which still continues today). Liberalism was important in the development and disintegration of the British Empire, but as a complex mixture of ideals, hypocrisy and unintended consequences.

Perhaps Hegel might have regarded this as 'the cunning of (liberal) reason'. Indeed, in the long run there was in empires a secular move away from predation and towards production – though even today the former is not entirely absent from the world economy. But whereas I believe that the world was brought great benefits by the European and especially the British miracle at home, the blessings brought by any imperial miracle are much harder to perceive. It is ultimately impossible to envisage a counter-factual world without modern empires in order to assess whether Asia, the Americas and Africa would have been better off without them. I suspect most of them would have been. Yet had European expansion been genuinely liberal, rather than imperial, embodying production rather than predation, as Gellner saw had happened within Europe and Britain itself, the benefits would have much easier to perceive.

References

Bartlett, R. 1994. *The Making of Europe: Conquest, Colonization and Cultural Change, 950–1350*. Princeton, NJ: Princeton University Press.
Bayly, C. 1998. *Origins of Nationality in South Asia*. Oxford: Oxford University Press.
    2004. *The Birth of the Modern World 1780–1914*. Oxford: Blackwell.
Blackburn, R. 1997. *The Making of New World Slavery: From the Baroque to the Modern, 1492–1800*. London: Verso.
Brenner, R. and Isett, C. 2002. England's Divergence from China's Yangzi Delta: Property Relations, Microeconomics, and Patterns of Development. *Journal of Asian Studies* 61: 609–62.
Cannadine, D. 2001. *Ornamentalism: How the British Saw Their Empire*. London: Allen Lane/Penguin.

Canny, N. (ed.) 2001. *The Oxford History of the British Empire*, vol. I: *The Origins of Empire*. Oxford: Oxford University Press, paperback edition.

Collingham, E. M. 2001. *Imperial Bodies: The Physical Experience of the Raj, c. 1800–1947*. Cambridge: Polity.

Crafts, N. 2004. Long Run Growth. In R. Floud and P. Johnson (eds.), *The Cambridge Economic History of Britain since 1700*, vol. II. Cambridge: Cambridge University Press, pp. 1–24.

Dalrymple, W. 2002. *White Mughals: Love and Betrayal in Eighteenth-Century India*. London: HarperCollins.

Deng, K. 2003. *Fact or Fiction? Re-examination of Chinese Premodern Population Statistics*. LSE Economic History Working Paper Series 76. London: LSE.

Drayton, R. 2001. Knowledge and Empire. In Peter Marshall (ed.), *The Oxford History of the British Empire*, vol. II: *The Eighteenth Century*. Oxford: Oxford University Press, paperback edition, pp. 231–52.

Eltis, D. 2000. *The Rise of African Slavery in the Americas*. Cambridge: Cambridge University Press.

Ferguson, N. 2003. *Empire: How Britain Made the Modern World*. New York: Basic Books.

2004. *Colossus: The Price of America's Empire*. London: Penguin.

Fissell, M. and Trim, D. 2005. *Amphibious Warfare and European Expansion 1000–1700: War, Commerce and State Formation*. Leiden: Brill.

Frank, A. G. 1998. *Re-Orient: Global Economy in the Asian Age*. Berkeley and Los Angeles: University of California Press.

Gelber, H. 2001. *Nations Out of Empires: European Nationalism and the Transformation of Asia*. New York: Palgrave.

Gellner, E. 1988. *Plough, Sword and Book: The Structure of Human History*. Chicago: University of Chicago Press.

1994. *Conditions of Liberty: Civil Society and Its Rivals*. London: Hamish Hamilton.

1995. *Anthropology and Politics: Revolutions in the Sacred Grove*. Oxford: Blackwell.

Gilmour, D. 2003. *Curzon: Imperial Statesman*. New York: Farrar, Straus and Giroux.

Goldstone, J. 2002. Efflorescences and Economic Growth in World History: Rethinking the Rise of the West and the British Industrial Revolution. *Journal of World History* 13: 323–89.

Hall, J. A. 1986. *Powers and Liberties: The Causes and Consequences of the Rise of the West*. Harmondsworth: Penguin.

Hall, J. A., Baechler, J. and Mann, M. (eds.) 1988. *Europe and the Rise of Capitalism*. Oxford: Basil Blackwell.

Hart, N. 1998. Beyond Infant Mortality: Gender and Stillbirth in Reproductive Mortality before the 20th Century. *Population Studies* 52: 215–29.

Herbst, J. 2000. *States and Power in Africa: Comparative Lessons in Authority and Control*. Princeton, NJ: Princeton University Press.

Hobson, J. 2004. *The Eastern Origins of Western Civilisation*. Cambridge: Cambridge University Press.

Ingham, G. 2004. *The Nature of Money*. Cambridge: Polity.

International Labor Office 1938. *Industrial Labor in India*. Geneva: author.

Jacobs, M. 1997. *Scientific Culture and the Making of the Industrial West*. New York: Oxford University Press.

2000. Commerce, Industry, and the Laws of Newtonian Science: Weber Revisited and Revised. *Canadian Journal of History* 35: 1–12.

Jones, E. 1987. *The European Miracle: Environments, Economies and Geopolitics in the History of Europe and Asia*. 2nd edn, Cambridge: Cambridge University Press.

Keen, M. 2001. Introduction. In Keen (ed.), *Medieval Warfare: A History*. Oxford: Oxford University Press.

Lal, D. 2004. *In Praise of Empires: Globalization and Order*. New York: Palgrave.

Landes, D. S. 1998. *The Wealth and Poverty of Nations: Why Some Are So Rich and Others So Poor*. New York: Norton.

Lee, J. and Campbell, C. 1997. *Fate and Fortune in Rural China: Social Organisation and Population Behavior in Liaoning 1774–1873*. New York: Cambridge University Press.

Lee, J. and Feng, W. 1999. *One Quarter of Humanity: Malthusian Mythology and Chinese Realities*. Cambridge, MA: Harvard University Press.

Lenman, B. 2001. Colonial Wars and Imperial Instability 1688–1793. In Peter Marshall (ed.), *The Oxford History of the British Empire*, vol. II: *The Eighteenth Century*. Oxford: Oxford University Press, pp. 151–68.

Louis, W. R. 1999. Introduction. In Judith M. Brown and Wm. Roger Louis (eds.), *The Oxford History of the British Empire*, vol. IV: *The Twentieth Century*. Oxford: Oxford University Press, pp. 1–46.

Lugard, F. 1922. *The Dual Mandate in British Tropical Africa*. Edinburgh and London: Blackwood.

Mann, M. 1986. *The Sources of Social Power*, vol. I. Cambridge: Cambridge University Press.

1993. *The Sources of Social Power*, vol. II. Cambridge: Cambridge University Press.

2005. *The Dark-Side of Democracy: Explaining Ethnic Cleansing*. Cambridge: Cambridge University Press.

2006. The Sources of Social Power Revisited: A Response to Criticism. In J. A. Hall and R. Schroeder (eds.), *The Anatomy of Power*. Cambridge: Cambridge University Press, pp. 343–96.

Marshall, P. 2001. Introduction and The British in Asia: Trade to Dominion 1700–1765. In Peter Marshall (ed.), *The Oxford History of the British Empire*, vol. II: *The Eighteenth Century*. Oxford: Oxford University Press, pp. 1–27, 487–507.

Marty, M. E. and Appleby, R. S. 2001. *Fundamentalisms Comprehended*. Chicago: University of Chicago Press.

Marx, S. 2002. *The Ebbing of European Ascendancy: An International History of the World, 1914–1945*. Oxford: Oxford University Press.

Mokyr, J. 1992. *The Lever of Riches*. Oxford: Oxford University Press.

2000. Knowledge, Technology and Economic Growth during the Industrial Revolution. In Bart Van Ark and Gerard Kuper (eds.), *Productivity, Technology and Economic Growth*. The Hague: Kluwert, pp. 253–92.

Morgan, K. 2000. *Slavery, Atlantic Trade and the British Economy, 1660–1800.* Cambridge: Cambridge University Press.

Motyl, A. 2001. *Imperial Ends: The Decay, Collapse, and Revival of Empires.* New York: Columbia University Press.

Muldoon, J. 1999. *Empire and Order: The Concept of Empire, 800–1800.* New York: St. Martin's Press.

O'Brien, P. 2001. Inseparable Connections: Trade, Economy, Fiscal State and the Expansion of Empire, 1688–1815. In Peter Marshall (ed.), *The Oxford History of the British Empire*, vol. II: *The Eighteenth Century*. Oxford: Oxford University Press, pp. 53–77.

Forthcoming. Economic growth: A Bibliographic Survey. In B. Stuchtey and E. Fuchs (eds.), *Writing World History*. Oxford: Oxford University Press.

Pagden, A. 2001. *Peoples and Empires: A Short History of European Migration, Exploration, and Conquest, from Greece to the Present.* New York: The Modern Library.

Pakenham, T. 1991. *The Scramble for Africa: White Man's Conquest of the Dark Continent from 1876–1912.* New York: Random House.

Pomerantz, K. 2000. *The Great Divergence: China, Europe, and the Making of the Modern World Economy.* Princeton, NJ: Princeton University Press.

Porter, B. 2005. *The Absent-Minded Imperialists: What the British Really Thought about Empire.* Oxford: Oxford University Press.

Ray, R. K. 2001. Indian Society and the Establishment of British Supremacy, 1765–1818. In Peter Marshall (ed.), *The Oxford History of the British Empire*, vol. II: *The Eighteenth Century*. Oxford: Oxford University Press, pp. 508–29.

2003. *The Felt Community: Commonalty and Mentality before the Emergence of Indian Nationalism.* New York: Oxford University Press.

Richardson, D. 2001. The British Empire and the Atlantic Slave Trade 1660–1807. In Peter Marshall (ed.), *The Oxford History of the British Empire*, vol. II: *The Eighteenth Century*. Oxford: Oxford University Press, pp. 440–64.

Roy, T. 2000. *The Economic History of India 1857–1947.* Delhi: Oxford University Press.

Said, E. 1979. *Orientalism.* New York: Vintage Books.

Sen, S. 2002. *Distant Sovereignty: National Imperialism and the Origins of British India.* New York: Routledge.

Sharkey, H. 2003. *Living with Colonialism: Nationalism and Culture in the Anglo-Egyptian Sudan.* Berkeley and Los Angeles: University of California Press.

Sinha, M. 1995. *Colonial Masculinity: The 'Manly Englishman' and the 'Effeminate Bengali' in the Late Nineteenth Century.* Manchester: Manchester University Press.

Stoler, A. 2002. *Carnal Knowledge and Imperial Power: Race and the Intimate in Colonial Rule.* Berkeley and Los Angeles: University of California Press.

Temin, P. 1997. Two Views of the British Industrial Revolution. *Journal of Economic History* 57: 63–82.

Weber, Eugén 1976. *Peasants into Frenchmen: The Modernisation of Rural France, 1870–1914,* Stanford: Stanford University Press.

Wheare, J. 1950. *The Nigerian Legislative Council.* London: Faber and Faber.

White, N. 1999. *Decolonisation: The British Experience since 1945*. London and New York: Longman.

Wilson, H. S. 1994. *African Decolonization*. London: Edward Arnold.

Wong, R. B. 1997. *China Transformed: Historical Change and the Limits of European Experience*. Ithaca, NY: Cornell University Press.

Wrigley, E. A. 1998. Explaining the Rise in Marital Fertility in the 'Long 18th century'. *Economic History Review* 51: 435–64.

Wrigley, E. A. and Schofield, R. 1989. *The Population History of England, 1541–1871: A Reconstruction*. 2nd edn, London: Edward Arnold.

3   Power, modernity and liberal democracy

Mark Haugaard

In this chapter I wish to explore the social conditions which made liberal democracy possible, arguing that Gellner's account is incomplete because his view of power was too narrow. Within Gellner's paradigm, modern political forms emerge from a process whereby 'Production replaced Predation' (1988: 158). Implicit in the trinitarian 'plough, sword and book' image, which informs this account, is the hypothesis that the realm of politics, thus power, is derived from the might of the sword. In Gellner's logic, if the norm of premodern societies is characterised by the dominance of the sword (and occasionally the book), and if it is an observed fact that modern society is not controlled by the might of the sword, the logical implication has to be dominance by one or other of the elements of this trinitarian universe. In short, the rise of one element of the trinitarian universe has to be explained in terms of the fall, or containment, of the other two. As modern societies are industrial societies, it follows that it is the plough economy that has become dominant over the others. While I agree with Gellner that modern democratic societies are historically particular in the fact that, as a routine, positions of dominance do not change hands through contests determined by the sword, it does not follow from this that the only possible explanation is containment of the sword by the plough. Gellner mistakenly assumes that the sword is the only possible basis for power. I would argue that the displacement of the sword (coercive power) was made possible by the emergence of new forms of social power, which were highly effective. This social power is not based upon violence but derives from new forms of internalised structural constraint made possible by a social and cognitive transformation of human agency which took place with the emergence of modernity.

This 'displacement of power' hypothesis should not be interpreted as a simplistic claim to the effect that in premodern societies politics was entirely based upon violence and, conversely, in modern societies coercion is entirely absent. Premodern societies also had non-coercive forms of power (as will be explained), but in the European context (which is what Gellner is describing) these societies tended to be backed by higher levels of coercion than modern democratic systems.

In many respects it is surprising that Gellner missed the point that modern political systems presupposed a change of the basis of power. Non-coercive power is based upon the possibility of controlling social agents through their cognitive process, rather than through fear of physical retribution, as is the case with coercion. The image contained in Foucault's *Madness and Civilization* comes to mind. Up until the nineteenth century the insane were chained and bound. Samuel Tuke, a reforming Quaker, released them from their shackles and replaced iron with self-restraint derived from control through reason and introspection (Foucault 1971: 249). For Tuke, power exercised through the soft tissues of the brain was substantially stronger and more effective than iron. According to Foucault this shift from power as coercion to modern power meant a displacement of one kind of power with another through the emergence of a better, more refined power.

The conceptual equivalent of chains and iron in the *polity* would be machines and technology in the economy. Viewing political change purely in terms of a transformation in relations of coercion would be analogous to holding a simplistic materialist view of history whereby technology is the sole motor of economic advancement. Far from arguing the latter, Gellner is clear that the emergence of *industria* from *agraria* in the economy presupposes a cognitive transformation. The logical extension of this argument is that the transition from feudalism to modern forms of power in the *polity* is similarly premised upon the same cognitive transformation. However, in order to make this argument one has to hold the premise that power is not necessarily reducible to the sword – a premise which, for whatever reason, was not apparent to Gellner.

Gellner was suspicious of the terms *democracy* and *liberalism* because, as he saw it, they were based upon false promises and inaccurate premises. The idea of democracy, as rule by the people, suggests that the latter actually control social order, which is false. The types of decisions made in democratic politics presuppose a complex social order that remains relatively stable (Gellner 1994: 184–9). This false premise leads to the promise of creating society anew, which is a misunderstanding that contributed to the Reign of Terror after the French Revolution.

Even though he was a liberal himself, Gellner was reluctant to invoke liberalism because of his strong disagreement with the philosophical premises of much of contemporary liberal thought. In particular, he was highly critical of the use of social contract within liberalism (Gellner 1988: 23–6) and also felt that most liberals mistakenly defined liberalism in terms of liberty, instead of openness (Gellner 1964: 112).

While I think there is some truth in these observations, it misses the central point. If we wish to understand what is unique about modern liberal democracies, we have to contrast them with what went before. In the European case, this was feudalism. Just as in modern democracies, when feudal lords and kings took power they did not have the capacity entirely to transform the political system but largely reproduced existing relations with different personae. The crucial difference between democracy and feudalism is that the former allows for the routine contestation and replacement of political elites without the threat or use of violence, and the principles underpinning this circulation of elites are entirely different. Similarly, Gellner may be correct that the basic normative premises of liberalism are nonsense on stilts, but it is a unique social fact that, as distinct from feudalism, members of the *polis* have individual rights which protect them from physical coercion by anyone other than the state and, in the case of the latter, this violence is strictly regulated and controlled by complex rules of procedure.

Gellner used the term 'civil society' in place of 'liberal democracy', which points to a general cultural transformation that facilitated modern politics. This is entirely consonant with my argument that modern power presupposes a fundamental cognitive transformation. I suspect that the only thing that prevented Gellner from arguing what I am about to argue was an impoverished concept of power. As a consequence, I will begin with a short synopsis of Gellner's account of the emergence of *industria* and 'civil society', which provides the background for my substantive argument concerning power, constraint and human cognition.

Gellner and the emergence of 'civil society'

One of the premises of Gellner's account of the origins of 'civil society' is that modernity entails a change of relations of domination. He interprets modernity in terms of a transition from agrarian societies in which the economy and polity were interconnected, with the former dominating the latter, to a society in which the two have been separated and the economy becomes dominant. Gellner was at pains to argue that this was a unique event in world history. He expressed the problem of understanding modernity in the following term: 'How could it happen that Production replaced Predation as a central theme and value of life? Everything in the standard condition of agrarian society militates against such a miracle' (Gellner 1988: 158).

To Gellner, agrarian society is a historical norm and has structural tendencies towards relative stability, whereas modernity is dynamic and based upon economic growth. The absence of growth in agrarian societies is explained by an inherent dilemma which is confronted by those who, for whatever reason, manage to produce economic surplus. The secret of modern sustained economic development is, of course, the continual reinvestment of surplus production in capital. However, in an agrarian society there is a disincentive to reinvest in the means of production and an incentive to convert economic wealth into the means of coercion. In *agraria* those with surplus are vulnerable to predation from those with the means of coercion. Consequently, those with surplus must invest in the means of coercion, so as to protect their newly acquired wealth. If they reinvest in the means of production they are, in effect, standing by to let their profits be coerced from them by others (Gellner 1994: 33–4). This resulted in an innate tendency for profit to be transformed into the means of coercion rather than reinvested in capital. Hence, certain forces within agrarian societies militated against the cycle of capitalism, of converting profit to capital because, essentially, wealth was more easily acquired through predation than production. Gellner characterises this as a historical norm whereby coercion by the thugs dominates producers.

The only exception to rule by specialists in coercion was domination by the clergy (specialists in ritual and doctrine), which was essentially another form of rule by fear. However, this took place only through the consent of, or alliance with, the thugs. The other alternative to dominance by the sword or book was domination by kinship structure, which necessitates a highly ritualised social order. However, this 'Durkheimian' social form is largely characteristic of hunter-gatherer societies rather than *agraria*.

A number of coincidentally occurring social events broke this agrarian cycle of domination by coercion. As observed by Weber, the Protestant ethic created a new class of hard-working producers who were theologically prevented from using their wealth for pleasure. Gellner added to this hypothesis the idea that the same religious faith would also prevent these hard-working 'God-fearing souls' from purchasing coercion as a means of protecting their wealth. Protestantism created a predisposition to reinvest surplus production in capital, rather than pleasure or coercion. However, on its own this is insufficient to prime the pump of capitalism since there were others who would coerce, thus destroy, these tender shoots of capitalism.

The Protestant ethic coincided with a second contingent event: the emergence of massive technological innovation. For the first time in history, those involved in production had wealth enough to create a 'bribery fund' of sufficient dimensions to buy off the specialists in coercion. From this emerged the modern state, which has a monopoly on coercion but does not use these means to kill the goose that lays the golden eggs. The specialists in coercion are given regular income (tax) which can be factored into the meticulous book-keeping of early capitalism. Contrary to Marxist assertions that the economy is always dominant, this was the first time in history that power shifted from coercion to production.

The conditions that allow the economy to develop contribute to a process whereby the economy and polity become separated. A strong economy that is partially independent of the state contributes to the creation of a civil society, which is an effective counterbalance to the coercive power of the state. Gellner's basic definition is as follows:

Civil Society is that set of diverse non-governmental institutions which is strong enough to counterbalance the state and, while not preventing the state from fulfilling its role of keeper of the peace and arbitrator between major interests, can nevertheless prevent it from dominating and atomizing the rest of society. (Gellner 1994: 5)

As has been argued by Hann (2003), the term 'civil society' is a kind of catch-all phrase which points to the process of transformation that made modern politics possible but without actually explaining the source of that transformation. In a sense, it is viciously circular. I would argue that what lies behind the efficacy of the term civil society, of which 'civil society' is a mere symptom, is the same cognitive transformation which made *industria* possible.

As argued by Gellner, Protestantism leads to a radical disenchantment of the world, which undermines the power of the clergy. As the industrial revolution advances, scientific rationality reinforces this aspect of Protestantism while also creating a sense of doubt, which makes modern pluralism possible. Arguably, this scientific doubt feeds upon evangelical Protestant doubt concerning salvation – although Gellner does not state this explicitly. Modern pluralism is not simply reducible to a diversity of beliefs. Agro-literate societies, especially the Habsburg Empire, were also characterised by pluralism. Modern pluralism is qualitatively different in that it is combined with the belief that there are no certain truths but only facts that have not yet been falsified. This cognitive doubt, which is central to scientific advances, leads to a rejection of dogmatism and turns pluralism into tolerance.

The Protestant faithful facing God on their own and the scientist who continually distrusts traditional communal truths embody a uniquely modern individualist identity central to capitalism and modern politics. If we take Descartes as paradigmatic, for him truth was arrived at by introspection into the self (Gellner 1992). By implication, the latter could exist in splendid isolation from the world. The liberal modern self seeks freedom not in community and culture but in a separation from it. Of course, in the phenomenon of nationalism we see a reaction against this kind of self. Gellner sees modernity as characterised by continual ideological conflict between the liberal individualists and romantic communitarians (Gellner 1998). While the liberal individualists are not the straightforward heroes of this story, they are responsible for a new type of social subject who is essential to the emergence of the modern conditions of liberty which constitutes one of the conditions of possibility for the essentially private realm of 'civil society'.

The liberal self views culture as a distortion of knowledge. In science, truth transcends culture and is arrived at through experiment which, essentially, strips external reality of cultural distortions. A scientific fact is a scientific fact everywhere in the world. Of course, it is true that scientists cannot actually escape their own culture but they work as though they can and, even if their underlying method is not entirely a mirror of reality, it delivers enormous technological innovation that legitimates the method.

This desire to see things 'in-themselves' leads to severing of the fact/value distinction. Consequently, a world that is epistemologically unified becomes separated into a descriptive vocabulary of science and a distinct normative one of social order. The incommensurability between fused and non-fused universe makes many of the ontologies of traditional society sound nonsensical to modern ears. For instance, one of the tribes of the Nuer identified bulls with cucumbers. How can the same object be both a bull and a cucumber? According to Gellner, one of the meanings concerns social solidarity, the other is descriptive, and both are fused into what, to us, appears an impossible concept. In premodern societies concepts were multistranded, being simultaneously observations about the world and statements of loyalty to a social order (Gellner 1988: 43). In contrast, our concepts are single-stranded – a concept is either an observation or a statement of normative solidarity. Once this separation takes place and science becomes freed from dogma, the 'Galileos' of this world no longer find themselves in conflict with the clergy. When this is combined with the escape from coercion, for the first time in history there is a realm of reason that has escaped from the domination of both priests and kings and it is this realm which forms the basis of 'civil society'.

The arena of international politics does not favour societies which are not effective at coercion, even in the modern world. Our explanation so far makes some sense of why predation does not take place within the jurisdiction of the modern state but is still possible from the outside. Why did early modern wealthy productive states not find themselves

objects of predation from coercively run states? The new modern
bourgeois states, in which coercion was divided from economic functions, counter-intuitively, proved more effective at war than those societies in which the specialists at coercion ran society. Regular taxes gave
the state predictable revenues to build up armies and navies, and the
technological revolution, derived from industry, gave them the most
sophisticated arms available. Just as the most otherworldly Christians
became the most effective at creating worldly goods, so too those who
prioritised the economy over the means of coercion became better at
coercion than those who pursued coercion as an end in itself. As
observed by Macfarlane, the added contingent fact that the most modernising of these states was England, and later the USA, which were both
geographically favoured against attack, reinforced this process (Macfarlane
2000: 282).

Power

While this model is broadly correct in many of its contours, it is only a
partial picture, which is rendered incomplete by Gellner's understanding
of power. For Gellner power is always power 'over' others and is
invariably based upon coercion. As is implicit in its definition above, civil
society is a counterweight to the state, which is entirely conceptualised in
terms of negative predatory and coercive power. While Gellner does
recognise that social order may be maintained through non-coercive
means, namely through legitimacy and conviction (Gellner 1988: 18),
this is divorced from power and relegated to the status of exceptional. In
Gellner's trinitarian universe of plough, book and sword, power is
exclusively equal to the sword. The conditions of liberal democracy are
created when the sword is kept in check by the economy and its offshoot,
'civil society'. This opposition mirrors the classic liberal distinction
between public and private. While I think this distinction has some
normative merit, it is sociologically misleading as it suggests a division
which is not consonant with the operations of power and social agency.
In fact, social actors are shaped by processes within society in general
(civil and otherwise) that ultimately create the conditions of possibility
for effective exercises of non-coercive power. However, in order to
explain why this is the case, we need to look at power generally.

In the literature on power there are two broad theoretical traditions.
Those who largely consider power as entirely conflictual include the
following: Weber (1978), Dahl (1961), Bachrach and Baratz (1962),
Mann (1986, 1993), Lukes (1974) and Poggi (2000). Opposed to this
there exists a minority consensual school, including Parsons (1963),

Arendt (1970) and Barnes (1988). An in-between position is taken by Giddens (1984), Morriss (2002), Clegg (1989) and Haugaard (1997, 2003), who argue that power has both conflictual and consensual aspects. Similarly, Foucault observes that power should not be theorised purely negatively (1979: 194), yet he would appear to have a negative view of it – as something one should resist. In the second edition of *Power: A Radical View*, Lukes acknowledges that power includes 'power to', which suggests a move away from the adherence to the exclusive 'power over' view but, as observed by Morriss (2006), Lukes does not develop the implications of this observation to any great extent.

In the work of Arendt, Parsons and Barnes, power is a *capacity* for action which social actors gain by virtue of their membership of a social system. In short, power is empowerment. For all three authors this form of power is very different from violence. The most categorical statement of this comes from Arendt, who argues that 'politically speaking, it is insufficient to say that power and violence are not the same. Power and violence are opposites; where one rules absolutely, the other is absent' (Arendt 1970: 56). For these authors violence entails control over the other through physicality, thus it is a form of natural power. In contrast, social power derives not from the physical world but from our membership of political systems.

Arendt goes on to argue that 'violence appears where power is in jeopardy... violence can destroy power; it is utterly incapable of creating it' (Arendt 1970: 56). What she has in mind here is that a political regime which continually resorts to coercion is using physical power as a *substitute* for social power because it is weak. If the only method that an agent has of controlling another is violence, or threat of it (coercion), their control is actually quite limited. In everyday life, a parent who continually has to slap a child to get him or her to do what they wish is a parent who lacks power over the child, rather than the converse. The same applies to social systems: a society in which social order is based upon the sword is both unstable and weak, and, I would conjecture, unlikely to survive in competition with societies in which the predictability of its members does not stem from coercion. The fact that the Chinese authorities had to use tanks in Tiananmen Square demonstrates that they lacked any other kind of power over the protesting students. That is not to deny that coercion can be effective in certain instances. Nevertheless it is a substitute for willing compliance and has the capacity to destroy the sources of such compliance or, in certain instances, can increase the social power of those over whom it is exercised. The use of coercion against Greenpeace in sinking the *Rainbow Warrior* may have been a successful episodic exercise of coercive power but it made Greenpeace more rather than less powerful; consequently, the incident was contrary to the long-term interests of those who engaged in that act of violence.

Even if the power–violence contrast is somewhat overdrawn empirically, what lies behind it is the insight that social order gives us a capacity for action which is different from the power that we derive from the natural world. Power from the sword is another variation of the power that a lion has with tooth and claw, which is a rather different source of power than is created by complex political systems. In order to understand where this kind of power comes from we have to understand social order.

What is social order? At its most fundamental, it is the predictability of others. What makes their actions ordered is the fact that their social action makes sense by being meaningful. Meaning is reproduced through the reproduction of structure. The furry creature that purrs and the word 'cat' are both the same concept whereby a word and an animal constitute 'carriers' of specific linguistic structure. They are carriers of structure by virtue of interacting social agents imposing these structures upon them in the moment of interaction. The use of the word cat by a single agent is an act of structuration. While Giddens' (1984) theory of structuration suggests that individual acts of structuration are sufficient for structure to be reproduced, I would argue (Haugaard 1997: 119–35) that structuration is a necessary though not sufficient condition. Social deviants do not engage in what for them is meaningless social action. As far as they are concerned, *they are structuring*. The point is that it is not meaningful to anyone else – which is why it is classified as deviant. As Wittgenstein argues in his private language argument (1967), the meaning of a word is created by actors in collaboration with others. Invented words are not real words, unless they are understood by actors other than those who invented them. Social order is a complex of interdependent acts of structuration and responses which confirm the initial acts of structuration. However, these acts of collective structural reproduction *are not* a foregone conclusion. Social actors frequently structure in a manner that others reject, and part of the process of socialisation constitutes learning from such receptions which acts of structuration are likely to be felicitously received in specific social contexts.

For the structuring self, the nub of the problem of social order is that acts of structural reproduction are culturally based. Chomsky and Kant may be correct in their view that our minds are pre-programmed. However, it is only to a certain extent, and a great variety of social orders are possible. To Chomsky and his followers the difference between

Chinese and English may appear trivial but to the social actor it is fundamental. Following Kant, it may be true that time is a priori, but there is such an enormous gap, in terms of predictability, between aboriginal 'walk-about time' and Western 'clock time' that interaction based upon both concepts would not constitute structural reproduction. The 'walk-about' appointment appears arbitrary to the 'clock timer' and vice versa. Hence, an act of structuration between such culturally different actors would not elicit appropriate responses. Of course, the (no doubt arrogant and well-armed) Westerner can produce a gun and get some kind of predictability out of the native Australian other, but this is a form of physical power that effectively bypasses social order. Imagine for a moment that a member of the Nuer tribe were transposed into modern society. Unless an interlocutor happened to be familiar with the writings of Gellner or were an anthropologist in his or her own right, any acts of structuration based on the cucumber–bull concept would fail to elicit appropriate responses from others and the structure would effectively cease to exist systemically, even if our unfortunate Nuer lived to a great old age endlessly repeating, or structuring, cucumber–bull social practices.

The ability of individuals to act in concert is premised upon shared ability to make sense of the world (common interpretative horizon) and willingness to confirm the meaning of each other's structuration practices. When reproducing social order through mutually predictable structuration practices they gain a mutual capacity for action. They gain *power to* or mutual empowerment. Counterintuitive though it may sound, this presupposes common shared constraints. Constraint is enabling. Let us take the example of language: my capacity to communicate with my readers is premised upon the fact that I am constrained by the rules of the English language. If I were a truly free agent thus creating words and grammatical constructions as I went along I would lose the power to explain the theory which I am promulgating. This joint capacity for action, through mutual constraints, applies not only to *power to* but also to *power over*, and in the case of the latter the workings of constraint are more manifest. Imagine that I enter a democratic election. My ability to win that election is premised upon the fact that all the contending parties are willing to be constrained by the rules of the game and, as distinct from the speech example, there is a clear incentive not to respect the rules if you are the loser. Power over the losers is premised upon the fact that the latter are constrained by the structures of the democratic system. Of course, violence and coercion are necessary when the loser is not bound by structural constraint, and most modern political systems do have coercive resources at their disposal for such contingencies. However, the remarkable fact is that this is exceptional and the routine exercise of power within modern political systems is based upon structural constraint. As observed by Parsons (1963) and Barnes (1988), the violence which the state has at its disposal is not nearly sufficient to explain the routine exercise of power in democratic systems.

The problem of social order is how to create the interactive context in which actors share common perceptions of social order and are willing to be constrained by them. It is a problem that is compounded by the fact that social order frequently presupposes relations of domination which, being culturally constituted, may be construed as arbitrary. In this case, why should actors reproduce an essentially arbitrary set of conventions which allow others to exercise power over them? If the meaning of 'peasant' and 'lord' are constituted by mere convention, why should the former not simply opt out of this social order? The easy answer is either coercion, or the sword. However, the other possibility is a set of structural constraints which have their roots somewhere in the agent's socialisation. This constraint can take many forms, but the most obvious is where the structures appear other than convention. For instance, if the structures of social life are interpreted as an act of God, they are no longer a matter of convention but a divinely ordained order which the agent cannot simply opt out of. If the feudal lord can gain compliance based upon the religious beliefs of the peasant, the lord would be entirely foolish to threaten violence. Coercion only becomes logical when the beliefs that sustain these relations of domination have been undermined in some way.

As argued by Gellner (1988), hunter-gatherer societies tend to be Durkheimian, in that routine and ritual ensure that the actor's perception of 'the order of things' is entirely normative. In *agraria* the social actor thinks multistrandedly, mixing the normative and the analytical, and/or in some instances sees both the social world and the natural world according to normative single-stranded social logic, which is a kind of Platonism (Gellner 1988: 76). In either case, in *agraria* the social actor does not see that the laws of physics have a cultural transcendence in a way that the laws of social interaction do not. To this actor the social world is entirely coterminous with the natural world, thus its predictabilities have the same ontological status. There is no juxtaposition between conventional social practice and natural facts. Gellner was interested in the way this limited the actor's capacity to make sense of the natural world scientifically. However, this fusion of 'is' and 'ought' has another aspect, which he does not explore. Not only do 'is' things become 'ought' things (and thus science cannot progress) but 'ought' things become 'is' things. A normative injunction (for instance, that 'you should obey your elders') becomes a statement of fact (you obey your elders) and thus not open to negotiation. Hence, even if in a particular interaction it is in the interest of an actor to reject the constraints of that society, that actor will feel compelled to reproduce these norms correctly because he/she believes that not to do so would be to violate the 'natural order of things'. So, for instance, in a patriarchal society that routinely gives men more power over women than vice versa, the latter will continue to reproduce that social order for fear of doing something which is against nature – Shakespeare's *Macbeth* was based upon such a violation of the order of things. This kind of social power is substantially more effective than continually having to coerce people.

In the great axial-age civilisations, the book and monotheism replace nature and ritual but the effect remains the same. Social structures are perceived as more than convention – they are the will of God who created both society and nature. Being an unreliable reproducer of social order becomes 'heresy'.

European feudal societies believed that their social order reflected the Great Chain of Being, which is another claim to the effect that the social system is not arbitrarily constituted. This belief was reinforced by teleology whereby it was thought that all objects moved as a reflection of essences within them. For Aristotle, an acorn becomes an oak, because it has the essence of oakness within it, which means it *should* become an oak.

Transposed to social life, this logic suggests that aristocrats and peasants have different essences. In his account of nationalism (1983), Gellner noted that in the feudal world the aristocracy and the peasantry were culturally different. This is significant in explaining the existence of that particular set of relations of domination. The empirical fact that the aristocracy are different reinforces the essentialist view that they are inherently different, in the same way that the oak is different from the beech. As examined in detail by Elias in his account of the 'civilizing process' (1994), the aristocracy reinforced their domination by continually creating more and more complex manners for themselves in order to distinguish themselves from the bourgeoisie. The object of this exercise was not simply a desire for quaintness but derived from a realisation that their power presupposed the belief that they were inherently different from the rest of society. When these behaviours are conjoined with the Great Chain of Being, the person who does not act in a fitting manner relative to their aristocratic 'superior' violates both the law of nature and that of God. The empirical visible evidence of this was the fact that the aristocrats did actually behave differently. Relative to the feudal interpretative horizon, or cognitive world, these beliefs were a form of constraint that created the conditions of possibility of specific forms of non-coercive power.

Like words, social roles are carriers of meaning and structure; from this follows that their reproduction presupposes constraint. However, they are not simply words, but are meanings that are directly implicated in complex relations of domination. Thus their collaborative reproduction is continually in jeopardy. A feudal lord who demands 'tribute' is structuring the meaning of the concept of 'lord'. The peasant who responds appropriately by giving tribute is confirming a shared system of meaning. However, the meaning of the concept of lord entails not only 'he who is given tribute' but also 'he who gives protection'. If the peasant complains that bandits rob him of his crops, the lord is expected to afford protection and in so doing social order and meaning are recreated. In this relationship both social actors are subject to constraints which render the actions of both predictable and intelligible to each other. The mutual reliability of both sustains a regularised relationship of power. Not only do they have 'power to', they also have 'power over' each other, even if the latter is far from symmetrical. They are both constrained and yet out of that constraint comes certain autonomy. Even though the lord has more power over the peasant than vice versa, there exists a virtual 'semantic compact' whereby being a 'lord' is not the same as being a 'robber'. If the feudal lord decides to plunder his subject peasants arbitrarily, he is substituting physical power or coercion for social power derived from structural constraint. This will have one of two consequences: the peasants may decide that the social order is not divinely ordained, thus a set of arbitrary customs which may be violated with impunity. Alternatively they may conclude that their erstwhile lord is not really a 'lord' but a 'robber'. If the former is the case, feudalism as a system becomes illegitimate; while in the latter case the particular local lord, or persona, of the system becomes contested.

Let us be clear: I am not suggesting that feudalism was an entirely legitimate system, in which social power displaced coercive power. In fact I use it as a worst-case scenario in which my general hypothesis, contra Gellner, still holds – i.e. that relatively stable complex social systems presuppose social power based upon structural constraint, which exists over and above the sword. What happened in the transition from agrarian to modern society was that a new form of social and political power *largely* replaced coercive power. The word *largely* deserves emphasis: feudalism was sustained by social power although less so than modernity. This does not entail the claim that modernity does not contain coercive power or that maybe coercion was (and still is) used to wipe out rival social forms. I do not dispute the fact that democracy has a dark coercive side (as argued by Mann 2003) but the routine reproduction of democratic power structures is not primarily based upon coercion. When based upon coercion, democracy is no longer stable and, over time, will collapse. I would argue that when the beliefs that sustained the reifications of feudalism became perceived as arbitrary, the system collapsed. Once the Great Chain of Being and teleology became perceived as nonsense, the only way of sustaining the system was through coercion, with the consequence that the system became unstable.

Modern social power replaces feudalism when power in the latter is largely exercised through coercion. This occurs when the cognitive frameworks of social actors are more consonant with structures of liberal democracy than they are with those of feudalism, which entails a change of cognitive social ontology. Modern social agents perceive the Great Chain of Being as entirely arbitrary but, for reasons of a cognitive revolution, do not consider routine elections or human rights as arbitrary.

An election entails power *over* others. In the act of acceding defeat, the defeated party reproduces the structures of the democratic system. The willingness to do this without being coerced is not something that a traditional social actor would countenance. In fact, it is entirely counter-intuitive that people are willing to invest huge amounts of time and money in standing for election and, even if defeated by a narrow margin, willingly concede power to another (George W. Bush is the exception who proves the rule), and then wait four or five years for another election, possibly to be defeated again. However, for reasons of social transform-ation in Western society in the beginning of modernity, it appears entirely 'natural' or 'right' to do this. Of course, there are elections in which this does not happen and the electorally defeated party reaches for the means of coercion. However, this is most likely to happen in a situation in which the social actors in question are not truly modern, for instance when democracy has been superimposed upon a traditional agrarian society. As observed by Dahl, democracies take about twenty years to become stable, which is evidenced by the fact that there are few if any instances of a democracy that has been established for longer than this reverting to non-democratic forms (Dahl 1989: 315). This is because it takes about twenty years for the interpretative horizon which sustains democracy to become internalised into the taken-for-granted tacit knowledge, or *habitus*, of a population. It is not the case, contra Gellner, that it takes twenty years to get the predators used to keeping the sword in its scabbard.

So, what is the transformation in social ontology that constitutes the conditions of possibility for modernity and liberalism? This entails that liberal democracy be based upon social power, not simply coercive power. It would be possible to take a set of traditional actors and coerce them at gun-point to hold elections and so on, but this would not constitute democracy. This is analogous to a Wittgenstein type argument

(Wittgenstein 1967) to the effect that getting members of a society in which the concept of a board game was absent to go through the motions of playing chess is not the same as actually playing chess. Different cognitive frameworks constitute conditions of possibility for different types of relations of domination because they entail the internalisation of specific constraints.

Power and the conditions of possibility for liberal democracy

In our analysis so far, we have already seen that feudalism presupposes a teleological world-view based upon essences. As argued by Gellner, one of the premises of *industria* is a continuous world-view in which there are no exceptions (Gellner 1992). Starting from *cogito ergo sum*, it should be possible to arrive at the truths of physics and from there, by way of biology, to theorise the social sciences – which was Comte's vision. This implies that the rules that apply in the physical sciences should apply to social life. Hobbes' description of politics as an artificial machine, a clock, following the laws of mechanics, would be typical. One of the central elements of the modern scientific revolution was to move away from teleology. When Galileo saw the moons of Jupiter, what was revolutionary was his interpretation of them as 'moons'. Astronomers had observed them before but no one had seen them as moons. The implications of Galileo's description of them as moons is a continuous science in which the laws of physics equally apply to Jupiter as they do on Earth. There are no exceptions. Everything can be reduced to the same laws which equally determine the path of objects falling off the leaning tower of Pisa and in space. When Newton discovered gravity his great concern was that others might think he had found another 'essence' and, consonant with the modern vision, was at great pains to claim that this was not the case.

Applied to social life, the demise of essences has huge implications. The feudal system was essentially a historical instance of Plato's myth of metals, as outlined in the *Republic*. This reinforced the entire social behaviour of different classes. They dressed differently, ate differently and, as argued by Gellner, spoke different languages. There is a medieval Danish saying which encapsulates this: 'An Aristocrat speaks Latin to scholars, French to his peers, German to the peasants and Danish to his dogs.' This did not stem simply from some desire to be different for difference's sake, but was absolutely essential to the maintenance of feudal power structures. The belief that the aristocracy, monarchy and members of the church were somehow different constituted a structural constraint upon the minds of the less powerful.

The modern individual has no essence. As described in *Reason and Culture* (Gellner 1992), this self is virtually an 'it'. Humans become the conceptual equivalent of atoms or monads all of which are interchangeable. This reductionism leads to the kind of egalitarianism which de Tocqueville observed to be central to American democracy. '[T]he more I studied American society, the more clearly I saw equality of conditions as the creative element from which each particular fact derived, and all my observations returned to this nodal point' (de Tocqueville, quoted in Macfarlane 2000: 183). The law of democracy is based not upon seeing people as different but upon seeing them as the same. We take this for granted, but someone like Plato would have seen this as odd; after all, treating dissimilar people as though they were the same constitutes an injustice. It is not that feudal law was arbitrary but that it became *perceived* to be arbitrary once the essentialist ontology of teleology was removed. In his account of the transition from sovereign to modern forms of punishment, Foucault argued that what was central was that the former became perceived as 'arbitrary'. This perception was factually incorrect: pre-modern punishment was far from arbitrary; for instance, there were exact weights and measurements for torture, sentencing and trial by ordeal (Foucault 1979: 40, 78–81). However, the point is that to the modern mind trial by ordeal (for instance, holding a person under water for a certain length of time in order to know if they are guilty or innocent) has nothing to do with justice. This procedure is not inherently arbitrary; it *becomes* so through a specific cognitive shift.

The decline of teleology was also central to meritocracy and the emergence of mass education. As described by Gellner (1983), the advent of modernity entailed mass socialisation, controlled by the state, which levelled cultural differences within the domain of the state. This was, of course, central to the legitimation of capitalism as a meritocratic system. Educational credentials replace blood and kinship as power resources. To modern social actors educational credentials are not arbitrary, whereas privilege based upon historical lineage is. Again, once blood lineage is perceived as an arbitrary accident of birth, a whole set of constraints simply fall away and with them a whole set of conditions of possibility for exercising power. Conversely, new conditions for relations of domination are created.

The creation of culturally homogeneous populations through mass education created the preconditions for liberal democracy in a number of other ways. Liberal democracy is premised upon the idea that policy decisions are based not upon might but upon argumentation – what

Habermas describes as 'ideal speech'. However the hypothesis that the best argument should win raises the issue: which rationality should we use? Putting social actors through a common curriculum socialises them into a common perception of what constitutes reason. Thus mass education creates a population who internalise similar processes of reasoning. To take an analogy, if a society were to decide to change elites by playing ritual games of chess, these chess championships would presuppose that everyone internalised the rules of chess as part of the logical order of things.

Reasoned argument not only presupposes a common method of reasoning but is also premised upon a convergence of systems of meaning. To continue the chess analogy: if this society of chess players does not play with the same pieces, their political system cannot work. Prior to mass education (which is really mass socialisation) society was made up of many local cultures each of which had embedded within it separate meanings. Even if the rules of reason were shared, divergence of meaning will make the other appear unreasonable and thus winning an argument becomes impossible. As observed by Ackerman, democratic citizenship presupposes the ability to participate in an intelligible way in a dialogue of justification (Ackerman 1980: 72–3). While social actors do not, by and large, have Wittgenstein's insight that justification takes place within specific culturally constituted local 'language games', it is an empirical fact that reasonable justification presupposes cultural uniformity which can be only be achieved through mass socialisation.

In this context it should be noted that Mann's argument, in chapter 2 and in *The Dark Side of Democracy* (Mann 2005), to the effect that many modern Western democracies were 'ethnically cleansed' at some point in time may be correct. Modern democracies may have seen high levels of coercive power at the moment of their inception but this does *not falsify* the point (sociologically speaking, although perhaps morally so) that, after 'ethnic cleansing', this homogeneity is functional to the creation of power resources which are largely non-coercive.

We have introduced democracy as central to our analysis, which raises the issue of Gellner's scepticism concerning the centrality of democracy. I would argue that his general point is correct. Democracy does not entail handing over the creation of social order or of social structures to government by the people. However, this does not falsify but rather reinforces my hypothesis. My argument hinges on the fact that any exercise of power presupposes a relatively static *habitus* (Bourdieu 1990) or 'practical consciousness knowledge' (Giddens 1984) that constitutes the conditions of possibility for the routine exercise of structural reproduction, thus social power. Essentially, modernity entailed a shift in tacit knowledge that is similar to a Kuhnian paradigm shift but is even more profound in the sense that it is not confined to science. In essence, I would argue that the possibilities of structural change through the democratic process are constrained by the *habitus* of social subjects, which constitutes the conditions of possibility for routine non-coercive exercises of power.

So far I have emphasised the democratic elements of modern political systems. Now I wish to shift focus onto the liberal elements. As has been argued by Gellner in his characterisation of the opposition between the early and the late Wittgenstein (Gellner 1998), modernity is caught in a dilemma between attempting to construct a value-free 'view from nowhere' and the realisation that this is in fact an impossibility. All interpretation is an imposition of meaning upon the world, consequently a reflection of culture. Gellner's disagreement with the late Wittgenstein is not that the latter perceived social agents as suspended in language games of their own creation but that Wittgenstein and others, including Geertz and Winch, considered this condition unproblematic. According to Gellner's interpretation of Wittgenstein, there is no need to transcend these holistic webs of meaning because 'local truth' is all that philosophical inquiry can deliver in any case. Of course, Gellner recognises that we cannot transcend culture, but he considers the attempt to do so by scientists a model of Enlightenment. Gellner interprets this quest for neutrality as a 'myth', which should 'not be taken literally, at face value' (Gellner 1998: 184). They are myths that have made possible the technological miracle which characterises modernity.

While Gellner endorses this Enlightenment quest with regard to the natural world, he ridicules the attempt by some liberal political philosophers to use this kind myth, in the form of social contract, as the basis for understanding justice (Gellner 1988: 23–34). The person at the centre of Rawls' original position is a Robinson Crusoe-like Cartesian agent, which Gellner criticises as entailing an absurd account of social life.

Gellner *is* correct that this is absurd as a *descriptive* account of social life. Who cares how 'the stone age vote swings' and, yes, of course, 'the original social contract' will never be found (see Gellner 1988: 23–34), but the point is that this thought experiment is not absurd as a regulative ideal from the perspective of moral philosophy. Ironically, this distinction can best be understood by using Gellner's analysis of the difference between single-stranded and multistranded thought.

A bull–cucumber is an absurdity when seen single-strandedly. The point of single-stranded thought is that it defines concepts relative to a single interpretative horizon. A single-stranded thinker can hold a single interpretation through a complex process of rational deliberation without allowing interference from alternative interpretative horizons. As such, it is a form of 'methodological bracketing'. Within this, concepts gain a gestalt quality whereby we know for instance that the picture of a duck–rabbit can appear as both, but for the sake of a particular logic and interpretative horizon we insist that it is only a duck. In *Thought and Change* Gellner relates a story told by Kafka concerning a man who wakes up in the morning and finds himself to be a beetle and goes on to explain how disorientating being a beetle–man is (Gellner 1964: 50). No doubt this is descriptively correct because we are not used to being a beetle–man. Gellner interprets the relationship between single-stranded and multistranded thought in terms of a conflation of 'is' and 'ought' – the social world and the natural world. However, this account of the distinction between single- and multistranded thought does not go far enough. If we think of Weber's account of four types of action, these are single-stranded modes of thought, which entail precisely a kind of metamorphosis as we switch from one to the other. From the perspective of bureaucratic purposive intrumental rationality, a person is a number while from the perspective of affective action she may be 'Mary who lives up the road and whom I care for dearly (although her mother is hard to take)'. When the bureaucrat has to deal with 'Mary up the road' in the course of administration, she metamorphoses into a number, but when the bureaucrat meets her in the local pub in the evening, she is 'Mary up the road' again. The *efficient* bureaucrat has the capacity to bracket methodologically everything they know about 'Mary up the road' from client number 4556. However, like a gestalt picture, she is never both at once. 'Mary up the road'–4556 is a kind of beetle–man or bull–cucumber for whom (which?) modern bureaucracy has no conceptual space. The latter would be an instance of interpreting single-stranded thought multistrandedly, which is what a traditional person would do when confronted by the modern world. Rawls' original position is a similar attempt at methodological bracketing which aims at single-strandedness. When persons in the original position methodologically bracket everything they know about their preferences, place in society and so on, what they are doing is to single out a specific strand of a given perspective. To use an analogy: in *The Order of Things*, Foucault describes how in the Renaissance period the naturalist Aldrovandi described natural and imaginary objects together. So, for instance, the entry on snakes included dragons and various myths surrounding them. Half a century later, in the 'Classical' era, the compilers of the Encyclopaedias excluded these elements, concentrating upon anatomical description (Foucault 2001: 39–40). The Classical Encyclopaedist would almost certainly have been familiar with these myths but he methodologically bracketed this information. This move towards singularising their interpretation of nature entailed a constraint upon knowledge, which is analogous to the way in which modern systems of justice and bureaucratic administration entail a bracketing-off of information concerning an interacting other. For the bureaucrat and the judge, competence entails a massive methodological bracketing where only very specific information is considered pertinent and all the rest is viewed as extraneous. Gellner's insistence on seeing Rawls' thought experiment descriptively or sociologically constitutes a misinterpretation of single-stranded thought as multistranded. It is analogous to but logically the reverse of ridiculing the Nuer for bull–cucumbers – ironically, Gellner is the multistranded thinker and Rawls the single-stranded one.

If we consider the contrast between these forms of thought in the more extended sense that I propose here, I do not know if it is correct to say that modernity is unique in developing single-stranded thought, while agrarian societies were multistranded. It could be the case that agrarian societies had different forms of single-strandedness which are difficult for us to recognise. For instance, the ability of the feudal warrior to switch from courtly love to the violence of battle suggests a switch from one form of single-strandedness to another. However, be that as it may, modernity is associated with the emergence of particular forms of single-strandedness and some of these are central to the conditions of liberal democracy.

Central to modernity is the ability to see other and self as essentially unencumbered beings. Rawls in *A Theory of Justice* (1971) may have been empirically mistaken, just like Kant, in thinking that the conceptual categories which he propounded were universal, but the attempt methodologically to bracket the socially contingent particularities of other and self is essential to *modern* liberal conceptions of justice. This does not just apply to the rarefied realms of political philosophy. Something similar is at work in everyday interaction when one actor is trying to convince the other that a specific outcome is just and the former retorts to the latter, 'Ah yes, but you would say that', meaning 'You would say that, *given your particular circumstances.*' The only reply to that comment, which is going to be successful, is to demonstrate that the principle of justice in question does not reflect contingent particularity: in other words, to demonstrate that one is arguing single-strandedly from a position which resembles the original position.

The ability to think single-strandedly entails a high level of internalised restraint. When an actor thinks of another or (even more difficult) thinks of the self single-strandedly, as in the original position, this entails a methodological bracketing. Kant correctly observed that making an exception of self is hugely tempting. The source of this difficulty is not only self-interest, as one might assume. We may know little about 'citizens', the abstract holders of human rights or other categories of single-stranded thought, such as 'consumers' or 'clients'. Yet we know a lot about ourselves (or our friends and relations), and what we are being asked to do is methodologically to bracket that rich information in favour of the thin knowledge of single-stranded description. Anyone who has ever corrected the examination paper of a student whom they know well feels the tension between this affective knowledge and the need to trump it with the single-stranded standards of measuring academic excellence. In short, single-stranded thought requires a self-imposed constraint, which comes only through discipline.

Modern societies are disciplinary societies, a fact which is usually considered antithetical to liberal democracy. The latter is intuitively so in the sense that discipline is a constraint upon liberty, but for the moment I wish methodologically to bracket this aspect of discipline in favour of its less obvious positive face.

Gellner argues that the late Wittgenstein discovered what everybody on the village green knows, but he did so discursively, unlike the actors on the village green (1998). The latter practise their culture as tacit taken-for-granted knowledge but Wittgenstein was responsible for turning it into a philosophy. In his account of nationalism, Gellner argues that state monopoly of education constitutes a unique shift of socialisation from the home and apprenticeship to centralised state institutions. Underlying this is a fundamental point about modernity: modernity is unique in making socialisation discursively problematic and, as a consequence, we are a civilisation that renders it a political problem.

The problem of socialisation is paradigmatically represented in Panopticism. The Panopticon is essentially a 'socialisation machine' in which anything can be taught. Children can be socialised in it and taught that two and two make five and the moon is made of green cheese (Foucault 1979: 204). Foucault concentrated upon the negative aspects of this, but this discipline is also essential to modern liberal democracy. Panoptical socialisation is, in a sense, a metaphor for self-internalised restraint. The point is that bars are replaced by light: 'no more bars, no more chains, no more heavy locks ... The heaviness of the old "houses of security" could be replaced by the simple economic geometry of "houses of certainty" ' (Foucault 1979: 202). As argued by Foucault, when Tuke freed those in his care from chains he replaced these with guilt and responsibility in which the madman 'promised to restrain himself' (Foucault 1971: 246). Tuke organised 'tea parties' where the mad were instructed to dress in their best clothes, act with the utmost politeness and judge themselves and each other for the slightest misdemeanour.

In this way the subject was 'obliged to objectify himself in the eyes of reason' (Foucault 1971: 249). In other words, the capacity to replace coercion with reason presupposes the internalisation of restraint. Foucault interprets this in a normatively negative light: contrary to his critique, the ability to be persuaded by the force of better argument, or methodologically to bracket information which you would like to use, presupposes the internalisation of a set of norms defining what constitutes reason, pertinence to specific situations, *and* the predisposition to be constrained by this knowledge. This internalisation presupposes discipline. Of course, coercion remains in the background. It is needed to create the disciplined agent (you could not leave the Panopticon at will) and after that it is used against those who have failed to internalise the norms of proper structuration practices. However, in the former case, coercion is there to beget social power and in the latter as a substitute when social power fails. You coerce the unpunctual children in the hope that they become punctual, in which case they will always be punctual irrespective of continued coercion. Social power is the preferred tool of domination, rather than coercion. If we think of education, especially in its early modern form, discipline is essential. How else can we interpret the endless attention to punctuality and neatness? This discipline is necessary for creating a social agent who is willing continually to bracket information methodologically according to single-stranded logic.

When viewed over time, the process of education itself is a massive deferral of gratification. Children are taught to sit inside for the best part of the day and the curriculum itself is directed at rewards which are years away. The agent who has been accustomed to studying for examinations that are years away is more likely to accept electoral defeat and wait for the next election than someone who has undergone socialisation in the home in which social life is taken up with immediate problem-solving tasks.

As we argued earlier, the problem of social order is that social structures are in fact entirely conventional. It has always been believed that if actors were to perceive this then anarchy would reign. In agrarian societies this unravelling was prevented by appeals to ritual, God or the 'Great Chain of Being'. In modern societies this will not do. However, belief in a transcendent reason performs the same function. The belief that it is possible to think about justice from an 'original position' or have democratic debate as 'ideal speech' is the functional equivalent of God.

In agrarian societies failure to acknowledge reification leads to damnation whereas in modern societies it is simply characterised as 'unreasonable'. However, the effectiveness of that presupposes massive disciplinary training and an education in which reason is given foundational status, which is the functional equivalent of being sacred. While this may appear contrary to liberal democracy as 'ideal speech', it is procedurally necessary. If a particular party loses an election, it accepts defeat and does so because it would be considered unreasonable not to, rather than because they are coerced into it or believe they will burn in hell. They are 'forced to be free' by their own powers of reason. Autonomy for Kant was not a state of doing what you want but of being self-governed through reason. This constitutes a kind of internal democracy in which order is maintained through the sovereign principles of reason, which entails massive internal restraint.

Modern liberal democracies are also societies in which the state has taken over the monopoly of violence. In civil society and politics everyday social interaction is *meant* to take place without coercion. Coercion is reserved for those who do not play by the rules of the game (the deviant and undisciplined) and is hidden at the margins of society. This removal of coercion from everyday life is also made possible by a kind of sociogenic transformation which Elias describes in the 'civilising process' (Elias 1994). Essentially Elias argued that the aristocracy, who were the traditional warrior class, tried to distinguish themselves from the bourgeoisie by adopting more and internalised constraint through the adoption of more and more complex 'manners'. However, the bourgeoisie followed suit and slowly adopted some of the etiquette of their 'superiors'. During the nineteenth century the petit bourgeoisie and finally the working classes followed suit. The aggregate result is a population which has internalised massive constraint in their everyday behaviour and has a dislike of violence. Modern social elites, as distinct from the feudal knights, find physical violence distasteful. Of course it is not that they are not capable of violence but they prefer to give orders to bomb from 20,000 feet to getting spattered in blood. The former can be done from single-stranded instrumental rationality: 'targets' are shot rather than 'people' killed (Bauman 1989: 103). Liberal democracy pre-supposes actors who do not engage in private violence but allow them-selves to be procedurally constrained, while single-stranded logic allows those very same actors to defend the state coercively. This internalisation of 'manners' entails a sociogenic (to use Elias' terminology) transform-ation whereby the self becomes substantially less spontaneous, which constitutes one of the conditions of possibility of the creation of the modern law-abiding democratic voter.

In his account of *industria*, Gellner discusses Weber's hypothesis concerning the elective affinity between Calvinism and capitalism (for instance, Gellner 1988: 167–8). Relative to this new set of restraints which I argue underpins modern power, a Puritan ethic adds to the creation of this law-abiding citizen who does not need to be routinely coerced. If God is no longer engaged in miracles, and the world has become a disenchanted place, this has a clear analogy with the singular modern political world in which exceptions are ruled out and the rule of law is paramount. The severe Puritan God who is constitutionally incapable of helping the sinner who has 'strayed' from the faith is analogous to the bureaucrat who insists that no exceptions can be made and endless application forms must be correctly filled in. If the judgement of heaven allows no exceptions, why should temporal justice?

The combination of modern disciplinary education, Elias' account of the 'civilising process' and Weber's account of the 'Protestant ethic' collectively entail a transformation of social agency in the direction of restraint. This modern restrained being does not find sword-wielding a legitimate basis for social order but is quite compliant and structurally constrained in the face of impartial justice, bureaucracy, regular elections and so on. Thus new forms of *power to* and *power over* become part of the conditions of possibility of politics.

Forces working against liberal democracy

So far I have methodologically bracketed aspects of the conditions of modernity which lead away from liberal democracy. However, in order to provide balance I conclude with a brief analysis of these darker forces. As there are many, I shall confine myself to the dual dark aspect of the very same social forces which I have singled out as contributing to modern social power, thus liberal democracy.

We discussed how the undermining of teleology was central to undermining feudal essentialism. The success of non-teleological thought was central to scientific advancement and liberal thought. However, following MacIntyre (1981), the decline of teleology in ethics has the potential to contribute to an essentially meaningless anomic existence, which undermines liberal democracy. If life has no ultimate end and there is no desire for self-development, as a realisation of *telos*, there is a danger that the self will become an empty being who strives for gratification after gratification in a directionless manner. As described by Bauman, the anomic actor of 'liquid modernity' is like Don Giovanni, who seeks seduction but the moment it occurs is dissatisfied and has to find new conquests (Bauman 2001: 53–4). This is a parable for the consumer who does not desire objects because they are *for* something but simply because consumption has become an end in itself. This kind of person is wonderful for capitalism but entirely weightless as a counterbalance to economic forces. Consequently, the *polity* becomes devoid of value rationality, subsumed by the economy and colonised by the logic of consumption. In agrarian societies, the *polity* and the economy are fused, with the former dominating the latter. In proper democratic modern society, political power and the economy are separate and in balance, resulting in a democratic liberal state. In liquid modernity, through neo-liberalism, the economy and the *polity* become fused again in a manner which undermines liberal democratic debate.

The ability to think about others single-strandedly makes possible liberal justice, democratic elections, the correction of examination papers, and many other associated structural practices. Unfortunately, this form of single-stranded thought also facilitated the Holocaust. While it can be argued that Bauman excessively downplays the significance of anti-semitism in *Modernity and the Holocaust*, he is broadly correct in arguing that the implementation of the 'final solution' would have been impossible without instrumental bureaucratic reason. When dealing with issues of bureaucratic justice it is often normatively desirable that the 'other' is a number with no name. However, once individual Jews became numbers this facilitated their transportation to factories of death. As was argued by Bauman, the key to the implementation of the 'final solution' was for 'ordinary' Germans *not* to think of Jews in terms of their Jewish neighbour. Reversing this, the key to preventing the Holocaust is the ability to see '4556' for transportation to 'resettlement' also as 'Miriam up the road'. In other words, when carried to excess, or in the wrong context, single-stranded thought contributed to the Holocaust.

Discipline makes self-restraint possible, which, in turn, facilitates rule-following. However, abject obedience to rules leads to the outcomes of the Milgram experiments. People who are so obedient they will carry out any action as long as it accords with the rules of the game are dangerous. In these situations it is the law-abiding person who is dangerous, not the deviant: the indiscipline of seeing multistrandedly can be an asset.

We referred to how the 'civilising process' contributes some of the conditions of democracy. Of course, the ideal of being 'uniquely civilised' also legitimates undemocratic and illiberal behaviour towards the so-called 'uncivilised'.

We have argued that reason, as embodied in ideal speech, is essential to democracy. This of course raises the question: whose reason? What about the unreasonable? The belief in the transcendence of reason is responsible for democratic closure but is, of course, also responsible for exclusion.

Each of the elements that I have singled out as contributing to the conditions of modern liberal democracy also has a dark side, which has the potential to undermine liberal democracy. However, my objective is not a normative one of endorsement but a sociological one in which I wish to show how modern democracy is based upon a transformation of human agency, both cognitively and emotionally, which renders these social agents particularly susceptible to certain relations of empowerment and disempowerment. The fact that aspects of the social transformation that characterises modernity also have the potential to lead to the legitimisation of relations of domination that are antithetical to liberal democracy does not falsify my general hypothesis. The decline of value rationality, subservience to market forces, the Holocaust, bureaucratic indifference and social exclusion are also a part of modernity. As with liberal democracy, these normatively undesirable aspects of modernity do not rest on the power of the sword. They are created and recreated by the modern social agents who have internalised the interpretative horizon and constraints described above.

In chapter 2, Mann argues that European liberal democratic states frequently practise imperialism, which seems to go against the normative principles of liberal democracy. In chapter 6, Malešević takes Gellner to task for viewing modern human agents as pacifists, while their traditional ancestors are sword-wielding, as this presupposes an implausible concept of agency. For Malešević one of the central puzzles of modernity is precisely that modern social agents profess peace, and would appear to have a sincere dislike of violence, yet they have the capacity to practise genocide and industrial war. While this may appear at odds with my insistence that modern liberal democracies are based upon new forms of social power, theoretically this is not the case. A single-stranded social agent who has internalised massive discipline and is 'civilised' in Elias' sense of the word, is a highly compartmentalised social agent. If the other is a 'target' or a 'terrorist', a massive methodological bracketing takes place which theoretically speaking entails the same discipline and ability at single-stranded logic as thinking yourself into the 'original position'. 'Extraneous elements' are entirely removed and the social agent perceives the other entirely one-dimensionally. The one-dimensional other can then be slotted into a massive and complex bureaucratically organised industrial mode of killing. Cognitive dissonance takes place when the actor thinking single-strandedly is confronted with situations when the methodological bracketing necessary becomes problematic – when 'Mrs Cohen up the road' becomes confused with '4556'. To take a trivial everyday instance, modern Western meat-eaters are at ease buying various cuts of meat, wrapped in cling-film off the supermarket shelves, yet when they travel to less developed societies and see entire animal corpses hanging up they feel revulsion and disgust. In the former case the animals are slaughtered through principles of industrial production and when they appear on the shelves in small packs are entirely divorced from the animal in the field, whereas the carcass hanging up is not separable in this way. The Western traveller is being confronted with what they normally methodologically bracket. Similarly, Western elites who would find cutting off the head of another with a sword traumatic, find the bombing of thousands is less problematic. Therefore, the very conditions which allow internal pacification of social life also create the conditions of possibility for extreme violence if presented correctly. This Janus-like quality is unfortunately functionally necessary. If liberal democracies were unable to go to war, they would be a dysfunctional social form which would have stood no chance of survival in the nineteenth and twentieth centuries. Functionality presupposes precisely the fact that there is counterintuitive elective affinity between the characteristics that make possible the replacement of elites without violence and the ability to wage war on a massive industrial scale.

This leads me to conclude with a more general comment. The claim, contra Gellner, that modernity entails a transformation of power, which is not reducible to a containment of the predators and wielders of the sword, should not be taken as a simplistic normative endorsement of these forces of transformation. The fact that social actors have internalised massive restraints, which facilitate liberal democracy and the removal of violence from everyday life, should not blind us to the fact these same restraints are also the conditions of possibility for other modern forms of domination which, relative to the normative criteria of liberal democracy, may be as reprehensible as the feudal forms which they replaced. As with liberal democracy, the conditions of possibility for these normatively objectionable forms of domination are based upon new forms of social power that have their source in a profound ontological transformation of social agency.

References

Ackerman, B. 1980. *Social Justice in the Liberal State*. New Haven: Yale University Press.
Arendt, H. 1970. *On Violence*. London: Allen Lane.
Bachrach P. and Baratz, M.S. 1962. The Two Faces of Power. *American Political Science Review* 56: 641–51.
Barnes, B. 1988. *The Nature of Power*. Cambridge: Polity.
Bauman, Z. 1989. *Modernity and the Holocaust*. Cambridge: Polity.
    2001. *Community*. Cambridge: Polity.
Bourdieu, P. 1990. *The Logic of Practice*. Cambridge: Polity.
Dahl, R.A. 1961. *Who Governs? Democracy and Power in an American City*. New Haven: Yale University Press.

1989. *Democracy and Its Critics*. New Haven: Yale University Press.

Elias, N. 1994. *The Civilizing Process: The Development of Manners*. Oxford: Blackwell.

Foucault, M. 1971. *Madness and Civilization: A History of Insanity in the Age of Reason*. London: Tavistock.

1979. *Discipline and Punish: The Birth of the Prison*. Harmondsworth: Penguin.

2001. *The Order of Things*. London: Routledge.

Gellner, E. 1959. *Words and Things*. Harmondsworth: Penguin.

1964. *Thought and Change*. London: Weidenfeld and Nicolson.

1983. *Nations and Nationalism*. Oxford: Blackwell.

1988. *Plough, Sword and Book*. Chicago: University of Chicago Press.

1992. *Reason and Culture*. Oxford: Blackwell.

1994. *The Conditions of Liberty*. Harmondsworth: Penguin.

1998. *Language and Solitude*. Cambridge: Cambridge University Press.

Giddens, A. 1984. *The Constitution of Society*. Cambridge: Polity.

Hann, C. 2003. Civil Society: The Sickness, Not the Cure? *Social Evolution and History* 2 (2): 55–74.

Haugaard, M. 1997. *The Constitution of Power*. Manchester: Manchester University Press.

2002. *Power: A Reader*. Manchester: Manchester University Press.

2003. Reflections on Seven Forms of Power. *European Journal of Social Theory* 6 (1): 78–114.

Laclau, E. and Mouffe, C. 1985. *Hegemony and Socialist Strategy*. London: Verso.

Lessnoff, M. 2002. *Ernest Gellner and Modernity*. Cardiff: University of Wales Press.

Lukes, S. 1974. *Power: A Radical View*. London: Macmillan.

2005. *Power: A Radical View*. 2nd edn, Basingstoke and New York: Palgrave Macmillan.

Macfarlane A. 2000. *The Riddle of the Modern World: Of Liberty, Wealth and Equality*. Basingstoke and New York: Palgrave Macmillan.

MacIntyre, A. 1981. *After Virtue: A Study in Moral Theory*. London: Duckworth.

Mann, M. 1986. *The Sources of Social Power*, vol. I: *A History of Power from the Beginning to A.D. 1760*. Cambridge: Cambridge University Press.

1993. *The Sources of Social Power*, vol. II: Cambridge: Cambridge University Press.

2005. *The Dark Side of Democracy*. Cambridge: Cambridge University Press.

Morriss, P. 2002. *Power: A Philosophical Analysis*. 2nd edn, Manchester: Manchester University Press.

2006. Steven Lukes on the Concept of Power. *Political Studies Review* 4: 124–35.

Parsons, T. 1963. On the Concept of Political Power. *Proceedings of the American Philosophical Society* 107: 232–62.

Poggi, G. 2000. *Forms of Power*. Cambridge: Polity.

Rawls, J. 1971. *A Theory of Justice*. Oxford: Oxford University Press.

Weber, M. 1978. *Economy and Society*. vol. I: *An Outline of Interpretive Sociology*. Berkeley: University of California Press.

Wittgenstein, L. 1967. *Philosophical Investigations*. Oxford: Blackwell.

4   Gellner versus Marxism: a major concern or a fleeting affair?

Peter Skalník

Marx's faith, I believe, was fundamentally a faith in the open society.
(Popper 1966: 200)

When the Revolution comes, both sides will shoot *him*.
(David Glass, according to Gellner 1996: 673)

Gellner's choice is a variety of democratic socialism.
(Wettersten 1996: 503)

Gellner's social theory rests on two pillars: civil society and modernity.[1] In both, Marxism has a stake. Lessnoff argues that Gellner saw Bolshevism as 'an effective agent of economic and social modernization' and that Marxism-Leninism as an ideology was for him 'a kind of functional equivalent, a collectivist substitute, for the "Protestant ethic" of Calvinism' (Lessnoff 2002: 55). This chapter is an attempt at a more subtle and diversified look at Gellner's relationship with Marxism. On the one hand there is the reality and practice of Bolshevism (Soviet Marxism or Marxism-Leninism) which Gellner viewed rather critically; on the other there is Marxism without adjectives as a general social and historical theory. I shall analyse both strands. Although Gellner did not submit the former to any deeper analysis (there are indications that after his one-year stay in Moscow in the late 1980s he envisaged a book on the Soviet communist system), I argue that he was attracted to the theory and practice of the Soviet experiment. In perhaps his last word on this theme, he wrote that he 'always knew that those beliefs were rubbish' but treated them with respect 'as one generally does with regard to the religion of others' (Gellner 1993: 141). In a way he liked the exchange between liberalism and socialism and, as a

---

[1] The first version of this chapter was read at the international conference 'The Social and Political Relevance of Ernest Gellner's Thought Today', held at the National University of Ireland in Galway, 21–22 May 2005. I am grateful to the participants for their comments and questions. Special thanks are due to Siniša Malešević at Galway and David Shankland at Bristol for their inspiring suggestions which led to some revisions of the text. However, I am the sole person responsible for the contents and form of the chapter as it now reaches the reader.

notorious maverick, regretted the 'total collapse of one participant in the Great Debate' (141). The latter, as it reflected itself in the theoretical disputations among Soviet ethnographers, fascinated Gellner as well and he spent relatively a lot of time in order to understand and explain to Western readers what preoccupies theorists such as Semyonov, Kabo or Bromley. I shall pay attention to these theories, their pitfalls and the trap into which Gellner fell while studying them.

Marxism for Ernest Gellner was a challenge of the day, in effect of all his life. Although his philosophy, as expressed in his first and last books, does not look like a part of this challenge, all his politics and thinking was marked by taking Marxism seriously. For Gellner, Marxism was a contender for primacy and a major opponent of the liberal theory of modernity. In his view Marxism was an alternative theory of modernity, and even though he paid a lot of attention to Islam as well I do not think that Islam (understood broadly as a life strategy) was really perceived by him as a candidate for a future socio-political order, at least in the Euro-Atlantic space. As I quote him above, Gellner always knew that Marxism was a set of *beliefs* which were untrue, which deserved respect only as an alternative religion. His former colleague in Cambridge stressed that Gellner rejected Marxism for its economic determinism, but that at the same time he 'emphasized a materialist standpoint ... [and] this Central European is painfully aware that decent human communities require stronger social foundations than those which liberal individualism has been able to provide' (Hann 2001: 5899, 5901).

Gellner 'believed' in an unbiased, falsifiable, quest for knowledge as the decisive characteristics of humankind. Man for him is a knowledge-seeking being, who maintains that beliefs are fictions which differ fundamentally from scientific knowledge. History is the history neither of class struggle nor of national conflict, he wrote in his last fully accomplished book on *Nationalism* (Gellner 1997). In a collection of essays which was published just a few years before *Nationalism*, he was more concrete: 'Marxism distinguishes *various* types of class-endowed society, it is we post-Marxist sociologists who bring together all agrarian societies in one great genus, contrasted with the industrial world' (Gellner 1994b: 185, Gellner's emphasis). Gellner's relation to Marxism is, however, ambivalent and more colourful than black and white. After all, Gellner lived nine-tenths of his active academic life while Marxism ostensibly ruled in a large part of the world and expanded into the less developed ex-colonial world. Arguably the best of Gellner's books, *Plough, Sword and Book* (Gellner 1988a), is subtitled 'the structure of human history' and as such is a response to the dogmatism of Marxist historical materialism (cf. Musil 2001). His guru here is Max Weber, who stressed ideology as a major ingredient of capitalism. However, neither Weber nor Gellner wanted to discount the role of production. Gellner wrote of Weber that

there is no question of his intending to replace a 'materialist' account by some kind of 'idealist' negation or inversion of it ... The most he claimed was that the indisputably indispensable material pre-conditions were to be supplemented by a further additional ideological one, without which, on their own, the material or structural causes would not have sufficed to produce the required result. (Gellner 1990: 146)

What Weber really changed in the theory of history was his tran-scendence of Marxist and Hegelian stress on the endogenous nature of historical process.

Weberianism most emphatically does not assume or postulate that all past social forms contain the later forms as seeds ... Capitalism was not, for Max Weber, the inevitable fruit of the internal contradictions of some generic pre-capitalist social formation ... The really important difference lies in the fact that this approach does not assume that all pre-capitalist class-endowed social formations are inherently unstable, nor does it see them as located along some permanent evolutionary ladder. (1990: 147–8)

Western historical theory, unlike Marxism, worked with 'the absence of a faith in a persistent and as it were internal mechanism of change, propelling human society in a specific direction' (148). To this rejection of teleology, inherited from Weber, Gellner adds what Marxism underscored in its theory but overutilised in its practice: coercion. Whereas Marxism rele-gated politics into superstructure, Gellner puts it into the infrastructure.

Gellner qualifies Karl Marx as 'the bourgeois to end all bourgeois. He did indeed anticipate the shedding by mankind of the most deplored alleged corollaries of our Neolithic work addiction, namely social stratification and coercion' (Gellner 1988a: 34). 'Neolithic work addic-tion' refers to Marshall Sahlins' theory of absence of work ethic among early humans, the 'affluent' hunter-gatherers. Only with the so-called Neolithic revolution, i.e. with the first peasants, came more work, its division and unequal acquisition of wealth. 'It was the acquisitive pri-meval proto-bourgeoisie of the late Stone Age which sets us off on the slippery path of Progress' (34). According to Marxism, division of labour would disappear in the future communist society, 'but *work as fulfilment* would remain and indeed constitute our fulfilment' (35, Gellner's emphasis). Putting it bluntly, Gellner writes in his *magnum opus*

Basically, Marxism is a bourgeois wish-fulfilment fantasy: work is to be its own reward, life really is *about* work and finds its meaning in work, and the secret of history is that, appearances notwithstanding, it is determined, not by the patterns of coercion, but by those of production. That is where the action really is. It is only the faulty organisation of work which engenders antagonistic relations between men, and their corollaries, coercion and socially instituted delusion ... The destiny of the proletariat was to fulfil the bourgeois ideal of peaceful, self-rewarding and unconstrained productivity. (35, Gellner's emphasis)

Marxism, argues Gellner, devalued the political in favour of forces of production. This is the most critical point where Marxism failed. That is also why Marxist orthodoxy did not and could not count with the Asiatic mode of production (irrespective of whether it existed or not) because it was stagnant and overtly politically coercive. Gellner, by putting 'Sword' in the central place in between the two other basic concepts, reminds his readers that besides production ('Plough') and knowledge ('Book') there is another moving factor in history: i.e. coercion, which belongs to the political sphere. As is well known, Marxism denies primacy to politics and puts what Gellner called forces of coercion into the so-called super-structure and not among the forces of production. There, according to Gellner, lies the crux of the 'misunderstanding' between Marxists and non-Marxists. The latter tend to view coercion as part of the material, along with economic forces. He rightly explains that the problem which the Soviet Marxists saw in the purported existence of a sixth, Asiatic mode of production was exactly that it was

a social order which contradicts, not merely the crucial Marxist thesis of the inherent instability of class-endowed societies, but also the view that power and coercion are parts of the super-structure. The Asiatic mode of production characterizes a society in which the political rulers do *not* reflect the interests of a pre-existent, economically defined class. The soldiers and bureaucrats who rule, administer and enforce a 'hydraulic' social order are themselves its beneficiaries, and only come into being *with it*. (Gellner 1990: 149, Gellner's emphases; cf. Gellner 1984)

Gellner views Marxism as a world religion, 'a political messianism', about the terminal outcome of the sequence of progression of social and economic forms (into which the Asiatic mode of production did not fit) which 'will be free both of coercive institutions and of private property' (Gellner 1988a: 143).

Here Gellner raises the question of the very foundation of Marxism which views political power as 'the mere handmaiden of pre-existing economic classes' and coercive mechanisms in society as part of 'super-structural reflection'. There he sees an interesting overlap with the contemporary Western idealism which appears under names such as hermeneutics, semantics and, one should hasten to add, postmodernism. These new directions in Western thought work with meanings as their basic concepts which are an integral part of languages and culture. So the causal sequences or generalisations are not that interesting or important; rather, the meaning-systems should be explained because they allegedly direct human behaviour (1988a: 143). Gellner, however, did not say a word about his previous pastime of his studies of Soviet *etnografiya*, and that is of course his hobby in reconstructing the beginnings of human society.

Before we turn to topics where Marxist-Liberal debate has been most visible, I would like to mention the problem with civil society. Gellner did not write his *Conditions of Liberty* (1994a) just because he wanted to paraphrase Popper or improve on him. He wanted, to my mind, to make a point about Marxism. It was the practical Marxism, so to say the 'really existing socialism', that suppressed pluralism of civil society. At the same time Marxism, while repeating empty slogans about the withering of the state, made state *the* central omnipresent and omnipotent behemoth which, as Gellner aptly wrote, 'tolerated no rivals'. Civil society emerged as a potent rival and Gellner hastened to remind us that, to Marxism, civil society must have appeared as a fraud, 'a façade for a hidden and maleficent domination' (Gellner 1994a: 1). So both the state and civil society 'are damned as redundant and fraudulent' (2). The practice of 'socialism' was a failure. The attempts to liberalise, improve it morally and remove its 'deformations' were not successful. Gellner's civil society book was written to prove that Marxism was wrong because there has been no better taming device for the state's inherent totalitarian tendencies than civil society. It is civil society, in Gellner's rendering, that 'prevents the establishment of monopoly of power and truth'. It does not allow what Gellner called 'Caesaro-Papism-Mammonism' and other types of *nomenklatura* (1994a: 4). At worst, it appeared to Gellner, fared Russia with her 'superimposition of Marxism on Byzantine theology and traditions'. The result was the demise of the Soviet Union, and the emergence of a badly felt need to resurrect the society taken by the plague of reproduction of the system which 'created isolated, amoral, cynical individualists-without-opportunity, skilled at double-talk and trimming within the system, but incapable of effective enterprise' (1994a: 5). The gist of the book is not only to reveal why Marxism failed and Islamic *umma* succeeded (at least for the time being). It shows why civil society is so essential for those who suffered or still suffer under the spell of state totalitarianism; it also shows that democracy is a slogan like civil society but perhaps less powerful because it is easily falsifiable by its own mechanics. For the sheer exercise of majority vote might suppress a sole person who is right but receives no votes. In a civil society this isolated but right voice can and should be heard better. *Conditions of Liberty* is a timely word against the void created by the disintegration of the Marxist world, now deprived of the faith in its central doctrine: 'Thugs and humbugs as Mediators with the other world are tolerated, sleazy mediocrities [of the Brezhnev period – P.S.] as agents of the Apotheosis of *this* world are not' (Gellner 1994a: 42). The solution appears to Gellner as being what he calls the International of Consumerist Unbelievers, committed 'to a pragmatic and pluralist pursuit of wealth'; and civil society (1994a: 211)

in which polity and economy are distinct, where polity is instrumental but can and does check extremes of individual interest, but where the state in turn is checked by institutions with an economic base; it relies on economic growth which, by requiring cognitive growth, makes ideological monopoly impossible.

Neither class nor nation: nationalism

The well-known discussion of the work of Miroslav Hroch is very important, not because of the question of whether Hroch was or was not a Marxist but because of the question of what were the forces which brought about modernity. Were these forces the class contradictions of the transition from feudalism to capitalism as Hroch believes, or, as Gellner argues, the *earlier* structural changes within European society when absolutist society engendered secular bureaucracy and pushed the church to the background, whereby centralised polity linked itself with 'a literate, normative, codified High Culture' (Gellner 1994b: 185)? The logic of Hroch's argument leads to what Gellner called 'phenomenology of nationalism', which in turn leads Hroch into a dilemma. The question, in Gellner's words, sounds: 'is it nations, or is it classes, which are the real and principal actors in history?' For Hroch it is 'the conception of the nation as a constituent of social reality of historical origin' which is opposed to 'the subjectivist conception of the nation as the product of nationalism, national will and spiritual forces' (which is, as is known, basically Gellner's position). Hroch admits that his 'generalising procedures' 'are derived from the Marxist conception of historical development' but actually, as Gellner stressed, end up in 'basic social ontology', where origin of the modern nations is to be found rather than in the historical structural change (all quotations from 1994b: 194). Thus Gellner brands Hroch's approach as 'semi-Marxist': 'nations do have an independent and irreducible existence, and ... none the less, the main historical reality remains the change in class relations postulated by Marxism' (195). Gellner summarised his position on Hroch in these words (ix):

The work of Miroslav Hroch ... represents a remarkable attempt to superimpose the Marxist and nationalist visions of history on each other: history is the account of changing class relations *and* yet the independent reality of nations is also conceded and affirmed. Moreover, he brings to his aid a wealth of historical and sociological documentation, and the case must be taken seriously by someone who, like myself, accepts *neither* of these two visions.

What I would stress here is that both class and nationalist options are *visions* for Gellner, not scientifically proven theories. This he further develops in his discussion of Szporluk's discussion of Marx and List. Marxian thesis on class struggle as the essence of history is refuted by both Szporluk and Gellner. Gellner reminds Marxism of its own idea that class struggle is there (was there) only temporarily. It was not there before; it will be not there after. But Gellner is careful not to give the impression that he would accept 'the doctrine that a genuinely classless society is feasible', stressing instead that 'the way in which society divides its members into sub-groups is … subject to radical change'. Class structure 'is in no way inscribed into the eternal nature and order of things'. Gellner crowns this discussion with the assertion which defeats both Marxist teleology and the historicist-evolutionist approach as such: 'There is no valid ideological justification for any one social order, and no one balance of power underlying a given order is permanent' (Gellner 1994b: 4). Thus that which he calls Social Metaphysics in Marxism is 'a very curious mixture of individualist anarchism and a pan-human communalism' (5). The substance of the Marxist vision is what Gellner characterised as realisation of species-being in the liberation of the constraints imposed on humanity by 'membership in class, ethnic or religious categories, and indeed by any social roles' which will climax in 'a harmonious universal community'. Gellner wonders about the 'nature of the hidden hand which is to perform this … miracle' because the founding fathers of Marxism did not specify on this point. What is obvious to Gellner is Marxist wishful thinking which excludes nations and classes (and he adds religion) from 'true human essence' (6).

However, Marxism, according to Gellner, does not admit that history is the history of national struggles. Why Gellner invoked Szporluk and List is precisely because 'List was right and Marx wrong' (1994b: 7). Friedrich List, a German economist and the author of a little-known but all the more important book 'The National System of Political Economy' (*Das nationale System der politischen Ökonomie*, 1841), was able to explain why nationalism is the result and concomitant of economic modernisation (rather than class or cultural antagonisms). This of course is grist to Gellner's mill, for Gellner's theory of nationalism rests on modernity and industrialism as its main ingredients. I think that here Gellner distanced himself very clearly from Marxism, which appears to him wrong not only factually but also as a visionary utopianism.

Lessnoff, who tried to characterise Gellner's attitude to Marxism in a few pages in his excellent book (Lessnoff 2002; cf. Skalník 2003b), like Gellner, contrasted the liberal society with authoritarian or totalitarian ones. Gellner discovered that civil or liberal society in the West was a result – or, as Lessnoff writes, a 'corollary' – of industrial capitalism which requires independence from the state. The pluralist state was an 'unintended gift to mankind' made possible by buying off the political class of the *ancien régime* by what Gellner termed a Social Bribery Fund created by capitalist accumulation (cf. Lessnoff 2002: 53).What makes liberal society free is not absence of rules but its openness, in the sense of Popper, meaning 'open to criticism, challenge and change'. There rests potential progressiveness, not in a command system of the Soviet Marxist-Leninist type. Lessnoff reminds his readers that for quite some time Marxism-Leninism seemed to Gellner to be 'a collectivist substitute for the "Protestant ethic" of Calvinism' (55) materialised in the undeniable successes of the USSR. Its collapse, according to Gellner, was caused by economic determinism, which was wrongly conceptualised as a determining force of history. Instead, history was rather dominated by those who held politico-military power.

According to Lessnoff, Marxism-Leninism was close to capitalism and civil society in its stressing of economic forces. But paradoxically, Marxism-Leninism made power-holders to rule over producers and thus eventually 'destroyed' economic dynamism. The result was something like an anti-modernising Counter-Reformation and certainly not a revolution. This 'real' communism also killed the work ethic which it had, at least in theory, shared with Calvinism. Market was substituted by a planned economy which in turn produced sleaze: 'it was Brezhnevian sleaze, not Stalinist terror, that discredited the system' (Lessnoff 2002: 57). Whereas terror was explainable as an indispensable part of revolution, corruption was not found in the Marxist-Leninist theory. A viable civil society was for example very difficult to create in the post-Soviet period, more difficult than in post-Franco Spain. What has increased in the post-communist Russia and its former satellites is nationalism. While Gellner saw nationalism as an inevitable feature of modernity, civil society was only a possible trait.

In Lessnoff's interpretation, and I can only agree, Gellner championed open (civil, liberal) society and politico-liberal pluralism. Democracy was not the same as civil society. Gellner was rather sceptical about democracy as it seemed to him an impossibility when institutions and culture shape people. Only less important things can be decided upon democratically. For example people could not vote about the transition from totalitarianism to democracy as it would go against all their values: 'liberal pluralism is

more important, and more meaningful, than popular sovereignty'
(Lessnoff 2002: 59). In other words, liberal pluralism gets stronger through
democracy but democracy does not, cannot and should not enable people
to rule. Here Gellner is Popperian according to Lessnoff but he (Gellner)
goes beyond Popper's piecemeal reform when admitting that violent
revolution is sometimes necessary. But Gellner does not believe that a truly
democratic revolution is possible, any more than a democratically chosen
transition to modernity.

Soviet Marxist anthropology

Gellner had an ambivalent relation to Marxist anthropology which for a
while was quite in fashion in Britain, France, the United States and other
Western countries. Although he maintained close relations with some of
the protagonists such as James Woodburn, he chose Soviet Marxist
etnografiya as his testing ground and, as Hann wrote, 'he maintained an
enthusiastic curiosity for Soviet Marxist anthropology' (Hann 2001:
5899). Recently I have written about this special relationship and readers
are referred to my text (Skalník 2003a). Nevertheless I shall repeat the
gist of the argument as far as the topic of this chapter is concerned.
Gellner, as a student of modernity and its role in history, was interested
in the Soviet communist experiment with accelerated modernity
undertaken in the name of Marxism (Marxism-Leninism was the name
which Soviet Marxists used). He wondered to what extent it was
grounded in reality or was in fact a hoax. When in the 1970s he became
interested in Soviet Marxist anthropology (Gellner 1974) it was hardly
predictable that the Soviet communist experiment was to fail by the late
1980s and early 1990s. Gellner wanted to know what were the alternative
moments in Marxist thought (if any) and especially to what extent
Soviet Marxism was really a scientific theory of history as was claimed by
Soviet anthropologists. He wanted to know the ways of conceptualisation: production and coercion, typology of human societies, nature of
ethnicity, ethnos as a guise of culture.

   In the preface to the proceedings of a conference of Soviet and Western
anthropologists which took place under the auspices of the Wenner-Gren
Foundation at Burg Wartenstein in Austria in 1976, Gellner explained
why he was interested in Soviet *etnografiya*. It was on its merits 'as
anthropology or as historical sociology' but also because it illuminated the
intricacies of Soviet (Marxist) thought, of how 'social and philosophical
problems are conceptualised in the Soviet Union'. He mentioned four
major issues. The first was the relationship between production and
coercion. Gellner maintained that coercion was omnipresent in human

societies and engendered economic inequality. Similarly, culture might also be a factor independent from economy. Marxism maintained the opposite. In the latter the economic base determined the political and cultural superstructure. The second issue is closely related to the first as it concerns the typology of human societies. Evolutionism versus Weberian *Herrschaft*-domination (Gellner calls it gate-keeping) was Gellner's question *par excellence*. The influential Soviet ethnographical theorist Yuriy Semyonov answered it in an original way by applying the law of human development to the totality of historical process, not to individual cases. Third, Gellner believed that the nature and role of ethnicity was 'supremely important – theoretically and practically'. It seemed to him that Yulian Bromley's insistence on *etnos* as subject matter of *etnografiya* and Semyonov's version of Marxism meant that 'ethnicity becomes historically necessary, instead of contingent' (Gellner 1980: xv). And fourth, in Gellner's view Bromley's reorientation of the whole Soviet discipline's research priorities from primitive society (and thus archaeology and ethnography of the primeval society) towards *etnos* enabled the study of contemporary ethnicity in the USSR. Ethnicity in its *etnos* version is manifested through culture, which is understood as leisure and intellectual activities. In the specific Soviet framework, manifestation of a new 'Soviet culture' is what is being studied by ethnographers.

Khazanov, who until the early 1970s lived and worked in Moscow and met Gellner there, wrote that Gellner was fascinated by Marxism without ever adhering to it (Khazanov 1996/7). Whereas Gellner concluded that the failure of communism was in its economic and military inefficiency, he, according to Khazanov, did not really wish the multinational Soviet Union to disintegrate and disappear from the world map. The reason for this, it seems from the available evidence, consisted in the fact that Gellner was interested not in practical politics which included political dissidence but rather in finding out whether the inconsistencies of classical Marxism-Leninism would lead to some theoretical research and a confrontation of new ethnographical data with the fairly ossified historical materialism. My thesis is that he did find it in some works of researchers who were dealing with the theory of primitive society and stages of socio-economic evolution (*formatsii*) rather than in the ethnos of the Bromley School.

Without any doubt the analysis of scholastic Marxist dogmatism fascinated Gellner. On the other hand, Gellner's well-known work on nationalism was telling him that Bromley and his colleagues might have something important to say as well. But again, Gellner was more interested in the Soviet *theory* of ethnicity than in the practical implications of reified *etnos* 'theory'. So there was a kind of split of mind in Gellner's encounter with Soviet *etnografiya*: his passion for the scholastics of historical reconstructivism on the one hand and a pragmatic interest in the Bromley School. I think that Gellner did not realise fully how an incorrect analysis of real ethnic processes prevented Bromley and his loyals from grasping their own inadequacies. He was fascinated by its seeming formal difference from dogmatic Stalinism (one should not forget that Stalin was, after all, the author of *Marxism and the National Question*) without noticing that it was equally unable to cope with the reality of national self-determination movements within the Soviet Union.

Probably the very last stage of Gellner's encounter with Soviet ethnographical Marxism took place in London in early April 1989 during a conference 'Pre-modern and Modern National Identity in Russia/USSR and Eastern Europe', organised by the London School of Slavonic Studies. Both Gellner and Bromley were present. The bankruptcy of Bromley's theory was by then obvious to many but in London he still tried to style himself as a reformer of his own theory. In spite of it, Bromley was unable to explain the then raging Armenian–Azerbaijani conflict over Nagorno-Karabakh. Neither was he able to accept the parallel of his *etnos* notion with the *etnos* concept of the South African *volkekundiges* about which I was reporting at the conference (cf. Skalník 1988). Although Gellner, freshly back from his year-long stay in Moscow where he was attached to Bromley's institute, by then realised the inherent falsity of Bromley's position, at the London conference he chose the diplomatic tact of a host. He listened quietly to a lively exchange between Bromley and his critics but did not reveal his opinion. His taciturn attitude was all the more puzzling when we realise that just few days earlier, many of those present in London were gathered in Paris in order to carry out an overall stocktaking of Soviet *etnografiya* at the conference 'Anthropologie soviétique et sociétés traditionnelles' (Berelowitch 1990).[2]

Gellner's Marxist counterpart in Moscow

Gellner considered some other important questions in Marxism, especially as it was further developed, interpreted or modified by the Soviet ethnographers, namely Yuriy Semyonov. According to Gellner, Semyonov wrote 'an elegant, coherent, beautifully argued and uncompromising defence of unilineal interpretation of Marxism' as a theory of

---

[2] Gellner, who was among the initiators of the Paris conference, was present. So were Semyonov, Pershits and other Soviet specialists but Bromley did not come. Memorably Vladimir Kabo, Soviet specialist on Australian aborigines and Gellner's close friend, came to Paris with a substantial criticism of Soviet *etnografiya* (Kabo 1990).

human history (Gellner 1980: 59). Gellner admired the philosophical realism of Semyonov, who argued that socio-economic formations are neither to be found in concrete societies, nor did they exist without them. According to Semyonov the formations existed as 'the inner essences of concrete societies' which determined the development of these societies. Semyonov thus defends the unity of human history and its one-way development following the sequence of formations (for a comparison of positions of Semyonov and Kabo, see Skalník 1992).

According to Gellner, Semyonov's theory posits that unity of history is meant only in a generic sense, not as present in each individual society. To require that every society passes through all the stages of history or the full sequence of socio-economic formations would be absurd, and Semyonov's reformulation is original. Gellner found Semyonov's argument 'entirely convincing'. Indeed, contends Gellner, 'there was presumably never a time when slave-owners were required to hand in their deeds of ownership of slaves, and have them replaced by land-deeds to appropriate territory, carrying with them a given number of serfs, and corresponding military obligations to overlords, and so forth' (Gellner 1980: 141).

Then, of course, Gellner had to ask the following question: What is the purpose of formations and why is their sequence important when it does not apply to any concrete society in its full sense? Semyonov's answer is what Gellner called 'torch relay theory of history'. A new formation arrives when the most advanced and influential area enters the particular stage. The radiation of the torch-carrying society or societies would be such that nowhere else is the same stage repeated or reinvented. It is a kind of diffusionism in a Marxist veil. Semyonov shows on the one hand that between the primitive society and socialist society there are many parallels, and on the other that in history the torch now goes to the Soviet brand of communism.

Creative orthodoxy of Soviet Marxist ethnography and historiography

A similar fascination with the creative orthodoxy and inconsistencies in the work of some Soviet Marxists is exemplified in several of Gellner's articles collected in the book on *State and Society in Soviet Thought* (Gellner 1988b). Kradin (2003) discusses the question of nomadism as treated by Gellner and there is no need to dwell on this topic here. Let us only mention that Gellner was fascinated by the attempts of Soviet authors, among them ethnographers, to force the data from non-European societies into the Procrustean bed of feudalism. Thus Gellner noticed interest-ing points in Lev Kubbel's treatment of state formation in Songhai

(West Africa) where the state must have appeared before the social classes. Nevertheless, Kubbel argued for Songhai's feudal character, but only after 'very thorough discussion of the arguments on the other side'. Kubbel's conclusion was that the transition from the primitive tribal society straight to feudalism is to be explained by the lateness of this transition in West Africa. Africa in the first part of the second millennium was peripheral and the only influence it could be inspired by was feudalism, whether the North African or the Portuguese. Gellner noticed that there is some strange contradiction between Kubbel's (and general Marxist) stress on endogenous development and this obvious diffusionist statement. Again, however, Gellner apparently liked to discuss 'the constraints and the flexibilities of Kubbel's conceptual scheme ... the elegance of its deployment, its overall style, the manner in which it meshes in with the concrete material at his disposal, the symbiosis of sensitivity and metaphysics in it ... and the way in which it overlaps with or diverges from some Western approaches' (Gellner 1988b: 90).

For similar reasons Gellner took issue also with V. N. Nikiforov's influential book *The East and World History*. Nikiforov's position was clearly on the side of the Marxist five stages, into which Asia did not fit. Nevertheless, for Gellner he was 'a distinguished, erudite, scholarly, pugnacious, fair-minded and committed *Pyatchik*', i.e. champion of the five-stage scheme (1988b: 39). In contrast, Gellner was 'a convinced Trinitarian' who along with other thinkers 'claimed that mankind passes through three, and only three, fundamental stages in its development', i.e. foraging, agrarian and industrial. Nikiforov's main goal was to refute Wittfogel's thesis about the existence of the Asiatic mode of production in both theory and practice. He found the substitute for it in the existence of primitive classless community, discovered by Morgan and embraced by Marx and his followers. What fascinates Gellner and what he found 'profoundly endearing' is the idea expounded by Nikiforov that domination and exploitation first needed inventing within the realm of primitive tribal communities before they could successfully subject or be subjected to the spread and penetration by higher formations (conquest by one tribe of another, the spread of feudalism to slaveless society, the spread of capitalism and the assistance to backward countries by socialist ones). Domination could not precede exploitation, which in turn had to be based on private property. Therefore also the Asiatic mode of production was impossible because it was domination without private property. Gellner evidently enjoyed this logic of 'the great collective passion play of history' without necessarily subscribing to it (Gellner 1988b: 66–7). But the ethnic theorising, as exemplified by Bromley, stands apart and Gellner paid special attention to it.

Gellner's overestimation of Bromley's *etnos*

Gellner was convinced that the question of the nature and role of ethnicity was supremely important. What is however unfortunate is that the English rendering 'ethnicity' is relational whereas *etnos* in Bromley's rendering is a reified substance. Did Gellner confuse ethnicity with *etnos* or would he rather like to see the two terms as identical or almost identical? I think that here Gellner did not think about the consequences. Elsewhere he goes as far as arguing that Bromley's *etnos* theory meant a 'minor revolution', at least within *etnografiya*. The latter appeared to him as an analogy of Western social anthropology. The revolution consisted in the shift of the main research focus within Soviet *etnografiya* from the reconstruction of the primitive formation to ethnoses defined synchronistically and culturalistically. 'The revolution consists of making *ethnography* into the studies of *ethnos*-es, or, in current Western academic jargon, into the study of *ethnicity*' (Gellner 1988b: 115). Gellner argues that this 'revolution' 'is of utmost importance for those preoccupied with nationalism and ethnicity' (116) and thereby apparently seems to identify some parallels with Western anthropology. In Gellner's understanding, the problematic of Bromley's *etnos* is not 'archaism-oriented', it is directed towards the present time, it is 'relatively synchronicist' and 'markedly universalistic', culture-oriented rather than structure-oriented, while the research methods are based on fieldwork or are sociological, rather than preferring historical reconstruction (118). If this were so, are Bromley and his followers still Marxists? Gellner rushes to defend the Bromley School on this crucial account: choosing relatively synchronistic and cultural research strategy by no means leads to rejection of evolutionist and structural orientation. Soviet *etnografy*, to be sure, do not bend away from Marxism and 'there is not the least indication' that they have 'the slightest wish or indeed the opportunity to do so' (120). Was Bromley 'the man destined to lead the ethnographers towards the promised land of the ethnos', as Gellner (121) seems to believe? Did he really carry out an 'ethnosist' revolution which pushed the Ideologists and Primitivists within Soviet *etnografiya* to the background? To grasp better the problem is to look more closely at the concept of *etnos*.

The main problem with Bromley's *etnos*, however, is its reified conceptualisation (cf. Skalník 1986, 1988, 1990). Bromley's main quest was to identify *etnos* with the main subject-matter of his discipline. It should be borne in mind that when he assumed the position of the director of the Institute of Ethnography of the USSR Academy of Science back in 1966, Bromley was an outsider to *etnografiya*. He had to justify his abrupt arrival by a quick feat which would attract attention of his superordinates within the academy and the Communist Party leadership. This he did by turning attention to the very term *etnografiya* (cf. Khazanov 1990: 214). He argued that it denoted description or study of ethnoses, or peoples, understood as bounded wholes. Thus *etnografiya* was not the study of ethnic features in societies, i.e. what in the West would be ethnicity, but a science of societies conceived as ethnoses. Gellner was apparently too eager to find a common language with Bromley and presented his ethnos theory as 'relatively untilled ... conspicuously important ... of practical use ... a legitimate area of study ... comparatively unperilous' (Gellner 1988b: 120–1). It may sound slightly ironic, but Gellner means it when he indicates that Yulian Bromley was a chosen man with an *etnos* mission.

Gellner is to some extent right that Bromley introduced some fresh air by taking *etnos* into the arena of Soviet *etnografiya*. Those whom he called Ideologists (such as Semyonov) or Primitivists (such as Kabo) were keeping *etnografiya* among the disciplines preoccupied with archaic phenomena which might be of use as a kind of inspiration only when Soviet society would reach the classless communist utopia. In contrast Ethnosists, led by Bromley, appeared to Gellner as promising to address a topical subject, namely the cultural pluralism of the multiethnic Soviet Union and its eventual transcendence by some supraethnic unity, i.e. *sovetskiy narod* (Soviet people). Gellner was, however, not naive as to the substantive contents of Bromley's new doctrine. He did not believe that Ethnosists went beyond 'a typology of ethnic phenomena' and 'certain generalizations articulated in terms of that typology' and some 'concrete research strategies based on these' (1988b: 125). If there was something new, at least within the Soviet Marxist circle, then it was 'the sheer stress on the existence of ethnicity' and 'a language in which to speak about it' (126).

Gellner realised that beyond that there was hardly any ground on which Bromley's theory could be useful. He was aware of the fact that Western research on ethnicity centred on nationalism, and nationalism basically deals with congruence between ethnic and political boundaries. If the congruence does not happen, nationalism is not satisfied and discontent may result in questioning legitimacy of ethnic boundaries, nay irredentism (1988b: 126). Of course, Gellner concludes, it would be undiplomatic to think of redrawing political boundaries both within the USSR and/or among its satellites. Asking questions like 'Will Ruritania survive, despite the tension between its diverse ethnic groups?' or inquiring about the status of 'groups which do and do not possess their own political formations, even though otherwise they are at the same "level of development"' would not be tactful. In other words, 'the language for posing this question is now available, but we may yet have to wait for a full utilization of it' (127). Gellner, much more than Bromley, was aware of the fact that ethnicity is primarily a political problem with lots of explosive potential exactly because it is so closely connected with nationalism. He perfectly well understood that Soviet students would rather avoid openly political issues in favour of tackling the political problem of ethnicity only in a rather formal and abstract way. In practice, the fact that equally developed Soviet ethnoses did or did not have their statehood (albeit limited by the membership in the Soviet Union) was enough to cause havoc once even a slightly more liberal regime might take over. This, of course, happened under Gorbachev's rule.

Under the changed conditions the very nature of Bromley's theory, its analytical sterility and political helplessness, prevented its 'utilization' in the analysis of ethnic contradictions, conflicts, ethnic wars and the disintegration of exactly those multi-ethnic 'Ruritanias' such as the USSR, Yugoslavia and Czechoslovakia. Neither Bromley nor Gellner predicted these processes, which had lots to do with ethnicity, of course, in the sense of ethnicity as politics of cultural difference, certainly not meaning *etnos* as a static academic construct. While Bromley, facing the truth of explosion of ethnic-driven conflicts, continued to repeat the same fallacies about the successful handling of the ethnic or national question in the USSR, Gellner indirectly admitted that he was too optimistic about 'utilization' of Bromley's theory. In December 1988 he wrote that ethnicity and nationalism are the most dangerous and uncontrollable aspects of perestroika (cf. Gellner as Philip Peters in an article entitled 'Moscow Notes', published in *The Times Literary Supplement*, 9–15 December 1988, pp. 1370 and 1382). Two years later, when talking about his one-year stay in Moscow to an interviewer, Gellner said that Bromley burnt his fingers by stressing the importance of ethnicity but insisting that there was no problem with it in the USSR (Gellner 1992; cf. Gellner 1993).

What Gellner made out of Soviet *etnografiya?*

Gellner's encounter with Soviet *etnografiya* and its peculiar brand of Marxism was an important episode in his academic career. But it seems to me that the place of this episode in his overall work was not properly understood. Lessnoff (2002) and Hall and Jarvie (1996) chose not to include that fairly voluminous production in their analyses of respectively Gellner's modernity studies and Gellner's social philosophy. It is certainly regrettable because Gellner's choice to study Soviet Marxism and namely some interesting trends within Soviet *etnografiya* are an integral part of his quest both to understand and to explain vagaries of modernity and modern social thought. By ignoring or avoiding this episode, Gellner's complexity remains incomplete. The only exception is Berelowitch, who among the Western writers best understood that *etnos* was not equal to Anglo-Saxon ethnicity and that reified *etnos* might be just another manifestation of the real concreteness of socio-economic formations à la Semyonov (Berelowitch 1998).

On the other hand we should not overestimate the importance of Gellner's encounter with 'the Soviet'. His deep interest and sometimes even enthusiasm when dealing with Soviet Marxist thought was to no small measure inspired by his idiosyncrasies, namely his passion for things doctrinal and quasi-theological, in this case his quest for finding some cracks in the Marxist monolith. There is a whole corpus of Gellner's writing about the politics and culture of Czechoslovakia and Central Europe which, quite apart from his work on Soviet academia, testifies about it. The other reason why there is a definite limit to the importance of Gellner's writing about *etnografiya* and Soviet Marxism is his swift shift away from these dry theoretical preoccupations towards the post-1989 authentic fascination with civil society, ethnic nationalism, ethnic wars, separatism and ethnic cleansing as they suddenly took over the scene in Gellner's third and fourth time zones, i.e. Central and Eastern Europe. After all, Gellner's studies on nationalism and its role within modernity were corroborated much more by these revolutionary changes than by anything contained in Soviet Marxism and Soviet *etnografiya*.

Is a conclusion possible?

At a risk of simplifying, I would contend that Ernest Gellner did not consider Marxism as a viable theory of social organisation and societal reorganisation. He witnessed at first hand both the power and the demise of the Soviet-type state totalitarianism, both the Brezhnevian sleazy decadence and the Gorbachev era of partly naive perestroika and glasnost. He recognised but did not analyse the escape route of China, Vietnam and even Cuba (but not North Korea) via accelerated economic growth without much political relaxation of the communist power structure. His main concern, however, was with the particular aspects of Marxist theory, be it primitive communism, Asiatic mode of production, feudalism, transition to capitalism with nationalism bearing nations as an accompaniment, ending with the question of the projected withering of the state. On all counts, eventually, Gellner seemed to out-argue Marxism, both Soviet and Western, by his theory of history, nationalism

120   *Peter Skalník*

and politics. However, in some minor points he conceded that Marxism had its logic and a historical role to play. It is now up to us to discover flaws in his social theory. Had he lived, Gellner would probably be delighted to see some of his points resisting criticism but equally delighted when his conclusions would not survive colleagues' critique. For Ernest Gellner was a creative Popperian, and as such he championed falsification of theories in the atmosphere of open society.

References

Berelowitch, W. 1998. Entre marxisme et ethnicité: l'anthropologie russe selon Ernest Gellner. *Genèses* 33: 128–33.
Berelowitch, W. (ed.) 1990. *Regards sur l'anthropologie soviétique*. Special double issue of *Cahiers du Monde Russe et Soviétique* 31 (2–3).
Gellner, E. 1974. The Soviet and the Savage. *Times Literary Supplement* 3789: 1166–8, reprinted in *Current Anthropology* 16(4): 595–601 and Gellner 1988b : 1–17.
(ed.) 1980. *Soviet and Western Anthropology*. London: Duckworth.
1984. Soviets against Wittfogel, or the Anthropological Preconditions of Marxism. In J.-C. Galey (ed.), *Différences, valeurs, hiérarchie: textes offerts à Louis Dumont*. Paris: Editions de l'Ecole des Hautes Etudes en Sciences Sociales, pp. 183–211.
1988a. *Plough, Sword and Book: The Structure of Human History*. London: Collins Harvill.
1988b. *State and Society in Soviet Thought*. Oxford: Blackwell.
1990. The Theory of History: East and West. In W. Berelowitch (ed.), *Regards sur l'anthropologie soviétique*. A special double issue of *Cahiers du Monde Russe et Soviétique* 31 (2–3): 141–50.
1992. A Year in the Soviet Union (An Interview with Nikki Keddie). *Contention* 1 (2): 107–20.
1993. Homeland of the Unrevolution. *Daedalus* 122 (3): 141–53.
1994a. *Conditions of Liberty. Civil Society and Its Rivals*. London: Hamish Hamilton.
1994b. *Encounters with Nationalism*. Oxford: Blackwell Publishers.
1996. Reply to Critics. In J. A. Hall and I. Jarvie (eds.), *The Social Philosophy of Ernest Gellner*. Amsterdam and Atlanta: Rodopi, pp. 623–86.
1997. *Nationalism*. London: Weidenfeld and Nicolson.
Hall, J. A. and Jarvie, I. (eds.) 1996. *The Social Philosophy of Ernest Gellner*. Amsterdam and Atlanta: Rodopi.
Hann, C. M. 2001. Ernest Gellner (1925–1995). In N. J. Smelser and P. B. Bates (eds.), *International Encyclopedia of the Social and Behavioral Sciences*. Oxford: Elsevier, pp. 5899–5901.
Kabo, V. R. 1990. Etude de la structure sociale traditionnelle dans l'anthropologie soviétique, hier et aujourd'hui. In W. Berelowitch (ed.), *Regards sur l'anthropologie soviétique*. A special double issue of *Cahiers du Monde Russe et Soviétique* 31 (2–3): 163–9.

Khazanov, A. 1990. The Ethnic Situation in the Soviet Union as Reflected in Soviet Anthropology. *Cahiers du Monde Russe et Soviétique* 31 (2–3): 213–21.

1996/7. Gellner and the Soviets. *Cambridge Anthropology* 19 (2): 50–8.

Kradin, N. N. 2003. Ernest Gellner and Debates on the Nomadic Feudalism. *Social Evolution and History* 2 (2): 162–76.

Lessnoff, M. 2002. *Ernest Gellner and Modernity*. Cardiff: University of Wales Press.

Musil, J. 2001. Gellner's Philosophy of History – Interpretations and Problems. *Czech Sociological Review* 9 (2): 153–72.

Popper, K. 1966. *The Open Society and Its Enemies*, vol. II. Rev. edn, London: Routledge.

Skalník, P. 1981. Community: Struggle for a Key Concept in Soviet Ethnography. *Dialectical Anthropology* 6 (2): 183–91.

1986. Towards an Understanding of Soviet Etnos Theory. *South African Journal of Ethnology* 9 (4): 157–66.

1988. Union soviétique-Afrique du Sud: les 'théories' de l'etnos. *Cahiers d'Etudes Africaines* 28 (2): 157–76.

1990. Soviet Etnografiia and the National(ities) Question. In W. Berelowitch (ed.), *Regards sur l'anthropologie soviétique*. A special double issue of *Cahiers du monde russe et soviétique* 31 (2–3): 183–91.

1992. Soviet Etnografiia: Marxist Methodology or Evolutionist Ideology? In C. W. Gailey (ed.), *The Politics of Culture and Creativity: A Critique of Civilization*. Gainesville: University of Florida Press, pp. 391–405.

2003a. Gellner's Encounter with Soviet Etnografiia. *Social Evolution and History* 2 (2): 177–93.

2003b. Gellner on Modernity. *Social Evolution and History* 2 (2): 203–24.

Wettersten, J. 1996. Ernest Gellner: A Wittgensteinian Rationalist. In J. A. Hall and I. Jarvie (eds.), *The Social Philosophy of Ernest Gellner*. Amsterdam and Atlanta: Rodopi, pp. 497–520.

Part II

Ideology, nationalism and modernity

5   Nationalism: restructuring Gellner's theory

Nicos Mouzelis

Introduction

The main thesis of this study is that, if one replaces Gellner's concept of *industria* with that of modernity, it is easier to identify mechanisms that non-teleologically link the structural conditions of modernity with the development of nationalism.

Modernity is here defined as the type of social organisation which became dominant in Western Europe after England's industrial revolution and the French Revolution. It entails the irreversible decline of the non-differentiated traditional community and the large-scale mobilisation and inclusion of the population into the centre. This unprecedented 'bringing-in' process portrays two unique structural features: (a) the deep, unmediated penetration by the state into the periphery, and (b) the top-down differentiation of a social formation's institutional spheres.[1]

State penetration

At the end of the eighteenth and the beginning of the nineteenth century, owing to growing inter-state geopolitical struggles, as well as the rapid development of new communicative and organisational technologies, the 'infrastructural' powers of the state assumed unprecedented dimensions.[2] Expanding state bureaucracies managed to break the relative self-containment of traditional, local communities and to penetrate the periphery to a degree that had been unthinkable in premodern social formations, however despotic.

This penetration led to a massive transfer of material resources from the periphery to the centre, to the concentration at the top of the means

---

[1] For a more detailed discussion of the concept of modernity viewed in structural rather than cultural terms, see Mouzelis (1999).
[2] For the concept of the infrastructural state powers, see Mann (1993, 1996).

not only of production but equally those of domination and violence.[3] In addition it meant a transfer of symbolic resources to the centre, as the means of persuasion and education also became concentrated at the top – people identifying less with their local community and more with the 'imagined community' of the nation-state (Anderson 1991).

The inclusion into the centre could be and was both autonomous and heteronomous. In the former case it saw the spread of rights – civic, political, social-economic – to the lower strata (e.g. in nineteenth-century Britain). In the second case people were brought into the centralised arenas of the nation-state (the army, the taxation system) but were 'left out' in respect of political rights (e.g. nineteenth-century Prussia). In both cases, however, the relations between rulers and ruled were *unmediated* – in the sense that there were no or only very weak feudal and/or patrimonial intermediaries between the population and the centralised state apparatus (Bendix 1969).

The combination of 'penetrative' administrative technologies and relations of domination in unmediated fashion concentrating material and non-material resources at the top constitutes a mode of domination which has an elective affinity with nationalism. From this perspective, nationalism can be conceptualised as a discourse adopted by political elites for promoting, institutionalising, and legitimising a mode of domination characterised by deep, unmediated state penetration of the periphery and the massive concentration of material and symbolic resources at the top.

Before illustrating this with a concrete example, I shall focus briefly on the second unique structural feature of modernity.

Top-down differentiation

As Talcott Parsons pointed out, modern societies are characterised by the differentiation of institutional spheres (economic, political, social, cultural), each one portraying, at least potentially, its own logic and values (Parsons 1977). Premodern complex social formations too portrayed a high level of socio-structural and cultural differentiation (Eisenstadt 1963, 1990), but there the differentiation was confined to the top, the social base being characterised by segmental forms of social organisation.[4] It was only in the modern nation-state that 'segmental

---

[3] See on this point Tilly (1990).
[4] Marx's concept of the Asiatic mode of production is a very good illustration of this type of differentiation at the top. See Hindess and Hirst (1975).

localism' declined irreversibly, this leading to a top-down differentiation of institutional spheres.

Following Parsons (1966, 1977), the differentiation of institutional or role structures generates problems of *social integration*. When we look at differentiated units in terms of roles, it is obvious that the replacement of rather diffuse by more specialised roles affects coordination. The difficulty can be solved only by the emergence of more abstract, more general and hence more flexible, less situation-specific values and ideas, able to subsume the more specific normative logic of the differentiated roles or role/institutional complexes (Parsons 1966: 22). Once 'value-generalization is achieved, a society acquires greater "adaptive capacity" for moving up the evolutionary ladder' (Parsons 1964).

As I have argued elsewhere (Mouzelis 1993), Parsons considers that the major differentiated institutional spheres of modern societies have a tendency to achieve integration or 'social equilibrium' in a quasi-automatic manner: social mechanisms establish a balance between the values of productivity/wealth creation in the economic (adaptation) subsystem, those of democracy in the political (goal achievement) subsystem, those of solidarity in the social (integration) subsystem, and those of value commitment in the cultural (latency) subsystem. However, looking at actual historical developments we find that, Parsons notwithstanding, integration is achieved less by inter-institutional equilibria than by the *dominance* of one institutional sphere over others.

In early modernity there was a marked tendency for integration to be achieved via the dominance of the *political* rather than the economic sphere (Mouzelis 1999). This is not surprising if one takes into account that, contra Marx, it was state rather than market expansion that constituted the chief motor force of modernisation. Indeed, given the relatively late development and dominance of industrial capitalism (middle to end of the nineteenth century), it was inter-state geopolitical struggles that were responsible for the decline of 'segmental localism' and the deep state penetration of the periphery. Particularly during the Napoleonic Wars, the creation of huge citizens' armies led to a phenomenal increase in military expenditure. In order to extract the required resources from civil society, state elites had to develop extensive administrative structures, which undermined the traditional, non-differentiated communities' relative self-containment (Mann 1993, 1996; Tilly 1990).

If political rather than economic mechanisms integrated the differentiated institutional spheres of early modernity, this more systemic perspective allows us to conceptualise nationalism as another one of those integrating mechanisms. More specifically, it can be linked with Parsons' 'integration/value-generalization' process. As a discourse stressing the value of identification of and commitment to a broad entity that transcends local kinship and communal institutions – i.e. as a more *context-free* medium of co-ordination and communication – it helps to integrate the differentiated role structures of modern societies.

To conclude this section: if nationalism from the point of view of actors' strategic conduct can be seen as a discourse by state elites who promote and legitimise a penetrative and centralising mode of domination, from a more systemic institutional-analysis point of view[5] it can be understood as a relatively context-free medium enhancing impersonal communication and, in various ways, integrating the differentiated institutional spheres of the nation-state's 'imaginary community'.

The development of Greek nationalism

I shall illustrate the above conceptualisation of nationalism by taking as a concrete example nineteenth-century Greek nationalism.

Before the final and successful national uprising in 1821 against Ottoman rule, the bulk of the peasantry, given the limited spread of nationalist ideas in the countryside, did not have any clear political goals. Most of the people were concerned less with political independence from the Turks than with a return of the 'good old days' when a strong Ottoman state was able to safeguard their traditional rights and so check the predatory conduct of landlords and local officials (Stavrianos 1959). The promoters of the 'modern', 'new', nationalist ideas were diaspora Greek merchants, Western-educated professionals, and an intelligentsia influenced by the ideas of the French Revolution. In other words, peasants and artisans constituted the raw material, the energy source of the nationalist uprising, whereas it was a fraction of the merchant class and the intelligentsia which operated as a catalyst directing popular energies into nationalist channels (Crawley 1957). It was they who provided leadership as well as material and symbolic resources in a society hitherto dominated by the anti-Enlightenment, anti-Western orientations of the Greek Orthodox Church.

In fact the church, the Phanariote aristocracy at the imperial centre, and the Greek landowners were very ambivalent towards the Greek national uprising.[6] At the beginning the church (especially the high

---

[5] For the distinction between institutional analysis and analysis in terms of 'strategic conduct', see Giddens (1984: 289).

[6] For the role played by the church, the Phanariotes (Greeks living in the Phanari district of Constantinople and occupying key positions in the Ottoman patrimonial administration) and the landowning classes during the nationalist uprising, see Stavrianos (1963: 17ff).

clergy) was downright hostile to any idea of overthrowing the Ottoman rule under which it occupied so privileged a position. The Patriarchate, exercising political and spiritual power over all the Orthodox Christian subjects of the empire (Greek and non-Greek), realised that the emergence of new autonomous states in the Balkans would fragment not only Ottoman rule but also its own power position. Moreover, the fact that Greek nationalism was greatly influenced by the Enlightenment values of the West provided an additional reason for opposition. In parallel, the Phanariote aristocracy at the *Porte*, although initially responsive to Western ideas, was rather opposed to the Greek nationalist movement. Their privileged position within the Ottoman administration, their close links with the church and their cosmopolitan orientation explain their reluctance to join the revolution (Svoronos 1972). As far as the Greek landlords were concerned, they – whether involved in trade or not – were initially against any idea of nationalist uprising because they feared that the peasants would demand land reforms. It was only when the above privileged groups realised the irreversibility of the nationalist revolt that they threw their weight behind the insurgents and so contributed to its final success (Stoianovich 1963).

Inevitably, as soon as the uprising gained momentum, the diverging interests of the various actors involved came to the fore and resulted in internecine fighting that seriously threatened the ultimate success of the insurrection.

The struggles among Greeks during the later phases of the revolt (in so far as they did not arise from purely regional differences and kinship alliances) were due to the basic conflict between those who wanted to 'modernise', 'Westernise' Greece by establishing a strong centralised state which would eliminate regional fragmentation and the politico-military autonomy of local potentates, and those who wanted simply to oust the Turkish overlords but not to change the traditional, decentralised patrimonial structures.[7] For obvious reasons the traditionalist policy appealed to the autochthonous landowning-cum-merchant groups, whereas the modernising, centralising policies attracted the intelligentsia and the diaspora merchants who, having kept their wealth abroad, did not risk very much by pursuing the 'progressive' strategy. At the end of the protracted civil war the 'Westernisers', despite their poor control of local resources, managed to impose their views on the *form* at least that the future political institutions of modern Greece were to take. This was

---

[7] For an account of social conflicts and the linkages between kinship, regional and class differences during the early nineteenth century, see Petropoulos (1968) and Diamandouros (1972).

due both to the fact that they possessed the legal and administrative skills for running the new-born state, and to the fact that they enjoyed greater support from the Western powers (Diamandouros 1972). This last point is crucial, given that the nationalist insurrection, jeopardised by the civil war, was finally salvaged only by the active intervention of the 'Great Powers' (England, France and Russia).

It was, therefore, the leading role of the diaspora merchant class and the Westernised intelligentsia before and during the War of Independence and their partial victory over the more traditional, autochthonous oligarchy that explain to a great extent why nationalist ideas prevailed from the very start. They resulted in a persistent effort to organise the newly formed state along Western, centralising, state-penetrating-the-periphery lines, despite the overall poor economic development and the absence of a strong, Western-type autochthonous capitalist class (Mouzelis 1978: 14–17).

On the other hand, the victory of the Westernisers was very relative indeed. Although they succeeded in imposing a centralising, Western mode of domination, the autochthonous elite did not accept the new state of affairs without putting up strong resistance. During the first three decades of the post-independence period there was constant tension between the centralising efforts of the monarchical administration and the centrifugal tendencies of the various regional potentates striving to maintain the autonomy they had enjoyed in the past. For instance, the anti-monarchical, so-called 'democratic revolutions' of 1844 and 1862 (which curtailed the powers of the crown and strengthened the political parties) were not so much popular victories as oligarchic attempts to stop the centralising tendencies of the state. Eventually the local revolts against state expansion and penetration petered out as local oligarchies, realising the irreversibility of the centralising and penetrative process, attempted to colonise the state apparatus from within (Mouzelis 1978: 141–4).

The same macro-historical process seen from a systemic institutional perspective shows a rather week socio-cultural differentiation during the pre-independence period. For instance, in view of the political-representation functions of the Orthodox Church vis-à-vis the imperial centre, there was no clear differentiation between religious, political, judicial and educational roles at local or regional level. Under Ottoman rule, the Church elites, although subjected to strict and often arbitrary, 'sultanistic' control,[8] not only enjoyed a high degree of autonomy

---

[8] For the term *sultanism*, implying an extreme form of arbitrary, despotic, patrimonial rule, see Weber (1978).

in religious, cultural and educational matters, but also acquired an important number of political functions. So, with the local notables, the church was responsible for the running of all municipal affairs (Papadopoulos 1952; Arnakis 1952: 235–50).

With the establishment of the modern Greek state, however, came a clean differentiation between religious, political, cultural and educational roles. Almost all the political functions that had previously been exercised by the church authorities were transferred to newly established ministries. Therefore, after independence political and religious institutions and roles were much more clearly differentiated on every level (village, community, region, nation).

This top-down differentiation took a specific form, of course: religious roles and institutions being definitely subordinated to political ones, it was via the dominance of the political that the differentiated institutional spheres became integrated. Given the ambiguous, weak role that the high clergy had played during the national uprising, it is understandable why the holders of the centralised means of domination managed quite early on (a) to establish the autonomy of the autochthonous church vis-à-vis the Patriarchate in Constantinople, and (b) to put religious authorities, now stripped of their political functions, under the direct control of state elites. As a matter of fact, the 1833 ecclesiastical constitution of the autonomous Greek Orthodox Church (which followed the lines of the German Protestant tradition), put the church under the strict control of the government (Frazer 1969). In fact, until the rise of the charismatic, populistically orientated and political power-seeking Archbishop Christodoulos in the 1990s, the church was more or less an administrative extension of the Ministry of Education and Religious Affairs.

If we now focus on nationalism as a generalised medium transcending localistic attachments which, at the same time, integrated the relatively differentiated religious, judicial, educational and political role structures of the Greek nation-state, we find two fundamental unifying themes. The first stressed the unbroken continuity of modern Hellenism with the civilisation of ancient Greece. The Western concern with classical antiquity, having been imported wholesale into Greece in the nineteenth century, was then incorporated into a nationalist discourse that established (particularly after the development of European Romanticism with its glorification of *la patrie*) linkages between ancient Greece, Byzantium and modern Hellas.[9]

---

[9] The major architect of this view of Greek history was Constantine Paparrigopoulos (1925), the nineteenth-century 'national' historian *par excellence*. His multi-volume magisterial *History of the Greek Nation* attempts to refute theories like those of Fallmerayer

This notion of the three-stage macro-developement of the Greek nation proceeded from the idealisation and glorification of the past to a grandiose vision of the future. It inspired – and this is the second unifying theme – an irredentism which, particularly during the middle of the nineteenth century, took the form of the *Megali Idea* (the Great Idea): the Romantic vision that it was the sacred mission of the newly established modern Greek state to reconquer Constantinople and resurrect Byzantium. The *Megali Idea* led, on the one hand, to the gradual broadening of the national boundaries via the incorporation into the Greek polity of not only Thessaly and the islands but also some of the northern territories of Epirus, Macedonia and Thrace. On the other hand it resulted, in the early 1920s, in the (for Greece) disastrous Greco-Turkish war, which put an abrupt end to the nationalist project of a Byzantine revival (Mouzelis 1990: 110ff).

What should be stressed from the point of view of this chapter is that both the notion of the 3000-year-long 'unbroken continuity' of the Greek nation and its irredentist consequences constituted during the late nineteenth century the most powerful symbolic resource for mobilising the Greek-speaking population, and so contributed to shifting orientations and attachments from the periphery to the national centre. It in fact constituted a very effective *integrating mechanism* of the differentiated economic, political, social and cultural institutional spheres of the Greek nation-state.

Restructuring Gellner's theory

Gellner links nationalism, as a predominantly modern social construction, to two core features: *industrialisation* and *cultural homogeneity*. As several critics have already pointed out (Hall 1998), both these features create difficulties for Gellner's theory.

To begin with the most obvious cases, the linkages between *industria* and nationalism in late-developing countries are tenuous. In the nineteenth-century Balkans, for instance, nationalist ideologies as well as the building of nation-states occurred in a context where large-scale industrialisation simply did not exist. Here the relatively rapid development of nationalist ideologies before and during the nation-building process took place at least a century before we can call these societies

---

(the *bête noire* of Greek nationalist historians), which deny any biological and even cultural connection between ancient and modern Greeks (see Skopelea 1997); as well as theories that do not consider Byzantium as the vital link between ancient and modern Greece (see on this point Dimaras 1986: 70ff). For Paparrigopoulos there can be no question of the unbroken continuity from ancient Greece via the Hellenistic empires and Byzantium to the modern Greek state. Throughout the ages he detects the hand of Divine Providence guiding the Greek ethnos in its unique destiny (Dimaras 1986: 183ff).

industrial. In 1870, for example, non-industrial Greece had seven times more civil servants per 10,000 population than the United Kingdom (Mouzelis 1986: 11). Pre-industrial Greece therefore experienced the phenomenal growth of a state bureaucracy penetrating the periphery in a non-industrial or proto-industrial context.[10]

Gellner may defend his theory by pointing out that it focuses on countries where nationalism had already emerged. But even if we confine ourselves to the West, in the light of what was said above (about inter-state struggles and state penetration rather than market expansion as the motor force of modernity), it is reasonable to argue that even in its birth-place nationalism precedes rather than follows the large-scale development and eventual dominance of industrial capitalism (in the late nineteenth century).

Similar difficulties arise with the second core characteristic of Gellner's theory, that of cultural homogeneity. According to Gellner,

there is a kind of inverse relationship between the importance of structure and culture. In a highly structured society, culture is not indispensable. Where relationships are fairly well-known (because the community is small, and because the types of relationship are small in number), shared culture is not a precondition of effective communication. (Gellner 1969: 154)

In industrial, complex societies on the other hand, where roles are more flexible and 'a man is not fully identified with his role, and can if he wishes divest himself of his role' (Gellner 1969: 155), communication via a *common cultural medium* becomes crucial. Therefore, national culture rather than structure becomes of the utmost importance. Because of this, nationalism entails a strong tendency towards the homogenisation of culture. Nationalism as a relatively context-free medium of communication and coordination of the actions of 'modular' subjects is based on a set of common cultural elements (language, religious beliefs, myths, etc.) inimical to the coexistence of other sets of common cultural elements shared by other groups within the same polity. When Gellner's critics refer to cases where cultural homogeneity does not exist (e.g. Switzerland, Canada, Belgium), defenders of his theory can argue that in such cases there is quasi-homogeneity – in the sense of an articulation of different cultures within which one is dominant (Hall 2005).

However, Gellner's theory clearly makes the assumption that in multicultural cases there will be a strong tendency for peripheral cultures to be eliminated by peaceful (e.g. cultural absorption) or more drastic

---

[10] A similar point can be made about the southern cone countries of Latin America (see Mouzelis 1986: 3–73).

means (e.g. ethnic cleansing, forced population exchanges, adjustment of national boundaries, etc.). His theory does not at all allow for cases of *relative multicultural stability* as in the cases mentioned above, or in the type of multiculturalism seen today in most developed societies hosting a large number of immigrants from poor countries.

The above difficulties can be much attenuated if Gellner's notion of *industria* is replaced by the concept of modernity conceptualised in terms of the two structural features already discussed: unmediated state penetration of the periphery, and top-down differentiation of industrial spheres. In terms of these two basic structural dimensions we can construct a fourfold typology of nationalism. To put this schematically:

In Box 1 we have high state penetration of the periphery and high top-down differentiation. This type of 'classical' nationalism characterises the majority of developed capitalist nation-states.

In Box 2 we have a high differentiation but low penetration of the central state administrative apparatus. This is the case of confederal polities like Switzerland, where the cantons enjoy a great deal of autonomy vis-à-vis the national government in matters ranging from education and migration to welfare policies. In the Swiss case of 'confederate nationalism' we have stable articulation of three identities: the national (Swiss), the regional (e.g. French) and the cantonal (e.g. Genevois).

In Box 3 we have high state penetration of the periphery but without full differentiation. The case of Iran suitably illustrates this variant of Arab nationalism. While given modern communicative technologies, the centralised state apparatus does penetrate the periphery, there is relatively low differentiation between religious, educational, juridical and political roles on both the national and the regional/local levels. Borrowing from the Parsonian conceptual armoury,[11] we can label this type of nationalism diffuse, given the lack of role specificity in low differentiation.

Box 4 finally (low state penetration and low differentiation) refers to the cases of several African polities where, as John Hall has put it, nationalist ideas do not extend beyond the boundaries of their capital city (2005: 21), the periphery being organised along tribal/segmental lines. In this type of 'proto-nationalism', the administrative penetration of the central state apparatus is minimal, and the shifting of loyalties from the segmental periphery to the national 'imagined community' is very feeble. Such cases can hardly be called nation-states therefore.[12]

---

[11] The dilemma of diffuse versus specific orientation to a social situation is one of the famous five-pattern variables of Parsonian sociology (see Parsons 1964b: 322–5).

[12] By nation-state in the sense used here I do not mean one nation in one state. I mean a state characterised by unmediated bureaucratic penetration and by top-down differentiation.

Primordialism versus constructionism

I suggest that the above typology of nationalism guards better against exceptions than Gellner's, and at the same time links the nationalist phenomenon with features of modernity which, much more *directly* than his *industria*, show its constructed rather than primordial character. Take for instance the transfer from the periphery to the centre, of identifications and attachments, the famous move from 'peasant to French person' (Renan 1882/1990). Gellner is right when he points out, contra Anthony Smith (1986, 1991), that the crucial factor for explaining that transfer is not cultural continuity[13] which may or may not exist (Gellner 1996; Calhoun 1997: 53–7).

But if the construction of national identities has very little to do with primordialism, it may have equally little to do with industrialisation, whereas it has always had very much to do with the process of state expansion and penetration of the periphery. This is to say that what is most crucial for the formation of national attachments is the drawing-in process that occurs with the construction of national systems of taxation, education, postal communication, military service, etc. As 'modular individuals' are pulled into the numerous national arenas, there is a shift of symbolic resources from the periphery to the centre. This shift can be concretely measured by the multiplication of direct linkages between the citizens and the administrative mechanisms of the central state apparatus. To come back to our Greek example, whereas in premodern, prenationalist times a peasant on the Greek mainland had little direct relationship with the Ottoman patrimonial administration, once the Greek state was established his/her direct linkages with the expanding state bureaucracy multiplied exponentially. It is this rather than continuity with primordial values and beliefs and/or industrialisation that explains the transition from peasant to citizen.

The issue of functionalism

Gellner has made it crystal clear that his theory is not based on *teleological* functionalism. He rightly points out that it does not explain the emergence of nationalism in terms of *industria*'s *needs* for a context-free, literary medium of communication. He explicitly states that it is methodologically wrong to transform needs into causes. His non-teleological functionalism simply posits an *elective affinity* between *industria* and nationalism

---

[13] For a defence of the primordialism/cultural continuity argument, see Hutchison (1994), Smith (1986, 1991) and Greenfeld (1992).

(Mouzelis 1998: 160–2). As far as this study is concerned, I find the methodology perfectly legitimate, but consider that the elective affinity is less between *industria* and nationalism than between modernity (conceptualised as unmediated state penetration and top-down differentiation) and nationalism.

Elective affinity means that whenever nationalist and non-nationalist discourses coexist in a context characterised by unmediated state penetration and top-down differentiation, the former has greater chances of becoming dominant. When this does not happen, when the shift from local/regional to central state identification does not take place, then the polities concerned have little chances of survival in a world dominated by nation-states (i.e. by states with highly developed 'infrastructural powers').

This becomes obvious if we take into account the key role that inter-state struggles play in the survival of a polity. In premodern European absolutism, for instance, the French model of centralised patrimonialism (as shaped by Louis XIV and his successors) rapidly spread to the rest of continental Europe, all major states adopting more centralised forms of tax collecting, army organisation, population surveillance, etc. Given this new system of inter-state relations, any state that failed to centralise (e.g. Poland) was condemned to peripheralisation, partition or extinction (Anderson 1974). Something similar happened when the inter-state system of European absolutism gave way to the system of European nation-states (eighteenth to nineteenth centuries). If European absolutism entailed the centralisation of the means of violence and taxation at the top, the nation-state (as already argued) dramatically accentuated the process of centralisation. Unlike all premodern states (including the absolutist one), the bureaucratic machinery of the nation-state destroyed segmental localism and drew the whole population into broader economic, political and cultural arenas of the national centre (Bendix 1969; Nettl 1967). Once the inter-state system of nation-states was consolidated, any state failing to 'modernise' (i.e. to make the shift from segmental localism to differentiated national arenas) tended to become peripheral or to break up (e.g. the Ottoman, Romanov and Habsburg imperial states).

Summary and conclusion

(a) A way to restructure Gellner's theory of nationalism so as better to satisfy its numerous critics is to replace his concept of *industria* with that of modernity, the latter notion being conceptualised in structural rather than cultural terms.

(b) There are two structural features which distinguish modern from premodern social formations. The first refers to the destruction of segmental localism and the mobilisation and inclusion of the whole population into the centre. This is achieved via the unprecedented and unmediated state penetration of the periphery. From this perspective nationalism can be conceptualised as a discourse by political elites trying to reduce the autonomy of local potentates and concentrate the means of production, of domination/violence and of persuasion/education at the top.

(c) The second unique structural characteristic of modernity entails the top-down differentiation of institutional spheres, each sphere portraying, at least potentially, its own logic and values. From this more systemic/functionalist perspective, nationalism can be seen as one of the main mechanisms that integrates a social formation's differentiated institutional spheres.

(d) I have tried to illustrate the utility of the above conceptualisation of nationalism by (i) applying it to the development of nineteenth-century Greek nationalism, and (ii) constructing a fourfold typology of nationalism based on the notions of unmediated state penetration of the periphery and of top-down differentiation (classical nationalism, confederal nationalism, diffuse nationalism and proto-nationalism).

(e) In the light of the above I have examined briefly the primordialism-versus-constructionism debate, as well as the issue of functionalist explanations of nationalism, both teleological and non-teleological.

References

Alexander, J. C. and Colomy, P. (eds.) 1990. *Differentiation Theory and Social Change*. New York: Columbia University Press.

Anderson, B. 1991. *Imagined Communities: Reflections of the Origins and Spread of Nationalism*. Rev. edn, London: Verso.

Anderson, P. 1974. *Lineages of the Absolutist State*. London: New Left Publications.

Arnakis, G. E. 1952. The Greek Church of Constantinople and the Ottoman Empire. *Journal of Modern History* 24 (3): 235–50.

Bendix, R. 1969. *Nation-Building and Citizenship*. New York: Action Books.

Brubaker, R. 1998. Myths and Misconceptions in the Study of Nationalism. In A. J. Hall (ed.), *The State of the Nation*. Cambridge: Cambridge University Press, pp. 272–306.

Calhoun, C. 1997. *Nationalism*. Minneapolis: Minnesota University Press.

Crawley, C. W. 1957. John Capodistria and the Greeks before 1821. *Cambridge Historical Journal* 13 (2): 162–82.

Diamandouros, N. 1972. Political Modernization and Cultural Cleavage in the Formation of the Modern Greek State 1821–1828. PhD thesis, Columbia University, New York.

Dimaras, K. T. 1986. *C. Paparrigopoulos* (in Greek). Athens: Educational Institute of the Bank of Greece.

Eisenstadt, S. N. 1963. *The Political Systems of Empires*. New York: Free Press.

Eisenstadt, S. N. with Arbitbol, M. et al. 1990. Modes of Structural Differentiation, Elite Structure and Cultural Visions. In J. C. Alexander and P. Colomy (eds.), *Differentiation Theory and Social Change*. New York: Columbia University Press, pp. 19–51.

Frazer, F. A. 1969. *The Orthodox Church and Independent Greece*. Cambridge: Cambridge University Press.

Gellner, E. 1969. *Thought and Change*. London: Weidenfeld and Nicolson.

1996. *Nations and Nationalism*. Oxford: Blackwell.

Giddens, A. 1984. *The Constitution of Society*. Cambridge: Polity Press.

Greenfeld, L. 1992. *Nationalism: Five Paths to Modernity*. Cambridge, MA: Harvard University Press.

Hall, J. A. (ed.) 1998. *The State of the Nation: Ernest Gellner and the Theory of Nationalism*. Cambridge: Cambridge University Press.

2005. How Homogenous Must We Be? Paper presented to a conference on 'The Social and Political Relevance of Ernest Gellner's Thought Today', National University of Ireland, Galway, May 2005.

Hall, J. A. and Jarvie, I. (eds.) 1996. *The Social Philosophy of Ernest Gellner*. Amsterdam: Rodopi.

Hindess, B. and Hirst, P. 1975. *Pre-Capitalist Economic Formations*. London: Routledge and Kegan Paul.

Hutchinson, J. 1994. *The Dynamics of Cultural Nationalism*. Rev. edn, London: HarperCollins.

Jelavich, C. and Jelavich, B. (eds.) 1963. *The Balkans in Transition*. Berkeley: University of California Press.

Mann, M. 1986. *The Sources of Social Power*, vol. I: Cambridge: Cambridge University Press.

1993. *The Sources of Social Power*, vol. II: Cambridge: Cambridge University Press.

1996. The Emergence of Modern European Nationalisms. In J. A. Hall and I. Jarvie (eds.), *The Social Philosophy of Ernest Gellner*. Amsterdam: Rodopi, pp. 137–66.

Mouzelis, N. 1978. *Modern Greece: Facets of Underdevelopment*. London: Macmillan.

1986. *Politics in the Semi-Periphery: Early Parliamentarism and Late Industrialization in the Balkans and Latin America*. London: Macmillan.

1990. *Post-Marxist Alternatives: The Construction of Social Orders*. London: Macmillan.

1993. Evolution and Democracy: Talcott Parsons and the Collapse of the Eastern European Regimes. *Theory, Culture and Society* 10: 145–51.

1998. Ernest Gellner's Theory of Nationalism: Some Definitional and Methodological Issues. In J. A. Hall, *The State of the Nation*. Cambridge: Cambridge University Press, pp. 158–65.

1999. Modernity: A Non-Eurocentric Conceptualization. *British Journal of Sociology* 50 (1): 141–59.

Nettl, P. 1967. *Political Mobilisation*. Englewood Cliffs, NJ: Princeton University Press.

Papadopoulos, T. H. 1952. *Studies and Documents Relating to the History of the Greek Church and People under Turkish Domination*. Brussels: Scaldis.

Paparrigopoulos, C. 1925. *History of the Greek Nation: From Ancient Times till the Reign of George I* (in Greek). 6 vols., Athens: Eleftheroudakis.

Parsons, T. 1964a. Evolutionary Universals in Society. *American Sociological Review* 29, June.

1964b. *The Social System*. London: Routledge and Kegan Paul.

1966. *Societies: Evolutionary and Comparative Perspectives*. Englewood Cliffs, NJ: Prentice Hall.

1977. *The Evolution of Societies*. Englewood Cliffs, NJ: Prentice Hall.

Petropoulos, J. 1968. *Politics and Statecraft in the Kingdom of Greece 1833–1843*. Princeton, NJ: Princeton University Press.

Renan, E. 1882/1990. What Is a Nation? In Homi Bhabha (ed.), *Nation and Narration*. London: Routledge.

Skopetea, E. 1997. *Fallmerayer* (in Greek). Athens: Themelio.

Smith, A. 1986. *The Ethnic Origins of Nations*. Oxford: Blackwell.

1991. *National Identity*. Harmondsworth: Penguin.

Stavrianos, L. S. 1958. *The Balkans since 1453*. New York: Holt, Rinehart and Winston.

1959. Antecedents of the Balkan Revolution of the Nineteenth Century. *Journal of Modern History* 29 (4): 335–72.

Stoianovich, T. 1963, The Social Foundation of Balkan Politics. In C. Jelavich and B. Jelavich (eds.), *The Balkans in Transition*. Berkeley: University of California Press, pp. 297–346.

Svoronos, N. 1972. *Histoire de la Grèce moderne*. Paris: Presses Universitaires de France.

Tilly, C. 1990. *Coercion, Capital and European States*. Oxford: Blackwell.

Weber, M. 1978. *Economy and Society*, ed. G. Roth and G. Wittich. Los Angeles: University of California Press.

6 Between the book and the new sword: Gellner, violence and ideology

Siniša Malešević

Introduction

We live in an age which abhors violence. Grounded in the spirit of Enlightenment rationalism and humanism, most modern-day individuals, as with a majority of international organisations, value the principles of dialogue and toleration over those of hereditary inequality and collective brutality. When compared to the ethical world of early medieval Europe our moral standards seem so greatly superior: we do not dismember the bodies of executed convicts at the carnivals to play football with their heads and limbs (Youngs 2006: 89), and neither do we burn people alive or force them to sit on iron-spiked chairs. Nevertheless, our age has surpassed all others when it comes to killing. As Charles Tilly (2003: 55) emphasises, the twentieth century alone produced 250 new wars with over a million deaths per year, which makes it by far the most violent century in recorded history. Moreover, as both Zygmunt Bauman (1989) and Michael Mann (2005) convincingly argue, systematic genocidal mass murder is largely an invention of the modern era, whether as an unintended consequence of modernity's obsession with the ordering of difference, or as a perverted attempt towards democratisation. Even though modernity loathes violence, it is, as the French Revolution and the Jacobin Reign of Terror illustrate only too well, created through violence, and violence has proved essential to its worldwide proliferation.

This inherent contradiction that characterises modern living, where coercive brutality is intensely disliked but systematically practised, is something that the great theorist of modernity and a staunch sociological realist, Ernest Gellner, was acutely aware of. As he put it: 'Generally speaking, human societies maintained order by coercion and superstition. The Enlightenment was right in perceiving this, but deeply misguided in its supposition that it would be possible simply to replace such a system by another, in which society was based on truth and consent instead' (Gellner 1994: 31). Yet despite this awareness about the importance of coercion and the need to justify it ('superstition'), Gellner could not reconcile this and similar insights with his distinctly optimistic theory of modernity. As will be argued in this chapter, Gellner's theory of social change, with its emphases on the unique and unprecedented nature of modernity, is built on presuppositions that epistemologically and ontologically stand in stark opposition to the view that sees coercion and ideology as fundamental to human sociability. Though in many of his books he acknowledges the independent role of shared cultural beliefs and collective violence in creating the foundation of modern order, and notwithstanding the fact that his *magnum opus* of historical sociology carries the very Weberian title *Plough, Sword and Book*, Gellner's understanding of modernity is distinctly non-Weberian in its sanguinity. While his analysis of the social changes that radically transformed *agraria* into *industria* is profoundly accurate, both his view of late modernity and his stress on the economic basis of this extraordinary transformation are highly problematic.

In other words, in this chapter I argue that Gellner's theory of social change unjustifiably prizes the plough over the book and the sword; that is, his account of modernity clearly and unduly favours production over culture and coercion. Not only is it that ideology and coercion require more attention than Gellner allowed for, but, as I argue, violence is also an indispensable ingredient of modernity which expands and intensifies as the modern way of life spreads throughout the globe. To counter this proliferation of collective brutality modern social order requires more effective and more persuasive mechanisms of justification. Hence the growth and excess of violence go hand in hand with the articulation of potent and all-encompassing normative and operative ideologies. Against Gellner's diagnosis where economy is more or less bent on swallowing culture and politics in late modernity, I contend that, far from disappearing or diminishing in influence, violence and ideology have been transformed and have become even more pervasive. Despite our progressivist upbringing and widely shared sense of moral superiority, it is our age more than any preceding era that is founded on and necessitates the use of coercion and ideology.

The miracle of modernity

From his first significant sociological book, *Thought and Change* (1964), to his last unfinished one, *Language and Solitude* (1998), Gellner's key preoccupation was and remained the origins and character of modernity. Following in the footsteps of the founding fathers of sociology, Weber, Durkheim and Marx, Gellner was baffled by the same central questions:

What is modernity? Why and how did it emerge in 'one small part of Europe, and on one occasion only' (Gellner 1989: 4)? And what were the structural causes of its current shape? Nevertheless, what set Gellner's apart from sociological classics was his unbridled buoyancy about the nature of modernity as well as his accidentalist view of its origins. All three classics interpreted the transition from the traditional to the modern world as a socially agonising process that results in the decline of social values and norms that causes a deep rupture in social order by creating estranged individuals. For Marx this was the product of the capitalist induced alienation. In Durkheim's view this breakdown of existing social norms is a principal cause of the state of anomie. For Weber the ever increasing bureaucratic rationalisation leads inevitably towards the disenchantment of modern human beings. In contrast Gellner paints a much more optimistic picture of modern life where, instead of the Weberian 'iron cage' of rational constraint, we live in a 'rubber cage' – a world of advanced industrialism where 'antinomian permissiveness' and self-satisfying consumerism coexist with scientific and technological rationality (Gellner 1987, 1996b). In addition, whereas the classics, with the possible exception of Weber, perceived this transition to modernity as an almost unavoidable process, Gellner understands it as a great 'European miracle'.[1] Hence, instead of seeing it as an unambiguous transition from a uniform moral order of mechanical solidarity towards complexities of organic solidarity, as in Durkheim, or through the prism of dialectical materialism with relatively fixed stages of historical development, as in Marx, or in the context of the unstoppable forces of rationalist bureaucratisation as in Weber, Gellner comprehends modernity as a profoundly contingent historical event that in most respects went against the grain of all known human experience.

Gellner offers, as he puts it, a 'trinitarian' and evolutionary vision of social change whereby humankind is seen as passing through three distinct organisational stages of development: hunting/gathering, agrarian and industrial (Gellner 1988, 1997). The three stages are understood as conceptual ideal types and as such sharply demarcated from each other: they are founded on utterly different coercive, economic and cultural institutional arrangements. While culture and coercion are acknowledged as important, what determines the structural differences of these three social orders is 'the economic or productive base'. As Gellner (1988: 20) acknowledges, his position is a form of economic materialism which 'assumes and claims that each of the three crucial productive

---

[1] Other influential theorists of the 'European miracle' include Jones (1981), Mann (1986) and Hall (1988, 1989), and Mann reiterates his position in chapter 2 of this book.

bases – hunting/gathering, agriculture, and scientific/industrial production – bestows on the societies which use it radically different sets
of problems and constraints'. In his view it is the distinct nature of
economic production more than anything else which makes the three
forms of social order into 'three fundamentally different species'.

What interests Gellner most in his analysis of the 'structure of human
history' is the peculiar, unprecedented and, historically speaking, rather
sudden character of transition from an agrarian social universe into the
industrial/scientific age. From his early diagnosis in *Thought and Change*
to his last books Gellner maintained a view which sharply separates the
two universes. Whereas *agraria* is a torpid, poverty stricken and slow
world involved in a permanent collective effort to secure and accumulate
enough food, *industria* is an energetic, socially mobile universe sustained
by continuous scientific development and economic growth. The profoundly hierarchical order characterised by the appropriation of wealth by
the Red and Black, that is by the 'coercion-and-salvation-monopolizing
rulers' and by the widespread destitution of the peasant majority of
agraria, is contrasted with the dynamism and egalitarian principles of
industria. The industrial age is rooted in, and structurally dependent on,
the complex division of labour, occupational flux and modular, adaptable
individuals thus valuing and promoting innovation and merit. In stark
opposition, the agrarian age is one of Malthusian zero sum brutality
where noble heritage and honour are prized, manual work despised, and
where one starves 'according to rank': 'The requirements of labour and
defence power make them [the inhabitants of *agraria*] value offspring or,
at any rate, male offspring; the stability of technology imposes a limit on
production ... the exponential growth of population, jointly with the non-
exponential growth (if any) of output, means that the society as a whole is
never too far removed from the point when it becomes incapable of
feeding all its members' (Gellner 1997: 17).

In addition to economic and political discrepancy between the aristocratic castes and the peasant majorities, the world of *agraria* is also a
world of two distinct and in many respects incommensurable cultures:
the high, mostly Latin, culture of royalty, upper clergy and warrior
nobility stands in sheer opposition to the ocean of low folk who are
immersed in the vernacular lifestyle of the village. In contrast, the
essential prerequisite of industrial society is a standardised cultural
medium expressed through universal state-sponsored literacy. Not only
does *agraria* not need cultural unity, the very role of culture serves to
reinforce the existing status hierarchies: the elaborate codes of dress,
speech, make-up and dancing are there to distinguish between peasant
and aristocrat. In contrast, industrial order requires a much greater

degree of cultural similarity, with context-free communication and universal literacy underpinning the semantic skills that characterise modern work relations.

This absolute polarity of the two social orders is, according to Gellner (1988: 158) reflected in the radical social transformation where, for the first time in human history, predation replaces production as a 'central theme and value of life'. Consequently the two worlds imply the existence of two different ontologies: whereas *agraria* values social over logical coherence, the world of *industria* prioritises logic over communal bonds. The rationalist, scientific and meritocratic foundation of *industria* 'butters no parsnips and legitimises no social arrangements', with individual autonomy and solitary anonymity looming large as 'publicly accessible truth fails to separate members of a community from nonmembers' (Gellner 1988: 272). Thus the radical and, historically speaking, swift transformation from the agrarian ontology to the industrial ontology appears as a true miracle indeed. There is no simple answer to account for this miracle and Gellner, following existing research, suggests a long list of probable causes – from the Protestant ethic thesis, to the notion of permeable aristocracy, free peasantry, plural state system, emergence of national bourgeoisie to restrained burghers, and 'the lifting on the ceiling of available technical discovery' (Gellner 1988: 158–70). However, the factors that stand out and appear most often in his books are 'the expanding bribery fund' and the European church–state stalemate. The separation of church and state in Europe and their intensive rivalry and power created an unintended outcome whereby the two strong institutions were forced to control and contain each other: 'Priests helped us to restrain thugs, and then abolished themselves in an excess of zeal, by universalising priesthood' (Gellner 1995: 58). By the 'expanding bribery fund' Gellner means the ability of modern social order to pacify rulers by making them wealthy without the need to resort to violence as well as to restrain aggression throughout the entire society by dramatically improving material living conditions.

To sum up, Gellner's central research theme[2] is the accidental and extraordinary emergence of modernity, a web of events and processes which have uniquely transformed a violent, hierarchical, economically backward, culturally divided and stagnant world underpinned by the monopoly of singular religion into an order characterised by cumulative

---

[2] In an interview in *Current Anthropology* (Davis 1991), Gellner explicitly states that this miraculous transition from the two social universes is 'the central fact about our world' and 'my central preoccupation'.

knowledge, rapid scientific discovery, value pluralism, economic growth, egalitarian ethics, cultural standardisation and peace. Although there is much to be commended in this diagnosis concerning the contingency of the modern miracle, there are also some profound epistemological and ontological weaknesses of this argument which find their full expression in Gellner's understanding of the modern condition. By attributing too much explanatory power to production over coercion and ideology, Gellner's argument falls short in accounting for the dominance and expansion of violence and ideology in late modernity. More precisely, Gellner's theory of modernity cannot explain two major processes of the contemporary epoch: the continued significance of coercion, and the omnipotence and complexity of ideological practice in modern life.

The expansion and externalisation of violence

The idea of social conflict looms large in Gellner's writings. He was a superb polemicist who cherished the opportunity to provoke and exchange intellectual punches with his opponents – whether linguistic philosophers, idealist social theorists or relativist anthropologists. Moreover his life's work was entirely devoted to unprecedented revolutionary changes filled with turbulent and conflictual transformations of the social world. Finally he had a passionate sociological interest in cultural collisions, conflicting secular ideologies and disparate religious *Weltanschauungen*. Notwithstanding this, Gellner was principally a sociologist of consensus who understood social relations through a prism which privileges normative accord over social conflict. As he would often point out: 'The dependence of the individual on the social consensus which surrounds him ... is the normal social condition of mankind' (Gellner 1996a: 140); or again, 'men are, all things considered, astonishingly well-disciplined and restrained in their conduct and their thought' (1995: 47). Nevertheless, Gellner was a far cry from traditional structural functionalism both in his adamant rejection of its organicist imagery as well as of its ahistorical idealism. Instead Gellner offers a particular twist on functionalist understandings of social order, with his materialist historicism making a strict distinction between the modern, industrial world and its predecessors. In this view social consensus characterises only modern social orders while its premodern equivalents are dominated by zero-sum violence, a cult of aggressiveness and intrinsic social conflicts. As already noted, Gellner's vision of historical transformation posits *agraria* firmly as an undesirable predatory environment and *industria* as a peaceful milieu underpinned by scientific growth and continuous production.

Despite the valuable structural contrasts noted above, Gellner's account is both ontologically and epistemologically unsound. The stark contrast of the two historical periods is interpreted as generating two highly diverse forms of sociability whereby in one era humans appear to be deeply conflictual beings and in another they are almost universally norm-governed creatures. Although most sociologists would have no difficulty is concurring with Gellner that humans are social beings vastly influenced by their environment and changing social structures, very few would go as far as Gellner in attributing so much explanatory power to historical forces. In Gellner's theory the people who inhabit agrarian premodernity are essentially different in kind from those living in industrial modernity. He does not hesitate in making this apparent by employing the inverted Kafkiesque metaphor of metamorphosis, so that the premodern, agrarian beetle turns into industrial man (Gellner 1964: 50). Furthermore this process is seen as total and irreversible: 'The most important thing about this transition is that it is one-way: beetle into man, but never man into beetle ... movement is possible in one direction only' (1964: 68). The problem with this view is not only its inflexibility and determinism, closing off as it does all doors for historical reversibility (of the kind Taliban attempted in Afghanistan for example), but more importantly Gellner leaves little or no room for human agency. In this radical form of historical structuralism[3] human action appears to be insignificant if not completely irrelevant. Premodern humans are no more than beetles – unthinking, weak and socially dependent creatures; only the modern condition allows for the emergence of the authentic human being. Such a position is both ontologically and epistemologically unsustainable as it completely divests social life from human agency and individual or collective choices. This is not to say that structural historical transformations are directed by conscious agents – as such events are obviously often beyond individual or group control. However, no dramatic historical change is possible without human action. As Rex (1980: 119) rightly argues, social structures arise from 'the continuity in time of interlocking patterns of interaction'. Although they involve activities of thousands or even millions of people over long periods of

---

[3] In *Thought and Change* (1964: 69) Gellner openly acknowledges his historicism: 'the present argument is "historicist", it abjectly prostrates itself before what it holds to be predetermined, a cosmic or at any rate global trend. In those cases (which are rather rare) when some social – or other – development is known with adequate certainty to be inevitable, it is better to adjust oneself to it and learn to like it rather than to condemn it.'

time and are influenced by geographical, environmental and other factors, social structure for the most part is, and remains, a distinctly human product. This problematic structuralist reasoning leads Gellner towards the conclusion that human beings are so feeble that the tides of history can mould them from being predominantly violent into peace-loving producers and traders. That is, in this view politics can be, and is, replaced by economics: coercion, brutality and rigid hierarchy give way to negotiation, calculation and reasoning. There is too much historical and structural determinism in this account.

A sociologically more plausible and ontologically more coherent interpretation would have to work with a stable and durable view of human action. Instead of the historical grand puppeteers who cast humans into either producers or coercers it is necessary to acknowledge the existence of some universal, trans-historical traits that characterise all social action. Although macro-structural events and processes have a powerful impact on individual and collective behaviour, they cannot eradicate universal biological, psychological, political and most of all sociological attributes of human life. In other words, the inherent con-flictuality of social relations does not vanish with the arrival of indus-trialisation. Far from it. Social conflicts do not fade away; they transform, mutate and find their outlets elsewhere. Although the modern world takes a very different stance on violent behaviour than its prede-cessors, this does not automatically imply the disappearance of conflict and coercion in modernity. In this respect there is no metamorphosis of a beetle into a man. There was a beetle–man before just as there is a beetle–man today. Instead of the Spencerian (1967) vision of a great transition from militarism to industrialism which Gellner obviously endorses, modernity retains a central place for violence.

In fact modernity requires violence. As the work of many historical sociologists, most of all W. McNeill (1984) and M. Mann (1993, 2005), reveals so well, mass-scale violence entails complex organisation, cen-tralised authority, technological development and advanced mechanisms of ideological persuasion, all of which are products of modernity. The birth and expansion of modernity goes hand in hand with the concen-tration and bureaucratisation of power in the institutions of the nation-state. The monopoly of violence that characterises the modern state creates an environment where nearly universal 'internal pacification' is achieved at the expense of the externalisation of conflict. As Giddens (1985) and Hirst (2001) point out, the reduction of internal conflict, the depoliticisation of the domestic sphere, and the eradication of violence within one's borders were accompanied by the simultaneous transfer of enmity and aggression outside of the nation-state. The most common form of the externalisation of violence is war, and in the modern epoch warfare has dramatically expanded. The centralisation and bureaucratisation of authority combined with scientific and technological advances stimulated the intensive proliferation of warfare, while the emergence of nationalism as a popular dominant ideology of the nation-state supplied a potent source of justification for warfare. Thus modern social order enforces a strict division which separates internal from external forms of violence: killing your fellow countryman is a heinous crime whereas killing the foreign enemy on the battlefield is a noble deed.

The expansion and externalisation of violence in modernity directly contradicts Gellner's theoretical optimism. Although he is absolutely right that modernity is normatively built on principles that abhor violence, the reality of the modern age is often the exact opposite of this. Gellner's theory of modernity cannot explain the central paradox of modernity whereby aggression, brutality and the murder of fellow human beings are universally denounced and despised at the very same time as they become systematically utilised on a mass scale. The unprecedented technological advancement, the unparalleled levels of educational attainment and near universal literacy in the developed world went hand in hand with the birth of ethnic cleansing, total war, revolution and the projects of systematic annihilation. Despite unmatched economic growth, increased standards of living and the proliferation of an egalitarian ethic, the last century was by far the bloodiest century in recorded history. As Tilly (2003: 55) argues and empirically demonstrates: 'In absolute terms – and probably per capita as well – the twentieth century visited more collective violence on the world than any century of the previous ten thousand years.' Mann (2001) estimates that ethnic cleansing and genocides account for up to 120 million deaths. In total more than 200 million human lives have been lost as a consequence of wars, political massacres, state terrorism, revolutions and rebellions (Holsti 1996). Furthermore twentieth-century warfare was also unique in gradually making little distinction between soldiers and civilians – with civilians making up 5 per cent of casualties in World War I, 50 per cent in World War II and 90 per cent of all deaths in the wars of the 1990s (Chesterman 2001). Instead of its alleged demise, violence in fact strengthens, deepens and accelerates with modernity.

Although *agraria* was infamous for its practices of boiling or burning people alive, foot roasting, impalement or body disfigurement, the gruesome nature of these procedures exaggerates their destructive effectiveness. This ritualistic use of violence was perhaps useful in spreading fear among rebellious peasants and thus reinforcing the feudal aristocratic or religious authority, but its detrimental utility was nonetheless modest.

Popular images of medieval brutality tend to disguise the very low intensity of violence in the premodern world. Not only were the armies of *agraria* fairly small, but they were rarely engaged in prolonged battles, and the outcomes resulted in few casualties by comparison to modern warfare. In contrast to contemporary cinematic depictions of medieval warfare with massive bloody battlefields and enormous killing fields, most conflicts were in fact decided with little actual fighting: 'Communications diffi-culties in ancient warfare were so great for both sides that their armies rarely met head-on ... Battles were usually unnecessary: Skirmishes showed the rough balance of force, the defenders' counsels were divided, someone opened the gates' (Mann 1986: 141). Premodern militaries were also very small by today's standards. The renowned emperor Sargon of Akkad subjugated the whole of Mesopotamia, Syria and Caanan with no more than 5400 soldiers (Mann 1986: 145; Gat 2006: 231). The famous Spartan army had fewer than 10,000 warriors at the peak of its power (Gat 2006: 317). William of Normandy conquered England in 1066–70 with fewer than 7000 soldiers, while the largest army ever gathered during the crusades in defence of Jerusalem (1183) had fewer than 15,000 soldiers (Beeler 1971: 249–50).

These figures stand in stark contrast to the armies of modernity which during wartime have numbered millions of soldiers and resulted in hundreds of thousands of human casualties. The famous battles of the First and Second World War such as Verdun, the Somme, Moscow or Stalingrad all involved millions of dead soldiers and civilians, and have no equivalent in the traditional world. Hence premodern social order spoke in the language of hate and violence but was fairly ineffective in their implementation. Modernity speaks in the language of equality, peace and toleration but exercises – with brutal efficiency – mass mur-der. We rarely impale or saw the genitals of our enemies; but we quite easily remain silent when tens of thousands die as 'collateral damage'. The grisly violence of the traditional world was a ritualistic spectacle, a morbid theatre of individual deeds of monstrous cruelty. In contrast the modern world dispenses with the irrationality of gruesomeness in favour of instrumental efficiency and high killing ratios. We cannot tolerate it when our soldiers humiliate their prisoners by holding them on a dog-leash, but we show little remorse when thousands of 'enemy casu-alties' are reported. It seems astonishing that such a perceptive mind as Gellner's could omit the simple fact that systematic mass-scale violence has expanded and multiplied with modernity. The probable cause of this grave oversight comes from Gellner's almost exclusive focus on internal societal developments without paying much attention to inter-state relations. And indeed when one looks internally at modern social order there is significantly less bloodshed and cruelty than in previous historical epochs. However, such a partial view neglects the fact that a particular *industria* emerges and grows in a specific geopolitical environment which includes not only other such *industrias* but also remnants of *agraria*. Our analyses of modernity cannot stop at the borders of the nation-state, because it is precisely here at the borders that violence and warfare find their full expression in industrial society. The internal pacification of modern society is not a spontaneous phenomenon caused by transformations in society's economic organisation; it is a process accomplished by the externalisation of violence. Modernity does not play Houdini tricks. Instead of their miraculous disappearance, modern nation-states displace social conflicts outside their boundaries. The industrial society requires the shell of the nation-state and the nation-state appears on the historical stage only with other nation-states. As Hirst (2001: 56) points out, the post-Westphalian international system of state sovereignty was built on the principle of mutual recognition: 'Legitimate membership of the system depended on acceptance by other states as the exclusive ruler of a definite territory. A defining feature of modern sovereignty is the recognition by states of the difference between internal and external policy, and thus arises the norm of non-interference in the internal affairs of other states.' In Schmitt's (1976) famous analysis, states originate and define their *raison d'être* through a friend versus enemy relationship. The state's monopoly on violence and unquestioned sovereignty involving internal pacification of society are a direct product of the externalisation of violence.

The Gellnerian image of the modern order characterised by continual production, system efficiency, scientific growth, social mobility and domestic peace is often the pleasant outcome of highly unpleasant processes – wars, ethnic cleansing or revolutionary terror. The successful economic transformation from *agraria* into *industria* owes little to economic factors, so dear to Gellner, and a great deal to political causes as the abundance, inclusivity and tolerance of modernity rests on the foundations of mass murder. As Mann (2005) argues, liberal democracy, class compromise and civil rights were built on top of ethnic cleansing and institutionalised coercion. Modernity was born with and has expanded through violence. Howard (1976), Giddens (1985), Dandeker (1990), Tilly (1995) and many others document well how the naissance and development of modern social order parallels the growth and spreading out of coercion and warfare. In fact all principal social movements of the post-traditional era – from the Enlightenment, Romanticism, Bolshevism, Scientific Racism, Fascism and Liberal Democracy – had to rely on coercive means to leave their stamp on the world. The outcome of their ideas has shaped the modern world: French, American and Russian revolutions, colonialism, two World Wars, Holocaust and so on. In many respects, and despite our moral inclination to think otherwise, modernity would be unthinkable without coercion and violence.

Furthermore, protracted warfare has also led to the gradual implementation of a central organising principle of modernity – bureaucratic rationalisation. If, as Weber (1968) argues, ever increasing rationalisation articulated in bureaucratic administrative organisation is a key feature of modernity, then there would be no modernity as we know it without major wars. Modern warfare requires sophisticated organisation, and it is the military sector that is a cradle of Weberian bureaucratic rationality and the elaborate division of labour. Gellner's emphasis on the importance of a division of labour for the emergence and functioning of industrial society ignores the fact that this structural development was initiated in the military, corresponding to a tripartite division of military activities into artillery, cavalry and infantry. Furthermore, the major technological and scientific innovations which have transformed our world, such as new modes of transport and communication, mass industrial production of goods, processed and pre-packed food or the professionalisation of occupations, were all discovered in, and for, the military sector (Giddens 1985; Dandeker 1990).

Although violence has been transformed in modernity through being largely externalised, coercion has not vanished from the domestic sphere. The fact that modern states have absolute monopoly on the use of violence within their borders means that they are in a position to mobilise and if necessary force entire populations to participate in warfare. The birth of total wars such as the First and Second World Wars where the *raison d'état* implied that the state could marshal all its existing human and material resources was an excellent indicator of the state's omnipotence in modernity. As Mann (1986, 1988) rightly argues, the infrastructural powers of modern states have dramatically increased as they are in a position to tax, police, censor, conscript and monitor nearly all of their citizens. When these powers connect with increased despotic powers as in the cases of Nazi Germany or the Soviet Union, then there is no escape from state-induced coercion. However, even when despotic powers are minimal, as for example in present-day Greece or Portugal, by withholding the citizenship or welfare rights of immigrants the modern state is in the position to delineate the rigid criteria of exclusion and inclusion.

Hence modernity is far from being free of coercion and violence. On the contrary, underpinned as it is by intensive scientific and technological development, the post-Westphalian separation between internal and external spheres of legitimacy and the secularisation of inter-state politics sees collective violence blossom in modern conditions.

The might of ideology

Although the twentieth century witnessed quantitatively more human bloodshed than any previous epoch, general attitudes towards the use of violence for pursuing economic or political goals have radically changed. In this sense Gellner's account is perfectly accurate as modern human beings live in a normative universe which utterly detests coercion and brutality. Instead of the medieval glorification of congenital hierarchy, torture, and unquestioned authority sanctioned by coercive feudal structures, we live in a post-Enlightenment world that prides itself on observing the universal humanist goals of equality, liberty and fraternity. Nearly all modern states have enshrined in their constitutions and other principal legal acts the right to life, to fair trial, and to freedom from slavery, serfdom, discrimination and cruel punishment, thus emphasising the moral equality of all human beings. While the premodern social order was fairly open to the use of excessive force and elaborate torture, industrial societies tend rigorously to proscribe not only violent behaviour on the part of individuals and groups, but also verbal or other incitements to violence. A civilised people does not condone revenge killings, does not burn heretics.

Nevertheless there is a great sociological irony in the fact that the social order which is normatively built on ideas and principles that cherish reason, rationality, humanism and peaceful reconciliation is the very same order that is responsible for the glut of systematic mass murder. It seems that the nominal rejection of violence is inversely proportional with its actual presence in modernity, with nearly universal disdain for coercive actions coexisting with the constant intensification of atrocities. And this is the core predicament of post-traditional order: how to reconcile this cognitive and ontological dissonance whereby universally shared principles deeply contradict social reality. Modernity's answer to this contradictory situation is the emergence of the most forceful device for the successful legitimation of violence – ideology. This concept is not to be understood in a narrow, Marxist sense, as a giant structural brain-washing apparatus, a form of false consciousness. Instead ideology is a historically novel but fairly universal social process through which social agents articulate their beliefs and actions. As the contents of ideological messages often transcend human experience by invoking grand vistas of collective authority they are nearly impossible to test. However, as powerful mechanisms of group mobilisation, ideologies succeed by making effective appeal to higher moral norms, advanced knowledge claims, and collective/individual interests or affects in order to justify particular social action (Malešević 2002; forthcoming).

The gradual decline of religious authority, in both its institutional and its doctrinal form has led to the delegitimisation of premodern social order grounded in the principles of the divine origins of monarchs. This simultaneous undermining of religious and political authority created an environment for the birth of modern ideologies underpinned by mass popular appeal. In this new social context religious doctrines had to compete with secular equivalents and were often forced to rearticulate their messages in the new ideological discourses, which in turn often transformed religious authority. The dynamism, restlessness and unpredictability of modern life produced an environment of constant ideological bifurcation with socialism, liberalism, conservatism and religious fundamentalism (among others) fighting for the souls of the new modern subjects. However, despite the potency and successes of the four ideologies noted above, it was nationalism, in all its varieties, that established itself as the dominant ideological doctrine of modernity.[4]

Ernest Gellner (1964) was the first who realised this and who provided a persuasive explanation of why nationalism was and had to be an essential requirement of modernisation. The structural disparity between the premodern and the modern social order is most visible in the cultural sphere where, as Gellner made it apparent, the agrarian society not only was an epitome of rigid social stratification but also was culturally divided. In contrast to this, a modern, industrial order requires a substantial degree of cultural homogeneity. In other words, before the age of Enlightenment and the French Revolution, the social realm was clearly divided between a small nobility concerned with status enhancement, and the masses of illiterate agricultural producers who were both socially and geographically immobile. While the world of Latin 'high culture' was preoccupied with the establishment of the Holy Roman Empire under a single Christian ruler, a mode of authority based on personalised royal warfare and intermarriage, the rest of the population consisted of an illiterate peasantry marked by a plurality of often mutually incomprehensible oral vernacular 'low cultures'. In traditional order, then, there is no congruence between polity and culture, as the two have rather distinct roles: 'in simple societies culture is important, but its importance resides in the fact that it reinforces structure – the style of being and expression symbolises, underlines the substance, the effective role, activities, relationships. In modern societies, culture does not so much underline structure: rather, it replaces it' (Gellner 1964: 155). A young baroness learns difficult and elaborate

---

[4] Elsewhere I have argued (Malešević 2006) that the dominance of nationalism in modernity comes in part from its symbiotic ability to coexist with all major ideologies on the operative level, thus making it in fact the dominant operative ideology of the modern age.

dancing routines not so much for personal enjoyment of dance as to reinforce her social status. A young Breton learns French not to take pleasure in its melodic quality but to get a job in a Paris factory. While learning the dance routine helps the baroness to dissociate herself from the inferior commoners, by mastering French a Breton boy makes sure that his progeny becomes and remains French for good. The historically rather sudden transformation from culture as structure to structure as culture was genuinely a miraculous development: a process through which nationalism become the dominant ideology of the modern era. The success of this transformation is so overwhelming that it is regularly taken for granted. Apart from a few academics and people on the political margins of their societies, few question the apparent normality and naturalness of nationhood. The ideological power of nationalism is so solid and internalised that it is generally assumed, as Gellner (1964: 150) puts it, that 'a man has a nationality just as he has a height, weight, sex, name, [and] blood-group'.

Gellner's pioneering understanding of the rise and spread of nationalism is in many respects still unsurpassed. Despite the brazen functionalist underpinnings[5] of his argument, Gellner provides a sociologically compelling and coherent theory of nationalism which rightly stresses its contingent nature, its modernity and its legitimising potency. However, what comes as a surprise in Gellner's account is his sanguine conclusion that nationalism is likely to wane in late modernity. In many respects this view directly contradicts Gellner's own theory of nationalism. Such an unsubstantiated conclusion is derived from two erroneous premises: (1) that the modern human being is principally *Homo economicus*, exclusively motivated and satisfied by gain maximisation; (2) that ideology plays little or no role in advanced modernity.

According to Gellner (1964: 114) the two central values of an industrialising order are 'the attainment of affluence and the satisfaction of nationalism'. Moreover these are also identified as the main principles of political legitimacy in the modern age (Gellner 1997: 25). However, while economic growth is understood as a variable, non-teleological category, nationalism is seen in much more static terms. So Gellner (1997: 25) argues that 'regimes are acceptable if they can, over a period, engender growth, and they lose their authority if they do not'. In other words legitimacy is linked to continuous economic success, without fixed parameters of how much economic growth is needed. In contrast, nationalism appears to be an either/or phenomenon: once a substantial

---

[5] For effective critiques of Gellner's functionalism see most chapters in Hall 1998.

degree of cultural homogeneity within a particular polity is attained then this criterion has been fulfilled for good. While both of these assumptions are highly problematic the second one is mistaken on two accounts.

First, the idea that the legitimacy of established nation-states comes exclusively from their ability to generate economic wellbeing represents quite a constricted understanding of both human action and social structures. The classics of sociology such as Weber and Durkheim demonstrated long ago that the social world is a complex network built on the unintended consequences of human action. Weber (1968) emphasised that we are motivated as much by instrumental rationality as by value rationality, tradition, habit or emotion, while Durkheim (1982) showed how and why social structures often acquire logic of action which departs from the motives of individual actors. Although economic growth might be a potent generator of action it is not the only one. The case of the Saudi Arabian middle classes (including al-Qaeda sympathisers) is a good example of how rulers cannot rely solely on the collective bribing of its population forever, as legitimacy is derived from a variety of sources. Non-economic conflicts polarise many contemporary societies. Ideological and political issues such as attitudes to the state's involvement in oversees military action, environment, abortion, euthanasia, animal rights or gun control can topple governments as much as the price of petrol, tax increases or unemployment. Rulers often lose credibility and thus the authority to rule over non-instrumental concerns such as the right to wear the hijab, to practise homosexuality or to contest the military adventures of some superpower. Most importantly these ideological and political disputes regularly traverse socio-economic divides within a particular society, and are present in economically advanced areas as much as in the poorest corners of the globe. Human beings are not just economic maximisers; they are also political and ideological animals.

Secondly, Gellner's view of ideology in general and of nationalism in particular stumbles over two related hurdles: (1) nationalism, as with any other ideology, is not an either/or phenomenon; and (2) ideology, and nationalism most of all, is a vital ingredient of late modern order.

Although Gellner correctly attributes the potency of nationalism to the period of transition from the traditional to the modern world, he also believes that when 'the marriage of nation and state' is completed, that is, once 'the satisfaction of nationalism' is achieved, then nationalism loses much of its might. In his own words: 'In advanced industrialism, the intensity of ethnic feeling diminishes' (Gellner 1996a: 122); or again 'the sharpness of nationalist conflict may be expected to diminish ... it was the social chasms created by early industrialism, and by the unevenness of its diffusion, which made it acute' (1983: 121). Here again one encounters a teleological view underpinned by a problematic ontology of human action. It is far from clear why social actors living in a world of nation-states, that is, in a nation-centric environment, would suddenly stop being nationalists. Though Gellner argues convincingly that the production of cultural homogeneity in the industrial world is confined to the borders of the nation-state, he is less convincing in his prognosis. Cultural homogenisation is heavily dependent on the imposition of a standardised high culture, exo-socialisation of state-wide education and context-free communication, all of which model genuine nationalists, and as long as these processes are in motion there is no obvious reason why nationalism will fade away.

On the contrary, universal literacy, the spread of print-capitalism (Anderson 1983) and advanced technological developments in communication and transport have increased the infrastructural powers of nation-states, transforming nationalism into a trans-class and trans-generational phenomenon that has expanded throughout the entire planet. The establishment of the nation-state as a dominant principle of organisation in modernity means that nationalism is unlikely to leave the historical stage any time soon. In fact the centrality of nationhood, as both an all-embracing cognitive and social form that penetrates everyday life (Brubaker 1996, 2004) and an indispensable ingredient of political rhetoric, makes nationalism the dominant operative ideology of the modern age (Malešević 2006). Nationalism is a more protean force than Gellner allows for. It is a meta-ideology of modernity that is able to accommodate a whole variety of social movements and political organisations. Any political party or social pressure group bent on attracting mass support has to embrace a nation-centric narrative, for to risk being labelled 'unpatriotic' is to invite automatic marginalisation on the political scene. Similarly, regardless of whether the state is nominally a democracy, monarchy, military dictatorship or theocracy, its leaders are bound to invoke nationalist principles and national solidarity as the key source of the regime's self-legitimisation. From Thai junta generals to Iranian ayatollahs to Cuban Communist Party central committee members, British prime ministers and American presidents, all state leaders mobilise public support through the discourse of nationalism and claim to act on behalf of 'their people'. Thus, instead of diminishing, nationalism has continued to strengthen and deepen with modernity.

The fact that Gellner perceives nationalist ideology in static, either/or, terms stems largely from his almost exclusive association of nationalism with the peripheral regions of the globe as they underwent a belated process of modernisation. Other forms of nationalist virulence are associated with separatist movements, with Gellner tending to ignore nationalism in the established nation-states. Instead of looking for and analysing the practice and rhetoric of nationalism in all modern societies, Gellner confines nationalist ideology solely to the social movements engaged in the establishment of new states. In this perspective there is no nationalism in the contemporary USA, Britain or France but only in such regions as Quebec, Scotland or Kurdistan. This leaves us with a very reductionist theory of nationalism which is unable to explain non-secessionist forms of nationalist expressions. In other words, with nationalism too tightly linked to economic forces such as uneven development, late industrialisation and a complex division of labour, Gellner's model allows no explanatory room for the political, military and other causes of nationalist ideology. Not only is it that this model has little to offer in terms of accounting for the radical middle-class nationalisms of Britain or France at the start of World War I, or the fact that all modern inter-state wars are almost by definition nationalist wars (Beissinger 1998: 176), but it also pays little attention to the political structure of states from which secession is sought. The authoritarian character of empires, the lack of political voice and collective humiliation can all feed secessionist nationalism much more than economic inequality (Hall 2002; Taylor 1998).

Although the nationalisms of established nation-states seem to be muted for the time being, manifest primarily in symbolic violence such as international sport and entertainment contests, or occasionally in anti-immigrant outbursts of rage, they are still far from being innocuous. Rather, historically speaking, they oscillate between everyday banality and periodic butchery, as all the wars and genocides of the twentieth century illustrate too well. The current dominance of banal – in contrast to 'hot' – nationalisms does not suggest, as Gellner hoped, the departure of nationalist ideology from the world stage. Instead its habituation, regularity and routinisation help normalise the nation-centric vision of the world, thus making nationalism a very potent ideological force of everyday life. Its banality is not a sign of blandness. As Billig (1995: 7) points out: 'Banal nationalism can hardly be innocent [as] it is repro-ducing institutions which possess vast armaments [that] can be mobil-ised without lengthy campaigns of political preparation.'

Thus the prolonged state of peace among wealthy Western states or the globalisation of the world economy provides no reliable evidence to support claims about the demise or impending death of nation-alism (Bauman 2004; Anderson 1997). Such short-sighted economic reductionism obscures more than it explains. It often flies in the face of catalytic, nationalism-inducing events such as 9/11 in the USA, or the political assassination of charismatic leaders such as President Habyarimana in Rwanda, which sparked the 1994 genocide, or, as another type of example, occasions seen as national humiliation as with the unsuccessful Italian occupation of Ethiopia and the 1939 Soviet defeat in Finland.

To sum up, Gellner's optimistic vision of modernity where coercion gradually evaporates and ideology has no role to play is unsatisfactory. In many respects modernity is constituted and sustained by both violent actions and ideological beliefs. Given that nationalism is the dominant operative ideological framework of the modern age, let us explore its workings in greater detail.

The authoritative and the mundane: nationalism in practice

One of the ideal types that seem to be central to Gellner's understanding of the birth and expansion of nationalism in modernity is the dichotomy between high and low culture. To explain the fundamental shift from the world of unstandardised vernaculars of an illiterate peasantry towards the linguistic and semantic homogeneity of modern nation-states, Gellner often invokes these two ideal types, pitting one against the other: as industralisation progresses so low oral cultures become obsolete and give way to a high, literate equivalent. In Gellner's theory there is no room for low cultures in modernity. As he explicitly states: 'In the industrial age only high cultures in the end effectively survive' (Gellner 1983: 117).

Although the intensity and prevalence of this historical change is not questionable, Gellner's judgement about 'low' cultures is somewhat hasty. Whereas modernity is structured around the nation-state model, which clearly privileges nation-centric high culture, this is neither the only nor necessarily the dominant form of cultural expression. What seems significantly to overshadow the high culture in modern everyday life is popular culture. Instead of its agrarian oral folk variant, popular culture is a relatively standardised mainstream process through which the vast majority of modern citizens express themselves. With techno-logical developments such as mass production, copying and distribution, the expansion of mass media industries and affordable entertainment, modern life is filled with the products of popular culture. An over-whelming majority of people in modern industrial/post-industrial soci-ety, and many beyond its borders, consume, interact with, experience and enjoy popular mass culture. Attendances at national operas, ballets or poetry readings cannot compare to those at football matches, rock concerts or cinemas, even in nation-states that pride themselves on having the pre-eminent tradition of ballet, opera or poetry. The turnout at the Bolshoi Theatre could never match that of football club such as CSKA Moscow, which does not even figure among premier clubs. However, despite its palpable popularity and strength, popular culture rarely stands on its own. Instead mass culture forms a symbiotic, if not fully parasitic, relationship with high culture. That is, modernity has room for and requires more than one culture.

Gellner's standardised high culture of the nation-state emerges actually in two forms – as an authoritative and as a mundane type. While the authoritative layer stands for a normative ideal through which nation-states imagine and present themselves to other nation-states, the mundane layer is how modern culture functions in everyday life. The authoritative layer is an ideal type which broadly corresponds to Gellner's notion of high culture, which is historically transformed from being the property of a tiny aristocratic and priestly minority to becoming the important, if not also essential, glue of national/state legitimacy in modernity. However, contra Gellner, 'high culture' never becomes a majority culture. Rather it becomes a normative ideal now recognised and often nominally treasured by most members of particular nation-states. As such it becomes an indispensable ingredient of a particular national narrative serving as 'an inner standard for the community, an *exemplum virtutis* for subsequent emulation' (Smith 1995: 63). In contrast the mundane layer feeds off high culture by drawing on its recognisable and stereotypical images. The popular, lived culture of the mainstream operates in the same normative frame of the nation-state (and of course beyond it as well) but it pays little attention to the substance of high culture. It is not necessary to know artistic merit or even simply to recognise the symphonies of Sibelius or the paintings of Čiurlionis for one to be deemed a good Finn or Lithuanian. What matters is only that one is well aware that these individual artists are 'ours', and as such represent the ingenuity and greatness of 'our' nation. In other words popular culture requires national status symbols provided by high culture.

Hence, the authoritative layer of modern standardised culture distinguishes itself from other national authoritative layers through internationally acclaimed works of art, architecture, and the unique inventions and successes in science, technology and medicine, or through exceptional examples of individual or collective courage, morality, responsibility or honour. The national high culture is built on the global prestige of individual or collective artistic genius. Although Chekhov's plays and short stories, Caravaggio's baroque paintings, Kierkegaard's existentialist philosophy or Bach's organ toccatas and fugues are all exceptional precisely because of a universality which transcends national attachments, they remain unambiguous products of distinct Russian, Italian, Danish and German high cultures. Furthermore, these extraordinary works are the fundamental and indispensable components of what constitutes a particular national culture. It is almost unimaginable to think of English literary culture without Shakespeare or French high culture without the philosophy of the Enlightenment. In addition to artistic excellence the authoritative layer of national culture is also built and sustained by scientific and technological successes, leadership genius, exceptional individual ethical commitments or marked charismatic appeal. Louis Pasteur and Antoine Lavoisier were brilliant scientists whose discoveries have changed the world, yet they also stand out as powerful symbolic representations of Frenchness. Their scientific triumphs are signs of the superiority of the French educational system, which is to say French high culture. Likewise the moral resilience of Mother Theresa, Neil Armstrong's landing on the Moon, Mahatma Gandhi's non-violent resistance, and the military brilliance of Alexander the Great are admired not only as formidable individual achievements but also as direct reflections of the distinct qualities of a representative Albanian, American, Indian or Greek culture.

The fact that the 'true origins' of some of these 'national icons' are regularly disputed only indicates the ferocity of status struggle for national recognition. Was Napoleon French or Italian? Was Kafka Czech, German or Jewish? Was Marie Curie French or Polish? Was Tesla Serb, Croat or American? Such open questions are most pronounced on the mundane layer of national culture. Unlike its authoritative counterpart, the focus here is on form rather than content. Popular culture regularly borrows from high culture by creating and dispersing clichéd images of national identification. It often operates through what Barthes (1957) and, more recently, Laclau (1996: 36) call 'empty signifiers'. While for Barthes this refers to signifiers with no definite signified, Laclau's understanding is more exclusive – empty signifiers are those without a signified. In other words this is a condition where a verbal expression has no actual concept attached to it but still maintains its signifying power. The typical example would be a 'war on terror' as an elastic term devoid of any precise content. In this sense an empty signifier is an expression that instead of referring to a relatively precise concept involves multiple sequences of meanings all of which are defined and exist solely through their opposition to other concepts. The high culture supplies precious 'national treasures', world famous artists, scientists, philosophers, leaders and other symbols of nationhood, some of which are commodified, some sacralised and most oscillating between the two. These images are reproduced and stereotypically reinforced through mass media, educational system, civil society activities and public ceremonies.

However, what makes the two layers of national culture highly distinct is the fact that while mass society acknowledges and often appreciates the importance of high culture as a symbol of 'our' authenticity and global pre-eminence, the actual high culture in itself plays little or no part in everyday life for most people. The authoritative layer is a static symbol of collective prestige which rarely if ever finds lived expression in daily activities of the great majority of those who nominally identify with it. How many nationally conscious Germans know or ever have read *Nibelungenlied*, that 'German Iliad'? How many Indians are familiar with the contents of Mahabharata or Ramayana? How many Japanese regularly read patriotic haiku poetry? How many Dutch can recognise, let alone analyse the meaning of, Hieronymus Bosch's paintings? Yet most of them will proudly claim all these products of high culture as uniquely and quintessentially 'ours'. Despite its obvious and important difference from the folk culture of the agrarian world the mundane layer is not and could never be Gellner's high culture. Instead popular culture requires the existence of high culture as it can articulate itself only in relation to it, whether as its exaggeration, its simplification, its caricature or its direct opposition.[6]

Although internationally recognisable symbols are the most potent markers of national signification, as there are very few individuals, events or cultural products of truly global stature most national symbols are confined to borders of the particular nation-states. As many of these national icons are associated with independence movements and the often violent establishment of particular nation-states, their significance is either localised or disputed and challenged by their neighbours. For example Vuk Karadžić occupies a distinctly high place in the pantheon of Serbian national heroes, as someone who standardised the Serbian language, while Croat and Bosniak linguists see him as an ideologue of early Serbian nationalism and hegemonism. Similarly the movement of Young Turks of the late nineteenth and early twentieth

---

[6] Obviously youth and other countercultures are often defined by their fierce opposition to dominant high culture. However, the initial rebellion, sarcasm and intentional profanisation of sacred national symbols often paradoxically become reincorporated into dominant national narrative. A good example is the British punk band the Sex Pistols which successfully parodied the national anthem 'God Save the Queen'. However this parodic song has gradually been reincorporated into the mainstream, thus enhancing the exemplary concept of Britishness as something associated with unlimited freedom and vitality.

centuries is a cornerstone of the contemporary Turkish secular state and as such holds high regard in Turkey, while most Armenians see the same movement as the chief executor of the 1915–17 genocide. However, the great majority of all national heroes and events remain externally undisputed. Instead their symbolic influence rarely stretches beyond the boundaries of respective states: Babak Khorramdin, legendary leader of the Persian resistance against Arab invaders, is celebrated in Iran but largely unheard of elsewhere; every schoolchild in the Philippines knows who Andres Bonifacio – the leader of the Katipunan revolution against the Spanish colonial rule – is, but outside the country he is mostly unknown; Eduardo Mondlane has banknotes with his image, and town squares, schools and a university named after him, but his name means very little to people who have no connection to Mozambique.

Although the authoritative and mundane cultural layers remain both mutually dependent and distinct, the relatively recent expansion of popular culture, followed by the gradual deconstruction of high culture, has created a situation where some products and representatives of mass culture find their place in high culture and vice versa. What traditionally was considered popular music, such as jazz, blues or even rock and roll, has recently assumed the status of classics, thus penetrating the domain of the authoritative cultural layer. Similarly opera singers and classical composers appear in popular TV shows. The fact that symbols and images of popular culture now easily mix with those of high culture has led some to conclude that we live in a postmodern age characterised by syncreticism, bricolage and anything-goes logic. The entire legacy of Enlightenment, with its search for a cognitive ascendancy capable of differentiating truth from non-truth, genuine aesthetics from trendy kitsch, or high ethical principles from moral decadence, has been deemed obsolete. In this context Tim Edensor (2002) argues that the two cultural levels are now barely distinguishable, thus indirectly inverting Gellner's argument that in the modern age 'we are all clerks' into the claim that all high culture in the end becomes popular culture. However this is not the case. Not only do the products of mass culture have a very limited expiry date, as they instantly replace one another and most are quickly forgotten, but also as the mundane layer parasitically draws on the existing authoritative layer, so the disappearance of high culture would automatically signal the end of popular culture too. While some cultural products and their representatives can be, and periodically are, 'promoted' from mundane to authoritative layer, an overwhelming majority are not. In addition high culture requires regular actual, lived experience that most are unwilling to act upon.

None of this is to suggest that authoritative and mundane layers of modern culture are fixed and unchangeable. On the contrary, both layers are objects of relentless and often severe ideological clashes. Being vital ingredients of nationalist narratives, both authoritative and mundane layers of culture are regularly incorporated and articulated into ideological storylines of various movements who offer distinct and other mutually incompatible interpretations of 'our culture', that is, of what it means to be Irish, Nigerian or Polish. As nationalism remains a dominant operative ideology of the modern era which easily blends with a variety of contrasting normative doctrines from conservatism or liberalism to environmentalism or religious fundamentalism, it is of paramount importance for every respectable social movement to legitimise its actions in nationalist terms. No political actor aspiring to gain or maintain state power can ignore this, just as no political order can operate successfully without encompassing national myths and symbols from high and popular culture. In the nation-centric world in which we live, all political ideologies, regardless of how universalist their official doctrine is, are bound to be nationalist, at the operative level. Even though normative ideologies of Hamas and Chechen Islamists differ radically from those of Vietnamese or Chinese communist apparatchiks, they all attempt to justify their political role by invoking the greatness of their respective nations. Similarly the actions and deeds of the Tibetan Buddhist monks, Moroccan kings and Hindu swamis, just as those of successive American presidents, are regularly judged and valued in so far as they protect the interests and values of 'our people'.

Thus, Gellner's understanding of high culture is obviously too narrow. The potency of standardised culture in modernity stems from the symbiotic cohabitation of the authoritative and mundane layers. The industrial age is not only an age of reason, economic progress, science and artistic sophistication. It is also a world stretched between everyday banality and periodic virulence which is propped up by the scaffold of nationalist ideology. In the modern era the logical coherence is just as easily sacrificed to communal coherence as it was in the agrarian age. In some respects modernity is even more prone to what Gellner calls 'collective falsehoods', with the communal bonds of a complex dynamic mass society built on sentiments which are fragile and scarce. The fact that we trust science more than our predecessors does not mean that we live in a culture-free world. On the contrary, as our world has lost certainties of extended kinship networks and the familiarity of the 'village green', we are forced to look for, and find, collective warmth and affection in 'imagined communities'.

Conclusion

The birth, survival and continuous expansion of modernity is one of the greatest riddles of human history. Values such as the moral equality of all human beings, toleration of different beliefs and creeds, or peaceful coexistence of neighbouring societies, values that we now mostly take for granted, would be perplexing if not entirely incomprehensible to our premodern predecessors. Not only would such principles directly challenge their fundamental convictions, more importantly they would seem worthless, if not counterproductive, in the worlds of hunter-gatherers and agrarian producers. As Weber (1968) made clear, there is an 'elective affinity' between collectively shared beliefs and distinct socio-political orders. He shows this well in the example of Rome, where the fact that most Roman soldiers were stringent followers of the Cult of Mithras was directly related to the bureaucratic organisation of the Roman Empire's military structure. The shared beliefs and the organisational structure were fully compatible as Mithraism rested on the hierarchy of religious ranks and initiatory ceremonies which was almost identical with the Roman military organisation.

Similarly there is no sociological reason why a society-wide egalitarian ethics would emerge before modernity. For this to happen the entire material and organisational basis of the premodern world would have to undergo a transformation. Hence the change in belief systems goes hand in hand with gigantic structural transformations: the development and mass application of science and technology and the industrialisation of production and consumption require an utterly different *Weltanschauung*. It was Gellner more than anybody else who provided a masterful diagnosis of the unique character and unprecedented magnitude of this structural change. In this sense he is a true heir of Weber, a comparative historical sociologist of world-transforming processes. His interpretation of the miraculous nature of modernity is potent, persuasive and elegant. However, whereas Gellner's understanding of the past is staunchly Weberian with its multilayered dissection of culture, economy and politics, his analysis of the present is significantly less so. By clearly privileging production over coercion and ideology in the post-traditional world, Gellner's sociology becomes a victim of a deficient ontology and epistemology. His structural determinism makes little, if any, room for human agency, thus preventing him from comprehending, let alone analysing, the intrinsic universality of social conflict and ideological commitments. Even if the modern human being has metamorphosed into an utterly different creature – from beetle into a proper man as Gellner claims – this can only mean that such a complex, interesting and ideas-driven species is even more likely to be conflictual and doctrinal. The institutional constraints of modernity can as easily be swivelled so as to rely on the sophisticated coercive and ideological machinery of the modern state to pursue distinctly regressive goals. In other words, the virtues of modernity are built on institutionalised human sacrifice – the proliferation of war, revolutionary violence and systematic mass extermination. To justify something that seems so incongruous with the spirit of Enlightenment the modern age needs much more than Socrates' sophisticated lies: it requires logical, coherent, scientifically embedded rationalisations, that is, ideological doctrines. In Gellner's cheerful vision of late modernity one can find many sufferers of the Dorian Gray syndrome – losing one's consciousness and sense of reality for the sake of fake eternal beauty. Such a tranquil ersatz perfection emerges from the shadows of the guillotine, Great War cemeteries, Auschwitz and Treblinka, Hiroshima and the labour camps of Siberia.

References

Anderson, B. 1983. *Imagined Communities: Reflections on the Origin and Spread of Nationalism*. London: Verso.

Anderson, P. 1997. The Europe to Come. In P. Gowan and P. Anderson (eds.), *The Question of Europe*. London: Verso.

Barthes, R. 1957. *Mythologies*. London: Vintage.

Bauman, Z. 1989. *Modernity and the Holocaust*. Cambridge: Polity.

1991. *Modernity and Ambivalence*. Cambridge: Polity.

2004. *Identity*. Cambridge: Polity Press.

Beeler, J. 1971. *Warfare in Feudal Europe 730–1200*. Ithaca, NY: Cornell University Press.

Beissinger, M. 1998. Nationalisms That Bark and Nationalisms That Bite: Ernest Gellner and the Substantiation of Nations. In J. A. Hall (ed.), *The State of the Nation-State: Ernest Gellner and the Theory of Nationalism*. Cambridge: Cambridge University Press, pp. 169–90.

Billig, M. 1995. *Banal Nationalism*. London: Sage.

Brubaker, R. 1996. *Nationalism Reframed: Nationhood and the National Question in the New Europe*. Cambridge: Cambridge University Press.

2004. *Ethnicity without Groups*. Cambridge, MA: Harvard University Press.

Chesterman, S. 2001. *Just War or Just Peace? Humanitarian Intervention and International Law*. Oxford: Oxford University Press.

Dandeker, C. 1990. *Surveillance, Power and Modernity*. Cambridge: Polity.

Davis, J. 1991. An Interview with Ernest Gellner. *Current Anthropology* 32 (1): 63–71.

Durkheim, E. 1982. *The Rules of Sociological Method*. Basingstoke: Macmillan.

Edensor, T. 2002. *National Identity, Popular Culture and Everyday Life*. Oxford: Berg.

Gat, A. 2006. *War in Human Civilization*. Oxford: Oxford University Press.

Gellner, E. 1964. *Thought and Change*. London: Weidenfeld and Nicolson.

166　*Siniša Malešević*

1983. *Nations and Nationalism*. Oxford: Blackwell.

1987. *Culture, Identity and Politics*. Cambridge: Cambridge University Press.

1988. *Plough, Sword and Book: The Structure of Human History*. London: Collins Harvill.

1989. Introduction. In J. Baechler, J. A. Hall and M. Mann (eds.), *Europe and the Rise of Capitalism*. Oxford: Blackwell.

1994. *Encounters with Nationalism*. Oxford: Blackwell.

1995. *Anthropology and Politics: Revolutions in the Sacred Grove*. Oxford: Blackwell.

1996a. *Conditions of Liberty: Civil Society and Its Rivals*. Harmondsworth: Penguin.

1996b. Reply to Critics. In J. A. Hall and I. Jarvie (eds.), *The Social Philosophy of Ernest Gellner*. Amsterdam: Rodopi, pp. 625–87.

1997. *Nationalism*. London: Phoenix.

1998. *Language and Solitude: Wittgenstein, Malinowski and the Habsburg Dilemma*. Cambridge: Cambridge University Press.

Giddens, E. 1985. *Nation-State and Violence*. Cambridge: Polity.

Hall, J. A. 1988. *Powers and Liberties: The Causes and Consequences of the Rise of the West*. Harmondsworth: Penguin.

1989. States and Societies: The Miracle in Comparative Perspective. In J. Baechler, J. A. Hall and M. Mann (eds.), *Europe and the Rise of Capitalism*. Oxford: Blackwell, pp. 20–38.

2002. A Disagreement about Difference. In S. Malešević and M. Haugaard (eds.), *Making Sense of Collectivity: Ethnicity, Nationalism and Globalisation*. London: Pluto, pp. 181–94.

Hirst, P. 2001. *War and Power in the 21st Century*. Cambridge: Polity.

Holsti, K. 1991. *Peace and War: Armed Conflicts and International Order 1648–1989*. Cambridge: Cambridge University Press.

Howard, M. 1976. *War in European History*. Oxford: Oxford University Press.

Jones, E. 1981. *The European Miracle*. Cambridge: Cambridge University Press.

Laclau, E. 1996. *Emancipation(s)*. London: Verso.

Malešević, S. 2002. *Ideology, Legitimacy and the New State*. London: Frank Cass.

2006. *Identity as Ideology: Understanding Ethnicity and Nationalism*. New York and Basingstoke: Palgrave Macmillan.

Forthcoming. Ideology. In K. Dowding (ed.), *Encyclopaedia of Power*. London: Sage.

Mann, M. 1986. *The Sources of Social Power*, vol. I: *A History of Power from the Beginning to A.D. 1760*. Cambridge: Cambridge University Press.

1988. *States, War and Capitalism: Studies in Political Sociology*. Oxford: Blackwell.

1993. *The Sources of Social Power*, vol. II: *The Rise of Classes and Nation-States, 1760–1914*. Cambridge: Cambridge University Press.

2001. Explaining Murderous Ethnic Cleansing: The Macro-Level. In M. Guibernau and J. Hutchinson (eds.), *Understanding Nationalism*. Cambridge: Polity, pp. 205–24.

2005. *The Dark Side of Democracy: Explaining Ethnic Cleansing*. Cambridge: Cambridge University Press.

McNeill, W. 1984. *The Pursuit of Power*. Chicago: University of Chicago Press.

Rex, J. 1980. The Theory of Race Relations: A Weberian Approach. In M. O'Callaghan (ed.), *Sociological Theories: Race and Colonialism*. Paris: Unesco, pp. 117–42.

Schmitt, C. 1976. *The Concept of the Political*. New Brunswick: Rutgers University Press.

Smith, A. 1995. *Nations and Nationalism in a Global Era*. Cambridge: Polity.

Spencer, H. 1967. *The Evolution of Society*. Chicago: University of Chicago Press.

Taylor, C. 1998. Nationalism and Modernity. In J. A. Hall (ed.), *The State of the Nation-State: Ernest Gellner and the Theory of Nationalism*. Cambridge: Cambridge University Press, pp. 191–218.

Tilly, C. 1995. *Coercion, Capital, and European State Formation*. Cambridge: Polity.

  2003. *The Politics of Collective Violence*. Cambridge: Cambridge University Press.

Weber, M. 1968. *Economy and Society*. New York: Bedminster Press.

Youngs, D. 2006. *The Life Cycle in Western Europe c. 1300–c. 1500*. Manchester: Manchester University Press.

7 Ernest Gellner and the multicultural mess

Thomas Hylland Eriksen

One of Ernest Gellner's most quoted statements is the definition of nationalism on page 1 of *Nations and Nationalism*, indeed the very first sentence in the book: 'Nationalism is primarily a political principle, which holds that the political and the national unit should be congruent' (Gellner 1983: 1). Adding nuance to the definition later on the same page, Gellner adds that 'ethnic boundaries should not cut across political ones, and, in particular ... ethnic boundaries within a given state – a contingency already formally excluded by the principle in its general formulation – should not separate the power-holders from the rest'. Gellner sees the national idea as one based on ethnic identity. In this, his theory of nationalism contrasts with Benedict Anderson's, whose *Imagined Communities* (1991/1983) explores nationalism as a symbolically integrating force and attaches little importance to its ethnic component or lack of such. Anderson's perspective is also more global than Gellner's rather Eurocentric vision.

One of the most important theoretical debates about nationalism since the almost simultaneous publication of these seminal books in 1983 has concerned its relationship to ethnic identity. While Anderson has occasionally contributed to this discussion (e.g. in his *Long-Distance Nationalism*, 1992), Gellner rarely, if ever, commented on the implications of migration and transnationalism for national identities. Moreover, he did not engage with the difficult questions arising from the rights claims of indigenous groups either, largely limiting his analysis of nationalism to West and East European history up to and including the postwar years.

Gellner was an open supporter of the same mix of cultural nationalism and political cosmopolitanism that he saw in his great hero Malinowski, who had experienced it first in the Krakow of the Habsburg Empire in its twilight years, later in the British colonies of Africa. In his celebrated or, to some, infamous exchange with Edward Said over the latter's *Culture and Imperialism* (Said 1993, cf. Gellner 1994), Gellner initially praised Said's insistence on the individual's right to choose his or her group allegiance – all said and done, both were liberal universalists, albeit of different persuasions – but dismissed Said's analysis of symbolic power and subordination as misguided and coming dangerously close to a relativisation of truth. Excluding his argument against Foucault-inspired anthropologists in *Postmodernism, Reason and Religion* (Gellner 1992), Gellner's public argument with Said may have been his closest brush with postcolonial theory and the dilemmas of multiculturalism. When he speaks of Islam, he concentrates on Muslim countries; when he talks of cultural pluralism, he is often content to linger with the Habsburg Empire; and when he speaks of the new millennium (in 'The Coming *fin de Millénaire*', Gellner 1995), he sees it essentially as a turning-point defined through the demise of the Soviet empire.

A couple of years before his death, I asked Gellner how he would analyse, within his own theory of nationalism, the rise of indigenous rights movements in the Amazon and elsewhere, and if he saw any solution to their predicament. He shrugged and said there was no simple answer, and seemed unwilling to discuss the issue further. During the same conversation, Gellner repeatedly described Norway as a culturally homogeneous country which in his view obviously enjoyed a strong degree of cohesion and national solidarity. He might have been forgiven for not thinking about the Saami, who are a smaller and arguably less oppressed minority than many other stateless peoples in Europe, but as we spoke, in a forest retreat in the hills above Oslo, our table was cleared by a brown-skinned waiter of Pakistani origin, dressed in a hybridised kind of Norwegian folk costume. A third of the schoolchildren in Oslo primary schools are defined as having a foreign-language background and, as in other West European countries, questions concerning immigration and the integration of immigrants had by the time of our conversation been at the forefront of public attention for more than a decade.

It would nonetheless be interesting to know what Gellner would have made of, for example, the Parekh Report (Parekh et al. 2000), which famously designates the UK as a 'community of communities', or of the public debate, begun by David Goodhart in the magazine of which he is editor, *Prospect* (Goodhart 2004), on the possible trade-offs between solidarity and diversity. Against this background it seems highly pertinent to explore to what extent the various elements of Gellner's theory of nationalism can shed light on contemporary European minority–majority relations.

Three interrelated questions form the framework of this enquiry.

- First, can the dual processes of incorporation, integration and exclusion of immigrant minorities that can be observed in European societies today be accounted for through Gellner's theory of nationalism?

- Second, are the conflicts arising from immigration of a kind that can be explained fully or partly through Gellner's theory?
- Third, do the new minorities constitute entropy-resistant groups, are they becoming assimilated, or does the pluralism entailed by their presence as apparently 'unmeltable ethnics' signify the advent of new political entities distinct from Gellner's concept of the nation?

Gellner's theory

Gellner's theory of nationalism, developed in numerous publications from *Thought and Change* (1964) to the posthumous *Nationalism* (1997), takes as its point of departure a recent watershed in cultural history, namely the industrial revolution. It led to a fundamental refashioning of social relations.

- First, industrialisation entailed an enormous growth in *scale*. Whereas agrarian society had been locally delineated in most respects, industrial society was based on large, anonymous markets where commodities, services and labour could all be bought and sold.
- Second, industrialisation led to *migration*. Millions moved where work was to be found, and were uprooted from custom and tradition, or – in Marx's pithy words – the idiocy of village life.
- Third, industrialisation created a need for *standardisation* of knowledge and skills, making workers and their skills interchangeable.
- Fourth, the *de facto* power residing in family and kinship was reduced, since the family was no longer a functioning unit of production.

In this new situation, the individual person no longer had an unequivocal belonging to a local community. His or her need for food, shelter and existential security could no longer be satisfied locally. In parallel with the economic changes, the state administration also grew, and along with it the state's need to govern its inhabitants. The ideology given the task of healing tendencies of fragmentation and alienation, a functional equivalent to ideologies of locality and kinship, was nationalism, in Gellner's view an ideology based on ethnic identity, that is a kind of identification which is metaphorically related to kinship.

The elites in a fully fledged nation need to consolidate their unity around a 'high culture' symbolically laden with claims to uniqueness, historical memories – real or fictional – and aspirations to aesthetic and moral greatness on behalf of the nation. This high culture, sometimes an upgraded version of peasant culture, sometimes a nationalised version of a cosmopolitan one, and more often than not a mix of both, is generally recognised, in a functioning nation, as *the* national culture.

The nation, seen as an abstract collectivity or imagined community whose members are loyal to the principle of the nation and its high culture, comes into being largely after the nation-state, whose institutions – including, notably, the educational system and the shared labour market – serve to homogenise the population culturally. Slowly, a majority is being mentally nationalised. However, Gellner adds, there are some groups which are so self-consciously distinctive that they come across as 'entropy-resistant'. The term entropy, taken from thermodynamics, refers to the ironing out of differences. Entropy-resistant groups, Gellner says, may have a different appearance, cultural and economic practices strikingly different from that of the majority, and/or a reflexive self-identity marking them off as different in ways that make them impossible to integrate. In his discussion of entropy-resistance, Gellner (1983: 64ff) points out that in prenational societies, cultural differences were in fact easily naturalised and endorsed; some people were held to be born rulers, while others were born serfs. In industrial societies, by contrast, difference becomes a problem, an obstacle to national cohesion and the egalitarianism presupposed, at least at the ideological level, by national sovereignty.

In the chapter of *Nations and Nationalism* titled 'The Future of Nationalism', Gellner discusses implications of international cultural homogenisation. While he recognises that people 'of a certain class' tend to speak the same language whichever language they speak, he also concedes that nations will, in the foreseeable future, remain culturally discrete, and if they fail to recognise their discreteness from others easily, they will invent national cultural traits in order to highlight their distinctiveness. Today, this is perhaps happening most visibly through the commercialisation of identity in tourism. Gellner also predicts that the intensity of nationalist conflicts, a product of the industrial revolution, will weaken in the future. This may be the case for Western and Central Europe (notwithstanding the rise of the new, populist right), but it is hard to see it happening elsewhere. Moreover, surprisingly and somewhat disturbingly, when Gellner speaks about the assimilation of immigrants and encapsulated diaspora nationalisms, he refers exclusively to historical examples. Here, he mentions language shift and successful participation in the national educational system as necessary conditions of assimilation; and in his discussion of diaspora nationalisms, he deals only with culturally stigmatised but economically successful groups like Parsis and Jews (a theme developed recently in a way consistent with, but ignorant of, Gellner's theory in Amy Chua's *World on Fire*, 2003).

The key terms to be extracted from Gellner's theory of nationalism in the present discussion are *culture, homogenisation* and *entropy-resistance*. In making his argument, Gellner implicitly assumes that identities, diasporic or not, tend to be coterminous with territories. This is a main problem when we try to address contemporary issues of identification and identity politics through his lens.

Cultural homogeneity versus social cohesion

One can have cultural similarity without social cohesion or a shared collective identity, and one can have a shared collective identity encompassing considerable cultural variation. The question is just how considerable. Gellner has little to offer on this issue; he does not problematise the concept of culture, and this is one of the reasons he was never very popular among anthropologists (see Hann 2003 for a sympathetic critique along these lines).

Three points may be made here, to add nuance to Gellner's crude conceptualisation of culture and identity.

- First: strong identities and fixed boundaries do not preclude cultural creolisation or mixing. Trinidadians of Indian origin have been strongly influenced by Anglophone, Afro-Trinidadian culture, but their ethnic identity and ethnic boundaries remain clearly delineated (Eriksen 1992). You can, in other words, have ethnic variation without cultural variation. Cultural mixing, creolisation or hybridity says nothing in itself about group identities and forms of boundedness.

- Second: fluid identities do not preclude cultural stability or continuity. For example, the ethnic or corporate identities of Caribbean peoples of African or mixed African-European origin are often extremely weak, yet the cultural similarities and continuities are strong. You can thus have cultural variation without ethnic variation.

  Both cultural variation and ethnic variation exist in non-random ways, but they refer to different aspects of social reality. Cultural similarity is associated with varying degrees of shared meaning, while ethnic identity is associated with clear (if disputed) group boundaries.

- Third: the widespread political manipulation of cultural symbols does not mean that the people in question do not have anything in common. (Being paranoid is no guarantee that nobody is after you.) Historiography, for example, tends to be selective and slanted in a nationalist way. Yet the stories related by historians within a nationalist epistemological framework may become self-fulfilling prophecies – they do give people a shared frame of reference – and moreover, the people in question may have other important cultural elements in common, such as language, which remain integrative notwithstanding the often dubious postulates by ideologues and historians about shared national identities. What have interested students of cultural hybridisation and creolisation are the situations where these frames of reference do not function; where they are contested, non-existent or being continuously rebuilt. It may just happen to be the case, in other words, that ethnic boundaries actually do coincide with certain cultural ones – but it cannot be taken for granted.

This entails that the ambiguous grey zones between categories and boundaries which are being challenged and contested can be privileged sites for studying the interplay between culture and identity. This is not because all boundaries will eventually disappear, but because they are made visible through their negotiation and renegotiation, transformations and reframing. What we need to look at in this respect are the *kinds* of boundaries that are being created, particularly in situations of change, and what they contain.

Many ambiguities surround notions of belonging and national identities in contemporary Western countries. With globalisation – increased travelling, intensification of trade and all forms of inter- and transnational exchanges – the cultural unity of the ethnic majorities is being questioned. With non-European immigration, which continues to grow, internal diversity is being enhanced in many, often uncontrollable, contested and poorly understood ways. Using the label 'diaspora' to describe immigrant minorities in contemporary European cities has long been inadequate: these groups include people in so different situations that a single term cannot cover the entire category – if it can be said to be a category at all. Steven Vertovec has recently (2005) proposed the term *super-diversity* to describe the current situation in the big European cities. The people adding to the cultural complexity of our cities include established minorities now into their third or fourth generation, recent refugees and asylum-seekers, illegal immigrants who either entered the country clandestinely or went underground after the expiration of their visa, prostitutes, beggars and drug dealers on tourist visas, students looking for ways to extend their stay, temporary or seasonal workers from Central Europe and elsewhere, highly skilled professionals on special quotas (from professors to football players), individuals who have married a citizen – and their children, the offspring of 'mixed marriages'; people who are 'here to stay' and people who are 'here to commute'; people with single, double and triple loyalties and people with none.

The state policies towards this motley conglomeration of persons seeping into the country tend to conform reasonably well to expectations that arise from Gellner's theory of nationalism. A key term in most West European countries is *integration*, and it bears a strong resemblance to Gellner's term *homogenisation*. The aim is to integrate immigrants through the school system and the labour market, to teach them the national language efficiently, preferably effecting a permanent language switch in the second or third generation, to discourage divided loyalties, and, recently, to attempt to depoliticise religion and to discourage transnational marriages (among immigrants, not in the majority).

All this could be predicted from Gellner's theory. However, the dynamics of ongoing social life point in other directions as well, and the direction is just as often away from homogenisation as it is towards it.

Inclusion and exclusion

The question of entropy-resistance is crucial in any test of Gellner's theory in the contemporary world. Which groups or categories of persons resident in a country are somehow being excluded, voluntarily or involuntarily, from the national unit?

Certain identities are marked, that is labelled *qua* identities, while others are not. Homosexuality is marked while heterosexuality is not. Criminals are marked while law-abiding citizens are not. The very poor and the very rich are marked to a greater extent than everybody else. And, naturally, ethnic, racial and religious minorities are marked. Indeed, the term 'identity' in everyday language increasingly refers to this kind of identity, not to gender, age, class or personal identity. In the football supporter culture of many countries, including Norway, anti-racism has become an institutionalised value. However, anti-sexism or anti-homophobia have not become part of the discourse. Race and ethnicity are visible in ways that other markers of difference are not.

Identities are, in other words, marked in different ways. Who the 'blue people' (Gellner 1983) are, those groups considered to be impossible to homogenise, changes historically. In the context of early twenty-first-century Europe, it seems clear that immigrants, and particularly Muslim immigrants, are considered, to varying degrees, to be entropy-resistant.

As a response to the perceived entropy-resistance, the European states have, to a much greater extent than the USA, resorted to ambitious integration programmes. The aim of these efforts is to help immigrants adapt to majority society through language acquisition and, in some cases, courses in culture and customs. In Amsterdam, there have been attempts to teach Somali women to ride a bicycle, while immigrants in Norway are taken on forest walks. Efforts are also made to facilitate the entry of immigrants into the labour market. All such measures fit with

Gellner's notion of national homogenisation, and seek to disprove claims about permanent entropy-resistance on the part of the immigrant groups, claims which are incidentally always seen as 'pessimistic' in the public and political discourses of European countries.

Regarding 'immigrant culture', concerns have been raised in many countries about marriage practices, though usually less in the political sphere than in general public debate. There have been allegations about incompatibility between arranged marriage and the individualist values on which Western societies are allegedly based, and it has been argued that marriage through family reunification slows integration down because it brings a continuous stream of new migrants into the country.

Interestingly, politicians and other public figures often praise the immigrants for 'enriching' the national culture. At the same time, they may worry about arranged marriages or Islam as impediments to national cohesion. This seeming contradiction indicates that cultural difference is not just one thing. Broadly speaking, we may state that *diversity* is seen as a good thing, while *difference* is not. A non-technical but potentially useful distinction could be made between 'shallow' and 'deep' cultural differences. The latter are the ones that mark a group or category of people as entropy-resistant, seen from the perspective of the state. The former are harmless and often enriching. As the late Robin Cook said in 2001, 'Chicken Tikka Massala is now a true British national dish' (quoted from Christensen and Hedetoft 2004: 8).

So far, I have claimed that European nation-states still favour cultural homogeneity, but accept and may even encourage certain forms of difference (diversity, that is) which are not seen as problematic in the context of 'national values'. Since the Rushdie affair (beginning in 1988), Islam has increasingly been perceived as a potential problem for democratic values, and many European Muslims have tried to show how their faith can be reconciled with the hegemonic values in their countries.

Among indigenous peoples, there has been a tendency to choose a certain degree of negentropy, through claims to exclusive land rights, language rights and so on. Among immigrants and their descendants, the right to equality has been more dominant than the right to differ, but all over Europe immigrant organisations also claim the right to be 'equal but different' (the slogan of a European anti-racist campaign in the late 1990s). The ongoing debates concern degrees and kinds of difference.

Negentropy can be chosen or imposed. What marks a group as negentropic also varies. In the early 1970s, substantial numbers of Pakistanis arrived in Norway, and were met by an expanding labour market and many job opportunities. Nobody complained about their language or religion then – if anything, the critics of immigration were left-wingers fearing unhealthy competition between immigrants and Norwegian workers. In the late 1990s, the right-wing populist party Fremskrittspartiet (the Progress Party) claimed that the reason for the high unemployment rates among some immigrant groups was their poor knowledge of Norwegian. However, it goes without saying that most non-white Norwegians today speak much better Norwegian than they or their parents did three decades ago.

Some time ago, an Oslo newspaper ran a story about a Pakistani-Norwegian who owned a flashy BMW car and who had been asked about his credentials by the traffic police ten times in the short period since he bought it. The newspaper had found seven ethnic Norwegians who owned almost identical cars, and only one of them had ever been interrogated by the police, after speeding. The Pakistani-Norwegian BMW owner, by profession a successful shopkeeper, might have been one hundred per cent integrated into Norwegian society at the level of culture – he may not even have been a Muslim believer – but at the level of ascribed identity, he remained as entropy-resistant as a black American under Jefferson.

This example merely says that things are more complicated than Gellner's theory of cultural homogenisation and entropy-resistance would suggest; it does not contradict it. All sorts of causes may lead to a group being disadvantaged in a nation-building context. Presently, race and religion are the most effective markers of exclusion in European countries, and objectively (or functionalistically) speaking, they are irrelevant. Nobody benefits. Unlike Gellner's favoured examples of elite diasporas, neither the minorities nor the majorities can be said to profit from the exclusion of minorities on the basis of criteria which bear no relation to their potential contribution to society. Take, as a final example in this section, the hijab debate, which ran across Western Europe and elsewhere in the first years of the new century. Some claimed that the Muslim headscarf was incompatible with secular values (in France), others claimed that it was oppressive to women (in Scandinavia) or at odds with 'common values' (the Netherlands). Some Muslims who had been indifferent to the headscarf began to take an intense interest in it. Some of their leaders said that it is the duty of a Muslim woman to cover herself, including her hair. To many Muslim girls and women, the result is a catch-22 – a double-bind situation. If they cover themselves up, they retain the respect and recognition of other Muslims, but are denounced as unwilling to integrate (voluntarily entropy-resistant) by the majority. If they choose not to cover their hair, they keep the respect and recognition of the majority, but lose their honour in the Muslim community.

This kind of situation, the intricacies of which were so well depicted in Orhan Pamuk's novel *Snow* (2004), has no relationship to culture in the Gellnerian sense, as Gellner was very much aware. It was, after all, he who said that being a Bosnian Muslim meant not that one believed that there was only one God and that Muhammad was his Prophet but that one had *lost* that belief. So Gellner was far from ignorant of the fact that cultural identity was created, often out of almost nothing – but he failed to apply that insight to the identity politics going on at the sub-national level.

Gellner's often cavalier treatment of cultural difference is, in this context, a minor point. A more serious objection concerns his tendency to emphasise functional, often economic, motivations for exclusion and inclusion. For as the recent and current politics of identity involving Muslim groups inside and outside of Europe on the one hand, and 'Western values' including American military force on the other, very clearly indicate, neither impediments to functional integration nor an economically competitive situation can account for the dynamics of inclusion and exclusion. Douglas Holmes (2000) has shown, in his *Integral Europe*, how the rise of the new, anti-immigrant populist right is linked to globalisation and the virtual disappearance of domestic working classes; but as regards the identity politics surrounding Islam, one would be hard pressed indeed to find a similar argument. No objective forces and no functionally relevant cultural differences seem to be at play here. I have argued earlier (Eriksen 2001), and repeat the argument here, that what is at stake in these identity movements is *recognition*. The key factors are, negatively, humiliation and, positively, respect. These are some of the main scarce resources in global identity politics today, and because of his robust, but inadequate concept of culture, Gellner failed to see this.

Beyond diaspora and territoriality

Entropy-resistant groups may, in a word, remain discrete – voluntarily or through external force – in spite of a high degree of cultural integration. Let us now move quickly to another huge question to be raised in relation to Gellner's theory of nationalism, namely that of territoriality. Gellner assumes, in all his writings about the topic, that cohesive cultural groups are territorial. He writes interestingly about diaspora populations in Central-Eastern Europe, for example. However, the time when the typical minority could be described either as indigenous or diasporic is long gone. The new migrations into Europe and elsewhere are trans-national in character, and to describe them as diasporic would be plainly misleading.

The term diaspora suggests a permanent state of emergency, an unfulfilled need for rootedness, insularity (entropy-resistance) in an alien context and severed links. Transnationalism, by contrast, suggests an active exploitation of opportunities, a dynamic and shifting identity, a creative and selective integration into the country of residence, and a continuous maintenance of links with the country of origin – or with transnationals of the same origin in other countries.

Now, transnationalism arguably has a greater appeal in contemporary intellectual life than diaspora: it suggests movement, freedom, flexibility, openness and global integration, while diaspora seems to suggest conservatism, cultural insularity and encapsulation. Quite clearly, if we choose to view immigrants as transnational persons instead of members of a diaspora, the normative evaluations of the outcomes of migration may shift from anxiety caused by imperfect integration to celebrations of the extent of social change effected by migration. The migrants will moreover be made to appear as cultural brokers rather than as second-class citizens and, given the acknowledged fluidity of social life, their varying degrees of integration into greater society need not be seen as a problem, but rather as part of the endless variation typical of complex, globally embedded societies.

This depiction of the transnational presupposes that the territorial logic of the nation-state is transcended. Nation-states can relate efficiently, if not always sensibly, to diasporas – minorities with a fixed abode and a clear-cut identity; minorities whose loyalties are perhaps still divided, but who can be won over. The state is much less comfortable when confronted with manifestly transnational groups, who may not be terribly interested in being 'integrated', and who care little about domestic politics, but who channel their economic surplus, their social capital and their political interests towards the country of origin – or who form part of a transnational or even global network of people with their origins in the same region, and whose main allegiances are towards that network.

The facts of transnationalism seem to explode the paradigm of nationalism and thereby to historicise Gellner's theory. Not all migrants are more transnational than they are diasporic; the point is that the territorial state consistently sees migration as the development of diasporas (and lacks a vocabulary for transnationalism), while migrants on the ground often see themselves as suspended in a both–and or neither–nor kind of situation regarding their territorial belonging. Like the dual character of light – it is made up of both waves and particles, but the two aspects cannot be seen simultaneously – migration and minority issues appear as radically different phenomena depending on the perspective chosen by the researcher. Now, although the transnationalist stance may be the more fashionable theoretical position, it is quite clear that a lot of current research on migration takes place within conceptual frameworks where notions of diaspora and integration are used. Partly this can be accounted for by the role of the state in commissioning research, but there are other reasons as well, to do with the traditional concepts used in social science, where 'society' and 'community' are privileged concepts and where 'movement' tends to be seen as an anomaly (cf. Urry 2001).

An evolutionary model popular in an earlier generation of migration researchers assumed that the minority moved from a diasporic situation – cohesive, bounded, longing for the homeland – through integration ('equal but different') to full assimilation. This was not to be. Instead, we are witness to a situation where transnationalism is replacing diasporas as the dominant mode of social organisation among migrants. The concerns, mentioned above, over South Asian immigrants who bring brides or grooms from the home village exemplify the continued dominance of a territorial model in European societies.

A telling example of new transnationalism could be the 'unmeltable ethnics' of the USA, who are not Scandinavian, Italian or Irish-Americans, but Spanish-speakers. Unlike in the nineteenth century, it is possible today to maintain a Spanish-speaking identity in a sea of Anglophones because the sea separating them from other Spanish speakers has shrunk. Even if they cannot necessarily travel physically, they are no longer cut off from communication with other Spanish-speakers in the USA and Latin America, no matter where in North America they find themselves.

For transnationalism does not, of course, just mean travelling back and forth. My Iranian friends in Oslo know everything about which films are screened in cinemas in Tehran and which ones are only available on the black market, even if they haven't been in Iran since the early 1980s. Moreover, developments in the country of origin influence the identity formation in the country of residence. In the early 1990s, the well-established and large community of Yugoslav immigrants and descendants in Sweden ceased to be Yugoslav: they began to identify themselves as Serbs, Croats and so on. Their pubs and restaurants were ethnicised, and their organisations split. And as a Norwegian-Pakistani long established in Norway says, back in the early 1980s, whenever he went to Lahore to visit his mother, he asked other Pakistanis in Oslo if they wanted him to bring a message for their relatives. About ten years later, when he asked the same question, they just laughed and held out their cell phones.

Fuglerud (1999) has shown that first-generation Tamils in Norway were strongly oriented towards Sri Lanka and had a modest interest in being integrated into Norwegian society. Tomba (2004), in a study of Chinese immigrants in Italy, quotes an informant who believes that Mandarin is more important for his everyday life than Italian. This is not because the Chinese community in Italy is very large (like Hispanics in the USA) or very compact (like Chinese in New York), but because of the economic and social importance of transnational connections with Chinese in other countries.

Seen from the territorial perspective of the nation-state, transnationalism is a threat to internal security because it entails divided loyalties. Seen from a more trans- or just international perspective, transnationalism mitigates and may prevent conflict precisely because it creates divided loyalties.

There is, in other words, a tension here – between diaspora and transnationalism. The former builds on ideas of multiculturalism, of bounded groups and cultures. The task of the state thereby becomes to ensure maximum loyalty and participation in the diaspora, perhaps with full assimilation as the ultimate goal. The latter entails a more fluid notion of sociality, with movement in networks and not society as a cohesive unit as the focus of research, where a main task becomes to identify flows through networks rather than gauging problems of integration.

John Urry has argued that '[c]orporeal mobility is … importantly part of the process by which members of a country believe they share some common identity bound up with the particular territory that the society occupies or lays claim to' (Urry 2001: 149). If this is true, then the increased corporeal mobility (as well as the huge increase in the traffic in signs) characteristic of the present age makes non-territorial forms of identity viable. This view, incidentally, conforms to the widespread view that contemporary information technology contributes to rendering old identities obsolete and new ones feasible.

Let me mention a few more examples of contemporary transnationalism, and its tense and conflictual relationship to the logic of the territorial state.

In Norway, concerns have been voiced over the tendency, not least among some of the most established immigrant communities such as the Pakistanis, to maintain close links, even after two generations, with the home village in the Punjab. They are 'here to commute', not 'here to stay', it has been said. This continuous contact, whereby not only are spouses brought from the home village, but children are sent there for months at a time, is believed to slow down the changes in values, language and family organisation supposedly necessary for a full integration into Norwegian society.

Seen from the perspective of transnationalism, this continuous contact can be seen as a strikingly efficient form of development aid. It enables people to transcend the insular and often unhappy existence of the diaspora and to achieve 'the best of both worlds', and it also contributes in no small measure to cultural changes in the original homeland. In villages in the Kharian area between Lahore and Islamabad, women can be seen carrying battered plastic bags from H&M as a sign of prestige, indicating a close link with Norway. A reasonable policy measure, if transnationalism were accepted, would entail setting up Norwegian schools in the Kharian area, to give the children a continuity in their education. This has been resisted by politicians so far – however, there are Norwegian schools for expatriate children scattered around the world, recently in southern Spain (which has become a haven not only for middle-class pensioners, but also for their support staff and a few others – thus the need for schools!).

Another obvious example, which shows the independence of trans-national connections from the state even more starkly, is the *hawala* system of economic transactions practised by overseas Somalis. As is well known, the money passes from person to person through this system until it finally reaches the recipient. It is efficient enough to be used by Somalis in many countries, and it is entirely based on interpersonal trust. After 9/11, some Somalis in Oslo were brought into custody by the police because it was suspected that they were funding terrorist organisations (foremost al-Qaeda). It was only during these investigations that the official Norway discovered the existence of the *hawala* system.

To the extent that migrants feel anchored in their country of residence, they often feel at home in a city. Vertovec (2005) remarks that as many as 300 languages are spoken in London today, suggesting that migration into the city is far more chaotic and multifarious than in the more orderly postwar decades, when most of the migrants came from the Commonwealth. Actually, in the borough of Holmlia in remote Oslo, more than a hundred languages are spoken. The city, as a focus of identity, has historically accommodated a variety of lifestyle options more easily than the state. Typically, the first sociologist of urbanity, Georg Simmel, emphasised the fleeting, flexible and liberating dimensions of urban life. However, this does not mean that city life precludes community and cultural conformity; only that it offers other options as well. One can live in and feel at home in a city without necessarily being or even wanting to be a citizen.

Add to this the issues of long-distance nationalism, addressed by Anderson (1992) in the aforementioned essay.

A focus on either diaspora or transnationalism leads to two different conceptions of the social, and to different formulations of the issues at hand. The state conceptualises its minorities as diasporas, as does much of the state-sponsored minority research, *as does Gellner*. There has been a great deal of attention to the varying forms of integration *within* states.

Time is now more than ripe to ask about the forms of integration that may take place *independently of* states. It has been argued that illegal migration is economically necessary for several of the most advanced economies, including the USA (Harris 2002); the *normative* question is if citizenship is the only source of salvation for the illegal migrants or if their current situation is better or worse than nothing. Some of the *research* questions to be asked ought to concentrate on coping strategies and ways of forging a sense of security, community and freedom independently of the state and territorial stability (see Malešević and Haugaard 2002 for some possible approaches).

Migration is an open-ended process. It simply never ends, and it represents a powerful counterdiscourse to that of the nation-state. My colleague Christian Krohn-Hansen, who was carrying out anthropological research in the Dominican Republic in the 1990s, realised after a few years that in order to complete his endeavour he would have to do some fieldwork in New York City. Only then could he tie up the loose ends and map out the social networks and cultural connections which were necessary to give a full account of both the Dominican village and the neighbourhoods on the Upper East Side. In this kind of world, the Gellnerian universe of clear-cut boundaries and state-led homogenisation processes is remote.

Some objections

All is not flow. It is a fact that non-European immigrants in Europe tend to form communities, both literally and metaphorically: they tend to live in the same parts of cities, and to interact more intensively with each other than with the host population. Many of them develop a strong sense of belonging to particular quarters or urban areas. Some would claim that this spatial concentration of immigrants is chiefly a result of exclusion and discrimination; possibly adding emerging identity politics among immigrants as a factor. However, it is also an obvious fact that people who share many of the same experiences and whose world-views overlap to a great extent tend to identify more closely with each other than with others. Norwegian Pakistanis, for example, share a cultural heritage, a mother-tongue, comparable childhood memories, food habits, a complex personal relationship to Islam and secularisation, customs and values. When they interact informally with each other, they do not play a zero-sum game, but confirm their selves in a backstage where they share taken-for-granteds that they do not, for the obvious reasons, share with the majority population. In our eagerness to deconstruct stereotypes and dubious generalisations about minorities, many of us have been too quick to neglect the internal cultural dynamics that contribute to maintaining group identities in complex multiethnic societies. Like language, the structures of relevance shared by individuals with similar experiences are supraindividual and exist not chiefly as the outcome of choice, but as the often unacknowledged conditions for choice. They must be read hermeneutically; they are not merely an aggregate outcome of intentional agency, but the complex institutional, symbolic and incorporated conditions for agency.

As pointed out years ago by Peter Worsley, one cannot simply exchange one's ethnic identity for another; life is not a self-service cafeteria (Worsley 1984). In addition, one cannot easily trade one's childhood experiences and personal network for others; one does not choose one's cultural universe. Culture is to some extent chosen and constructed, but it is also to a great extent implicit; it has an element of fate, or destiny. Similarly, reflexivity, mobility, creolisation at the level of lived culture and the bewildering and massive onslaught of signs do not seem to have dampened people's enthusiasm for anchoring their identities to places. If you only have two places, you belong to the diaspora of fixed abode more than to the world of transnationalism.

As some of the examples earlier in this chapter also suggested, both processes are taking place at the same time: a strengthening of boundaries *and* the evaporation of boundaries; strengthened community feeling and enhanced individualism; diasporic entrenchment, transnational flows and assimilation/conversion. But, and that is the main point here, the lofty dichotomy between homogenisation and entropy-resistance is totally inadequate as a tool for grasping the intricacies of cultural complexity in contemporary Europe.

Immigrants and their descendants in contemporary Europe are faced with four kinds of option. (i) They can opt for a diasporic identification, seeing themselves as living in a foreign country and having a clear idea of what and where their true country is. This creates, by necessity, a divided loyalty. (ii) They can decide to try to become assimilated, leaving the past behind as so many migrants to North America still do today. This option suggests a single loyalty. A Korean-American is American. (iii) The third possibility is transnationalism, where the state becomes less important and loyalty to any state is uncertain and situational. (iv) The final option is that of creole or individualist identification, where the migrant forges his or her own portfolio of cultural identities and mixes thereof, in critical dialogue with both hegemonic culture and ancestral culture. The two final options, I have suggested, are more widespread than the state would like us to believe, and may perfectly well satisfy both individual and collective needs for security and freedom.

Conclusions

Rereading Anderson and Gellner on nationalism, I tend to get the same feeling as I do when rereading Huxley's and Orwell's respective dystopian novels, *Brave New World* (Huxley 1932) and *1984* (Orwell 1949). While Huxley got almost everything right, Orwell seems stalled in the mid-twentieth century. His prophecy, reeking of coal fumes and the smell of boiled cabbage, has as much in common with the UK of the immediate postwar years as it has with Stalinism; while Huxley, writing a decade and a half earlier, predicted just about anything from package holidays in Spain to infotainment TV and Prozac. Yet, Orwell is the more interesting author to discuss (and disagree) with.

What, then, is left of Gellner's theory of nationalism? One can have mass communication creating a shared cultural identity and a high degree of homogeneity without industrialism – industrialisation is neither necessary nor sufficient as a condition for nationalism. One may have transnational identities, such as that of global Islam, which place strong demands on their adherents and have homogenising effects without being associated with a territory or a clear political project. And one can have reasonably well-functioning societies which are partly made up by communities with a minimal degree of integration into the majority culture, with a tenuous and weak relationship to the state, and which are yet able to offer a great deal of security and continuity to their members. One may even have societies where a large proportion of the population are transnational in their political identities, their social networks, their media consumption and their economic activities. And one can have societies where it is exactly the process of cultural homogenisation that leads to identity-based conflicts by creating tensions and experiences of humiliation. It is often the very fact that the different groups 'speak the same language' that makes conflict possible.

In this chapter, I have argued that Gellner's theory of nationalism draws on a limited and simplistic notion of culture, failing among other things to distinguish properly between culture and identity, and thereby assuming that cultural homogenisation leads to a shared identity. I have also argued that his treatment of entropy-resistance fails to take symbolic dominance into account, focusing too one-sidedly on economic and material factors. Finally, I have noted that in limiting himself to diaspora nationalisms and not considering transnationalism as a viable framework for stable identification, Gellner fails to address some of the most burning issues in today's world.

Yet, at the end of the day there remains a great deal of sociological common sense and original insight in Gellner's theory – in spite of its limitation to European history – which can be tapped in current research on the politics of culture and identity. His analysis of diasporic elites, where he predicts conflict between diasporas and nations when the latter have got their act together, has recently been confirmed in Amy Chua's influential book *World on Fire* (2003), which shows how elite minorities are being victimised as a result of democratisation. His emphasis on communication as a necessary condition for a shared identity remains as relevant as ever, not least in research on transnational networks and the implications of the new media for identity formation. His analyses of institutional differentiation and cultural entropy are good, Weberian sociology which can still offer a starting framework for detailed empirical research. Finally, the problems of identity currently experienced by the nation-state, some of which have been identified here, confirm Gellner's most controversial claim, namely that the nation-state is a product of particular historical circumstances; it has arisen, flourished, and eventually will go away. The human need for belonging and security may be constant, but it has to be realised under very differing circumstances.

References

Anderson, B. 1991/1983. *Imagined Communities: Reflections on the Origins and Spread of Nationalism*. 2nd edn, London: Verso.

1992. *Long Distance Nationalism: World Capitalism and the Rise of Identity Politics*. Amsterdam: Centre for Asian Studies.

Christiansen, F. and Hedetoft, U. 2004. Introduction. In F. Christiansen and U. Hedetoft (eds.), *The Politics of Multiple Belonging: Ethnicity and Nationalism in Europe and East Asia*. Aldershot: Ashgate, pp. 1–23.

Chua, A. 2003. *World on Fire: How Exporting Free Market Democracy Breeds Ethnic Hatred and Global Instability*. London: Arrow.

Eriksen, T. H. 1992. *Us and Them in Modern Societies: Ethnicity and Nationalism in Trinidad, Mauritius and Beyond*. Oslo: Scandinavian University Press.

2001. *Bak fiendebildet: Politisk islam og verden etter 11. september* (Behind the Enemy Image: Political Islam and the World after 9–11). Oslo: Cappelen.

Fuglerud, Ø. 1999. *Life on the Outside: The Tamil Diaspora and Long-Distance Nationalism*. London: Pluto.

Gellner, E. 1964. *Thought and Change*. London: Weidenfeld and Nicolson.

1983. *Nations and Nationalism*. Oxford: Blackwell.

1992. *Postmodernism, Reason and Religion*. London: Routledge.

1994. The Mightier Pen: The Double Standards of Inside-out Colonialism. In Gellner, *Encounters with Nationalism*. Oxford: Blackwell, pp. 159–69.

1995. 'The Coming *Fin de Millénaire*'. In Gellner, *Anthropology and Politics: Revolutions in the Sacred Grove*. Oxford: Blackwell, pp. 241–52.

1997. *Nationalism*. London: Weidenfeld and Nicolson.

Goodhart, D. 2004. Too Diverse? *Prospect* 95: 30–7.

Hann, C. 2003. Civil Society: The Sickness, Not the Cure? *Social Evolution and History* 2 (2): 55–74.

Harris, N. 2002. *Thinking the Unthinkable: The Immigrant Myth Exposed.* London: I. B. Tauris.

Holmes, D. 2000. *Integral Europe: Fast-Capitalism, Multiculturalism, Neo-fascism.* Oxford: Princeton University Press.

Huxley, A. 2004/1932. *Brave New World.* London: Vintage.

Malešević, S. and Haugaard, M. (eds.) 2002. *Making Sense of Collectivity: Ethnicity, Nationalism and Globalization.* London: Pluto.

Orwell, G. 1990/1949. *1984.* Harmondsworth: Penguin.

Pamuk, O. 2004. *Snow.* London: Faber and Faber.

Parekh, B. et al. 2000. *The Future of Multi-ethnic Britain* (The Parekh Report). London: Profile.

Said, E. 1993. *Culture and Imperialism.* London: Chatto and Windus.

Tomba, L. 2004. Looking Away from the Black Box: Economy and Organization in the Making of a Chinese Identity in Italy. In F. Christiansen and U. Hedetoft (eds.), *The Politics of Multiple Belonging: Ethnicity and Nationalism in Europe and East Asia.* Aldershot: Ashgate, pp. 93–109.

Urry, J. 2001. *Sociology beyond Societies.* London: Routledge.

Vertovec, S. 2005. Super-diversity. Talk given at the 'Cultural complexity' seminar, University of Oslo, 13 June 2005.

Worsley, P. 1984. *The Three Worlds.* London: Weidenfeld and Nicolson.

Part III

Islam, postmodernism and Gellner's metaphysic

Michael Lessnoff

Gellner on modernity and Islam

Ernest Gellner's definition of modernity stressed two elements: a mode of cognition (science) and a mode of production (industrialism). He stressed also that industrial-scientific society needs (and has) a uniform and universal literate culture, whereas premodern ('agro-literate') societies were divided between a literate 'high' culture and one or several illiterate 'folk' cultures (Gellner 1990: 16–21, 62–7; 1998: 21). Muslim civilisation, accordingly, was divided between 'high' and 'folk' Islam, the former being the central, orthodox tradition (Gellner 1992: 9–12). Adapting Christian terminology, Gellner dubbed it (generically) 'protestant', in contrast to 'folk' Islam. There was significant conflict between the two versions, although, unlike the Christian case, no formal break occurred (Gellner 1981: 4–5).

What did Gellner mean by calling high Islam (generically) protestant? First, it is strongly oriented to holy texts, valuing learning based on these. It is sober and puritanical, averse to 'hysteria and excess, and to the excessive use of the audio-visual aids of religion'. It is orderly and rule-observing. Above all, it stresses the 'severely monotheistic ... nature of Islam', discountenancing saintly and other mediators between man and God. It is thus spiritually egalitarian (like Luther's 'priesthood of all believers'). It is a religion for a literate urban stratum of merchants, scholars and others (Gellner 1992: 11).

Folk Islam, being the religion of illiterate masses, inevitably focuses (focused) much less on texts and textual scholarship. Instead it focuses on holy persons – Sufi saints and mystics – and on rites and festivals associated with them. It is joyous and ecstatic, often to excess. It indulges in 'music, dance, intoxication, trance ... possession'. 'Its ethic is one of loyalty [to special holy individuals]', not rule-observance (Gellner 1981: 48).

On this analysis Gellner erected a diagnosis of the relation between Islam and modernity which, in my judgement, is partly correct and partly very wrong. Compared to other traditional non-Western cultures,

Islam, Gellner believed, is uniquely well placed to modernise without 'Westernising' or denying its own central tradition. The confrontation with modernity has enormously strengthened 'high' Islam at the expense of 'folk' Islam, partly because the social structures that made the latter appropriate for rural tribesmen have undergone great changes, but also, importantly, because it was possible, in a new version of an old theme, to *blame* the folk version for Islam's decline vis-à-vis the West – to blame its suspect, heterodox practices as '*shirk*' or idolatry: a debilitating corruption of the pure faith (Gellner 1992: 13–15, 21; 1981: 4–5, 156, 161).

So far, I believe, Gellner is correct. In modern times the Sufi-influenced mystical-ecstatic version of Islam is everywhere under attack, excoriated, interestingly, by fundamentalists and purists and by would-be modernisers alike. But Gellner also argued that high Islam offers an appropriate Muslim response to the modern world, precisely because of its 'protestant' nature – its egalitarianism, sobriety, respect for script-based learning, hostility to emotionalism, mysticism and magic, etc. – which match the functional requirements of modern society (Gellner 1992: 17, 19–21; 1981: 5, 58, 61, 65, 171).

The second part of Gellner's diagnosis, clearly influenced by Weber's 'Protestant ethic' thesis, seems to me profoundly wrong. (It is also very different from Weber's analysis of Islam: Weber 1965/66: 86–8, 262–6). Clearly Gellner has in mind one aspect of modern society – the industrial economy. I have argued elsewhere that the parallel Gellner suggests, between Weber's 'ascetic Protestantism' and 'generically protestant' high Islam, is not specific enough to make his case (Lessnoff 2002: 80–1). More importantly, Gellner seems to focus on a single element of modernity as he defines it, to the exclusion of another – science, the scientific mode of cognition. I shall argue that when due weight is given to science and its social and cultural implications, Gellner's diagnosis appears shaky in the extreme.

Also, Gellner's way of dichotomising Islam is itself misleading. Islamic high culture was far from being just the 'generically protestant' orthodoxy he identifies. This orthodoxy did (and does) exist, and is important: but we should not identify its heterodox, un-protestant rival with 'folk' Islam. Folk Islam was (I think) indeed overwhelmingly of the non-protestant variety Gellner describes: but the converse is not true. Non-protestant Islam (Sufism, in a word) was not predominantly a folk religion: it was pervasive at all levels, including the urban elites. The tension between the two brands of Islam was likewise pervasive throughout Islamic history. (In fairness to Gellner, it is clear from various asides that he was aware of this (for example, Gellner 1992: 12) – but these asides play no real role in his analysis).

We can now turn to our main business: to examine the two styles in their relation to one aspect of modernity, science. I shall argue that the orthodox, 'protestant' style – the Islam of the ulema, the scholar-jurists – has absolutely no affinity with the scientific spirit and its intellectual preconditions; while the Sufi mystic style, however 'un-modern' it may be, was for centuries a nurturer of science – of a science whose important achievements, in its medieval heyday, made Islamic civilisation the world leader in such disciplines as optics, astronomy, mathematics and medicine.

(A brief 'health warning': as Gellner knew, his dichotomy, used here in a modified way, simplifies the reality. Each side – the learned legalistic orthodoxy of the ulema and the mystical heterodoxy of the Sufis – contains a range of positions. At their moderate ends the two could accommodate each other. Ulema could be Sufis, in some cases; and the great orthodox theologian al-Ghazzali, famous as the scourge of Greek-influenced philosophy, equally famously embraced Sufism. Nevertheless the tension between the two was a recurrent and important feature of Muslim civilisation. The more extravagant forms of Sufism were unacceptable to the orthodox, and to the ultra-orthodox all forms of Sufism were and are anathema. The dichotomy, though a simplification, is justifiable and serviceable).

The ulema, the class of accredited scholar-jurists, were absolutely central to Islamic society. The law of which they were exponents and guardians – almost the entire law of Islamic society – was the Sharia. But as Gellner (1981: 42) noted, the ulema were theologians as well as jurists – no hard-and-fast line can be drawn between jurisprudence (*fiqh*) and theology (*kalam*). Both must be considered in delineating Islamic orthodoxy.

Islamic rationalism

I shall begin by discussing a school (*madhhab*) of theologians, the Mutazilites – not because they were orthodox, but because, after an early period of influence and even ascendancy, orthodoxy decisively and definitively repudiated them. The Mutazilites were rationalist theologians, much influenced by Greek philosophy, who flourished (more or less, off and on) from about the eighth to the eleventh century CE. They were, inter alia, moral rationalists, believing in objective standards of right, discoverable by reason. God's decrees are just because they conform to this rational standard (contrary to the 'voluntarist' view that God wills as he pleases, thereby making what he decrees right or just). In general they considered the world to be rationally comprehensible, allowing only a limited role to the miraculous. Revelation, though necessary, can never conflict with reason – any apparent contradiction must be resolved by an appropriate, non-literal interpretation of the revealed text (for example, passages in the Quran that appear to attribute bodily attributes such as hands to God must be understood metaphorically) (Martin and Woodward 1997: 1–18; EOI 1993: 783–4, 789–92).

The Mutazilites' rationalism makes them attractive to modern commentators, but they had an Achilles heel – they were out-and-out elitists. They considered it inappropriate, indeed dangerous, for theological issues to be discussed by the masses. The masses wholeheartedly reciprocated their distrust. Their influence, therefore, depended largely on the support of rulers. Most famously, the Caliph Ma'mun (813–33 CE) attempted to enforce acceptance by his judges, officials and others of a controversial Mutazilite doctrine regarding the Quran – that it was created (not uncreated, eternal) – a policy known in Muslim history as the *mihna* (inquisition), which continued under Ma'mun's successors until 849. Some who refused to conform were executed, others imprisoned, the most celebrated being Ibn Hanbal; Hanbal's resistance to successive caliphs made him a popular hero, whose treatment provoked riots. Eventually the Caliph Mutawakkil released him from prison and reversed Ma'mun's policies (Fakhry 1983: 62–4; Watt 1963: 101–3). The followers of the triumphant though now aged Hanbal later established what would become the most obscurantist of the four 'orthodox' schools of law. The Mutazilites found support again from the Buyid sultans, the effective rulers of the Abbasid Empire in the late tenth and early eleventh centuries; but the overthrow of the Buyids by the Seljuk Turks was effectively the end for Mutazilite rationalism within Sunni Islam. Their doctrines were anathematised by the now dominant theological schools (EOI 1960: 696), most importantly the Asharites, followers of al-Ashari. So matters remained until recent times (EOI 1960: 694–6; 1993: 789; 2000: 27; Fakhry 1983: 204–8, 212).

Islamic orthodoxy

As the dominant theological school of orthodox Sunni Islam from the eleventh century, the Asharites deserve attention. Their theology has interesting similarities to Calvinism (no doubt one reason why Gellner dubbed the Islamic mainstream 'protestant'). Like Calvin, they stress the absolute sovereignty of God and corresponding powerlessness of men. God's creation of the world was an act of absolute freedom, and the world depends on God at every moment for its existence and behaviour. 'Nature' in itself has no power, causal or other. God decrees what he wills

and this is the definition of 'right' and 'just'. Injustice is disobedience.
Like Calvin, Ashari denied human freedom and upheld predestination,
but denounced disobedience as sinful. The Asharites reject metaphorical
interpretation of the Quran: texts like those referring to corporeal attributes of God must be taken literally, although incomprehensible to
human reason. They must simply be accepted (Fakhry 1983: 204).
Although the Asharites did not totally reject reason (unlike some rival
schools), they accorded it a strictly subordinate role. Ashari had himself
been a Mutazilite; at the age of forty however (in 912 CE) he publicly
recanted his earlier 'scandals and follies' (Fakhry 1983: 206–7). Thereafter, as one commentator puts it, he used Mutazilite methods to defend
Hanbalite positions (Watt 1963: 58–9, 65–7, 115).

Something similar applies to the greatest Asharite theologian, Ghazzali
(1058–1111) who, somewhat later, set himself to destroy the other main
manifestation of rationalism in Islam: the Greek-influenced philosophy
(*falsafa*) whose leading exponents included al-Farabi and, above all,
Avicenna (Ibn Sina). Such philosophy was always viewed with disfavour
by the orthodox as a 'foreign science'. Ghazzali (from 1091 to 1095 the
head of the Nizamiyah, a theological school established by the Seljuk
vizier Nizam al-Mulk) took *falsafa* more seriously. He made himself
expert in its arguments and Greek sources, in order to destroy his
enemies by their own methods. He used Aristotle's logic, but ferociously
attacked the metaphysics accepted by Aristotle's Muslim followers (Watt
1963: 115). In his famous polemic *The Incoherence of the Philosophers*
(*Tahafut al-Falasifah*), twenty doctrines are picked out for refutation:
seventeen as heresy, three as so seriously faulty that their holders must be
characterised as infidels, non-Muslims (whom, Ghazzali remarks elsewhere, it is no crime to kill) (Schacht 1974: 392). Among these is
Aristotle's doctrine of the eternity of the world, deemed to contradict the
dogma of divine creation.

By common consent Ghazzali succeeded in discrediting Greek-
inspired philosophy within Islam, at least in the Muslim heartlands. In
the Islamic West, the famous Aristotelian Ibn Rushd (Averroes) coun-
terattacked Ghazzali with his 'Incoherence of the Incoherence'; but
(what Westerners often fail to realise) Averroes had very little influence
on Muslim thought – far less than he was to have in Christian Europe,
through Aquinas and the Latin Averroists.

Philosophy and theology have their importance, but more important
for present purposes is Islamic law, 'the core and kernel of Islam'
according to one authority (Inalcik 1973: 63). That law is based on
principles utterly different from those familiar in the West, where legis-
lation is a function of government, often the responsibility of a designated

legislature, in latter times popularly elected. By contrast, Islamic law (Sharia) was formulated by learned and pious jurists, the ulema, interpreters of a divine law which the government of caliph or sultan was (in theory) required to enforce. But the ulema played a major part in enforcement also, in the role of judge, or *kadi*, who had complete freedom to judge and punish as he saw fit. Members of the ulema class also filled administrative positions, often including that of vizier. In Ottoman Turkey, ulema endorsement was formally required to legitimate a sultan's accession, and could equally justify rebellion and deposition. (One example is the overthrow of Sultan Ibrahim in 1648, on the grounds that he had violated holy law, among other misdeeds) (Watt 1998: 257–61; Calder 1996: 980).

What was the nature of the law formulated by this potent class of jurists? An important point is that it took shape early, and remained essentially unchanged until the nineteenth century, when it was to a degree disrupted by contact with the West. A central element is the concept of *usul al-fiqh*, the 'roots' or 'sources' of law. First among these is the Quran. But ever since the prescriptions laid down by the jurist al-Shafi (d. 820 CE) equal status has been accorded to the Sunna, understood as the practice and opinions of the Prophet Muhammad. Shafi decreed that, to be accepted in the Sunna, a rule must qualify as a tradition (*hadith*) with an accredited chain of descent from one authority to another, back to Mohammed's lifetime (*isnad*). In quantitative terms the Sunna soon enormously outweighed the Quran as a source – in the ninth century the hadiths or traditions that make it up were collected in six books accepted as 'canonical'. One authority has defined Islamic law as revelation understood through tradition (Schacht 1974: 394–5).

The central role of tradition is of the first importance. It is a feature of 'high Islam' far from 'protestant' in character (it is more like Roman Catholicism). It has also made Islamic jurisprudence extremely conservative. Although theoretically derived from Muhammad, in practice the Sunni hadiths usually reflected social norms of the time and place of their formulation. Thus was created a fateful blending of the sacred and the traditional. In effect, norms of ninth-century societies were sacralised and given an eternal and final status (Watt 1998: 294; Adams 1933: 133).

That Islamic law was not totally inflexible is perhaps due to the fact that, although the Quran and the Sunna had primacy, they were not the only recognised 'roots'. Two others were *ijma* (consensus of the community, as understood by the scholar-jurists) and *qiyas* (analogy), which could be used somewhat creatively to extend ancient principles to new situations. However, there was no general agreement on the status of these 'roots'. After the seminal writings of Shafi Islamic jurisprudence crystallised into four orthodox schools – if one adds Shia Islam there were five schools. Of the orthodox (Sunni) schools, one was the Hanbalite; the others are the Shafite (followers of Shafi), the Malikite (followers of Malik ibn-Anas), and the Hanafite (after Abu Hanifa, who died in 767 CE, before the time of Shafi). This multiplicity of equally authoritative schools, which were also the de facto legislators, is strange to Western eyes, for the schools were obviously liable to disagree. They disagreed on the relative status and acceptability of the four 'roots' of law. Two, the Shafite and the Hanafite, are described as relatively liberal, the Malikite and the Hanbalite being highly conservative – they are known as Traditionists because of the heavy emphasis they place on the hadiths at the expense of consensus and analogy. Most conservative are the Hanbalites, followers of Ahmad ibn-Hanbal (780–855 CE), who restricted the sources of law to the Quran and Sunna, dismissed reasoning by analogy and indeed all independent reasoning as heretical, and upheld *taqlid*, unquestioning obedience to authority (not only religious authority but – ironically in view of his own life-story – secular also) (EOI 1971b: 1026).

The position of the Hanbalites is important. They are, relatively speaking, extremists, but also recognised as orthodox – as much as the other three schools. In Islamic history the spokesmen for extreme rigorism have often been Hanbalites or neo-Hanbalites: two examples – important because of their considerable influence – are Ibn Taymiyah (1263–1328 CE) and his eighteenth-century follower Abd al-Wahhab, founder of Wahhabism, still potent today. Even the more moderate mainstream was liberal in only a very relative sense. It was Shafi, for example, whose teachings brought about, from around 900 CE, the notorious 'closing of the door of *ijtihad*' – of independent reasoning, which up till then was freely practised in interpreting the law. This 'closing' meant that, in the jurists' view, all controversies on major issues were now settled, for all time. All four schools became traditionalists if not Traditionists, preservers, primarily, of their founders' doctrines. The principle of *taqlid* came to loom large. The ulema became *muqallids*, a term translated as 'imitators' (though 'followers' or 'disciples' might be better) (EOI 1986: 1123, 1129–34; EOI 1960: 816–17).

Not surprisingly, the ulema were intimately involved in education. They controlled the institutions of higher education – the madrasas – whose principal function was to train the next generation of ulema. Usually, a madrasa was controlled by one of the juristic schools. The madrasas grew out of the mosque schools, and were located close to mosques. (The institutions of elementary education, the *maktabs*, which taught and teach reading and writing, also developed from, and within, the mosques, and put a heavy emphasis on religion).

The curriculum and teaching methods of the madrasa followed from their function. The main curriculum consisted of the Quran, the hadiths, *fiqh* (jurisprudence), theology, and some philological and linguistic science. Other disciplines, if taught, were so only for the sake of these 'primary' sciences. Despite the great achievements of Muslim scientists, the physical sciences had a very subordinate role. For example, astronomy (at least in the Sunni madrasas) was studied, if at all, for information related to religious needs such as the time of prayer. For this, apparently, Ptolemaic astronomy was considered adequate, and is taught (in Shia and Sunni madrasas) even to the present day (de Santillana 1968: xi).

The madrasas were not collegial institutions like Western universities – rather, they were locations where individual scholars taught their own students. Nor had they any concept of research, whether scientific or in the broader sense of extending knowledge. The aim was transmission of received wisdom. Lecturing took the form of dictation to students, whose prime task was to memorise texts, so as to be able to repeat them. Obviously the Quran and hadiths were memorised; otherwise it seems that, latterly at least, it was manuals, commentaries and glosses that were intensively studied and learned by heart. There was no examination at the end; simply, the teacher certified a student as adequately proficient, and awarded him the *ijaza*, or licence to teach. Holders of the *ijaza* were qualified also to act as lawyers, judges, preachers, leaders of public prayers, and so on.

Attempts in modern times to challenge this system have encountered fierce resistance. A notable example is the sustained but ultimately unsuccessful effort of Mohammed Abduh to reform Al-Azhar in Cairo, the premier Islamic institution of higher learning, at the end of the nineteenth century (for Abduh this was to be the first step in a wholesale modernisation of Islam). At first Abduh, with the Khedive's support, made some progress, but when that support was withdrawn his project foundered, and in 1905 he resigned from Al-Azhar in despair (Adams 1933: 27–30, 70–8).

The moral of all this is, I think, obvious: the mind-set of orthodox Islam could hardly be more alien to that 'cognitive growth' which, according to Gellner, characterises modernity. Could anything be further from Popper's 'critical rationalism'? Gellner himself refers to Islam's 'proscription of innovation' (stemming from the dogma that Muhammad is 'the seal of the prophets') and to the pervasive Islamic view that Mohammed's revelation provides a 'blueprint, [a] scheme to be implemented [such that] no new schemes are to be countenanced' (Gellner

1981: 2, 24). The puzzle is that he apparently gave no weight to these features in assessing orthodox Islam's affinity with modernity.

Islamic mysticism

Let us now turn to what Gellner called 'non-protestant' Islam – Sufism, or Islamic mysticism (*tasawwuf*). Sufism is both theory and practice, or rather a range of practices: to adapt Gellner's terminology, there is a 'high' Sufism and a 'folk' Sufism. The theory, of course, belongs to 'high' Sufism. Its leading principle is ontological monism, or unity of being (*wadat al-wujud*). God is not separate from his creation. As it is sometimes put, only God exists (EOI 2000: 313–15; Homerin 1999: 228; Nasr 1976: 13), for everything is God. Ibn Arabi (1165–1240 CE), probably Sufism's greatest and most influential theorist, expresses these ideas in a form owing much to neo-Platonism: the created world existed originally in the mind of God as a series of eternal archetypes, that were bodied forth in the act of creation. The prophet Mohammed finds his place in this scheme less as a historical person than as such an archetype, the 'perfect man', and fullest manifestation of God (Fakhry 1983: 252–4).

We can gauge the influence of neo-Platonism on Ibn Arabi by comparing him with the neo-Platonist Plotinus. In Plotinus' system, all existence arises from a single principle, the One. From the One emanate further stages of being, in which, however, the One always remains present – it might be said to unfold itself in these further stages. The first emanation is the World-Spirit (*Nous*), the sphere of ideal forms or archetypes; the second is the World-Soul (*Logos* of the World-Spirit); the last is the multiplicity of things that make up Nature (*Physis*), constituted by a combination of matter with the *Logoi*. For Plotinus Nature is not separate from the One, but is infused by it via interposed orders of being; for Ibn Arabi likewise the natural world is not separate from God, but infused with him via an intermediate level of existence (Dijksterhuis 1961: 46–7).

As well as a theory of being, Sufism is also a doctrine of salvation, known as the Path. The two are closely linked, for salvation is achieved through *gnosis* – knowledge of an esoteric, mystical kind (*irfan*). The goal of the Path is to know God, and thereby achieve mystic union with the divine (EOI 2000: 314–15; 1971a: 101; Bowering 1999: 45). This might seem to contradict the fundamental Sufi doctrine of monism, which suggests that man is of necessity in union with God – rendering the Sufi Path superfluous. I shall return to this. For now, however, let us note that in the Sufi view the Path reverses the order of creation. As a sympathetic commentator expresses it, there is one Supreme Being from whom all creation derives and to which all creation yearns to return (Gibb 1993: xvi). The Sufi is concerned with return by the human creature, in which the necessary first step is *tawba*, a radical moment of conversion and repentance. The necessary knowledge is not achieved by ordinary intellectual means but requires moral purification. It is more vision than conceptual knowledge – a vision of God, which involves a total submission of the human to the divine will, to the point of self-extinction: the Sufi adept no longer has a separate existence (Nasr 1995: 290; 1968: 23). As the Persian mystical thinker Mulla Sadra (1571–1640 CE) put it, the soul's journey is first to God, then in God, then with God. Sometimes this is referred to as self-annihilation (the Indian influence seems obvious); sometimes, less sympathetically, as self-deification. The famous Sufi al-Hallaj (857–922 CE) claimed to have achieved the 'essence of union', in which all the mystic's thoughts and actions are permeated by God (Fakhry 1983: 245).

How is the Path to be consummated? The answer provides the link between 'high' and 'folk' Sufism, and introduces another key element of Sufism – its hermeneutics of symbolism. It also shows why Gellner described 'folk' Islam as non-protestant and certainly non-puritan, even though many Sufis have used extreme, rigorous asceticism as a technique of salvation. Other techniques are more typical, especially at the 'folk' level; most characteristically those for achieving mystical ecstasy (*wajd*), presumably conducive to a vision of the truth. Many are hardly orthodox from a strict Islamic point of view. They include special postures and breathing techniques, rhythmic chanting, music and dancing (Gellner's 'audio-visual aids of religion'), even indulgence in carnal love and wine-induced intoxication (Gibb 1993: xvi). It is not hard to see how these can induce an ecstatic state, and also – in the case of carnal love, for example – can be given a symbolic interpretation, as figuring the reciprocal love of God and the believer. Indeed, according to one Western commentator, a consequence of Sufism was that Muslims came to inhabit a world of symbols (Gibb 1993: xvi; cf. Nasr 1968: 24). Ontological monism then means that nature is a series of symbols of the divine.

How did Sufism become not just an intellectual but a very potent social force, at both 'high' and 'folk' level? First, through the Sufi brotherhoods and 'dervish' orders (*tariqats*), who devote themselves to the Path under the guidance of a leader called, for example, a *shaykh* or *pir*. Other individuals, not members of these orders, are attached to them as followers and much influenced by them. The *shaykh* or *pir*, is not an ordinary person, but possesses a special sacred charisma. Typically he claims descent from Muhammad; he also claims, and is accorded by his followers, the exalted status of a *wali*, or 'friend of God'. Many, it seems, see him as quasi-divine. Routinely, he is believed to have magical powers, including that of intercession with the Deity (EOI 2000: 315; Bowering 1999: 53; Homerin 1999: 239–40; Buehler 1999: 468; Babayan 1996; Adams 1933: 161–2). Sufism, in theory and in practice, denies the spiritual egalitarianism that for Gellner characterises 'generic Protestantism': leading Sufis combine within Islam the functions of priesthood and sainthood in the Roman Catholic Church. Their tombs often become objects of pilgrimage, with shrines attached, where rituals such as circumambulation are performed, from which the believer expects spiritual benefit (EOI 2000: 316; Gaborieau 1999: 459–60). (In North Africa, Gellner directly studied a variation on this theme – the marabouts, hereditary saints who belong to saintly lineages: Filali 1999; Gellner 1969). We should not suppose, as Gellner seems to have done, that such manifestations were purely or even predominantly 'folk' religiosity. Sufism and its institutions were often patronised by the highest social levels.

Sufism has been for many centuries a pervasive force, but that does not mean it is or was generally accepted. Many features of Sufism are obviously highly suspect to Islamic orthodoxy. As mentioned, some accommodation between the two wings is possible, at their less extreme ends – each may tolerate, and even concede a positive value to, the other. One expression of this, expounded and endorsed by the Muslim scholar Seyyed Hossein Nasr, is a popular image which likens Islam to a circle: its centre is Truth (or God), its circumference is the Law, and the Sufi Path is (like) a radius leading from the circumference to the centre (Nasr 1968: 28). It will be noticed that the place here given to the law, and by implication the ulema, is far from central. Truth is reached only by following the Path. Nasr's approval of the image accords with his own evident Sufi sympathies and also with more moderate or philosophically inclined Sufism such as Ibn Arabi's: exoteric, explicit knowledge (such as the ulema have), and rational argumentation, are necessary but not sufficient – and inferior to the direct, visionary, esoteric, gnostic knowledge achievable by the Path.

Not all upholders of Muslim orthodoxy were or are happy to relegate the holy law to this subordinate role; moreover, many other aspects of Sufism irked them, not least the exalted spiritual status prominent Sufis were wont to claim for themselves. Al-Hallaj, the famous ninth/tenth-century mystic, famously asserted 'I am the Truth' ('Ana al-haqq'), which to Muslims equates to 'I am God' – a perfectly logical claim for one who has followed the Path to its culmination. However Hallaj, despite or because of his large popular following, was tried and executed for making it, thus becoming a saint and martyr to many Muslims (EOI 1960: 100–1). Another early Sufi, al-Bastami (d. 875 CE) is credited with the claim

'I am Thou' (again 'I am God') (Fakhry 1983: 244). A feature of Sufism that again offends the orthodox is the superior importance accorded to the state of the believer's soul, over obedience to the law and performance of exoteric ritual, even such a fundamental one as the pilgrimage to Mecca – Hallaj elevated the 'Ka'ba of one's heart' above the literal, material Ka'ba at Mecca. (Here, arguably, the Sufis are more 'protestant' than the orthodox.) One justification given for Hallaj's execution was his alleged claim that he had authority to release pious Muslims from ritual duties of the Sharia (Fakhry 1983: 246). Equally deplorable, to the orthodox, is the Sufi manner of interpreting the Quran, in esoteric, symbolic terms – understandably, because this threatens to deprive the words of objective meaning, making them say whatever the interpreter wants. As bad or worse is the claim some Sufis have made to receive revelations direct from God, giving their views a status equal to the Quran and the Prophet himself. The reverence accorded to Sufi saints, manifested in pilgrimages to their tombs, etc., is denounced by the orthodox as idolatrous worship of human beings (Gaborieau 1999: 452–3, 459–63).

Persecution of Sufism, therefore, has recurred throughout Islamic history – Sufis have been (I quote) denounced, exiled, imprisoned, tortured, executed and confined in lunatic asylums, by their orthodox enemies (Bowering 1999: 54). In Ottoman Turkey in the sixteenth century, for example, the leaders of a number of Sufi orders were executed following a *fetwa* (fatwa) pronounced by the *seyhulislam* (official head of the Ottoman ulema) (Inalcik 1973: 192; Ocak 1999: 607–8). A more recent example is the murder in 1994 of the moderate Kashmiri cleric Nisar Ahmed by fundamentalists, almost certainly because of his friendly relations with Hindus (de Jong and Radtke 1999: 1–2). One of the most instructive cases, perhaps, is Safavid Iran. Iran has for some centuries been the main homeland of Shia Islam – a form which, to many orthodox Sunni, seems to share some heretical features of Sufism, such as quasi-worship of a human being (the Imam, credited with powers of intercession and unique access to divine truth), and the attribution of esoteric meanings to the Quran. Furthermore, the Safavid dynasty (1502–1720) originated, unusually, from a Sufi brotherhood. Nevertheless tension soon developed between the Iranian Sufis and the Shia ulema, culminating in a devastating anti-Sufi onslaught led by Mulla Muhammed Baqir Majlisi (1628–99). So effective was this that Iranian Sufism went into abeyance until the nineteenth century (Nasr 1966: 262–3; de Jong and Radtke 1999: 16; Bayat 1999: 624–7).

Clearly the root problem with Sufism, for the orthodox, is its ontological monism, which flouts orthodoxy's transcendent concept of Deity and the unbridgeable gap between the divine and the non-divine, including the human, entailed thereby. One of the greatest virtuosi of anti-Sufi vituperation, the neo-Hanbalite Ibn Taymiyah, who denounced Ibn Arabi as a heretic, described the fight against monism as jihad, holy war. According to Taymiyah the monism of Arabi equates God with demons, infidels, dogs and pigs; the notion of human unification with God is tantamount to polytheism and to Christian-style 'incarnationism'. Naturally he denounced the cult of saints and all its trappings, and the ecstatic dancing and chanting of popular Sufism (Chodkiewicz 1999: 98–102; Homerin 1999: 231–3). Ibn Arabi and Sufism likewise incurred the wrath of Taymiyah's latter-day disciple, Abd al-Wahhab. In Wahhab's view most so-called Muslims have through Sufi influence become infidels and idolaters (EOI 2002: 40–1, 64; de Jong and Radtke 1999: 8; Gaborieau 1999: 463, 465; Buehler 1999: 473–4, 477–82). The speciality, therefore, of Wahhab's followers has been to destroy the objects of this idolatry, the shrines of saints. When they became powerful in Arabia they destroyed some of the most revered holy places of Islam (many feared that they might even destroy the Prophet's tomb in Medina); as recently as 1984 militant anti-Sufis destroyed saints' tombs at Lahj in Yemen (de Jong and Radtke 1999: 1). 'Generic protestantism' with a vengeance.

Within Islam not only the orthodox dislike Sufism – so too do Islamic modernisers: Sufism, with its mysticism and extravagant behaviour, seems the very antithesis of modernity, utterly at odds, in particular, with the scientific world-view. This assessment may be justified, in the end; however, the relation between Sufism and science is more complex than it suggests. In the premodern period Islamic society could boast the most advanced scientific culture in the world; yet this was somehow aborted, and 'modernity' failed to emerge. To understand this we shall need to explore the relations between Islamic science and Islamic society in general, but it will be useful first to have some appreciation of the Islamic scientific achievement itself.

Islamic science

Islamic science was, in the beginning, heir to the Greeks. Within two centuries or so from the inauguration of the Muslim calendar, virtually all the important Greek scientific texts had been translated into Arabic (Dijksterhuis 1961: 110–11). For present purposes, however, I shall concentrate on one particular science, astronomy. There are good reasons for this. For one, it was a prominent part of Muslim intellectual life for centuries. Secondly, the West's scientific revolution began with the astronomy of Copernicus, so it is appropriate to consider the relations between Islamic and Western developments. Thirdly, astronomy raises fundamental cosmological issues, central to a society's world-view. Finally, even if (as Thomas Kuhn asserts) Muslim astronomy did not amount to a fundamental revision of the Greek theory, nevertheless its achievements seem highly impressive. In fact practically all significant advances in astronomy between Ptolemy and Copernicus were made by Islamic astronomers; furthermore, in the opinion of many scholars Copernicus' revolution would have been impossible without their work.

The starting-point for Islamic astronomers was the astronomy of Ptolemy and the cosmology (and physics) of Aristotle. According to Aristotle, the universe is a great sphere, and the earth a much smaller sphere at its centre. The universe is divided into two parts – sub-lunar and supra-lunar – made of different elements, which behave quite differently. The sub-lunar elements are earth, water, air and fire; the earth we inhabit is at the centre because the natural motion of the element earth is towards this. The other sub-lunar elements naturally occupy an ascending series of spherical bands between earth and moon – when they are not in their natural positions, this is because the sub-lunar realm is a place of violent motion and change, birth and extinction, generation and decay. Quite different is the supra-lunar realm of the stars and seven planets (Moon, Mercury, Venus, Sun, Mars, Jupiter and Saturn) which endlessly circle the earth carried by spherical shells of ether, a crystalline substance of utmost purity. The shells' spherical form (and the consequent circularity of the planets' orbits) expresses the perfection of the celestial realm, for the sphere is the most perfect shape – it alone can rotate forever on itself without changing place or appearance. The celestial realm is thus eternal and unchanging. The outermost sphere is that of the stars. Its motion is transmitted by physical contact to the lower spheres; but the ultimate source of all celestial motion is itself unmoving, Aristotle's Unmoved Mover. Even terrestrial forces and motions ultimately derive from this, via the motion of the spheres (Kuhn 1957: 79, 82, 85, 91; Blumenberg 1987/2000: 135, 138).

Two aspects of this world-picture are noteworthy. One, already mentioned, is the radical division of the universe into sub-lunar and supra-lunar realms, with quite different physics. Secondly, this difference is also a value-hierarchy. The supra-lunar realm is in every way superior, closer to the Unmoved Mover, made of purer stuff, its motions more perfect, beyond change; the sub-lunar realm, made of grosser material, is subject to generation and decay. Lowest of all is the earth, at the centre. (Christians found it relatively easy to accept this hierarchy, with some modifications – for example, placing Hell at the centre of the earth, and Heaven beyond the sphere of the fixed stars) (Kuhn 1957: 92; Blumenberg 1987/2000: 140).

Generally Aristotle's cosmology was adopted by Greek astronomers, including Ptolemy (though they found they could economise on ethereal shells – Ptolemy reduced Aristotle's fifty-five shells to eight: one for the stars, one for each of the 'planets'). But Ptolemy was interested in precisely predicting the heavenly bodies' movements as seen from the earth, not least for astrological reasons; and here the Aristotelian framework presents problems. It appears incompatible, for example, with observed planetary 'retrogression' (in geocentric terms, planets sometimes appear to move backwards). Such problems led Ptolemy and others to introduce a well-known battery of supplementary devices – epicycles, deferents, eccentrics and equants. (A planet supposedly moves not only in its circular orbit round the earth (the deferent) but also in a secondary circular orbit (the epicycle) whose centre is on the deferent's circumference. The eccentric is a deferent whose centre is displaced from the centre of the earth; the equant is a point displaced from the centre of the earth, round which – rather than the geometrical centre – a planet is held to move regularly, sweeping out equal angles in equal times.) Using these devices, Ptolemy produced detailed, comprehensive and precise predictive tables (a remarkable intellectual feat) while remaining more or less faithful to Aristotle in ascribing only circular motions to the heavenly bodies (Kuhn 1957: 45, 50–1, 54, 59, 61–2, 64, 69–73, 80). In other respects, however, his astronomy is hard to reconcile with Aristotle. He seems to have supposed that the ethereal shells carrying the planets were thick enough to accommodate epicycles; and that, to accommodate eccentrics, it should be possible for the shells to pass through one another. But whence came the forces that could cause these rather complex movements? More generally, Ptolemy seems to have held that any physical difficulties in reconciling his astronomy and Aristotelian cosmology can be explained by the fact that our physical ideas derive exclusively from terrestrial experience. Celestial physics, in other words, is beyond human understanding. Ptolemy's prime concern was accurate prediction – to 'save the appearances', not explain them (Kuhn 1957: 8, 104–5; Blumenberg 1987/2000: xiii, xv–xvi, 211–14, 216–17).

Muslim astronomers, it seems, did not take this view. The advances they achieved were both observational and theoretical. They built the world's most advanced observatories, with new and more accurate instruments, thus revealing more and more difficulties and discrepancies in Ptolemy's system, necessitating ever more complex and ad hoc additions. Most significant is the attitude of Muslim astronomers to Ptolemy's epicycles, eccentrics and equants. Some of the philosophers denounced them as un-Aristotelian; but what mainly concerned the astronomers was their basis in physical reality. They did not object to epicycles, but did seek to rid astronomy of eccentrics and equants – because they appear to require motions physically incompatible with the cosmology of revolving spheres (Nasr 1976: 20–3, 97; Emperor Babur 2002: 58; Nasr 1968: 170; Saliba 1994: 6, 11, 20–4, 275–7). In this programme they achieved an impressive degree of success.

One of Ptolemy's earliest and most influential critics, on grounds of physical impossibility, was Ibn al-Haytham (b. 965 CE), known in the West as Alhazen (Saliba 1994: 13–14) (and best known for his work in mathematics and especially optics). Islamic astronomy's greatest achievements, however, are associated with the 'school of Maragha'. Maragha, in north-west Iran, was the capital city of the Ilkhanid dynasty, established by the Mongol invaders who captured Baghdad in 1258 CE. The great observatory at Maragha, founded in 1259, was a well-funded enterprise employing many astronomers and advanced techniques of observation. Two great innovators, al-Urdi and al-Tusi (1201–74 CE), were associated with it from the outset: the latter was its chief astronomer; the former was brought from Damascus to supervise its construction. Among Urdi's contributions is the Urdi Lemma, which enables the astronomer to dispense with eccentrics by replacing them with epicycles. Urdi applied this technique to the 'upper' planets (Mars, Jupiter and Saturn). More celebrated, perhaps, is the Tusi Couple, an ingenious geometrical construction by which linear motion can be transformed into circular motion, and vice versa. (The method uses two circles, one with a radius half that of the other. The former rolls within the latter on its circumference, with one circumference tangent to the other. The smaller circle revolves at twice the speed of the larger and in the opposite direction, so that a point on the smaller circle's circumference moves along a diameter of the larger.) Tusi's pupil al-Shirazi (d. 1311 CE) used the Couple to solve the orbit of Mercury; Ibn al-Shatir (d. 1375 CE), at a daughter observatory of Maragha in Damascus, did the same for the Moon. The planetary models of Shatir, who inherited the achievements of his predecessors, seem to have been the culmination of the Maragha School's achievement: a physically consistent model of the movements of heavenly bodies, postulating only circular orbital motions round the earth as centre, and without resort to equants or eccentrics (Saliba 1994: 12, 23, 26, 113–22, 258–77; EOI 1971b: 1137; 2000: 751; Nasr 1976: 20, 105, 109, 132; 1995: 216, 222–4; 1968: 172–4, 177; Iqbal 2002: 65–8).[1] Ibn al-Shatir made another interesting modification to Ptolemy's physics: since the planets and stars are so different in appearance from the

---

[1] According to Saliba, only Ibn al-Shatir among the major Muslim astronomers wished or was able to eliminate eccentrics.

spheres that carry them, they cannot all be made of the same ethereal substance but must be composite in structure (Saliba 1994: 24).

The achievements of the Maragha School have been appreciated only in the last fifty or so years, and the history of Muslim astronomy after Ibn al-Shatir has, it seems, still not been adequately studied. But it certainly did not come to an end. Another important observatory was established in 1420 at Samarkand (its ruins remain visible) by the Timurid ruler Ulugh Beg (himself reputedly keenly interested in astronomy) (EOI 1971b: 1137–8; Nasr 1976: 23, 105). We have no knowledge of further theoretical advances. Yet it seems that the achievements of Maragha were not lost to the world: they were very probably inherited by Copernicus himself, who has even been called the last and greatest member of the Maragha School.

Copernicus objected to Ptolemy's equants on exactly the same grounds as the Maragha astronomers, and he uses both the Urdi Lemma and the Tusi Couple in his model exactly where they did. One scholar has found that Tusi and Copernicus use the same alphabetical references for identical points of their diagrams; according to another, the parallels between Copernicus and his Maragha predecessors are so great that they 'could not be attributed to coincidence' (Nasr 1976: 111; Iqbal 2002: 68–9; Saliba 1994: 12, 26–8). The probable channel of transmission is via Byzantine scholars, known to have been in touch with the Muslims and to have translated their work. A Byzantine manuscript which entered the Vatican Library after the fall of Constantinople clearly shows the Tusi Couple and perhaps also a version of Shatir's lunar model. Copernicus' use of these ideas has no known precedent among European astronomers. Since Copernicus read Greek, and spent some years in Italy, it is not impossible that he even knew the Vatican manuscript directly (Saliba 1994: 28–9, 265–71). And this does not exhaust the contribution of Muslim astronomy to the Copernican Revolution. Tycho Brahe's famous observatories at Uraniborg (founded 1576) and Stjerneborg (1584) provided observations of unprecedented accuracy crucial to Kepler's revolutionary breakthrough, and were equipped with instruments of a kind pioneered by the observatory of Samarkand and its successor at Istanbul (EOI 1971b: 1138; Nasr 1976: 23).

Nevertheless it was in the West, not the Islamic world, that the revolution initiated by Copernican heliocentrism, and the Scientific Revolution as a whole, occurred. Why did Muslim astronomy stagnate? And why did Muslim scientists and intellectuals show no interest in the Copernican and Scientific Revolutions for centuries – in stark contrast to the voracious interest in foreign learning displayed by Muslims of the eighth to the tenth centuries, when a host of Greek philosophical and scientific texts were translated into Arabic (O'Leary 1922: 112)? It must be relevant here to investigate the relations of Muslim science to the two world-views mentioned earlier.

Science and religion in Islam

Orthodox Islam, as one might expect, generally looked on Greek-inspired science with suspicion if not hostility (calling it a 'foreign science'). Astronomy, however, could and did serve important religious functions: calculating the distance and direction to Mecca (and thus the direction of prayer) as well as religiously significant times (Nasr 1976: 92–3; Saliba 1994: 32–3, 79). From the eleventh century mosques employed an astronomically competent time-keeper (*muwaqqit*) who might be an astronomer of distinction – the great Ibn al-Shatir was *muwaqqit* of a Damascus mosque. On the other hand, orthodoxy had reason to be particularly suspicious of astronomy's close association with astrology, held to contradict the dogma of divine omnipotence. Arabic texts up to the thirteenth century often made no distinction between the two, calling both *ilm al-nujum* (science of the stars) (Saliba 1994: 33, 6–8; Nasr 1976: 95; 1993: 132, 151–2). Astrology had many clients in Muslim society, including at its highest levels, and some leading astronomers were also famed astrologers, among them Tusi. It seems clear that Tusi's prowess in astrology, rather than pure astronomy, motivated the lavish political patronage he and others received – incurring the wrath of the ultra-orthodox Ibn Taymiyah, who attacked Tusi vehemently, attributing the favour shown to him and his like by 'the Tatars' to 'the lies of astrologers and the tricks of deceivers which are contrary to reason and religion' (Saliba 1994: 44, fn 43). An interesting illustration of this attitude and its influence is the observatory established at Istanbul in 1575 by the Ottoman Sultan, by then the only observatory in the Muslim world. It survived for just three years. The Sultan's motivation, it seems, was primarily astrological, and incurred the hostility of a powerful group of ulema. They prevailed thanks to an outbreak of plague, which they interpreted as divine punishment for the astronomers' sacrilegious attempt to probe God's secrets. The observatory was destroyed (Inalcik 1973: 179–80).[2] One might speculate that by the sixteenth century the views of Ibn Taymiyah on such matters had come to prevail among the orthodox.

What, however, of Sufism? As mentioned, would-be modernisers have generally assailed Sufism as irrational and anti-scientific – understandably

[2] Inalcik's dates for the observatory are 1577–80; others give 1575–7.

if over-simply. It certainly looks as if some Sufis denigrated natural science by comparison with mystical illumination; an example is a poem by a Persian Sufi, Shaykh Bahili al-Din Amili (1546–1622), quoted by Seyyed Hossein Nasr (who calls Amili an outstanding Sufi and a fine poet):

> Formal science is nothing but altercation:
> It results in neither intoxication nor contemplation …
> There is no science but the Quran commentary and Hadith,
> The rest is the deception of the perverse Satan …
> A heart which is empty of the love of [divine] Beauty,
> Count it as a stone with which the Devil cleans himself.
> These sciences, these forms and imaginings,
> Are the excrements of Satan upon that stone …
>
> (Nan an Halwa, or Bread and Sweat)

Yet Amili was, perhaps surprisingly, also a famous mathematician and astronomer, who wrote a treatise on the astrolabe (Nasr 1995: 243–6).

On reflection, however, it is not surprising that Sufi thinkers should practise natural science, given the monism fundamental to Sufi metaphysics. If everything that exists is God, everything partakes of the divine, including the natural world. As a popular Sufi maxim has it, 'The Truth [i.e. God] is water, the world is ice' (Nasr 1976: 341) – and ice is water in one of its aspects. The adept has an obvious motive to understand nature. As Nasr puts it, 'All knowledge concerns some aspect of God's theophanies' (God's self-manifestation to man) (Nasr 1976: 13). In this light, natural science is a sacred achievement. Nasr also suggests that Islamic mysticism is mysticism with a difference, more rationalistically tinged than, for example, Indian mysticism, because it subsumed elements of Greek philosophy (Nasr 1995: 41; cf. Fakhry 1983: 20–1). For such reasons the Sufi world-view provided the main nurturing context for Islamic natural science: as Nasr puts it, most of the great Muslim scientists operated within the matrix of Gnosticism (Nasr 1976: 23; cf. Nasr 1997: 94).

This is certainly true of some of the greatest astronomers. Tusi was not just an astronomer but a typically polymathic Muslim scholar who wrote on philosophical and religious subjects (he is said to be better known to Muslims for this than for his astronomy). One book, *Rawdat al-Taslimya tasawwurat*, teaches how the soul may travel from the physical to the spiritual world, using the neo-Platonic framework integral to Sufi thought: this journey requires 'perfection of ascertainment of reasoned knowledge' but also esoteric knowledge. Another, the *Aswat al-Ashraf*, is a guide to the path from belief to union with and self-extinction in God (EOI 2000: 247; Nasr 1995: 161; 1976: 322; Dabashi 1996: 568–9). Another sign of his allegiances is his veneration for Hallaj, the great tenth-century Sufi martyr

(EOI 1971a: 103). Tusi's Maragha student and successor al-Shirazi was another polymath, famous for his scientific work (in optics as well as astronomy) but equally as the author of a treatise on a giant of theoretical Sufism, Suhrawardi (of whom more later). Nasr tells us that in the first widely accessible publication of the latter's major work, the *Hikmat al-Ishraq* or *Theosophy of Light*, in 1315 CE, Shirazi's commentary was appended, and it has been studied as a guide to Suhrawardi's thought ever since (Nasr 1995: 146, 161–4, 219–21). Also relevant is the thinking of an earlier (perhaps even greater) scientist, al-Biruni, another polymath whose scientific achievements embraced not only astronomy but pioneering calculations of the Earth's circumference, the specific density of minerals and much more besides. In Biruni's view, man has been equipped with sense, especially sight, in order to see the 'signs of God' (i.e. the physical world), and endowed with reason so that he can journey from the 'company of creatures' to the 'company of God' (Nasr 1976: 51–2; 1993: 107, 114–15, 117–18, 126–31, 150, 173). This is not exactly Sufism (the element of gnostic or esoteric knowledge is absent) but nonetheless it resembles the Sufi Path.

The Scientific Revolution

However impressive the achievements of medieval Muslim astronomers, they did not amount to a cosmological revolution – that occurred instead in Christian Europe, in the Scientific Revolution initiated by Copernicus (1473–1543) and culminating in the great synthesis of Isaac Newton's *Principia* (published 1687). Our next task is briefly to survey this revolution, with a view to throwing light on the Muslim stasis in the same period.

In substituting a heliocentric for a geocentric universe, Copernicus was motivated, inter alia, by cosmological considerations very similar to those of the innovators of Maragha and after: the inconsistency of the Aristotelian and Ptolemaic systems and the physical impossibility of equants (Kuhn 1957: 71, 138–9, 141–2). Copernicus, like his Muslim predecessors, succeeded in getting rid of equants, but not epicycles: although his heliocentrism explained the appearance of retrograde planetary motion that motivated epicycles in the first place, he failed to eliminate epicycles because he retained the Aristotelian–Ptolemaic idea that heavenly bodies move in circular orbits. The superiority of heliocentrism was not fully demonstrated until Kepler based his laws of planetary motion on elliptical orbits, which make epicycles unnecessary.

The cosmology of Copernicus and his followers destroyed Aristotle's division of the world into radically different realms, sub-lunar and supra-lunar. (In the sixteenth and early seventeenth centuries Aristotle's changeless celestial realm was also discredited by new evidence, owing principally to Tycho Brahe's observatories and Galileo's telescope: Kuhn 1957: 206–8, 219–24). Copernicanism also undermines Aristotle's physics – inseparably connected to his geocentric cosmology – but provides no adequate substitute to explain terrestrial or celestial motion. The Scientific Revolution was still incomplete.

It was completed, in this sense, during the seventeenth century by (among others) Descartes, Galileo and Newton. Descartes' crucial contribution was his corpuscular philosophy, according to which all matter consists of particles governed by laws imposed by God at the creation, discovery of these being the task of science. Descartes formulated one fundamental law of motion, the law of inertia (Descartes 1983 [1644]: 57–9). Galileo famously studied bodies moving near the surface of the earth, and formulated laws governing such motions. Finally Newton's *Principia* subsumed the contributions of his predecessors in the famous three laws of motion and the theory of gravitation, whose inverse square law subsumes both Kepler's laws of planetary motion and Galileo's laws of terrestrial motion. A unitary physics that treats all nature equally had been achieved.

Limitations of Islamic science

Medieval Muslim astronomy produced no scientific revolution. Why not? I shall offer some suggestions, focusing on philosophical and religious differences between European and Muslim civilisations. Some have offered a different kind of explanation: the Mongol conquest of the Abbasid caliphate in the thirteenth century, and consequent destruction and social dislocation in the Muslim heartlands. But the greatest achievements of Muslim astronomy came after the Mongol conquest. Indeed Tusi, first head of the Maragha observatory, had entered the Mongol conqueror Hulagu's service in 1256 and was in his entourage when he took Baghdad in 1258 (Dabashi 1999: 531–2). Hulagu greatly valued Tusi's astrological skills, seeking his advice as to propitious timing of his assault on Baghdad. Thereafter he patronised Tusi's work generously, lavishly funding the observatory at Maragha, his capital city. The victorious Mongols soon converted to Islam, and Hulagu's successors ruled as the dynasty of the Ilkhanids, active patrons of Islamic culture. Although Baghdad never fully recovered its preconquest position, other centres of learning arose (in Tabriz, Isfahan, Istanbul and Delhi, for example). The greatest, most powerful and wealthiest Islamic empires arose after the caliphate's violent overthrow: the Ottoman Turks (1290–1922), the Safavids in Iran (1501–1722) and the Mughals in

India (1526–1857). These empires produced wonderful art and architecture, although nothing comparable was achieved in science. Politically, Muslim decadence vis-à-vis the West was not evident until after 1683, when the Ottomans besieged Vienna for the last time, and were repulsed – just four years before the publication of Newton's *Principia*.

Science and religion in the West

How then can one attempt to understand the trajectory of Muslim science? My approach will be comparative, and therefore indirect. In the West, two concepts, I believe, have played a key role in linking religious and scientific thought: the Laws of Nature and the Book of Nature. Both are theological, although the former is also juristic and philosophical. They differ in one significant way. The Book of Nature was also expressed using somewhat different terminology, for example the Book of God's Works – it is the idea, not any specific wording, that is of interest. In the case of the Laws of Nature, by contrast, wording is crucial: what is significant is that different though related ideas were linked by a shared terminology.

We can see the significance of these concepts for Western science by examining the thought of figures such as Isaac Newton. Newton was a deeply religious man. The wellspring of all his work was his conception of God and of his own and the world's relation to God. His Christianity was not exactly orthodox – the focus of his interest was God the Father rather than the Son, to such an extent that commentators often describe his faith as Arian (an ancient Christian heresy). In a famous passage in the General Scholium to the *Principia*, Newton explains his view of God:

> This Being governs all Things, not as a Soul of the World but as Lord of the Universe; and upon Account of his Dominion, he is stiled Lord God, supreme over all. For the word God is a relative term, and has reference to Servants, and Deity is the Dominion of God not (such as a Soul has) over a Body of its own … but (such as a Governor has) over Servants. (Manuel 1974: 16–17)

Elsewhere he wrote: 'The word God is relative and signifies the same thing with Lord and King, but in a higher degree' (Manuel 1974: 22).

Newton's conception of Deity implies that the entire universe, including humanity, is subject to God's commands and reflects God's will. Newton had a passionate desire to know that will (he may even have thought himself divinely appointed to reveal it) (Manuel 1974: 23–4, 64) – hence his lifelong effort to understand both the natural world and the Christian Bible, especially the prophetic books (Daniel and Revelations), on which he wrote copiously; to understand, as Frank Manuel puts it, both 'God's word and God's works' (Manuel 1974: chapter II, and 22–3, 88). Francis Bacon, the great advocate of natural science, had expressed the same idea in the *Advancement of Learning*, where he preached study of both 'the book of God's word [and] the book of God's works' (the Book of Scripture and the Book of Nature) (Manuel 1974: 30). Newton told his follower Richard Bentley that the main business of the natural philosopher (scientist) is to investigate causes until he arrives at the First Cause; one of his great hopes for his own science was that it should 'work with considering men for the belief of deity' (Westfall 1958: 193).

Newton expressed his Principles of Natural Philosophy in the form of Laws, of Gravitation and of Motion. But why 'laws'? Here is Newton's own account:

It seems probable to me, that God in the beginning form'd Matter in solid, massy, hard, impenetrable, moveable Particles ... with such properties ... as most conduced to the end for which he form'd them ... It seems to me further, that these Particles have not only a Vis inertiae, accompanied with such passive Laws of Motion as naturally result from that Force, but they are also moved by certain Principles, such as that of Gravity ... These Principles I consider ... as general Laws of Nature. (Dampier 1971: 170, 155)

These laws are laws for nature made by God. To discover them is to decipher the Book of Nature. And Newton elsewhere applied the phrase 'laws of nature' to the commandments in God's other book, the Book of Scripture (Manuel 1974: 56). Both nature and humankind are subject to God's laws.

Here Newton was no innovator. Descartes (1596–1650) had already expressed similar views: God created 'the parts of matter', is the 'primary cause of [their] motion', and 'still maintains all this matter ... subject to the same law' as at the creation. From this 'immutability of God, we can obtain knowledge of ... the laws of nature' (Descartes 1983 [1644]: 57–9). Galileo (1564–1642) agreed that 'Nature is immutable ... never passing the bounds of the laws assigned her', she acts only 'through immutable laws which she never transgresses'. For Galileo, also, 'Philosophy is written in that great book which lies ever before our eyes – I mean the universe'; a book written in the language of mathematics (Burtt 1932: 75, 83). The views of Robert Boyle (1627–91), author of *The Christian Virtuoso* as well as Boyle's Law of gases, are similar: God 'is the creator of matter', sole author of its 'local motion' and of the 'mechanical laws of nature'. To Boyle it seemed evident that 'the laws of motion were ... arbitrary to Him and depended on His free will', necessarily so, for 'inanimate bodies are utterly incapable of understanding what a law is ... and therefore [their] actions ... are produced by real power', i.e. God (Westfall 1958: 91; Israel 2001: 257). The Lutheran Kepler (1571–1630) again was a passionately religious man, and perhaps took more seriously than anyone the idea of God's Book of

Nature. Astronomers, he wrote, are priests dedicated to the glory of God above all else: he rejoiced to 'behold how through my effort God is being celebrated in astronomy'. The universe is 'the most glorious temple of God', wherein God is 'to be celebrated, venerated and admired in true worship' (Hooykaas 1972: 105; Howell 2002: 110, 112–13). In Kepler's mind, his scientific studies were such an act of worship, and an interpretation of God's divine will explicitly compared to biblical exegesis (Howell 2002: 115). These views of Galileo, Kepler, Descartes, Boyle and Newton are quite typical of their era; to understand them, however, we must look to earlier centuries.

The law of nature in Western thought

The expression 'law of nature' (or 'natural law') has a long history in the West (of course in other languages besides English). Like so many ideas, it originated in Greece, where at first it seems to have carried an air of contradiction; contradiction, that is, of earlier Greek ideas, which drew a sharp contrast between *physis* (nature) and *nomos* (custom or convention, as well as law). Passages in Aristotle's *Rhetoric* indicate that by the fourth century BCE some Greek thinkers made a distinction between 'particular law' (of a specific community) and 'universal law' common to all, which 'accords with nature' and represents 'natural justice' (Burns, 2003: 1, 6–12) – thus associating *physis* and (one kind of) *nomos*. But it was from the later school of Stoicism that this crucial juxtaposition entered the post-Greek Western tradition. Not only did the Stoics (unlike Aristotle) use expressions like *nomos physeos* ('law of nature') and *nomos physikos* ('natural law') (Morrow 1948: 19; Pollock 1961: 126),[3] they also constructed a philosophy to which the idea expressed by these phrases is integral. In the Stoic conception, the world is purposively governed by an omnipotent, good and rational God (according to Zeno, founder of the school, God can be identified with *logos*): 'nature' means the way this world necessarily behaves. Men, alone in the world, share with God the divine faculty of reason, which, rightly used, enables them to understand the world and understand and share the divine purpose: to live 'according to nature'. (In this all men are fundamentally alike.) Stoicism distinguishes two kinds of law that men are under – that of the city (or of custom) and that of the world-city (the law of reason). The latter, the law of nature, is superior. Reason, which is man's nature, gives all men a universal, eternal, rational natural law (Sandbach 1975: 31–7, 69, 72–3, 79–80, 110–11; Sabine 1948: 148–51).

[3] I am grateful to Tony Burns for these references.

It was clearly as a juristic and moral, not a physical concept that Stoic natural law passed into the discourse of the post-Greek West. When the Greek world became part of the Roman state, Stoicism was its dominant philosophical school and the one that appealed most to the Roman elite. Towards the end of the second century BCE the school was headed by Panaetius of Rhodes who (according to G. H. Sabine) put its doctrine into a non-technical form easily assimilable by Roman aristocrats (Sabine 1948: 152–3). Later, Stoicism had a hugely significant influence on two great Roman institutions – Roman law, and the Roman lawyer, politician and philosopher Cicero.

Cicero is significant not for any theoretical originality but for his enormous influence on European thought. He it was who translated the Greek terminology of natural law into Latin, and bequeathed it to the Latin-speaking civilisation of Europe. In his dialogue *De Legibus* (The Laws), Cicero expounds orthodox Stoic doctrine on the world, God (or the gods), nature, reason and mankind. All men share the faculty of reason, which gives them something in common with the divinity that rules the world – and thereby the capacity to understand nature's rational plan and 'live according to nature, or ... live by her law'. Law in the true sense is 'the highest reason, inherent in nature, which enjoins what ought to be done and forbids the opposite' – and superior to the written injunctions commonly called law. Any 'law' contrary to nature is a bad law, not genuinely a law at all (Cicero 1998: 103–9, 112, 116–18, 124–7; Sabine 1948: 161–5; D'Entreves 1970: 25–6). In his *Tusculan Disputations* Cicero used (and perhaps coined) the pregnant phrases *lex naturalis* and *lex naturae* (Ritchie 1916: 36, 39; Robson 1935: 244).[4] According to Sabine, 'he gave to the Stoic doctrine of natural law a statement in which it was universally known throughout Europe ... down to the nineteenth century' (Sabine 1948: 163).

Most importantly, he influenced both Christian thought and Roman law. Lactantius repeats Cicero's definition of natural law, while both Augustine and Ambrose wrote of the 'lex naturalis in corde scripta' ('natural law written in the heart') (D'Entreves 1970: 26, 39: Sabine 1948: 163). In the seventh century, St Isidore of Seville in his *Etymologiae* wrote: 'Divine laws are based on nature, human laws on custom' (D'Entreves 1970: 39). And in 534 CE, the Roman emperor Justinian published the famous *Corpus Iuris Civilis*, one part of which (the Digest) is a compilation of the views of Roman jurists over some centuries. The Roman lawyers' terminology famously designated three types of law,

---

[4] I am again grateful to Tony Burns for these references.

ius civilis (civil law), *ius gentium* (law of nations) and *ius naturale* (natural law – translated from the Greek of the Stoics) (D'Entreves 1970: 22–7, 31; Sabine 1948: 157, 160, 163, 167–70). Although the meaning of these terms was not entirely stable, the third-century lawyer Paulus gives definitions very close to Stoic ideas: 'We can speak of law in different senses: in one sense, when what we call law is always equitable and good, as is natural law; in another sense, what in each city is profitable to all or to many, as is civil law' (D'Entreves 1970: 29). Justinian himself, elsewhere in the *Corpus Iuris Civilis*, defines the law of nature as 'those laws which are observed by all nations ... always stable and immutable', because they have been 'enacted by ... divine providence' (D'Entreves 1970: 32). This in effect Christianises the Roman doctrine.

When the Western Roman Empire collapsed, Roman law was not lost: it was painstakingly revived in the medieval period by, significantly, the canon lawyers (the nearest Christian equivalent to the Muslim ulema). In the twelfth century Gratian, a canon lawyer at the University of Bologna, compiled his famous *Decretum* (later incorporated into the church's *Corpus Iuris Canonici*) which opens: 'Mankind is ruled by two laws: Natural Law and Custom. Natural Law is that which is contained in the Scriptures and the Gospel' (D'Entreves 1970: 37). Because it is divine, Gratian says, natural law is absolute and superior to any other: 'Whatever contradicts natural law must be considered null and void'. According to A. P. d'Entreves, the Canonists 'gave natural law an unprecedented coherence and force'; canon law was thus the primary vehicle of natural law doctrine in the medieval West (D'Entreves 1970: 37–8).

It was not, however, the only one. Natural law has a central role in the thought of the most influential medieval European philosopher, Thomas Aquinas. Aquinas is famous for synthesising Christian theology and the philosophy of Aristotle; his thinking on natural law, however, is strikingly Stoic. 'The world is governed by Divine Providence', that is, by 'divine reason', which government Aquinas calls the eternal law. Human beings have 'a certain share in the divine reason'; this 'natural reason' enables men to discern the natural law, by which we distinguish good from evil. Natural law is the 'participation' of divine reason and the eternal law in rational creatures. It is thus common to all men, Christians or not (the divine law, revealed directly by God, adds to the natural law but does not contradict it). Human law must conform to natural law: 'Whatever has been recognised by usage, or laid down in writing, if it contradicts natural law must be considered null and void' (Sabine 1948: 249–55; D'Entreves 1970: 42–6).

As late as the eighteenth century Thomas Jefferson, seeking to justify the American Revolution, invoked 'the Laws of Nature and of Nature's

God'. But long before that the expression 'laws of nature' had acquired that other equally important meaning, central to the Scientific Revolution. When Alexander Pope wrote, also in the eighteenth century, of 'Nature and Nature's Laws', he was celebrating the science of Newton.[5] The similar terminology across such diverse subject matter is obviously of great significance; it seems safe to say that the physical conception of natural law could never have arisen without the long pre-history of natural law thinking in the West.

Islam and natural law

Islamic science, by contrast, did not develop the concept of natural law. This might seem surprising. Like Christianity, Islam posits a transcendent, all-powerful Deity who created and governs the world; and like the West the Muslim world assimilated in significant measure the Greek intellectual heritage. Why did this combination not produce a similar outcome?

One answer often given invokes the exalted conception of divine power posited by the dominant orthodox – that is, Asharite – theology of Sunni Islam. Not only did God create the world *ex nihilo*, its existence depends at every moment on a continuous series of divine creative acts. Matter in itself is utterly impotent; its qualities depend directly on God's will and power. In this sense there is no such thing as nature (*tabia*), i.e. matter having its own causal power. Contrary to Aristotle, there are no necessary connections between events in the world. In Ashari's words, 'Anyone who holds *tabia* to be necessitating is mistaken' (EOI 2000: 27). Unlike the Christian Fathers and the Scholastics, the Asharites deny so-called secondary causes. This view or something like it was accepted not only by the Asharites but by theologians of virtually all schools (Wolfson 1976: 518, 543, 560).

The most celebrated and sophisticated exponent of Asharite orthodoxy was al-Ghazzali. His argument (from *The Incoherence of the Philosophers*) is worth quoting at some length:

According to us the connection between what is usually believed to be cause and what is believed to be an effect is not a necessary connection; each of two things has its own individuality and is not the other, and neither the affirmation nor the negation, neither the existence nor the non-existence of the one is implied in the affirmation, negation, existence or non-existence of the other, e.g. the satisfaction of thirst does not imply drinking, nor satiety eating, nor burning contact with fire … nor decapitation death … [To take] one simple example, namely the

---

[5] 'Nature and Nature's Laws lay hid in Night; God said: "Let Newton be!" And all was Light' (Pope 1966).

burning of cotton through contact with fire, we regard it as possible that the contact might occur without the burning taking place, and also that the cotton might be changed into ashes without any contact with fire ... For fire is a dead body that has no action, and what is the proof that it is the agent? Indeed the philosophers have no other proof than the observation of the occurrence of the burning, but observation proves only a simultaneity, not a causation. (Bosley and Tweedale 1996: 28–9)

Ghazzali concedes that most people believe in causal connections, but he is able to explain this: 'Protracted habit time after time fixes [things] in our minds according to the past habit in a fixed impression' (Bosley and Tweedale 1996: 33).

Nobody, I believe, can read these words without being struck by their extraordinary similarity to the argument advanced centuries later by David Hume. However, Ghazzali's argument does not stop there. For him denial of natural necessity is (in stark contrast to Hume) the logical consequence of the absolute, exclusive and unlimited power of God. He continues:

The connection between these things is based on a prior power of God to create them in a successive order ... It is in God's power to create satiety without eating ... and to let life persist notwithstanding decapitation, and so on with respect to all connections ... [Likewise] we regard it as possible that a prophet should be thrown into the fire and not burn ... For strange and marvelous things are in the power of God ... [Thus] the bringing back to life of the dead and the changing of a stick into a serpent are possible. (Bosley and Tweedale 1996: 29, 35)

Although the possibility of miracles is very important to Ghazzali, he is equally concerned to account for the regularity of the world, on which our lives depend. 'God has created in us the knowledge that he will not do all these possible things' that are in his power; or, more precisely, it is his 'custom' not to depart from the normal constancies. But these are not necessary. God can and does depart from his custom as and when he sees fit (Bosley and Tweedale 1996: 33; Wolfson 1976: 548–9; EOI 2000: 27).

To many commentators it has seemed that we need look no further to explain the failure of Islamic civilisation to bring forth a Scientific Revolution. Charles Adams (biographer of the moderniser Muhammad Abduh) speaks for many: 'There is no place [in orthodox Islam] for natural law in the scientific sense, because of the absolute predominance given to the will of God as the active, immediate cause of all existence' (Adams 1933: 140). However, the similarity of Ghazzali's argument to Hume's suggests that it is perfectly compatible with the modern scientific world-view. Hume did not share Ghazzali's views on God or miracles; however these do not differ much from those of Boyle and Isaac Newton. As we saw, they held matter to be inert, dependent on God for its ability to move and act. Even the Deist Voltaire took this view: 'The whole philosophy of Newton leads of necessity to the knowledge of a Supreme Being, who created everything, arranged everything of his own free will. If matter gravitates, it does not do so by virtue of its very nature ... It received gravitation from God' (Hampson 1968: 79). The laws of nature would have been different had God chosen otherwise. Both Boyle and Newton accepted the possibility of miracles (Israel 2001: 256–7, 284; Gay 1967: 140–1; Manuel 1974: 37–8). And in any case, Muslim scientists seem not to have been unduly influenced by the orthodox theological view about nature. It did not inhibit the astronomers from modifying Ptolemaic astronomy, on the grounds that the equant is incompatible with the nature of a solid sphere, and therefore physically impossible.

I conclude that we need to look to another difference between the Western and Islamic traditions. In the West natural law discourse belonged at first to moral and juristic philosophy. Islamic jurisprudence did not receive the influence of Roman law and hence did not incorporate its idea of natural law; instead it took its inspiration almost exclusively from the Quranic revelation and prophetic tradition. More generally – and importantly – Islam was not heir to the Roman contribution to classical thought. There was no Arabic-speaking equivalent of Cicero; nor did the Arabic-speaking world receive Stoicism directly from Greek sources. The Arabic reception of Greek culture, though impressive, was far from comprehensive: in philosophy it was limited almost exclusively to Aristotle, Plato and the neo-Platonists (O'Leary 1922: 53, 105–6, 113–15; Peters 1996: 40–4). I shall return to this important point.

The Book of Nature in Western and in Islamic thought

In contrast to the clear disparity regarding natural law, that other key concept, the Book of Nature (which, as I remarked, can be expressed by various phrases) is found in both Western and Islamic religious traditions. However, its implications were not necessarily the same.

In Western thought the concept of God's Book of Nature (like the law of nature) long predates the Scientific Revolution. Hugh of St Victor, a leading Scholastic, stated it very explicitly in the twelfth century: 'The whole sensible world is like a book, as it were, written by the hand of God, that is to say, created by divine power, and each of its creatures are like forms ... established by the divine will in order to make manifest the wisdom of the invisible things of God'. According to Kenneth Howell, this belongs to a long tradition, echoing St Paul in Romans (1:20): 'The invisible things of [God] ... are clearly seen, being understood by the things that [he has] made, even his eternal power and Godhead' (Howell 2002: 209). Another, more vivid biblical passage often quoted by exponents of the Book of Nature is Psalm 19: 'The heavens declare the glory of God; and the firmament showeth his handiwork.' According to the gloss in the King James Bible, this means that 'The creatures shew God's glory', not just the heavens. Francis Bacon quoted the Psalmist to show that 'next to the word of God, the image itself of the world is the great proclaimer of the divine wisdom and goodness'. Bacon found the same message in the book of Genesis, where God, after the six days of creation, 'saw everything that he had made, and, behold, it was very good'; words that moved Bacon to proclaim that if men 'labour in [God's] works' they will be made 'partakers in [His] vision' (Howell 2002: 15). Before Bacon, John Calvin had warned against neglecting the study of nature, which leads to 'knowledge of God' – on this ground he praised natural science (Hooykaas 1972: 106).

If we turn now to the Muslim world, we find an extremely interesting state of affairs, for the idea of nature as God's book was well entrenched there also. But there are significant differences.

The concept of God's two books is expressed in Arabic as two Qurans: the Quran of creation (*al-Qur'an al-takwini*) and the recorded Quran (*al-Qur'an al-tadwini*) (Nasr 1976: 91; 1997: 94–5). The parallel to the Western duality seems close. There are, furthermore, many verses in the (recorded) Quran that suggest an attitude to the created world very like that underlying the Western concept of the Book of Nature. God is the creator of the world *ex nihilo*: thus the natural world manifests God's power and wisdom. As the Quran (2:164) has it: 'Lo! In the creation of the heavens and the earth, and the difference between night and day … are signs [of God] for people who have sense.' Similar things are said about the regular movements of sun, moon and planets. Collectively the many verses of this kind are known to scholars of Islam as 'sign verses' because they employ, in a rather stereotyped way, phrases like 'And this is the sign for those who reflect' (16:11) or 'or those who listen' (16:65) (Iqbal 2002: 29–30, 113; Nasr 1976: 91).

Undoubtedly some Muslim scientists undertook their work in this spirit. Thus, for the zoologist al-Jahiz, the goal of his science is to demonstrate the existence and wisdom of God (Nasr 1976: 62). One of the leading Maragha astronomers, al-Urdi, claimed 'excellence' for astronomy because it studies 'God's most admirable achievements, the most magnificent things he has created', and demonstrates 'God's existence and magnificence' (Saliba 1994: 116). Al-Biruni, the great polymathic scientist and scholar, considered scientific study to be a religious duty because it obeys the Quranic injunction to contemplate God's creation.

Biruni saw a divine 'economy' in nature, ensuring that nothing is ever wasted: 'The Vis Naturalis [Creative Force], in all the work it is inspired and commissioned to carry out, never leaves any material unused.' 'There is no waste or deficiency in God's work.' Springs have 'the most copious water in winter' because this fits the plan of 'the All-Wise and Almighty Creator'; leaves and fruit perish each year, making room for new ones to replace them, because this 'realises the result ... intended in the economy of nature'. At times Biruni sounds like Leibniz: 'Praise be to him who has arranged creation and created everything for the best.' Apparent anomalies in nature 'only serve to show that the Creator who has designed something deviating from the general tenor of things is infinitely sublime, beyond anything which we poor sinners may conceive' (Nasr 1993: 114–15, 122–4).

Given these similarities between Islamic and Western thinking, and given that the Quran even speaks of God decreeing natural regularities, it may again seem surprising that Islam did not anticipate (or follow) the Western development of science. I have suggested one reason: the lack of a concept of natural law. But I believe other factors may have contributed. I suggest three interconnected points. First, Muslim natural philosophy, despite its 'Quran of creation', never freed itself from Aristotle's hierarchical conception of nature, but rather reinforced it; second, its evaluation of nature from the standpoint of human salvation was ambivalent, and partly negative; thirdly, a powerful current of thought understood nature not in matter-of-fact terms but as symbols of a higher reality – to be interpreted through an esoteric hermeneutic.

What is most relevant here is the intellectual universe of Sufism. Esoteric symbolic interpretation of the world (*ta'wil*) is of its essence and inevitably affected the way nature was understood; and likewise the Quran. The Sufi habit of interpreting the Quran symbolically, however distasteful to the orthodox, could, theoretically, have encouraged scientific progress. The Quran like the Bible contains passages which, taken literally, appear to conflict with modern science, for example references to the motion of the Sun (rather than the Earth), and to God's creation of 'seven heavens' one above another and above a centrally placed Earth.[6] Symbolic interpretation could, in theory, have removed the apparent contradiction. This, however, requires that natural phenomena be treated as literal facts. Instead – in the words of Seyyed Hossein Nasr – nature, like the Quran, is seen as a fabric of symbols to be read. Nasr notes also that the Shi'ite attitude to nature has been very similar to that of Sufism

---

[6] See for example verses 2:29, 55:5 and 36:39 (I am grateful to Lloyd Ridgeon for these references). See also Iqbal (2002: 32).

(Nasr 1976: 64; 1968: 24, 36–7, 127, 295–6, 335; 1993: 10). An example is the way a Persian Shi'ite thinker, Mir Damad, discerned a correspondence between the Books of Nature and of Revelation. 'The world of letters corresponds to the world of numbers, and the world of numbers to the world of Being.' Letters, he believed, came into existence as a result of planetary conjunctions, and he worked out detailed correspondences between the twenty-eight letters of the alphabet and the twenty-eight stations of the Moon (Nasr 1995: 253–4). By the time of Mir Damad, the golden age of Islamic science was long over.

Perhaps we can now see how the Sufi view of nature is ambivalent. If nature is a fabric of symbols of a higher reality, it is important and worthy of study; but it is valued not for itself but for what it signifies. Nasr gives illuminating expression to this ambivalence. From the gnostic (Sufi) point of view, he says, nature is positive but secondary, a 'mirror' where reality is reflected. He quotes Ibn Arabi, who (in language reminiscent of Plato and neo-Platonism) called the natural world a world of 'shadows' of the archetypes. For the gnostic, says Nasr, nature is both positive symbol and negative illusion, which both 'veils and reveals' reality (Nasr 1968: 37, 338; 1997: 21, 95). According to Jami, the great Sufi poet, the Truth, which is One, begets an 'imaginary' multiplicity of natural entities (bodies, species of minerals, plants and animals) (Nasr 1976: 343). Another Sufi poet cited by Nasr, Afdan al-Kushani (an associate of the astronomer Tusi) contrasted the 'real' world of archetypes, universals and eternity with the 'symbolic' world of nature, particulars and existents (Nasr 1976: 296). It is now perhaps easier to understand how a Sufi such as al-Din Amili could be a leading scientist, and denigrate science.

These matters are, of course, linked to the Sufi Path. If the natural world is symbolic of the divine, knowledge of nature can help the Sufi to attain his goal. He uses nature to transcend nature; his Path is an upward Path which leaves the natural world behind. It is not hard to see how this fits with a hierarchical conception of nature. I remarked earlier that Sufism's metaphysical monism seems to be in some tension with the Path, which posits union with God as an aim, not a given. There might seem to be some tension also between metaphysical monism and a hierarchical conception of nature. However, as Nasr says (explaining the ideas of one of his heroes, Mulla Sadra), 'Being ... is a single reality but with gradations and degrees of intensity ... The Being of God, of a man, of a tree, or of a heap of earth are all one Being but in various degrees of intensity or manifestation.' All being shares the same attributes: 'A stone ... has knowledge, will, power and intelligence like men or angels. However, since at the level of a stone the manifestation of Being is very weak, these attributes are ... not perceptible' (Nasr 1995: 279).

The thinker whose system most strikingly expresses the hierarchical conception of being is, I suggest, the Persian Suhrawardi (1153–91 CE). Suhrawardi's life was short and his end violent because he fell foul of the orthodox jurists, of whom he was a bitter critic. Despite this, he has been immensely influential – according to Nasr, equal to Ibn Arabi for pre-eminent influence on Sufi thought (Nasr 1995: 125, 145–6). His philosophy is known as Illuminationism (*ishraq*); his major work is the *Hikmat al-ishraq*, and he is known as Shaikh al-ishraq, master of illumination. He was clearly influenced by the Zoroastrianism native to Persia before the Muslim conquest, but he drew on other sources, including Hermeticism (Suhrawardi considered Hermes Trismegistus to have been the recipient of divine revelation and the founder of true philosophy), Pythagoras and neo-Platonism.

Illumination is a multivalent concept. In one sense it is a mode of knowledge – ultimate knowledge, insight into the Divine, the goal of the Sufi Path. Such illumination is achieved not by rational means but by ascetic practices and self-purification. This knowing is a kind of seeing, and seeing is dependent on light. Suhrawardi uses the Zoroastrian opposition between light and darkness to construct a hierarchical world-picture, embracing both the visible and the invisible worlds. In crude summary, light equates with good, noble and spiritual, darkness with evil, base and material. Also, light is identified with the Orient (where the sun rises), darkness with the Occident (where it disappears). The material world, in this cosmology, is base and ignoble, a prison or 'crypt' from which the soul of the seeker after salvation must be liberated. Suhrawardi's hierarchical world-picture contains a hierarchical physics. The highest level of his cosmos is the invisible Supreme Light (beyond human comprehension) from which all being derives. Indeed light is being, present to a greater or lesser degree in all (inferior) existents, which are mixtures (in varying proportions) of light and darkness – darkness in itself is nothingness, non-being. The highest world is the Orient, the visible world of matter is the Occident; but within the latter there is also a hierarchy, which parallels and partly incorporates Aristotle's: the heavens are called the 'middle Occident' and are superior to the world of the (Aristotelian) elements. The elements are 'powerless' before the heavens, which in turn are dominated by the souls, and so on upwards to the Supreme Light. Within these broad strata there appear to be sub-hierarchies, for the Supreme Light has 'vice-gerents' in them: in the heavens the Sun, among the elements fire. The hierarchicalisation is obviously based on how far different beings manifest light – both the stars (in the heavens) and fire (among the elements) are forms of 'accidental' (i.e. dependent) light. All change is due to hierarchies of light. If anyone should wonder (as did many orthodox ulema) in what way this is a form of Islam, Suhrawardi found a place for Muhammad in his system. For example, Muhammad's famous Ascension (or Night Journey) is a journey upwards through the hierarchy of being – which the Sufi initiate too must achieve (Nasr 1995: 127–41, 144).

Suhrawardi's system has obvious implications for physical science. The lower world is of little or indeed of negative value, presumably hardly meriting the attention of a serious seeker. Much more valuable are the heavens, especially the sun – so it is not surprising that the Illuminationists were interested in astronomy, and that Tusi admired Suhrawardi (Nasr 1995: 161); nor that the greatest achievements of Muslim science were in astronomy and the physics of light. Another major Maragha astronomer, al-Shirazi, wrote the best-known commentary on Suhrawardi's *Hikmat al-Ishraq* and was plainly much influenced by it. Besides his astronomical work he developed a physics of light whose debt to Suhrawardi is obvious – it classifies bodies as transparent or opaque, and posits light as the source of all motion. That of the heavenly spheres is due to the illumination of their souls by the Divine Light (recall that according to Suhrawardi 'the heavens' are dominated by 'the souls'). Shirazi is also credited with reviving Islamic optical science, and being the first to explain correctly the physics of the rainbow (Nasr 1997: 97; 1995: 161, 219, 221, 225; 1976: 130) – a subject that could obviously interest an adept of Illuminationism.

A philosophy like Suhrawardi's could and did stimulate scientific investigation, up to a point. However, its hierarchical world-view is incompatible with the idea of laws (possibly, laws of God) governing all nature. It rules out anything comparable to Newton's unified physics, applicable both to heavenly bodies and terrestrial objects.

Islamic mysticism and Islamic philosophy

I remarked above that Seyyed Hossein Nasr points to a difference between Muslim mysticism and others – the former is, he contends, markedly more philosophical, incorporating significant elements of Greek philosophy, notably neo-Platonism. Equally important, I suggest, is the obverse of this: 'falsafa', the philosophy inspired by the Greeks, and often called Aristotelian, includes a large element of mysticism. One of the most celebrated 'Aristotelians', Ibn Sina (Avicenna), perhaps surprisingly, figures among Suhrawardi's prime sources. Suhrawardi translated one of his books (*Risalat al-tair*) into Persian, and acknowledged him as a pioneer of his own Illuminationism. As Nasr says, 'Ibn Sina's doctrines served as one of the main components … of the synthesis achieved by Suhrawardi' (Nasr 1993: 278). In fact Ibn Sina was much more than an Aristotelian, and in his later works (little known in the West until recently) veered to a mystical world-view. In one, significantly entitled *The Logic of the Orientals*, he downgraded the Aristotelian philosophy that had earlier preoccupied him, as only for the common people: for the elite, he offered his 'Oriental philosophy', which describes and prescribes a gnostic journey 'from the "world of shadows" to the Divine Presence, the Orient of Light'. Clearly Suhrawardi's Illuminationism is prefigured here. Nevertheless in these later 'Visionary Narratives' Ibn Sina did not discard his Aristotelian cosmology, but reinterpreted it as a universe of symbols 'through which the gnostic journeys towards ... beatitude' (Nasr 1968: 297). Given Ibn Sina's acknowledged influence on his thinking, this may well be why Suhrawardi likewise retained a quasi-Aristotelian cosmic hierarchy. It is striking, also, that two of the foremost Maragha astronomers, Tusi and Shirazi, wrote commentaries on Ibn Sina, and took a leading role in rehabilitating his thought, which had been neglected since the onslaught of Ghazzali (Nasr 1968: 55, 321–2; Nasr 1995: 220; EOI 2000: 747).

The nexus linking Ibn Sina, Suhrawardi, Illuminationism and the scientists of Maragha seems to me only the most striking manifestation of a crucially important fact: the continuities linking Hellenistic philosophy (*falsafa*) and Sufi mysticism, and the consequent interpenetration of mysticism, philosophy and science. According to a familiar account, the Muslims (or Arabs) preserved the Greek achievement (especially in philosophy and science) and later passed it to the West. The reality is more complex. The Muslims did not merely preserve Greek thought, they developed it. But, importantly, the Greek thought they inherited was in some ways unrepresentative, even erroneous. Translations of Greek texts into Arabic for Muslim patrons were largely the work of Syriac-speaking Christians, from Syriac versions made when the centre of Hellenism was no longer Greece but Alexandria (O'Leary 1922: 53; Peters 1996: 42–4; Nasr 1997: 54–5). The dominant intellectual force in Alexandrian Hellenism was neo-Platonism, a mystically tinged philosophy; among other powerful influences were Hermeticism (which envisages a journey of the soul after death through the celestial spheres to union with God) and Pythagoreanism, another strongly mystical philosophy (Peters 1996: 42, 46; Nasr 1997: 54; Whitfield 2001: 147). The Alexandrian neo-Platonists preserved Plato's and Aristotle's philosophy, but in a way that played down differences between Plato, Aristotle and themselves. The Muslim Aristotelians thus inherited a neo-Platonised Aristotle. A work they called the *Theology of Aristotle* is in fact an abridgement of part of Plotinus' *Ennead*; another 'Aristotelian' work, *Elements of Theology*, was actually by the neo-Platonist Proclus. Both expound the neo-Platonist doctrine of emanation. As Majid Fakhry, author of a *History of Islamic Philosophy*, sums it up: 'Aristotle ... was confused with Plotinus, reconciled with Plato, declared to be a disciple of Hermes' (Fakhry 1983: 273–5). Neo-Platonism is a common thread linking *falsafa* and Sufism. One reason, I suggest, for the limitations of Islamic science (despite its great achievements) is that it was embedded in a potent blend of Aristotle and mysticism, which it did not transcend.

References

Adams, C. C. 1933. *Islam and Modernism in Egypt*. London: Oxford University Press.

Blumenberg, H. 1987/2000. *The Genesis of the Copernican World*, trans. R. M. Wallace. Cambridge, MA: MIT Press.

Bosley, R. and Tweedale, M. 1996. *Basic Issues in Medieval Philosophy*. Peterborough, Ontario: Broadview Press.

Bowering, G. 1999. Early Sufism between Persecution and Heresy. In F. de Jong, and B. Radtke (eds.), *Islamic Mysticism Contested*. Leiden: Brill, pp. 45–67.

Buehler, A. 1999. Charismatic versus Scriptural Authority: Naqshbandi Response to Deniers of Mediatory Sufism in British India. In F. de Jong and B. Radtke (eds.), *Islamic Mysticism Contested*. Leiden: E. J. Brill, pp. 468–91.

Burns, T. 2003. The Tragedy of Slavery: Aristotle's *Rhetoric* and the History of the Concept of Natural Law. *History of Political Thought* 24 (1): 1–22.

Burtt, E. A. 1932. *The Metaphysical Foundations of Modern Science*. Rev. edn, London: Routledge and Kegan Paul.

Calder, N. 1996. Islamic Law. In S. H. Nasr and O. Leaman (eds.), *History of Islamic Philosophy*. London: Routledge, pp. 979–98.

Cicero, 1998. *The Republic and the Laws*, trans. N. Rudd. Oxford: Oxford University Press.

Dabashi, H. 1996. Mir Damad and the Founding of the School of Isfahan. In S. H. Nasr and O. Leaman (eds.), *History of Islamic Philosophy*. London: Routledge, pp. 597–634.

Dampier, V. C. 1971. *A History of Science and Its Relations with Philosophy and Religion*. Cambridge: Cambridge University Press.

de Jong, F. and Radtke, B. 1999. *Islamic Mysticism Contested*. Leiden: E. J. Brill.

d'Entreves, A. P. 1970. *Natural Law*. Rev. edn, London: Hutchinson University Library.

de Santillana, G. 1968. Preface to S. H. Nasr *Science and Civilization in Islam*. Cambridge, MA: Harvard University Press.

Descartes, R. 1983 [1644]. *Principles of Philosophy*, trans. V. R. and R. P. Miller. Dordrecht: Reidel.

Dijksterhuis, E. J. 1961. *The Mechanization of the World Picture*. Oxford: Oxford University Press.

Emperor Babur. 2002. *The Baburnama*, trans. and ed. W. M. Thackston. New York: The Modern Library.

EOI 1960. *Encyclopaedia of Islam*, vol. I. London and New York: E. J. Brill.

EOI 1971a. *Encyclopaedia of Islam*, vol. II. London and New York: E. J. Brill.

EOI 1971b. *Encyclopaedia of Islam*, vol. III. London and New York: E. J. Brill.
EOI 1986. *Encyclopaedia of Islam*, vol. V. London and New York: E. J. Brill.
EOI 1993. *Encyclopaedia of Islam*, vol. VII. London and New York: E. J. Brill.
EOI 2000. *Encyclopaedia of Islam*, vol. X. London and New York: E. J. Brill.
Fakhry, M. 1983. *A History of Islamic Philosophy*. London: Longman.
Filali, K. 1999. Quelques modalités d'opposition entre marabouts mystiques et élites du pouvoir, en Algérie à l'époque ottomane. In F. de Jong and B. Radtke (eds.), *Islamic Mysticism Contested*. Leiden: Brill, pp. 248–66.
Gaborieau, M. 1999. Criticizing the Sufis: The Debate in Early Nineteenth-Century India. In F. de Jong and B. Radtke (eds.), *Islamic Mysticism Contested*. Leiden: E. J. Brill, pp. 452–67.
Gay, P. 1967. *The Enlightenment: An Interpretation*. London, Weidenfeld and Nicolson.
Gellner, E. 1969. *Saints of the Atlas*. London: Weidenfeld and Nicolson.
   1981. *Muslim Society*. Cambridge: Cambridge University Press.
   1990. *Plough, Sword and Book*. Chicago: University of Chicago Press.
   1992. *Postmodernism, Reason and Religion*. London: Routledge.
   1998. *Nationalism*. London: Phoenix.
Gibb, H. A. R. 1993. Foreword to S. H. Nasr, *An Introduction to Islamic Cosmological Doctrines*. Rev. edn, Albany, NY: SUNY Press.
Hampson, N. 1968. *The Enlightenment*. Harmondsworth: Penguin.
Homerin, T. E. 1999. Sufis and their Detractors in Mameluk Egypt. A Survey of Protagonists and Institutional Settings. In F. de Jong and B. Radtke (eds.), *Islamic Mysticism Contested*. Leiden: Brill, pp. 225–47.
Hooykaas, R. 1972. *Religion and the Rise of Science*. Edinburgh: Scottish Academic Press.
Howell, K. 2002. *God's Two Books: Copernican Cosmology and Biblical Interpretation in Early Modern Science*. Notre Dame: University of Notre Dame Press.
Inalcik, H. 1973. *The Ottoman Empire: The Classical Age, 1300–1600*. New Rochelle, NY: Orpheus Publishing.
Iqbal, M. 2002. *Islam and Science*. Aldershot: Ashgate.
Israel, J. I. 2001. *The Radical Enlightenment*. Oxford: Oxford University Press.
Kuhn, T. S. 1957. *The Copernican Revolution*. Cambridge, MA: Harvard University Press.
Lessnoff, M. 2002. *Ernest Gellner and Modernity*. Cardiff: University of Wales Press.
Manuel, F. 1974. *The Religion of Isaac Newton*. Oxford: Oxford University Press.
Martin, R. C. and Woodward, M. R. 1997. *Defenders of Reason in Islam*. Oxford: Oneworld.
Morrow, G. R. 1948. Plato and the Law of Nature. In M. R. Konvitz and A. E. Murphy (eds.), *Essays in Political Theory*. Ithaca, NY: Cornell University Press, pp. 17–44.
Nasr, S. H. 1968. *Science and Civilization in Islam*. Cambridge, MA: Harvard University Press.
   1976. *Islamic Science*. London: World of Islam Festival Publishing Co. Ltd.
   1993. *An Introduction to Islamic Cosmological Doctrines*, revised edn, Albany, NY: SUNY Press.

1995. *The Islamic Intellectual Tradition in Persia*. London: Curzon Press.

1997. *Man and Nature*. Chicago: ABC International Group.

O'Leary, D. L. 1922. *Arabic Thought and its Place in History*. London: Kegan Paul, Trench, Trubner and Co. Ltd.

Pollock, F. 1961. *Jurisprudence and Legal Essays*. London: Macmillan.

Pope, A. 1966. *Essay on Man*. London: Macmillan.

Ritchie, D. G. 1916. *Natural Rights*. 3rd edn, London: Allen and Unwin.

Robson, W. A. 1935. *Civilization and the Growth of Law*. London: Macmillan.

Sabine, G. H. 1948. *A History of Political Theory*. London: Harrap.

Saliba, G. 1994. *A History of Arabic Astronomy*. New York: New York University Press.

Sandbach, F. H. 1975. *The Stoics*. London: Chatto and Windus.

Schacht, J. 1974. *The Legacy of Islam*. 2nd edn, Oxford: Clarendon Press.

Watt, M. 1963. *Muslim Intellectual: A Study of Al-Ghazali*. Edinburgh: Edinburgh University Press.

1998. *The Formative Period of Islamic Thought*. Oxford: Oneworld.

Weber, M. 1965/66. *Sociology of Religion*. London: Methuen.

Westfall, R. S. 1958. *Science and Religion in Seventeenth-Century England*. New Haven: Yale University Press.

Whitfield, P. 2001. *Astrology: A History*. New York: Harry Abrams.

Wolfson, H. A. 1976. *The Philosophy of the Kalam*. Cambridge, MA: Harvard University Press.

Kevin Ryan

Introduction: the open society

As a philosopher, sociologist and anthropologist, Ernest Gellner was resolute in his defence of reason and objectivity as the path to truth, perceiving both the infallibility of doctrinal beliefs and the epistemic relativism of postmodern thought as the enemies of the one true path to knowledge. Gellner developed his epistemology through an extended critique of Karl Popper, although it was also the case that his debt to Popper was never in question (see Gellner 1985; 1993a: xi–xviii; 1993b; 1994b). Popper himself described epistemic relativism as 'a betrayal of reason and of humanity' (Gellner 1993b), and yet he also seems to have shared a core concern with at least some thinkers gathered under the umbrella term of postmodernism. In particular I am thinking of how Popper's thesis, as set out in *The Open Society* (1962; 1966) and *The Poverty of Historicism* (2002b), resonates with Foucault's argument, derived from his reading of Kant, that we should engage in a 'permanent critique of ourselves', and that we should be suspicious of all ideas and conceptual frameworks that promise a final emancipation (Foucault 1984). In the case of Foucault, the rationalism so dear to Popper (and Gellner) would be among such conceptual frameworks, which is where an imagined conversation between these thinkers would probably terminate. I have found no evidence of direct dialogue between Popper and Foucault, but a little book published by Gellner in 1992 brought them into an interesting, though indirect, relation. I say indirect because in this text, titled *Postmodernism, Reason and Religion*, Gellner draws heavily on a single essay by Paul Rabinow. While the shadow of Popper forms at least part of the background to Gellner's thought, Foucault stands behind Rabinow. This characterisation may seem unfair as it risks turning two original thinkers into the mere apostles of Giants, but there is a purpose to my strategy. Despite the obvious disagreements that may have resulted, it is at least possible to imagine a fruitful dialogue between Popper and Foucault. Gellner however foreclosed on the possibility for such a dialogue, and went to some lengths to create a categorical distinction between rationalism and the critical standpoint he characterised, or rather caricatured, as postmodernism.

The aim of this chapter is to recast Gellner's interpretative scheme by teasing out its Popperian aspect and bringing it into a dialogue with Foucaultian-inspired research. I think this has the potential to further our understanding of the relation between modern and postmodern social thought. Between the modern impulse to know and to order, and the postmodern impulse to deconstruct that which is known and has been ordered, we find a relation which is one of neither total commensurability nor incommensurability. The problem I want to examine can be stated in the form of a question which conjoins Popper, Gellner and Foucault: what is the *source* of critique which is so essential to the open society?

The spectre of contingency: 'strong' and 'weak' articulations

In the work of Gellner and Popper, Rabinow and Foucault it is possible to detect competing research paradigms, and I want to characterise these before moving on to Gellner's encounter with postmodernism. These thinkers will be treated as exemplary representatives, noting in advance that this entails glossing the internally heterogeneous nature of a paradigm. I will be working with the assumption that a paradigm is not constituted through consensus in the naïve sense of that term, but through disagreements and petty disputes which are structured by a general level of agreement on such things as principles, procedures and objectives. The paradigms will be presented as (1) a problem-solving approach (Popper and Gellner)[1] and (2) a problem-driven approach (Foucault and Rabinow). The conception of contingency employed by the problem-solving approach is 'weak', while that of the problem-driven approach is 'strong'. While this terminology lacks a certain conceptual precision it allows me to proceed without having continually to specify different interpretations of terms such as 'historicism' or 'holism', both of which have paradigm-specific meanings.

Problem-solving research

A useful place to begin the task of mapping the general contours of problem-solving research is Popper's own account of critical rationalism,

---

[1] The reader may be asking whether I am justified in casting Gellner as a 'problem-solver'. Gellner wrote repeatedly about his empiricist/positivist-inspired 'granular' theory of world, which I think is consistent with the problem-solving paradigm. For Gellner's views on scientific problem-solving, see his *Relativism and the Social Sciences* (1985: 54–9).

which includes both the principle of falsification and the technical domain of piecemeal tinkering, which is Popper's preferred alternative to whole-scale social engineering[2] (1966: 157–68). We should also note Popper's solution to the problem of demarcation – distinguishing science from non- or pseudo-science – which hinges on what he defines as a crucial 'asymmetry' between verifiability and falsifiability: we can never prove the absolute truth of a theory because it makes an indefinite number of empirical predictions, and only a finite number of these can be tested. We can, however, prove a theory to be false, and a single reliable observation will suffice (2002a).

Popper was aware that the meanings of both 'reason' and 'rationalism' were subject to some degree of interpretation; interestingly, he also acknowledged that to adopt the attitude of the critical rationalist was an act of faith – an irrational decision, in fact. However, and this is his point, once the decision is taken and the attitude adopted, then its scope extends to any and all problems that can be solved by an appeal to reason, meaning 'clear thought and experience' rather than emotions and passions. More specifically, to be rational is to adopt an 'attitude of readiness to critical arguments and to learn from experience', so that the rationalist is willing to admit that 'I may be wrong and you may be right, and by an effort, we may get nearer to the truth' (Popper 1962: 224–5). I will return to this quote later when we examine Gellner's critique of postmodernism. For now I suggest we take Popper at his word and note that genuine scientific method is embedded in a particular type of culture. As can be discerned from the short quotation above, Popper was something of a radical on this point. Moving beyond the subject–object world to a three-world ontology, Popper accorded a crucial role to World Three, or the social world of communicative interaction[3] (see Gellner 1985: 107–9). As individuals we may on occasion argue with ourselves through critical self-reflection, but we have learnt to do this only by arguing with others. Reason is directed outwards at external nature and inwards at social relations, and when the individual utters her theory or claim to truth, so she is subjected to the constraints both of nature and of the exacting standards of rational thought and argumentation. Ultimately it is the argument, and not the person

---

[2] Gellner's equivalent can be found in his defence of piecemeal empirical investigation (1992a: 80–1).

[3] In *The Open Society* Popper explains that the attitude of reasonableness has a 'social character', so that 'reason, like language, can be said to be a product of social life' (1962: 225). He goes on to employ a Robinson Crusoe example, arguing that the lone individual may be clever enough to master many difficult situations, but she or he would invent neither language nor the art of argumentation. See also Habermas' theory of communicative action (1984: 76–9).

arguing, that counts (Popper 1962: 225, 217–18). Anchored in science and social organisation, Reason is the lifeblood of modern liberal culture, and as long as people are free to engage in rational debate and disputation, and thus free to falsify each other's hypotheses and statements, then the Open Society is secure against ideological closure (cf. Gellner 1992a: 75–96; 1994b: 95–6, 188–93, 211–12; 1992b: 116).

While he did not follow Popper to the letter (having much to say about Popper's neglect of 'falsifiers', or facts), Gellner did stay true to the core Popperian principle: knowledge must be falsifiable, which excludes all a priori or revealed truths, whether emanating from the religious prophet or the Marxist scientist. Discovery need not preclude intuition or even ideas inspired by dreams, but the justification for knowledge, as distinct from mere opinion, is its rational basis, which is to say genuine knowledge is subject to a verdict imposed by constraints – natural and social *facts* – which are more than subjective experiences and capable of dispelling collective illusions.

Gellner also departed from Popper in his emphasis on Worlds One and Two (external reality and the internal world of mind respectively), in the first instance exemplified in the work of Hume, and in the second by Descartes and Kant (1992b). Dissenting from what he saw as a naïve faith in World Three on the part of Popper, Gellner followed Descartes into the space of pure mind only to emerge in the empiricism of Hume. This might seem like an uncomfortable liaison to some, but Gellner insists that it is the best we can do. From Descartes comes the technique of seeking distance from the contingent – subjecting the arbitrary accretions of culture and experience to doubt, while from Hume comes the need for empirical facts – the stuff of falsification (Gellner 1992b; 1985). It is by adding an empirically informed World Three sociological dimension to this epistemology that Gellner arrives at his 'Big Ditch' thesis: one tradition, with its origins in seventeenth-century Europe, 'completely transformed the condition of human life by engendering the scientific and industrial revolution'. And this 'transformation of our cognitive and productive styles' is essentially an accident of history – an earthly Miracle, which gave birth to a style of thought capable of cumulative cognitive growth. However, and here Gellner rejects Popper's 'amoeba-to-Einstein cognitive optimism', this would never have happened without the World Two innovation of the Cartesian cogito, or something like it. The rational agent born with the Miracle learns how to adopt an attitude which, with the assistance of factual constraints, aims to purify the relation between mind, language and world. From the Big Divide emerges a style of cognition which treats all like cases in a like manner, attends as far as is possible only to the facts of the case, and ignores as far as possible the rich social context – this is Gellner's understanding of rationalism. And yet despite the best efforts of the giants of modern philosophy, and here is the pinch, we can only hope for, or express faith in, the possibility of discovering an essential causal structure or body of laws which originates in mind, or world, or both. Gellner did not subscribe to the mythical view from nowhere, and so like Weber's Calvinist we must look for auspicious signs in our practical achievements. It is the ability to improve our lot by understanding and controlling the world which is the most reliable sign that we are in possession of knowledge rather than in the grip of illusion (Gellner 1992a; 1992b: 160, 165–6; 1975: 337–8; 1985). As this Weberian-inspired thesis is grafted to Popperian-inspired method we get a sharp outline of Gellner's pragmatism: though fundamentally distinct from the merely contingent, the Sovereignty of Reason is nonetheless fallible; indeed its essential fragility – the elusiveness of a final guarantee or ultimate foundation for knowledge – can only be offset by the 'demonstration effect' of technological achievements.

So the Rule of Reason is not without its problems, and in particular Gellner detects something of a dilemma at the heart of Popper's World Three. On the one hand, even when it operates correctly – i.e. in an Open and not a Closed Society – it turns out to be a version of Adam Smith's Hidden Hand, and is capable of all manner of mutations. On the other hand, it may dupe the critical thinker into accepting the conventions of a particular culture, and here Gellner turns out to be even more of an individualist than the libertarian Popper.

Earlier I suggested that the nature of a paradigm was one of agreement, but not in the naïve sense of a cosy consensus, and Gellner's critique of Popper is precisely the kind of petty dispute which plays an integrative role. Whether we stay with a World Three rationalist like Popper and call the paradigm in question 'critical rationalism', or follow Gellner and call it 'rationalist fundamentalism', then we are not dealing with a dispute over 'fundamentals' in Kuhn's sense of that term (1996: 11; cf. Foucault 1994: 262). On the contrary, the fundamentals are set in stone, as we will see a little later. For the rationalists the relation between Reason and (what Weber and Habermas call) Rationalisation is one of difficult and indeterminate progress, and the danger of insurrection intrinsic to the latter (the Holocaust, environmental degradation ...) makes the former the proper authority. The benefits of the technologies born out of the Miracle must be weighed against their destructive potential, and a historically specific agent is responsible for striking the balance. In his *Conditions of Liberty* Gellner describes this agent as 'modular man'. At once introspective and discursive, the subject of *Gesellschaft* rather than *Gemeinschaft*, Modular Man is Modern Rational Man: individual, egalitarian, willing to stand against the coercive state, and capable of performing a dazzling range of practical and intellectual tasks[4] (1994b: 97–102). Whether located in the laboratory, the boardroom or the public sphere, Modular Man is disposed to open debate and is receptive to criticism. With a capacity for logical reasoning, and attending as far as is humanly possible only to the facts, the Agent of Reason clears away error so as to leave a solid kernel of truth. But this kernel is never free from scepticism – it remains fallible, and must be subjected to continuous and rigorous testing. In other words the knowledge which counts as truth is never more than provisional, hence contingent. This mode of contingency is weakly articulated, however, because it adopts a problem-solving approach to subject–object and subject–subject relations. While non-teleological, the problem-solving approach is an evolutionary theory of social change: a process of social learning which takes the existing structure as given, or at least as the given framework for improvement. The aim is to solve problems and account for anomalies as they arise within the complex whole, attempting to smooth the overall functioning of something which *is* beyond the understanding of any single mind and *should remain* beyond the control of any single authority. What the paradigm of rationalism does not do, as a rule, is question the complex whole itself (see Cox 1981: 128–30; Howarth 2004: 318).

In summary we can note that the paradigm of problem-solving locates Reason at the centre of a particular style of philosophical thought and a specific mode of scientific practice and social organisation. As to the source of critique, it takes the form of an asymmetrical relation between question and answer. As a problem to be solved the question is born within its context, but the corresponding answer is enunciated in a language which is for all people everywhere, and possibly even for all time – if it can withstand the scrutiny of testing. Though articulated within a context which is saturated by contingency, Reason itself transcends all contexts: the property of no one and available to everyone. Thus it is no accident that Reason is nominated as the official language of the Open Society, which of course in lay terms goes by names such as 'civil society' and 'liberal democracy'. Rationalism brokers no dialogue with paradigms outside of itself, or at least it cannot converse with others as equals. To do so would mean its demotion as the Sovereign Parent of all other language games, whereupon it would be become a mere relative among orphans (see Gellner 1992b: 53).

---

[4] Gellner also identifies an important ambiguity in Modular Man insofar as he (*sic*) is compatible both with liberalism and nationalism (1994b:107; for a cogent theory of this phenomenon see Haugaard 2006).

Problem-driven research

In contrast to the problem-solving approach, problem-driven research goes all the way down to a 'historical ontology of ourselves' (Foucault 1984: 48–9), not with a view to disclosing historical laws or predicting a future course of events, which is Popper's understanding of historicism, but in order to problematise and redescribe the present. In Foucault's work for example, the Enlightenment is an 'event' which gave rise to historically specific 'practical systems' (1984: 42, 48). As with Popper, Foucault examines knowledge as a social practice, but departing from Popper, he argues that the way we think, speak and act, indeed the very subjectivity we embody, is circumscribed by historical events which mark a transformation in the order of things. From the event is born specific 'theoretico-practical matrices' which order nominally distinct truth claims, or what Foucault calls 'statements', into strategic relations (Miller and Rose 1990: 23). A theoretico-practical matrix encompasses a number of domains: control over things, ways of acting upon the action of others, and forms of self-government (Foucault 1984: 48). Here we see Foucault's thought overlapping with Popper's three world ontology. However, as noted, Foucault is interested in the discontinuities created by historical events, and he works through an analytics comprised of three axes: knowledge, power and ethics (1984: 48–9). In this way Foucault examines how specific 'grids' of possibility are assembled from the intersection of systems of knowledge, relations of power, disciplinary technologies and regulatory apparatuses: ways of knowing and ways of doing that circumscribe the parameters of 'the true' (Foucault 1991: 79–82).

In the problem-driven approach then, 'truth is a thing of this world' (Foucault 1980: 131), which is to say it is *made by* rather than *reflected in* our representational systems (Laclau and Mouffe 1987: 106; Rorty 1980). And because society is ordered through discourses which distinguish true from false statements – ordered in the sense of technological and institutional hierarchies, and relations of empowerment and disempowerment between people – so social order can be characterised as a 'regime of truth' (Foucault 1991: 82). A truth regime is implicated in the organisation of social space, with certain possibilities ordered into the realm of the sayable and the doable while others are excluded. In this way the formation of truth can be conceptualised as a mode of foreclosing, or a form of political 'decision' (Torfing 1999: 67–9). Problem-driven research aims specifically to retrace the discursive formation of truth regimes: to open out the possibility of deconstructing and reassembling the present by disclosing its (our) contingency (Foucault 1972; 1977; Rabinow 1986: 239–40). This latter point can be elaborated through a direct contrast with the problem-solving approach.

In discussing the possibility of a unity of method between the hard and soft sciences, Popper discussed a way of modelling social action which he called 'the method of logical or rational construction', or alternatively the 'zero method', more commonly known as rational choice. Based on assumptions such as 'complete rationality', which may be supplemented with other assumptions, such as the possession of perfect information, the value of this way of analysing social action is that it can be used to evaluate 'the deviation of the actual behaviour of people from the model behaviour, using the latter as a kind of zero coordinate' (2002b: 130–1; cf. Weber 1978: 20–5, 63–8). But what happens when model behaviour – and here Popper's use of the term 'deviation' is important – is coded in normative terms as socially desirable, so that deviations are coded as problems to be corrected, cured or eradicated: defective intelligence, deviant behaviour, 'immoral' conduct, and the like? The relation between facts and norms very often turns out to be strategic, with those who practise the scientific disciplines implicated in the objectification of certain dispositions and conducts. Techniques such as the zero method are rarely innocent, but neither are they *necessarily* bad (Foucault 1984: 343). This is why the problem-driven approach is concerned with making certain things into a problem, thereby *problematising* aspects of the world which might otherwise go unquestioned. The zero method itself is only possible in a context where social knowledge is derived from the application of specific statistical techniques, and it is important to note that the latter have attained an inordinate degree of authority in modern Western societies (Hacking 1990). Historically, the zero coordinate of model behaviour has gone by a more familiar name: the 'normal' – a statistical average derived simultaneously from living individuals and a living population. But by the time this has been abstracted into standards and measurements of normal health, normal intelligence, etc., it no longer corresponds to any particular individual. Furthermore, as standards of normalcy are discursively consolidated – a World Three phenomenon – and built into instruments and techniques of administration, so they close off the fact–value distinction and begin to articulate specific forms of subjection. There are consequences attached to being coded as a person with above-average or below-average 'intelligence', or defined as a 'risk' to self and community following psychological evaluation.[5] The problem-solving approach provides a weak source of critique in the face of this type of problem, because

---

[5] For a brief history of the word 'normal', and an account of how it 'dances and prances' all over the fact/value distinction, see Hacking 1990: 162–3.

we are confronted with the power of shared systems of meaning – the cohesiveness of a Kuhnian paradigm, or in Foucault's terminology, a truth regime. I will provide a more concrete example of this shortly, but first I want to consider the question of contingency in more detail.

The manifestation of contingency can be coded in many different ways.[6] In the search for order, predictability and certainty, contingency may be coded as a crisis (a sudden downturn in the economy), as a threat to social security (an uncontrollable increase in long-term unemployment), as an internal threat to be controlled (a subversive movement or infectious disease) or an external threat which must be eradicated ('terror'). On the other hand, it may be interpreted as a horizon of possibilities. Perspective remains crucially important, as do differentials in status, authority and power resources pertaining to specific social subjects. Stepping back from these concerns so as to focus on the more general problem of order, then we can note that contingency is a 'surplus' (of meaning, of possibilities) made manifest. For the problem-driven analyst, a given ordered whole, whether a language or a society, is a relational system of elements, with each element both differing from the others and deferring meaning to itself (Saussure 1998). This presupposes a relation of presence and absence between the positivity of the elements which have an identity within the system and the possible meanings which have been excluded, a relation with both synchronic and diachronic dimensions (Derrida 1997: 65–7). This surplus can be defined as an 'outside' which is *immanent to* and *constitutive of* that which has the presence of being (Staten 1985). There is a kind of metaphysics to this, albeit one cast in a negative register of absent-presence, and I will attempt to clarify it a little later. For now we can simplify by noting that there is always more to a given context than what we can think or say or do, with the contingency of knowledge both the condition of possibility for truth and that which prevents a regime of truth from fully constituting itself, from achieving a state of perfect presence. Problem-driven research assumes from the outset that order is permanently vulnerable to the possibilities which have been excluded, and is thus necessarily unstable.

For the problem-solvers the contingency of knowledge is both desirable and disturbing. Problems to be solved are interesting and challenging, but they are also potentially menacing and threatening, for reasons explicated by Kuhn.[7] Unless it can be mastered, then contingency is a spectre which threatens the paradigm. For Popper this kind of scenario is central to the

---

[6] Readers familiar with Kuhn's work will see a trace of his anomaly in what follows.

[7] For Gellner's views on Kuhn see his review of Barry Barnes' 'T. S. Kuhn and Social Science' (1982; also 1992b: 112–15 and 1985: 110–27).

process of learning, and we should remain open to the contingency of knowledge. In practice, however, knowledge of who we are and what we are can be extremely precious – and strategic – particularly in contexts where the manifestation of contingency appears threatening. An example is the way 'terror' is being used today to symbolise the enemy of the Open Society. The fact of cultural pluralism in democratic societies leads to a second fact: the enemy is both within and without, and so the freedoms that characterise the Open Society must be constrained in the name of security, which is another way of saying that freedom must be limited for the sake of freedom. 'Terror' does not simply define the edge between two fully constituted entities; instead there is a mutually constitutive relation between the discursive construction of an 'inside' (the Open Society) and an 'outside' (Terror). This is precisely how the problem-driven approach examines a regime of truth. In situations where our theoretico-practical matrices lead to the marginalisation, exclusion or destruction of specific individuals and groups, then it might be possible – dare we say necessary, and here the ethical implications of particular standpoints, identities and objectives come into play – to create new meanings so as to redescribe the context. For analysts working within the problem-driven paradigm, the immanent horizon of contingency which haunts our systems of knowledge is simultaneously truth's condition of possibility and its condition of impossibility.

The source of critique

In both paradigms the source of critique is found in the way that contingency is specified. Problem-solving research confronts novel questions and data which – at least in terms of how they are encountered – are external to the existing state of knowledge. Solving problems may lead to the modification of truth, and even the death of branches of existing knowledge, yet the process invigorates and feeds the paradigm so that it grows in stature and strength. Problem-driven research on the other hand is a form of immanent critique, a method that aims to disturb and unsettle meanings which have become reified as they sediment in the social order and acquire the authority of truth. Problem-driven research takes the existing order as its field of inquiry, the objective to examine how regimes of truth have been assembled. While these research paradigms do not see eye to eye, they do share an important normative concern – keeping the Open Society open – and in both cases contingency is both the possibility for critique and the impossibility of ideological closure. However, an over-reliance on the problem-solving paradigm has proven to have dangerous implications, and an example will help to demonstrate what is at stake.

Problem-solving as a social practice

The example I want to use has been well documented and long since discredited: eugenics. As a paradigmatically 'biopolitical' field of discourse, which is to say a politics of living individuals and populations, eugenics brings together a heterogeneous body of knowledges and practical techniques which has as its logic a double-articulation between science and administration, between facticity and normativity. My main concern here lies not in the detail of a historical account but in underlining the role of problem-solving in the constitution and consolidation of a truth regime.

Social Darwinism is often used interchangeably, and somewhat uncritically, with eugenics, and it should be noted that I am using 'Darwin' as a statement within a formation of discourse which includes not only earlier thinkers such as Jean-Baptiste Lamarck and contemporaries of Darwin such as Thomas Huxley and Herbert Spencer, but also the administrative apparatus of the liberal state as well as reform projects driven by social inquiry and philanthropic organisation. While the works of Darwin provide a useful point of departure it would be erroneous to equate the author of a theory with discursive authority.

In his *Origin of Species* Darwin examined the problem of novel differences in nature, a question which had a profound resonance with the concerns of public officials, social inquirers and philanthropists at that time, and it is here that we can locate Darwin*ism* as discourse. When confronted with pure difference, that is, difference that awaits assignment in our systems of classification, Darwin explained that the scientist:

is at first much perplexed to determine what differences to consider as specific, and what as varieties ... Certainly no clear line of demarcation has as yet been drawn between species and sub-species ... or again, between sub-species and well-marked varieties; or, again, between lesser varieties and individual differences. These differences blend into each other in an insensible series; and a series impresses the mind with the idea of an actual passage. (Darwin 1998: 41)

Here Darwin invokes one of the axioms of post-Enlightenment thought: linear time. This could be coded equally well as evolution in nature, historical laws or social progress, and as it entered the social domain so it was brought to bear on the problem of governing individuals and populations. The problem Darwin formulates is this: in a given environment which is host to a dominant species, it is not unusual to find what he calls 'doubtful forms' which exhibit similarities to and differences from the dominant species. The problem for the classifier is how to interpret a doubtful form, which may be a simple variety of the dominant species, or alternatively an 'incipient species' in its own right, on its way to becoming a new dominant species. The relation between the struggle for existence and the conditions of existence was complex, and the implications of this interpretative scheme extended well beyond the intended reach of Darwin's investigations.

From the turn of the nineteenth century the notion of primitiveness was among the conditions of possibility not only for European colonial expansion, but also for novel approaches to the ordering of domestic social space (Jacques 1997; Kahn 2001). The relation between an evolved or 'civilised' life form and its primitive counterpart articulated the distinction between progress and regress, order and disorder, which at the level of social practice was coded by the difference and the relation between the normal and the abnormal. Encompassing such objects as crime, intelligence and sexuality, the normal/abnormal distinction underpinned technologies of surveillance, regulation and reform, coupling the disciplines of science to the disciplinary mechanisms of the modern state and forming an apparatus which extended from the prison and the poor house to the school and the family (Foucault 1977; 1998). How falsifiable was it though?

In the closing pages of his *Descent of Man*, Darwin placed a question mark over the validity of his thesis in a way that Popper might have approved of:

False facts are highly injurious to the progress of science, for they often long endure; but false views, if supported by some evidence, do little harm, as everyone takes a salutary pleasure in proving their falseness; and when this is done, one path towards error is closed and the road to truth is often at the same time opened. (Darwin 1981 [1871]: 385)

In this instance however bold conjecture had already met with approval, with Darwin's research incorporated into a truth regime concerned with plucking the weeds from the social body so that the garden could flourish (see Bauman 1991). And as the distance between the natural sciences and the social sciences was closed off, so the unstable relation between facts and norms was effaced. The discursive construction of novel problems such as the 'dangerous individual' (Foucault 2003), the 'moral lunatic' (Kitching 1857) and the 'morally defective child' (Still 1902) brought scientific practice and state administration into a productive relation, passing through Darwin's invitation to falsify his hypothesis and culminating in pervasive discourses of hereditary degeneracy, mental deficiency and racial hygiene. It was these concerns that would help to generate a range of eugenic engineering projects that were highly resistant to falsification (Castel, Castel and Lovell 1982; Rose 1985; Broberg and Tydén 1996; Walmsley 2000).

Nicole Hahn Rafter's (1988) research into the Eugenic Family Studies in the US, spanning the period 1877–1919, provides compelling evidence of how the practice insulated itself against falsification (cf. Kuhn 1996: 36–9). Emulating the method developed by Darwin's cousin Francis Galton, practitioners took specific 'tribes' as their object, which is to say families identified as exhibiting an inferior hereditary endowment and considered to be the source of crime, alcoholism, feeble-mindedness, laziness, licentiousness and pauperism. Rafter concludes that the practice depended for its continued existence on the positing of problems for which it was the solution. Problems to be solved included the correct definition of a 'family', with disputes over this object helping to consolidate the practice. Gathering evidence in the field also provided a problem in need of resolution, with the search for an approved method helping the practice gain an institutional footing. Other types of 'problem' also existed, but these were overlooked: the fabrication of evidence in order to verify preconceived assumptions; the role of persuasion and conjecture in writing reports; the objectification of people as things to be known, with the tribes described in the Eugenic Family Studies silenced by the monological gaze of normal science. In the British context research into the heritability of intelligence was led by scientists such as Sir Cyril Burt. It later transpired that Burt had been manipulating his data, often guessing the parental IQ of suspect children and then treating his guesses as objective facts (Rose 1985: 112–45). For Nikolas Rose what is interesting here is not the falsification of theory (quite recent in Burt's case) but how a strategic alliance was formed between techniques such as scientific intelligence testing and the administrative imperatives of eugenic practices, an apparatus which successfully established its claims to truth.

The problem-solving paradigm proceeds by identifying specific problems, by assimilating anomalies, and by overlooking or repairing its own inconsistencies, with the community of practitioners deferring those problems for which it cannot find solutions and selecting those for which it can (see Kuhn 1996: 37; Foucault 1972: 223–4). Problem-solvers such as Gellner and Popper certainly recognise the insidious nature of practices such as eugenics, which is why they abhor the idea of utopian engineering projects whether they originate on the left or the right of the political spectrum. However, they also fail to really engage with the liberal-Enlightenment origins of such practices, and the extent to which they are *commensurate* with the Open Society and the Rule of Reason. Interpreting itself as a learning paradigm, rationalism turns away from the errors of the past and claims to have learnt the lesson, gathering the past into itself as it expands in the present. However Burt's research in the UK and the Family Eugenics movement in the US were no isolated aberrations. They were part of a 'systematic explanatory structure which made the claims of certain arguments so strong as to require little in the way of justificatory evidence' (Rose 1985: 122). In short they were statements within a truth regime that came into existence not through the ignorance of a Closed Society (Popper), the utopian blueprints of 'collectivists' (Hayek) or the doctrine of a secular Hegelian priesthood (Gellner), but through manifold conflicts waged in the name of Reason – between psychologists and doctors, doctors and teachers, those who supported negative eugenics (sterilisation) and those who supported positive eugenics (family welfare), between a patriarchal liberal state and the opportunities for social work created by educated women.

The Open Society governs by 'directing' conduct – or what Nikolas Rose calls 'governing at a distance' – which presupposes a historically specific mode of authority. While the authority of liberal democracy is diffuse rather than concentrated, its power more constitutive than repressive, it nonetheless structures the social field in such a way that subjectivity is tied to subjection, freedom to discipline (Cruikshank 1999). When the Open Society is examined through Foucaultian analytics then we are confronted with the problem of practice, and the specific ways in which social practices articulate the relation between facts and norms: Gellner's Modular Man is not only the subject of knowledge but also its object. As certain categories of person are defined as a 'problem', so they are subjected to an objectivising gaze that derives its authority and its legitimacy from its claim to truth. The problem is this: can cognition ever be fully independent of value-orientated practices, and should we accept it when it appears to be so? Is the Habermasian normative ideal of domination-free discourse not also – *depending on the context of its articulation* – a dangerous idealisation? Gellner's encounter with postmodernism can shed some light on this.

In defence of truth and reason

Towards the end of his life, Gellner gave a sermon on 'the uniqueness of truth' before the University of Cambridge (1992c). Published in the *Times Literary Supplement* and later in Gellner's *Anthropology and Politics*, this sermon is a measured, eloquent and at times extremely sympathetic account of what Gellner called the 'triangular predicament' characterising the 'modern attitude to truth'. It is measured in the way it gives equal weight to the three positions defining Gellner's triangle – Relativism, Fundamentalism and Enlightenment Puritanism – and it is sympathetic in its empathy for the peoples of Eastern Europe who were just then emerging from what Gellner described as the 'secular absolutism' of the

Soviet Union. In this sermon, Gellner aimed to 'square the *ménage à trois*': to confront the predicament by acknowledging that, in the practices of everyday life at least, the modern attitude to truth was about compromise: the Open Society can accommodate different attitudes to truth, even if its technological achievements and its liberal culture are based solely on a blend of scientific method and rational thought. However, in a lengthier essay, published the same year as *Postmodernism, Reason and Religion* (1992a), Gellner flattened the triangle into a line of opposition, moulding his three-way relation into a standoff between two adversaries.[8] Between one essay and the other is something of an inconsistency, or perhaps the difference in mood, tone and texture is an indication of something else: of how academic texts are the product of belief and passion as much as reason. I am inclined to insist on the latter, first because whatever else Gellner might be accused of, he was never inconsistent. But there is also something more, which is why, in the remainder of this chapter, I want to examine *Postmodernism, Reason and Religion* in detail. This is not because I think the style of argumentation to be found in this book is entirely characteristic of Gellner (in fact it is not), but rather because a close reading of this text – tracing the contours of its normative convictions – shows us the extent to which Gellner's epistemological position is founded on values which cannot be entirely uncoupled from 'facts'. Indeed, this falsifiable-resistant element of belief is something Gellner openly acknowledged (Gellner 1985: 4–67), but here I want to underline its ethico-political rather than its epistemological implications.

Squaring the ménage à trois

Gellner begins his *Postmodernism, Reason and Religion* by noting the binary nature of human conflict – schismatic disagreements which have 'polarized mankind': the wars of religion pitched Catholics against Protestants; later came the confrontation between reason and faith; and

---

[8] It is worth comparing Gellner's book to Popper's *Poverty of Historicism*. Beginning with three positions (rationalism confronts anti-naturalistic and pro-naturalistic doctrines of historicism), Popper ends with two (rationalism versus historicism). Popper was working within a historical and cultural context where the liberal ideal of the Open Society was posed as *the* antidote to the totalitarian impulse, the only guarantee against 'collectivism' (cf. Hayek 1991 [1944]). Gellner was writing in a context where state socialism had come and gone, while the established discourses of social and scientific progress had been turned inside-out, laying bare the many forms of exclusion and domination perpetrated in the name of Enlightenment and Reason. Gellner is thus confronting a resurgent rather than declining enemy of Reason, one which for him spans two extremes: absolutism and relativism. Yet, as we will see shortly, he replicates Popper's argument by reducing his three positions to two.

more recently we have witnessed the standoff between liberal capitalism
and state socialism (Gellner 1992a: 1). But things have changed, and the
world is now structured by 'three fundamental and irreducible positions': Religion, Relativism and Reason. In the case of religion we can
be forgiving, because the emergence of monotheism is among the historical preconditions for the development of a rational culture (Gellner
1992a: 95; 1992b: 43–54; 1994b). Postmodernism on the other hand
makes the unforgivable mistake of abandoning this gain, and allows
itself to become an accomplice to divinised authority (1992a: 74, 85).
Furthermore, in a situation where a society is in the grip of a repressive
doctrinal truth, postmodernism is impotent because it cannot provide a
universal standard of right.

The plot then is one of three 'characters', but Gellner's treatment of
the three R's exhibits both a quantitative and a qualitative difference.[9]
Gellner gives far more space to postmodernism than to religion, and he
also provides an *account* of Islamic fundamentalism within the context of
modernity, which is consistent with his intellectual investment in this
topic (see Lessnoff in this volume). His treatment of postmodernism on
the other hand is a demolition job which lacks any indication of
impartiality. Religion plays the role of an alibi, a cover story for the main
event, and as it turns out there is a twist in the plot: relativism and
absolutism (i.e. religion) are not separate problems but part of the same
problem. There are three key moments in Gellner's argument that
I want to trace out: the charge of subjectivism, the problem of relativism,
and the moulding of religion and relativism into the single movable
object.

Subjectivism

In his reading of postmodernism Gellner seizes, correctly as it happens,
on the centrality of meaning. However, he does not engage with postmodern theories of meaning but instead goes straight to the epistemological problem. Because postmodernism locates the subject within
systems of meaning which are historically and culturally constituted, so
there is no way of gaining an objective vantage point on the circumscribed whole. The postmodern thinker (whom Gellner identifies as a
hermeneutist) abandons objectivity and operates within the space of a
particular perspective, hence the problem of subjectivism: the 'idealist

---

[9] Gellner also genders his argument, calling his own position 'the third man'. In another
work published the same year (1992b) he used a distinctively feminine register to
characterise Reason. The gendered style of Gellner's writing warrants a paper in itself.

liberation of theorising from empirical constraints' (1992a: 23; 1980: 299; 1985: 122). Hermeneutic-subjectivism is a version of the 'egocentric predicament' which has long confronted the empiricist: how to escape the circle of immediate sensations. The hermeneutist however is not trapped by sensations but enclosed by a circle of meanings. Furthermore, against the grain of rationalism, this is no longer a problem to be resolved so much as something to think about and write about (1992a: 35–6). Subjectivism turns out to be a self-sustaining puzzle, for having eliminated 'all clarity, all objectivity' the hermeneutist revels in the pleasure of feeling guilty about a 'residue of observer's intrusion'. In the impossible attempt fully to disclose her standpoint, the hermeneutist is drawn into the infinite regress of subjective reflection. Looking at this from the point of view of anthropology, Gellner identifies two sides to subjectivism: one of world creation (on the part of those who are studied) and the other of interpretation and representation (on the part of the researcher) (1992a: 29–30). As everything is, and can only be, created, interpreted and represented in context, so (with a nod to Derrida, though without citing him directly) everything becomes text. For Gellner this is simply nonsense.

Postmodernism then is the latest chapter in the story of idealism which, insofar as this concerns social reality, ignores the constraints engendered by political and economic power, or what Gellner calls 'objective structures' with 'real independent existence' (1992a: 63–6). Here Gellner seems to subscribe to a number of sociological axioms which are, strictly speaking, no longer axiomatic. First is a tendency to counter constructivism by opposing the realm of ideas and language to some kind of extra-linguistic 'material' domain or substrate, and second is an understanding of power as something constraining, coercive, limiting or otherwise negative in its effects (see Haugaard in this volume). These are not unrelated concerns, and I think Gellner's critical position can be captured by contrasting two statements: (1) 'The construction of social reality' (Searle 1995) and (2). 'The social construction of reality' (Berger and Luckman 1966), and the difference in emphasis is apparently important. John Searle defines the first as a concern with what he calls 'institutional facts', which are distinct from, but also necessarily related to, an external reality of 'brute facts'. The second statement, however, belongs to what Searle describes as the current 'philosophical trend' of social constructivism, which apparently denies the existence of a reality which is totally independent of our systems of representation[10]

[10] Searle does not actually mention Berger and Luckman's earlier work, which is a little strange given the title and concerns of his book, but he does devote a whole section to

(cf. Gellner 1985: 121–2). Consider Ernesto Laclau and Chantal Mouffe, two thinkers influenced by Foucault and associated with social constructivism, on precisely this point:

> We have [argued] that the 'being' of objects is different from their mere exist-ence, and that objects are never given as mere 'existences' but are always articulated within discursive totalities … Human beings socially construct their world, and it is through this construction – always precarious and incomplete – that they give to a thing *its being*. (Laclau and Mouffe 1987: 89, original emphasis)

Here responding to the charge of idealism, Laclau and Mouffe explicitly reject the way idealism tends to bring word, thought and thing into a fixed/essential relation as thinkable form. Accepting (rather then deny-ing) brute existence, they insist on an irreducible gap or distance within a relation which is *other* than that of the real and the ideal: between the 'discursive totality' of beings and the 'field of discursivity' which makes the relational whole possible. What they call the 'being' of an object is contingent, unlike its brute facticity which is not, with the being of an object articulated within a discursive totality which is socially con-structed and thoroughly penetrated by a surplus (i.e. 'the field of dis-cursivity'). The social and political significance of this is that the surplus (of meaning, of possibilities – see above) is a potential 'solvent in which the knowable and speakable could lose its form' (Staten 1985: 16). A more mundane way of putting this is to suggest that at the level of brute existence an object does not contain within itself the means of its own representation (Torfing 2004: 18; Heller 1989). A rock exists, but it is *meaningful* in different ways in specific contexts: to a geologist, a mountaineer who needs something to drive her tent peg into the ground, a Palestinian freedom-fighter, and so on – a definitive list is impossible. And the discursive articulation of brute facticity draws in the question of power. However, in contrast to Gellner's interest in power as con-straining and coercive, problem-driven analysis is interested in power as constitutive of the discursive totalities within which meaning is con-tested, fixed and inscribed into the social field of objects and relations (see Haugaard 2003; Clegg 1989). Gellner's critique is coloured by the way he projects categories and their contents from his paradigm onto the problem-driven paradigm.

---

refuting what he calls 'attacks on realism' which would apply to Berger and Luckman (Searle 1995: 149–76). For Gellner, who does make reference to Berger and Luckman (1985), it is Wittgenstein who is to blame for leading the hermeneutist retreat from reality into a subjectivist world of meanings.

Relativism

Gellner's encounter with postmodernism is limited not only by his reluctance to engage in a serious consideration of theory but also in the way he restricts his reading to a limited number of texts. In *Postmodernism, Reason and Religion* the charge of relativism relies almost solely on a single essay by Paul Rabinow (1986). The title of this piece – 'Representations Are Social Facts' – provides a clue as to why this particular contribution was selected from an edited collection, although Gellner seems to have interpreted it rather too literally. Anyone familiar with Rabinow's work knows that he has written extensively on Foucault, and indeed he uses Foucault in this particular essay precisely to argue that a Foucaultian analytics 'avoids the problem of totally relativising reason or of turning different conceptions of truth and falsity into a question of subjectivism' (Rabinow 1986: 237). Rabinow adds that historically circumscribed styles of reasoning determine specific criteria of objectivity, which is to say they establish definite (im)possibilities regarding what *can* count as a truth statement. Gellner's main concerns are all anticipated here: relativism, subjectivism and objectivity, yet we hear very little about the mechanics of this in Gellner's account, that is, beyond a few quotes originating with Rorty, with whom Rabinow does not in fact entirely agree. A more faithful reading of the text in question requires moving Gellner's interpretation to one side.

Unlike Gellner, who begins his Big Ditch story with Descartes and finds a relation of continuity between Descartes, Hume and Kant, Foucault finds this relation to be one of rupture (1994). With Kant 'man' becomes simultaneously part of the empirical world and the transcendental source of knowledge, and this places the Subject of Reason in a strange relation to itself. Tracking this problematic through key nineteenth-century discourses, Foucault argues that, as both the source of knowledge and an object to be known, the Subject of Reason is immersed in a horizon of obscurity – the unthought – which exceeds mind and subverts its status as the source of all intelligibility. And yet paradoxically this becomes the condition of possibility for the sovereignty of Rational Man (Dreyfus and Rabinow 1983: 31, 90–100). Moving in the shadow of Kant we think of ourselves as autonomous, and as we strive to bring the horizon of unthought into the realm of consciousness, of knowledge and technical control, so we come to understand ourselves as the authors of our own destiny. In doing so we tend to overlook the fact that we are the subjects of, and subjected to, discourses which exceed the kind of design and control functions associated with Reason. Within the paradigm of problem-driven research it is precisely this 'ontological' problematic – the discursive construction of social knowledge, subjectivities and social practices – which is the primary concern, the overarching question one of understanding how we have come to be what we are. To interpret this, as Gellner does, as a hermeneutic retreat into relativism is really to miss the point.

Anti-reason

Perhaps Gellner is simply unconvinced by the Foucaultian approach, but the careful crafting of his argument suggests that he was never open to the possibility of a genuine dialogue between equals.[11] Gellner has already made up his mind, and there is a more strategic purpose to his account of postmodernism than objective analysis: he is defending his paradigm, and this becomes explicit as his 'three fundamental and irreducible positions' become two oppositional identities.

The crux of this lies in the way that Gellner identifies Marxism as one of the 'intellectual ancestors' of postmodernism. While at first Marxism may seem an unlikely candidate – scientific, concerned with objective truth, and with the realm of ideas (or meaning) merely epiphenomenal to the material substrate – it is Gellner's contention that all of this was part of the original 'Marxist revelation' which did not accompany its development. The reference to a 'revelation' alerts the reader to what is going on here: it was the religious impulse at the heart of the Marxist enterprise that apparently made it possible to transform historical materialism into 'historical subjectivism'. In the original Marxism, truth was the possession of a secular priesthood, and it was this which insulated it against the critical standards of the Open Society and provisioned for its transformation into subjectivist doctrine, a move completed by the Frankfurt School. The Frankfurters moved steadily to a practice of writing and disseminating ideas no longer grounded in the world as it is, being solely concerned with the world as it should be – a matter of private revelations and intuitions (Gellner 1992a: 31–5; 1994a). Moving in the groove of the Frankfurters, the postmoderns have simply turned a style of thought into a movement.

So the Frankfurt School, as an idealist outgrowth of the secular religion called Marxism, provides a hinge which articulates the relation between religious absolutism and postmodern relativism. However, these are not

---

[11] I am grateful to the anonymous reader for CUP for drawing my attention to Foucault's comments on the 'game of discussion', which is relevant to the point I am making here. Foucault draws a distinction between 'interlocutors', who engage in 'reciprocal elucidation', and the 'polemicist'. Even before dialogue commences, the polemicist has decided to wage war upon and annihilate her or his adversary (Foucault 1984: 381–3).

made into a seamlessly singular object. The movements within Gellner's text are more subtle and can be explained by the tropes of metonymy and metaphor. Both opponents of Reason retain their separate identities, but now they can stand in for each other. Just as the phrase 'on the couch' stands in for 'psychoanalysis', or 'on the bottle' stands in for 'drunkenness', 'religion' and 'relativism' have become interchangeable and each can be used to articulate the meanings invested in the other. This metonymic extension occurs only on one level however: the level of detailed analysis. At this level Gellner cannot be accused of conflating his objects, but at the level of the overall argument the metonymic moment gives way to the much stronger movement of metaphoric condensation (Torfing 1999: 98; Laclau and Mouffe 2001: 112). Standing back from the specifics of analysis so as to consider the overall logic of the argument, then it becomes clear that Gellner has constructed two levels of signification.[12] On level one, the shallow level, Gellner moves a set of meanings under two signifiers which supplement each other: 'Absolutism' and 'Relativism'. But at level two, the deeper level, the entire ensemble is condensed as a unified sign which derives its significance from 'Reason'. As the absolute negative of Reason, the Absolutism–Relativism complex is given a singular identity: 'Anti-Reason'.

Far from taking up the attitude of Popper's rationalist and admitting that 'I may be wrong and you may be right, and by an effort, we may get nearer to the truth', Gellner moves in the opposite direction, at once foreclosing on the possibility of falsifying his own position, and more importantly, closing off the possibility of an open dialogue with his interlocutor. While claiming the 'attitude of reasonableness' for Rationalism, Gellner's position turns out to be a hegemonic strategy to define and defend his standpoint against its constitutive outside. But first he has to construct this space of exteriority, and the series of movements within his text tends to affirm Kuhn's analysis of just how resilient a paradigm can be (1996: 77–9, 146–7).

The question we might ask ourselves is whether any of this matters. I think is does matter. Though beginning with 'three primary colours', Gellner's argument ends in a binary relation,[13] with the categories created within the game of truth production itself: through a process of interpretation, by metonymically grafting elements together, and by metaphorically condensing the field into a dichotomous relation. In this

---

[12] Similar to Roland Barthes' distinction between denotation and connotation (Barthes 1993).
[13] Gellner takes Popper to task for doing something very similar in the latter's Reason/ Violence dichotomy (Gellner 1985: 42–6).

rendering of 'postmodernism' we lose sight of its internal complexity, of the fact that the envelope contains a plurality of approaches to problems such as authority, power and freedom. The 'irrational' foundation of rationalism – Popper's leap from faith – is not without its political consequences.

On the one hand Gellner affirms the basic structuralist argument that identity is constituted within a system of differences, but by limiting the contingency of his own position he also affirms the more radical post-structuralist insight that the relation between identity and difference, between inclusion and exclusion, is articulated by power as the moment of foreclosing, i.e. the 'decision', attempts to arrest the play of meaning by fixing the identity of things in place. Ultimately Gellner fails to engage with the fact that the heterogeneous body of research projects that he calls 'postmodernism' has levelled a compelling indictment against the Rule of Reason, showing just how perspectival and dangerous the notion of Universal Truth can be when it becomes a form of authority, when it operates as the standard of legitimacy, and when its repressive dimension is disavowed by claims to objectivity. In analytical structure and argumentative style, *Postmodernism, Reason and Religion* resembles one of those old Hollywood Westerns where the orderly chaos of frontier life is brought to a sudden halt by a single gunshot, which also punctuates an ensuing event. The milling crowd peels back to enframe two gunslingers engaged in a dual to the death, the protagonist symbolically dressed in white, the antagonist garbed in black: a confrontation which – within the broader narrative structure of culture/nature, reason/emotion, civilisation/barbarism – is also a divine judgement upon the quick and the dead. The mythical gunfight also narrates the story of Western modernity, with violence routinely dispensed in the name of science, progress, truth and justice.

Conclusion: 'incommensurability' as problem and possibility

What will come after postmodernism? … Our hopes [are for] the emergence of an intellectual culture that would be rationalist but not dogmatic, scientifically minded but not scientistic, open-minded but not frivolous, and politically progressive but not sectarian. But this, of course, is only a hope, and perhaps only a dream. (Sokal and Bricmont 1999: 198)

In his sociology of Reason, Gellner followed Weber in explaining that the rationalisation of science, industry and statecraft has engendered a civilisation which has learnt how to exploit what Gellner called the 'orderly predictability' of the world. We have, and increasingly so, become aware of the ambivalence of this civilisation. Orderly predictability is not simply there, in nature, to be found and exploited in the name of Human Progress. Orderly predictability is also made, which is the moment when bodies and minds become the raw material of scientific, industrial and administrative technologies, and this is also done in the name of Human Progress. Some Rationalists maintain that the scientific attitude can deliver a way of knowing and doing which is value-neutral, others – and I think Gellner falls into this group – accept the impossibility of this ideal but still insist that it can, and ultimately should, deliver a form of social organisation which is truly progressive in the sense of emptying the world of force and coercion. In his use of terminology ('postmodernism'), in the thrust of his critique (epistemic relativism), and in his interpretation of the problem ('subject-ivism'), Gellner shares much with the physicists Alan Sokal and Jean Bricmont quoted above. The yearning for a unity of method and an Open Society governed by the Rule of Reason is alive and well.

The question threaded through this chapter concerns the Open Society. So does Gellner help us here? The answer is not straightforward, partly because Gellner was an original thinker and fluent in more than one discipline. On the whole, I think Gellner does help us, though we may at times have to read against the grain of his own reasoning and argumentation. In this respect we might draw a lesson from contem-porary debates in democratic theory, with at least some contributors arguing that the Open Society requires a healthy dose of contestation (see Dryzek 2000). Perhaps the Open Society *presupposes* agonistic dis-agreements, some of which are irresolvable precisely because of the incommensurability of language games, discourses or research para-digms (Mouffe 2000). There is no need to lament the lack of consensus between the problem-solvers and the problematisers, that is, we will hardly see an alliance between them, although we may find examples of practitioners defecting from one and joining the other. More promising is what follows from the coexistence of these paradigms, both of which, it should be said, emerge from and identify with, albeit in different ways, Enlightenment modernity. So if we follow Gellner in 'seeking our identity in Reason' (1992b: 182) should this foreclose on Agnes Heller's argument that we should 'transform our contingency into our destiny' (Heller 1989: 321)? Maybe this is a dilemma rather than a simple either/ or choice; and let us remember that Gellner was also willing to recognise it as a predicament we could live with. Taken together, the moderns and the postmoderns articulate a double movement from truth-formation to its deconstruction, and this helps to prevent ideological closure without abandoning the goal of an emancipatory social order. It ensures, but not in the sense of a final guarantee, that we continue to engage in what Foucault called 'a permanent critique of ourselves'.

References

Barthes, R. 1993 [1957]. *Mythologies*. London: Verso
Bauman, Z. 1991. *Modernity and Ambivalence*. New York: Cornell University Press.
Berger, P. and Luckman, T. 1966. *The Social Construction of Reality: A Treatise in the Sociology of Knowledge*. Harmondsworth: Penguin.
Broberg, G. and Tydén, M. 1996. Eugenics in Sweden: Efficient Care. In G. Broberg and N. Roll-Hansen (eds.), *Eugenics and the Welfare State: Sterilisation Policy in Denmark, Sweden, Norway, and Finland*. Michigan: Michigan University Press, pp. 77–149.
Castel, R., Castel, F. and Lovell, A. 1982 [1979]. *The Psychiatric Society*. New York: Columbia University Press.
Clegg, S. 1989. *Frameworks of Power*. London: Sage.
Cox, R. 1981. Social Forces, States and World Order: Beyond International Relations Theory. *Millennium: Journal of International Studies* 10 (2): 126–55.
Cruikshank, B. 1999. *The Will to Empower: Democratic Citizens and Other Subjects*. Ithaca, NY and London: Cornell University Press.
Darwin, C. 1981 [1871]. *The Descent of Man*. Princeton, NJ: Princeton University Press.
    1998 [1859]. *On the Origin of Species*. Ware: Wordsworth.
Dean, M. 1999. *Governmentality: Power and Rule in Modern Society*. London: Sage.
Derrida, J. 1997 [1976]. *Of Grammatology*, corrected edn. Baltimore, MD: Johns Hopkins University Press.
Dreyfus, H. and Rabinow, P. 1983. *Michel Foucault: Beyond Structuralism and Hermeneutics*. 2nd edn, Chicago: University of Chicago Press.
Dryzek, J. 2000. *Deliberative Democracy and Beyond*. Oxford: Oxford University Press.
Foucault, M. 1972 [1969]. *The Archaeology of Knowledge and the Discourse on Language*. London: Tavistock.
    1977 [1975]. *Discipline and Punish*. Harmondsworth: Penguin.
    1980. *Power/Knowledge: Selected Interviews and Other Writings 1972–1977*, ed. C. Gordon. New York: Pantheon.
    1983. The Subject and Power. In H. L. Dreyfus and P. Rabinow (eds.), *Michel Foucault: Beyond Structuralism and Hermeneutics*. 2nd edn, Chicago: University of Chicago Press, pp. 208–26.
    1984. *The Foucault Reader*, ed. P. Rabinow. New York: Pantheon.
    1991. Questions of Method. In G. Burchell, C. Gordon and P. Miller (eds.), *The Foucault Effect: Studies in Governmentality*. Hemel Hempstead: Harvester Wheatsheaf, pp. 208–26.
    1994 [1966]. *The Order of Things*. New York: Vintage Books.
    1998 [1976]. *The History of Sexuality*, vol. I: *The Will to Knowledge*. Harmondsworth: Penguin.
    2003 [1999]. *Abnormal: Lectures at the Collège de France 1974–1975*. New York: Picador.
Gellner, E. 1975. Beyond Truth and Falsehood (Review Article on Paul Feyerabend's *Against Method*). *British Journal for the Philosophy of Science* 26 (4): 331–42.

1980. In Defence of Orientalism (Review Article on Bryan S. Turner's *Marx and the End of Orientalism*). *Sociology* 14 (2): 295–300.

1982. The Paradox in Paradigms (Review Article on Barry Barnes' *T. S. Kuhn and Social Science*). *Times Literary Supplement*. 4125, 23 April: 451–2.

1985. *Relativism and the Social Sciences*. Cambridge: Cambridge University Press.

1992a. *Postmodernism, Reason and Religion*. London and New York: Routledge.

1992b. *Reason and Culture: The Historic Role of Rationality and Rationality*. Oxford: Blackwell.

1992c. The Uniqueness of Truth. In his *Anthropology and Politics: Revolutions in the Sacred Grove*. Oxford: Blackwell, pp. 1–10.

1993a [1985]. *The Psychoanalytic Movement: The Cunning of Unreason*. Evanston, IL: Northwestern University Press.

1993b. The Rational Mystic (Review Article on Karl Popper's *In Search of a Better World*). *The New Republic*, 19 April: 35–8.

1994a. The Last Marxists: Pretensions, Illusions, and Achievements of the Frankfurt School. *Times Literary Supplement* 4773, 23 September: 3–5.

1994b. *Conditions of Liberty: Civil Society and Its Rivals*. London and New York: Allen Lane/Penguin.

Habermas, J. 1984 [1981]. *The Theory of Communicative Action*, vol I: *Reason and the Rationalisation of Society*. Cambridge: Polity.

1999a. *The Inclusion of the Other: Studies in Political Theory*, ed. C. Cronin and P. De Greiff. Cambridge: Polity.

Hacking, I. 1990. *The Taming of Chance*. Cambridge: Cambridge University Press.

Halliday, J. 1999. 'Popper and the Philosophy of Education', *Encyclopaedia of Philosophy of Education*, www.vusst.hr/ENCYCLOPAEDIA/popper_and_the_philosophy_of_edu.htm, accessed 24.3.05.

Harding, S. 1998. *Is Science Multicultural? Postcolonialisms, Feminisms, and Epistemologies*. Bloomington: Indiana University Press.

Haugaard, M. 1997. *The Constitution of Power*. Manchester: Manchester University Press.

2003. Reflections on Seven Ways of Creating Power. *European Journal of Social Theory* 6: 87–113.

2006. Nationalism and Liberalism. In G. Delanty and K. Kumar (eds.), *The Sage Handbook of Nations and Nationalism*. London: Sage, pp. 345–56.

Hayek, F. 1991 [1944]. *The Road to Serfdom*. London: Routledge.

Heller, A. 1989. From Hermeneutics in Social Science: Toward a Hermeneutics of Social Science. *Theory and Society* 18: 291–322.

Howarth, D. 2000. *Discourse*. Buckingham: Open University Press.

2004. Applying Discourse Theory: The Method of Articulation. In D. Howarth and J. Torfing (eds.), *Discourse Theory in European Politics: Identity, Policy and Governance*. Basingstoke: Palgrave Macmillan, pp. 316–49.

Jacques, C. 1997. From Savages and Barbarians to Primitives: Africa, Social Typologies, and History in Eighteenth-Century French Philosophy. *History and Theory* 36 (2): 190–215.

Kahn, J. 2001. *Modernity and Exclusion*. London: Sage.

Kitching, J. 1857. Lecture on Moral Insanity. *British Medical Journal*, 25 April: 334–6.

Kuhn, T. 1996 [1962]. *The Structure of Scientific Revolutions.* 3rd edn, Chicago and London: University of Chicago Press.

Laclau, E. 1990. *New Reflections on the Revolution of Our Time.* London and New York: Verso.

Laclau, E. and Mouffe, C. 1987. Post-Marxism without Apologies. *New Left Review* 166: 79–106.

2001 [1985]. *Hegemony and Socialist Strategy: Towards a Radical Democratic Politics.* London: Verso.

Miller, P. and Rose, N. 1990. Governing Economic Life. *Economy and Society* 19 (1): 1–31.

Mouffe, C. 2000. *The Democratic Paradox.* London: Verso.

Popper, K. 1962 [1945]. *The Open Society and Its Enemies,* vol. II. 4th edn, London: Routledge and Kegan Paul.

1966 [1945]. *The Open Society and Its Enemies,* vol. I. 5th edn, London: Routledge and Kegan Paul.

2002a [1935]. *The Logic of Scientific Discovery.* London and New York: Routledge.

2002b [1957]. *The Poverty of Historicism.* London and New York: Routledge.

Rabinow, P. 1986. Representations Are Social Facts: Modernity and Post-Modernity in Anthropology. In J. Clifford and G. E. Marcus (eds.), *Writing Culture: The Poetics and Politics of Ethnography.* Berkeley, Los Angeles and London: University of California Press, pp. 234–61.

Rafter, N. H. 1988. *White Trash: The Eugenic Family Studies 1877–1919.* Boston: Northeastern University Press.

Rorty, R. 1980. *Philosophy and the Mirror of Nature.* Oxford: Blackwell.

1989. *Contingency, Irony and Solidarity.* Cambridge: Cambridge University Press.

Rose, N. 1985. *The Psychological Complex: Psychology, Politics and Society in England, 1869–1939.* London: Routledge and Kegan Paul.

Saussure, F. 1983 [1916]. *Course in General Linguistics,* trans. Roy Harris. London: Duckworth.

Searle, J. R. 1995. *The Construction of Social Reality.* Harmondsworth: Penguin.

Sokal, Alan and Bricmont, Jean. 1999. *Intellectual Impostures: Postmodern Philosophers' Abuse of Science.* 2nd edn, London: Profile.

Staten, H. 1985. *Wittgenstein and Derrida.* Oxford: Blackwell.

Still, G. F. 1902. The Coulstonian Lectures on Some Abnormal Psychical Conditions in Children. *The Lancet* 1: 1008–12, 1077–82, 1163–8.

Torfing, J. 1999. *New Theories of Discourse: Laclau, Mouffe and Žižek.* Oxford: Blackwell.

2004. Discourse Theory: Achievements, Arguments, and Challenges. In D. Howarth and J. Torfing (eds.), *Discourse Theory in European Politics: Identity, Policy and Governance.* Basingstoke: Palgrave Macmillan, pp. 1–32.

Walmsley, J. 2000. Woman and the Mental Deficiency Act of 1913: Citizenship, Sexuality and Regulation. *British Journal of Learning Disabilities* 28: 65–70.

Weber, M. 1978. *Economy and Society,* vol. I. Berkeley, Los Angeles and London: University of California Press.

10   Gellner's metaphysic

John A. Hall

Ernest Gellner was most often termed a polymath by those impressed by his achievements. This is entirely comprehensible because he had distinct reputations in several fields, notably as theorist of Islam and nationalism and as both anthropologist and philosopher. But Gellner himself was wont to bridle at this sort of description, stating that beneath these different fields lay a common set of concerns. What was on Gellner's mind at this point is straightforward: he was claiming intellectual greatness. It is easy to see what he meant. Significance in a thinker derives from the presence of an underlying metaphysic rather than from facility in different fields of endeavour. The purpose of this chapter is to identify Gellner's metaphysic and to subject it to analysis. Two immediate words of caution are in order. First, to capture every element of Gellner's core concerns in a single essay is impossible. Accordingly concentration here is more on the philosophical than on the sociological elements of his metaphysic, on the grounds that these were crucial to Gellner himself, at all times of his life, yet have been almost wholly neglected in the secondary literature. Of course, there is no easy divide between philosophy and sociology within Gellner's work, and his metaphysic has historical and sociological elements at its core. Still, concentration here is on philosophical claims rather than on his sociology of open and closed societies. Second, my own analytic stance combines elements of appreciation with suggested modifications in a slightly unstable mix. The reason for this is simple: my own mind is not yet wholly clear on the issues under discussion.

Most of what follows can be best understood within the context of Gellner's life experiences. What is at issue follows rather closely from what is now fairly well known about his personal experiences with nationalism – that is, the move from the tricultural world of multiple identities in which he grew up to a new order of homogeneous nation-states. One point to be made about this is that he himself never felt fully at home in any of the latter, all of which were in a sense contingent and arbitrary. But a more important consideration is that such entities were real, the providers of different forms of life. This fact points to the larger biographical consideration. Gellner knew alternative social worlds viscerally, saw and felt Pascal's dictum that truth was different on the other side of the Pyrenees. It is worth illustrating this point immediately. One might have expected his contribution to a volume on the responsibility of intellectuals to be predictable, given that its focus was on Julien Benda's famous analysis of the betrayal of the intellectuals. Surely a Central European intellectual of Jewish background would endorse the view that far too many intellectuals had not stood up for the ideals of the Enlightenment? Gellner did no such thing, preferring to write about the treason of the treason of the intellectuals. His argument was that there was much that was question-begging and worrying about facile liberal rationalism – which was not, in a word, well grounded. At least some of the philosophers of the anti-Enlightenment – and his own first enthusiasm had been for Schopenhauer, with unstinting admiration for Nietzsche at all times – were honest and brave, doing their best to find firmer grounds for morality (Gellner 1990).

All sorts of positions, philosophical, therapeutic and political, were known to Gellner, and he had deep interest, especially as an anthropologist, in seeing how these different worlds functioned. Further, he certainly had friends with beliefs different from his own, and one had the impression that he cultivated this diversity. This is really his starting point. People have believed and believe now in all sorts of things, many of them ridiculous. Can a way be found to ground a morality for our times? Much of the answer to the general question will depend upon the understanding of what 'our times' comprise. But something else of greater generality and of utmost importance should be noted immediately. Gellner himself had to find some form of identity once the world in which he grew up was destroyed, and this perhaps made him particularly sensitive as to the need to find grounds for morality. The end result of this is a paradox. Gellner understood different worlds and appreciated fully the appeal of relativism, yet insisted – perhaps more than any other thinker of his generation – on the need for universal standards. Relativism was a real problem, whose very power demanded a solution.

A negative critique

Gellner did not make his task easy. His negative critique of established positions is exceptionally forceful and deeply felt, amounting to an insistence that *no* established morality is well grounded. Some of his most brilliant passages deconstruct the pretensions of varied theories. The fourth chapter of *Thought and Change* (1964) goes through several philosophical approaches, from Platonism to utilitarianism and with much in between, and finds the assumptions of each to be open to question. Great sympathy is shown to utilitarianism, but it is judged to work only within a settled world, being wholly insufficient as a philosophy able to help us reach such a world. More important still is the fact that the whole process of rational calculation cannot really work. Reason is good when dealing with small and discrete issues, when an ego can choose and will retain its identity whatever choice is made. But really large decisions change one's identity, making genuinely rational calculation impossible (Gellner 1985).

Roughly speaking, Gellner felt that three intellectual traditions mattered in the modern world. He devoted enormous attention to the 'world growth stories' present in Spinoza, Hegel and Marx and to the instinctualist theories of Nietzsche and Freud. In both cases, for myriad reasons, he found contradiction and implausibility. Rather than going over his critiques of these great traditions, however, attention will focus on the third tradition of liberal rationalism, of which he was a self-professed adherent. Nonetheless, a brief word about his views of these other positions is in order. His Popperian critique of Freudianism is well known, albeit the most interesting part of the treatise in which it occurs is the sociological explanation for the success of therapeutic ideologies. That book ends with praise for Nietzsche, whose view of power-hungry but confused humanity Gellner endorses (2003). But Gellner insists that there is incoherence in Nietzsche as well. If we really value hardness and choice – if our drives demand such – then how can passivity and cowardice, so present for Nietzsche, be explained (2003: 20)? The critique of world growth stories is quite as much positive as negative (Gellner 1964: 1–32). There is a great deal to be said in favour of creating a morality that makes sense of historical development, and Gellner will adopt this strategy, albeit in a limited way that avoids the harsher strictures of Popper's attack on the slavishness of historicists. The difficulty for Gellner with the world growth stories on offer, however, is that they are not powerful. The theory of social evolution tends to be logically flawed, whilst the warmth provided by Spinoza and Hegel is simply spurious. Gellner paid most attention to Marxism, of course, both practically and theoretically – and with especial reference to the theories of actually existing Marxist regimes (see especially 1988a; 1988b). His critique in a nutshell stressed that Marxism had no appreciation of the autonomy of power, and therefore no real protection against the depredations of the powerful.

What is most noticeable about Gellner's account of liberal rationalism is his refusal to cheat. He privileged David Hume and Immanuel Kant, and sought, as we shall see in a moment, to spell out the ways in which the principles exemplified by their thought combine in the practice of modern science. But he insists that neither of these thinkers was able fully to ground his position; neither presents universal justification. One can indeed go further: the measure of doubt, scepticism and uncertainty present in the ideas of these pillars of the Enlightenment far outdoes that claimed by any later postmodernist.

Most obviously, if nothing exists but sensation, as Hume stressed, we are then deprived of any certainty about the existence of an external world and have no reason to believe in causality. Just as importantly, we find our very selves prone to disappear – we are but a continuing set of fleeting sensations. Hume noted that contemplation of these findings drove him first to despair, and then to a remedy for this condition:

The *intense* view of these manifold contradictions and imperfections in human reason has so wrought upon me, and heated my brain, that I am ready to reject all belief and reasoning, and can look upon no opinion even as more probable or likely than another. Where am I, or what? From what causes do I derive my existence, and to what condition shall I return? Whose favour shall I court, and whose anger must I dread? What beings surround me? and on whom have I any influence, or who have any influence upon me? I am confounded with all these questions, and begin to fancy myself in the most deplorable condition imaginable, inviron'd with the deepest darkness, and utterly depriv'd of the use of every member and faculty.

Most fortunately it happens, that since reason is incapable of dispelling these clouds, nature herself suffices to that purpose, and cures me of this philosophical melancholy and delirium, either by relaxing this bent of mind, or by some avocation, and lively impression of my senses, which obliterate all these chimeras. I dine, I play a game of backgammon, I converse, and am merry with my friends; and when after three or four hour's amusement, I wou'd return to these speculations, they appear so cold, and strain'd and ridiculous, that I cannot find in my heart to enter into them any further. (Hume 1985: 316)

Gellner felt that it was difficult 'to read this part of his work without embarrassment'. Hume commends his own moral convictions 'with the tone of a man whose vantage point is fixed and secure. In the theory of knowledge, he is not like this ... Had Hume shown the same honesty and self-knowledge in ethics, which he had shown in logic, he would have been that much more lovable' (Gellner 1964: 58).

But these problems – the lack of a sense of reality, the presence of a ghostly self – are not the only ones from which empiricism suffers. The picture of the human mind suggested by empiricism is deeply implausible. For Gellner follows Quine in seeing behaviourism as modelling empiricism. But admiration for the practical working through of a key philosophy did not mean that Gellner in any way endorsed behaviourism as a model of human behaviour. To the contrary, the merit of the practical applications of the behaviourists was to demonstrate conclusively that

human behaviour had an entirely different character than that envisaged
by empiricist sensationalism. At this point, Gellner relied heavily on
Chomsky's (1959) famous assault on B. F. Skinner's *Verbal Behavior*
(Gellner 1975: 32–6 and chapter 5). On the one hand, Chomsky pointed
to the vacuity of the conceptual language of stimulus/response and of
reinforcement. These terms seem 'tough' because they seem practical
and are familiar to us. In fact, this is a sign of appalling cognitive weak-
ness, of the basest mentalism, for behaviourism illicitly rules out of
consideration, as explanatory variables, forces not present to consciousness. On the other hand, he demonstrated, conclusively in Gellner's eyes,
that the fundamental claim of the behaviourists was simply nonsense. We
do not learn to speak by hearing sentences that we then repeat. This must
be wrong, for new sentences are created all the time; differently put,
human language competence allows for creativeness and flexibility. In
this context it makes sense to turn to Kant – or, rather to the mechanical,
reductionist philosophy he exemplifies – as does Gellner's reading of
Chomsky.

Gellner's admiration for Kant was even greater than that for Hume: he
dubbed him quite simply 'the greatest philosopher of them all' (Gellner
1975: 184–91). Kant's basic philosophic move is well known. Recog-
nising the full force of Hume's scepticism, he sought most immediately
to save knowledge. He did so by saying that we could but see the world
in causal terms because of the way in which our minds are structured. It
may in fact be the case that the world runs on irregular lines, but we will
never be able to appreciate this as we are doomed to seek for order. But
quite as important to Kant was the consequent 'need' to save a measure
of human autonomy from the mechanical nature of our schemata.
Gellner calls the Kantian solution both desperate and left-handed. A
philosophy that in general insists on the importance of not making
exceptions does make an exception for itself: because it is we who impose
schemes on nature, we can exempt ourselves from their force.

If one problem with the orderly and mechanical vision of Kant is that it
fails to tell us how the world actually works, another problem results
from the way in which it undermines our humanity. Mechanism diminishes us as much as empiricism, but for a very different reason. What is at
issue is the nature of reduction. Reduction has two meanings. The most
common meaning stresses, so to speak, cheap and facile reduction, that
is, the failure to catch the complexity of the object being studied. A classic
instance of this is that of behaviourism: humans are simply more complex
than stimulus-response models allow. This should not be allowed to
diminish the Kantian point that genuine explanation, based on full
appreciation of the object to be explained, must be reductive in a different

sense. To explain is to reduce the complex to the simple, the personal and idiosyncratic to some publicly available model or mechanism. This matters enormously for the way in which we see our very selves. The fact that parts of nature are to be explained in mechanical terms may not affect our self-image, but there is no way in which the principle of explanation can somehow be limited to the external world. Rather, science can be applied to human beings. This point is made particularly neatly against Arthur Koestler, who sought by means of science to establish or find some entity that would ensure that human beings were more than simple models – notably, of course, behaviourism – allowed. The trouble with this view is that it would necessarily snatch defeat from the jaws of victory. The precise location of any quality would immediately make it public rather than private, explicable rather than unique (Gellner 1975: 105–6).

An even clearer way in which this point was underlined was with reference to Chomsky. It is not the case, Gellner insisted, that Chomsky, for all his radical political leanings, was content to rest his argument at the moment at which he had established the creativity of linguistic competence. Rather Chomsky has sought to explain the nature – its workings, its range, its limits – of human linguistic competence. Differently put, Chomsky wishes to replace the false and cheap reductionism of behaviourism with genuine explanation based on appreciation of the real character of the object in question. The resulting situation is characterised powerfully:

Any explanation of human conduct or competence in terms of a genuine structure is morally offensive – for a genuine structure is impersonal, it is an 'it', not an 'I'. Chomskian structures are also known to be, in part, well hidden from consciousness; he himself lays great stress on this. If this be the correct strategy in the study of man, then the *I* is ultimately to be explained by an *it* (alas). The Freudian *id* was beastly but, when all is said and done, it was cosily human in its un-housetrained way; at worst you could say it was all too human: it was human nature seen in the image of conscious man, but with the gloves off. (Like us, but without the advantages we've had, if you know what I mean.) The explanation of our unthinking, quasi-automatic competence into explanatory schemata, outlining structures which are not normally accessible to us at all, is far more sinister. This kind of *id* is not violent, sexy and murderous, it is just totally indifferent to us. (Gellner 1975: 99)

Gellner adds one last critical point to what is already a heavy indictment. Both strategies imagine that one can act like Robinson Crusoe, a 'pure visitor' to the world freed from all earthly assumptions. A second's thought makes one realise that this is impossible. Neither Hume nor Kant was describing any sort of universal human condition. Very much to the contrary, Kant's world partakes of Weber's puritan ethic, a viewpoint without appeal to many. Given all of this, it is almost tempting to throw one's hands up in despair. But Gellner insists that standards are needed. Reliance on customary rules is far from attractive at any time, as they can be the filled with nonsense and prejudice. This is especially so given the speed of social change. That sensation was felt by Descartes and by the great Enlightenment philosophers whose attempt to find a way to swim in a new world deserves praise, even if their attempts to ground knowledge were not wholly successful. There can be no doubt but that change in the twentieth century has been still more total. We have to find guiding posts by means of which to live our lives.

The positive position

There is a basic presupposition behind the positive answer that needs to be spelt out immediately. Bluntly, scientific knowledge *is* powerful. If that is stressed particularly clearly in *Thought and Change*, it is only in the later *Legitimation of Belief* that the manner in which this is possible is explained. Crucially, Gellner argues that a certain division of labour has taken place as between Kant and Hume – or, rather, as between the intellectual principles that they exemplify. Mechanism must be accepted, not least as it is the only plausible candidate for a model of human behaviour. And if empiricism fails in that regard, its role in testing theories – and above all, in making theories sensitive to evidence – is essential. In the end, the world may not work on puritanical and orderly principles, and reality may not be separable into atomistic entities. Nonetheless, presuming this to be so has unquestionably produced powerful knowledge. Differently put, empiricism and mechanism are ethics for cognition, social practices that deliver technical power (Gellner 1976a). The presence of such power may make us feel that genuine truth is being discovered, but there is no proof that this is so.

Gellner's positive philosophy contends that a social order in our time is and ought to be justified if it provides a decent standard of living and allows for rule by those co-cultural with other members of the society (Gellner 1964: 33–49). The former condition can be seen as that of passing a transition to an industrial and scientific age, the latter as the demand that the principle of nationalism be accepted. It is worth underscoring the fact that the claims made are at once sociological and moral. Certain social processes are clearly on the agenda of world social and political development, although we do not know enough, in his view, about the variations in form that they allow. Equally, these developments are to be endorsed morally; differently put, we should quite self-consciously commit the naturalistic fallacy. Two preliminary considerations must be noted before seeing how Gellner justifies committing himself to this historicist position.

On the one hand, even greater clarity is lent to the picture by the fact that there is really only one principle at work here. His theory of nationalism depends, in all its versions, upon the impact of industrialism. Gellner explicitly rejected that interpretation of his theory of nationalism which stressed its efficacy as a means of late development, although he recognised that nationalists do seek national development and saw homogeneity as probably good for economic development and for democracy (Gellner 1996).[1] Differently put, the causal pattern in his explanation of nationalism is from industrialisation to nationalism, and not the other way around.

On the other hand, Gellner was not in fact as clear as he wished. For the initial description of the new social contract suffered from a particular confusion. What is the place of knowledge? Is it somehow a third, autonomous force? This is suggested when he speaks of knowledge as 'the principal agent' of the transition to modernity (Gellner 1964: 72, 65). Or, is modern science merely the style of thought characteristic of industrial society? This too is suggested in a passage that claims that science 'is the form of cognition of industrial society' (1964: 72). This more passive view of science fits, it should be noted, much better with the general sociological position that Gellner adopted, early and late, in which great reluctance was shown to allowing much independent power to ideological innovation within the historical record. Gellner never explicitly admitted that his early work was open to two rather different readings at this point, let alone that his mind on the matter had either not been made up or was genuinely confused. Nonetheless, it is a fact that his later work did manage to sort out this confusion. The mapping exercise that is *Legitimation of Belief* notes explicitly that its focus is on the way in which science works within society, rather than on the extent to which science actually caused a new social world to emerge. That latter task is, however, performed in later books, notably in *Plough, Sword and Book* and in *Reason and Culture*. New forms of knowledge are there seen as playing some creative role, making it as well to read the nature of industrial society in a strong sense as distinctively including styles of thought quite as much as of social organisation.[2]

---

[1] He writes here against the views of Roman Szporluk, as I have made clear elsewhere (Hall 1998).

[2] For amplification of this argument, see my biography of Gellner, forthcoming from Verso.

There are no equivalent difficulties when dealing with industrialisation: as a principle it is primary, and its workings are absolutely clear.

The mechanics which ensures the necessity of the transition seems to me quite simple. Its crucial premise is simply that men in general will not tolerate a life of poverty, disease, precariousness, hard work, tedium and oppression, when they recognize that at least most of these features can be either obviated or greatly mitigated. (Gellner 1964: 70)

Gellner notes explicitly that this is a brutally simple argument, suggesting as prime mover a matter of general psychology rather than a feature of social organisation. But this is sociologically sound given that 'the secret is out' that affluence is possible. This was not the case with the very first European industrialisation, or indeed with its initial European emulators. But the name of the game since 1945 has been that of development. Any regime which fails to provide development is likely, in Gellner's view, to be short lived. Equally, any social theory that imagines that the members of industrial society are prepared to forgo the comforts to which they have become accustomed is held by Gellner to be merely risible.

The moral claim is equally straightforward. It is entirely proper to commit the naturalistic fallacy as we must prefer a mode of social life which brings comfort, health, long life and the possibility of decency to those for whom scarcity makes it virtually mandatory to advance at the expense of other human beings (Gellner 1964: 145–6). This is a brutal and banal point, stated more clearly in *Thought and Change* than anywhere else in his work, and Gellner clearly feels that it scarcely needs justification. Two points are, however, made. First, Gellner aligns himself with John Stuart Mill's response to those who claimed that utilitarianism – with its insistence on such 'philistine' concerns as decent sewage, health and food production – was a philosophy fit for pigs. Bluntly, it was such critics who were the real exemplars of a callous and piggish mentality (Gellner 1964: 73). It is important to note, secondly, that Gellner's general viewpoint is not, so to speak, passive and complacent.

To say this is not to say that existing liberal affluent societies are things of great beauty and warrant complacency. They aren't and they don't. The surviving areas of poverty and underprivilege are obscene precisely because they are now totally unnecessary. (Gellner 1964: 118–19)

The claim that Gellner is making can be underscored with reference to the notion of evolution. The sociological and ethical claim being put forward is specific rather than general, a neo-episodic view of evolution rather than a new version of some world growth story capable of solving all intellectual problems and of providing general meaning to our lives. Gellner is here hoping to insulate his general theory of modernity, indeed his philosophy of history as a whole, from the charge that it is messianic and total, and so inherently dangerous. He insists that this is not the case. The transcendence he seeks is not of everything, merely of certain particular features of social life central to human experience that can now be avoided.

Exclusions

Gellner liked to stress that power is lent to philosophies less by what they include than by what they rule out. Utilitarianism is given bite not by the attention given to pleasure and pain but by the insistence that nothing else matters. In his own case, Gellner is saying and means to say that nothing matters except industrialism and its corollary nationalism. It is as well to highlight, as does Gellner, two exclusions.

We have already seen, first, that Gellner claims that the cognitive style of modern society does more to undermine received opinions than to replace it with new certainties. It is not at all likely that the real and the rational, the desirable and the actual, will somehow inevitably combine in a beneficent way. Science does produce powerful knowledge, even though its assumptions are not well grounded. But the operations of rational science – questioning, doubting, splitting up taken for granted block beliefs, continually refuting beliefs that anyway can only ever be tentatively held – mean that science provides no comfortable place within which to live. The opportunity/cost of modernity is simple: the goodies that science brings come at the price of diminished certainty. This is Gellner's endorsement of Max Weber's thesis that modernity must be disenchanted. And no critic in recent times has been more effective than Gellner in puncturing the illusions of facile re-enchanting creeds.

Secondly, Gellner argues that it is extremely unlikely that the political liberty to which the West has grown accustomed will spread in some sort of automatic and facile manner to all of humankind. Allegiance is likely to be given to regimes which take one to the modern world. But this is most likely to occur through imitation, and by forcible means. Such concentration of power puts liberty at a discount. It is not hard to see what Gellner has in mind here. The initial breakthrough to modern industrial society was in effect an accident, the creation by happenstance of something completely new. Thereafter, there was something to copy. For a short period, it seemed as if the secret of the leading edge of power might lie in constitutional liberty. After that came the realisation that social planning from above could speed development. Industrial economies do not have large rural workforces, thereby making it seem rational to encourage urbanisation. As important is nation-building. In the Algerian case, national homogeneity was to be increased by making Arabic the language of the state. This required force both so as to make the Arabic-speaking peasants send their children to school and so as to prevent the use of either Berber or French as an alternative lingua franca. But what matters still more is the philosophical point made at the start of this chapter, namely that choice only makes sense within worlds. Utilitarianism is useless as a guide to the transition because the change involved is so great that in fact nobody would choose to undergo the pain that it involves (Gellner 1964: 98–100). Further, he asks rhetorically, 'during something inherently so painful, what hope is there for government by consent? It seems almost a contradiction' (1964: 141). He did not change his mind on this point, as can be seen from this passage – which appeared decades after those just cited:

> What one consents to depends on what one is, and what one *is*, in the end, springs from the society which has formed one. Could a vote have been taken in the late Middle Ages, on whether mankind was to move onwards to a secular and industrial world? The question would have been unintelligible. Those who were capable of thought at all endorsed the world they knew…The changes that have taken place since then have given us a humanity which, in the main, prefers itself as it now finds itself to be. But which third man, encapsulated in both, or independent of either, could possibly choose *between* them, and endorse that transformation 'democratically', by consent. There is no such third man. He cannot possibly exist.
> *Fundamental changes transform identities.* Yet without a single, persisting and somehow authoritative identity, there is no one available to give his full consent to a radical transformation … (Gellner 1988b: 193–4, 249–57)[3]

Gellner stresses that liberty is not necessarily on the cards of social and economic development in a different way, namely by noting the relative feebleness of argument for political liberty. Let us follow his treatment of this question (1964: 115–19).

1. A first argument has the character of 'sour grapes'. Essentially this is the Popperian view that science is based on refuting conjectures, rather than on establishing universal and unchanging knowledge. Nonetheless, uncertainty is, so to speak, reliable. Unfortunately, this view of science is most likely to appeal to those already living inside a liberal society.
2. It may be that political liberty is necessary for the knowledge upon which modern science depends. However, whilst this might have

---

[3] *Plough, Sword and Book* ends by saying that we had to be tricked into the new world.

been true of the initial breakthrough to a new cognitive style, it is not at all certain that it applies to later imitative development.

3. Liberal societies may have greater capacity to change than illiberal and rigid regimes. At this point Gellner noted, honestly, that the second and third argument do not fit with the first – for they offer the very certainty that had initially been ruled out.

4. The argument that clearly appealed to Gellner himself was Kantian in spirit. The fact of openness, of being free from any established state of affairs, whether institutional or intellectual, is attractive to those who wish to be masters of their own fate. Liberty and equality but no fraternity seems to be the message here.

5. In the long run, affluence will be generalised, thereby suggesting that concentration on other political values – above all, the establishment of safeguards against tyranny – is of great importance. This argument is likely of course to have greatest appeal only to those convinced that affluence really is on the cards.

The comment that Gellner makes on all this deserves quotation:

This set of arguments, not fully consistent with each other, and at widely divergent levels of abstraction, does not, alas, amount to a rousing manifesto for liberty. The very disparateness of the arguments may worry one: any one of them alone might have sounded more convincing than their conjunction. One must heed Kant's warning against supporting one's values by a mishmash of argument, which weaken rather than reinforce each other. But if the arguments one can muster do not match up to the degree of one's conviction, it is perhaps as well to confess it. (1964: 119–20)

It is as well to end this section with a warning. The fact that Gellner did not feel that political liberty would necessarily and easily spread throughout the world should not be interpreted as meaning that he himself did not have the utmost commitment to this form of polity. One way in which one can stress this is by remembering much of his later academic work. In a key later paper he argued that a vital question of the age was that of whether one could move from 'revolution' to 'liberalization' (Gellner 1976b). He was deeply interested in the possibility of decompressing regimes which had often gained much of their power as the result of claiming to modernise their societies by centralising power. He clearly felt that the question applied to authoritarian capitalist societies of all types as well as to socialist regimes, and he took care to visit examples of each type. Nonetheless, his most sustained interest lay in the future of state socialism, and it was this that took him to the Soviet Union in 1989 for his final period of extended anthropological fieldwork.

Assessment

This assessment of Gellner's claims is a mixed affair, moving from approval and endorsement to questioning, with the very final points being those in which the critique offered is the least certain.

There is a very great deal to be said in favour of Gellner's view of science. By this statement more is meant that his insistence on the power of science and admiration for his attempt, in the mapping exercise of *Legitimation of Belief*, to explain how it works. Rather, I believe that Gellner's arguments about the philosophy of social science will in the end be seen to be amongst his greatest contributions. A full account of those views cannot be given here, but the nature of the argument made can at least be noted. Genuine social scientific knowledge often depends upon taking the discoveries of Western natural science seriously. One can only investigate the role played by varied social beliefs when one knows that they are not in fact 'physically' accurate. A brilliant and lengthy exchange dealing with kinship made this point with particular force.[4] The social character of various kinship states can only be understood in the light of Western scientific knowledge about actual conceptions. Without this knowledge, an anthropologist would not seek to investigate, as is necessary, the strains that can arise from treating an adoptive child as one's own.[5]

A second consideration brings us closer to moral matters. Gellner's view of the disenchantment purportedly characteristic of modern life is somewhat intellectualist. There is no personal animus behind this critique: very much to the contrary, I am deeply attracted to an emptier and colder world, not least for the Kantian-inspired reasons suggested by Gellner. However, there is something a little strange about the notion that the vast majority of humankind once lived a warm, meaningful life, but is now condemned to a colder existence. Do we know this to be true? How much consolation did a peasant in the past gain from religion when faced with poverty and perhaps the death of a child? Is there perhaps not something to be said for the notion that the current era is the most enchanted known in human history – less exciting perhaps, filled with trivia too, but comfortable nonetheless? There remains much to be said at this point for the sociology of Adam Smith. The great Scottish

---

[4] This debate – in *The Philosophy of Science* – began when Rodney Needham objected to a 1957 article by Gellner dealing with kinship as an ideal language. Gellner's reply to Needham drew a comment from John Barnes. Gellner reviewed the whole debate (1963), with details to the papers mentioned herein.

[5] For justification of this view, see my forthcoming biography of Gellner.

moralist claimed that most humans sought the admiration of their fellows, and so sought wealth in order to command respect. The 'wise' readers of *The Theory of Moral Sentiments* were told that the possession of goods of all sorts would not bring happiness, given the certainty of death. Nonetheless, Smith maintained that the illusion that this was so, enjoyed by the 'vulgar', that is, the belief of the many that striving to keep up with the Joneses would ensure happiness, was beneficent for humanity, encouraging industry and replacing zero-sum political conflict (Smith 1976). Of course, this critique amounts in the end to only a slight difference from Gellner's position: it is to place an even higher value on industrialism than he himself does. Let us turn to weightier matters.

There is a very great deal to endorse in Gellner's privileging of nationalism and industrialism as the key elements of the modern social contract. I have dealt with his views on nationalism on other occasions, and note here that a defence of Gellner can be mounted – less for industry as the cause of nationalism than for the insight that nationalism has homogeneity so very often at its core (Hall 1998). It is useful to remember here a comment of David Laitin to the effect that Gellner wrote his own life and presumed it to be sociology. We will see the critical edge implied here in a moment, but should reverse the tables at this point. Gellner's life was *representative* of the heartland of European modernity, lending fundamental power to his thought. The Dark Continent of the twentieth century, that is, Europe, had at the core of its history homogenisation of peoples, through assimilation at best and population transfer, ethnic cleansing and mass murder at worst.

Still more obvious is the fact that industrialisation has scarcely lost its appeal, with the endless talk of globalisation being in part further evidence of the extent to which the world has become one. Recent scholarship has supported some of what Gellner claimed about the way in which forced industrialisation was likely to diminish political liberty. Atul Kohli's exceptionally powerful work is relevant at this point (Kohli 2004). The economic success of South Korea rests upon a coercive-capitalist route, in which the state works with leading capitalists, accumulates by repressing wages, and establishes from above clear developmental strategies. In contrast, development has been in part stymied, in part merely slowed in both India and Brazil, according to Kohli's careful account, because democratic pressures prevented either the adoption or the maintenance of developmental strategies which involved short-term social costs. Kohli further analyses the case of Nigeria, wholly bereft of an effective state and accordingly with the gloomiest prospects for political and economic development. Interestingly, Kohli ends up with moral qualms similar to those of Gellner, noting that development may be at the expense of democracy. It may be that the fifth and last of Gellner's arguments noted in the previous section applies to Brazil and India. But added moral complexity is lent by the recent history of South Korea. Its developmental regime certainly provided improvements in living standards. But this in turn does seem to have done something to provide a social base for political liberalisation. The chances for consolidated democracy now look greater in South Korea than in Brazil, perhaps greater even than those of India. So here is a case in which great social pain was followed by successful political decompression.

However, one must note quite as much that Gellner's views about both nationalism and industry are open to serious negative critique. The point implied by the comment of Laitin noted immediately above is that homogenisation is not an absolute functional requirement of modernity. Homogenisation certainly characterised European history, and one may further add that the presence of national homogeneity – as in South Korea in contrast to Nigeria – can help economic development. But this is not to say that forcible homogenisation should be nor need be encouraged. For one thing, many attempts at forcible homogenisation, especially in Africa, have been dismal failures, bringing misery to millions without corresponding benefits. For another, some federal and consociational schemes have worked, even though there have been quite as many failures. India works, as a state-nation rather than as a nation-state, and its example suggests a better way forward for many countries of the world than does the European experience. It may be that a measure of unity sufficient for the workings of a modern economy can be gained by the recognition of diversity.

Somewhat similar points can be made about industrialisation. The fundamental point that essentially goes against Gellner's view is that of the forcible imposition of the Soviet Model of industrialisation. Perhaps there is something to be said for the rise in educational standards in erstwhile socialist countries, since this might help economic development now that the Cold War has ended. But against that must be set genuine economic disaster. Russia was one of the world's great grain exporters in 1914: collectivisation so ruined Russian agriculture that it is now dependent on the outside world for its supply of food. More generally, it seems certain that socialist planning from above, bereft of any market forces, is a dead end. Further, the fact that socialism was so suspicious of civil society groupings made liberalisation impossible: there were no representative groups with whom deals could be struck, so as to allow decompression. Perhaps the Chinese route favouring perestroika before glasnost will prove more efficient economically, thereby perhaps providing conditions for political decompression. But the scars left by the millions who died in both China and the former socialist bloc are likely to have long-term detrimental effects on social and political development. Two final but related points should be made. First, coercive-capitalist development when protectionist can be dangerous as well, as the relative decline of Argentina since the 1930s so clearly attests. Secondly, a good deal of scepticism must be shown to Gellner's view that Islam has gained especial salience in recent years because it avoids the opposition between populism and Westernisation, having at its core a sense of discipline that can serve as an ersatz protestant ethic. There is almost no evidence of economic development being aided by fundamentalist Islam, and a very great deal to be said against this putative connection.

The world polity then presents a more varied picture than that allowed in Gellner's work. There are cases which support him, and cases which distinctly go against him. The latter suggest adding an argument in favour of liberty additional to the five that he himself suggested. Absolute catastrophe – notably the great famines caused by collectivisation and the Chinese Great Leap Forward – results from the absence of any checking power. Despite the difficulties of development in India, the ability to curtail disastrous policies has meant, as Sen so famously argued, that this huge south Asian country has never experienced a truly catastrophic famine (Sen 1978). Liberty may not be on the cards, easily, generally and automatically, but one can reasonably seek to give it a slightly more central place in the scheme of things than that allowed by Gellner. In this connection, two further arguments can be made against his pessimism. First, Michael Lessnoff (2002: 60–1) points to a measure of contradiction in Gellner's position. Gellner's appreciation of relativism (and so his insistence that a choice of worlds is impossible) is undercut by a generalised awareness that affluence is possible. Development may thereby have democratic elements to it after all. Secondly, there is something to be said for the view that political liberty is recognisable slightly more widely than Gellner allowed. One element of modernity seems to be that of anti-imperialism, whether in Poland or in Iraq. It would be madness to presume that anti-imperial sentiment automatically translates into the consolidation of democratic regimes. Nonetheless, there is here, so to speak, a moral base for liberty that Gellner ignored.

One final consideration should concern us, even though it points in exactly the opposite direction. In the final analysis, Gellner was an optimist, believing that the industrial mode of production would spread to all mankind. The failed states of sub-Saharan Africa suggest that one should not take this for granted. More generally, the scourge of war, now more intra-state than hitherto and with the possibility of the spread of weapons of mass destruction, seems to be with us more than Gellner and his intellectual generation had imagined. A pessimistic case can be set against Gellner's fundamental optimism.

Conclusion

We can conclude with a reflection about the nature of liberalism. Gellner can usefully be seen as an audience-hopper. On the one hand, he is writing for 'us', the members of advanced Western societies. He seeks to help us to understand ourselves better, so that we may defend a particular way of life, if the need arises. But Gellner was loath to accept relativism, the view that we must accept, as Wittgenstein had it, forms of life without question. So he seeks, despite himself, to stand outside all forms of life, encouraging rational discussion as to which is the best. We can do this only because the forms of life present to us are uneven, with that which happens to be in the West offering unprecedented cognitive and material power. It is scarcely necessary actually to point this out to people in other societies because they can already see it: that is what underdevelopment actually means.

A contrast of an ironic and amusing character can be drawn between Gellner's audience-hopping and the position of other contemporary social philosophers. The broad tendency within much modern social theory is to suggest that inter-faith dialogue can manage diversity. My own experience of this approach suggests that at the deepest level it does not recognise diversity at all, presuming rather that discussion will bring agreement because humans share so very much in common. Gellner was rather different, a Weberian aware of genuine difference, of allegiance to different Gods. There is a sense in which he sought to respect such difference, suggesting merely the likelihood of a shared interest in technical power. But his approach was, so to speak, sly and Machiavellian: adopt the technical means, and the bastions of closed belief systems would eventually fall.

References

Chomsky, N. 1959. A Review of B. F. Skinner's *Verbal Behavior*. *Language* 35: 26–58.
Gellner, E. 1963. Nature and Society in Social Anthropology. *Philosophy of Science* 30: 236–51.
    1964. *Thought and Change*. London: Weidenfeld and Nicolson.
    1975. *Legitimation of Belief*. Cambridge: Cambridge University Press.

1976a. An Ethic of Cognition. In R. S. Cohen, P. K. Feyerabend and M. W. Wartofksy (eds.), *Essays in Memory of Imre Lakatos*. Dordrecht: Reidel, pp. 161–78.

1976b. From the Revolution to Liberalization. *Government and Opposition* 11: 257–72.

1985. The Gaffe-avoiding Animal or a Bundle of Hypotheses. In E. Gellner, *Relativism and the Social Sciences*. Cambridge: Cambridge University Press, pp. 68–82.

1988a. *State and Society in Soviet Thought*. Oxford: Blackwell.

1988b. *Plough, Sword and Book*. London: Collins Harvill.

1990. La trahison de la trahison des clercs. In I. Maclean, A. Montefiore and P. Winch (eds.), *The Political Responsibility of Intellectuals*. Cambridge: Cambridge University Press, pp. 17–27.

1996. Reply to Critics. In J. A. Hall and I. C. Jarvie (eds.), *The Social Philosophy of Ernest Gellner*. Amsterdam: Rodopi, pp. 625–87.

2003. *The Psychoanalytic Movement*. 2nd edn, Oxford: Blackwell.

Hall, J. A. 1998. Introduction. In J. A. Hall (ed.), *The State of the Nation: Ernest Gellner and the Theory of Nationalism*. Cambridge: Cambridge University Press.

Hume, D. 1985. *A Treatise of Human Nature*. Harmondsworth: Penguin.

Kohli, A. 2004. *State-Directed Development: Political Power and Industrialization in the Global Periphery*. Cambridge: Cambridge University Press.

Lessnoff, M. 2002. *Ernest Gellner and Modernity*. Cardiff: University of Wales Press.

Sen, A. 1978. *Poverty and Famine*. Oxford: Oxford University Press.

Smith, A. 1976. *The Theory of Moral Sentiments*, part VI. Oxford: Oxford University Press.

Index